Jewish Legal Writings
by Women

Jewish Legal Writings by Women

edited by

Micah D. Halpern and Chana Safrai

URIM PUBLICATIONS
Jerusalem
1998 / 5758

Jewish Legal Writings by Women

Copyright © 1998 by Urim Publications and Lambda Publishing Inc.

Urim Publications, P.O. Box 3116, Efrat 90435 Israel.

First Edition

Distributed outside of Israel by:

Lambda Publishers Inc.
3709 13th Avenue Brooklyn, New York 11218 U.S.A.
Tel: 718-972-5449 Fax: 718-972-6307

ISBN 965-7108-00-4

Contents

HEBREW SECTION

INTRODUCTION

This volume reflects the newest era in the history of Jewish women as they enter into a new realm of knowledge—the world of Halakha (Jewish Law). The generation of women represented here is more learned and empowered than any of their predecessors in history. In the pages of this book, seventeen women articulate, engage, and debate essential halakhic issues in the rigorous spirit of rabbinic Judaism, adding new and richly textured voices to the ceaseless dialogue of Torah study.

Every contributor to this volume is a devout Jewish woman. Each, in her own way, engages in rabbinic discourse from the inside, from the point of view of a participant in the halakhic world, as an individual whose life is immersed in Jewish tradition, Jewish learning, and Jewish family. The arguments the authors pose are both personal and academic. Like any rabbi approaching a halakhic subject, these authors approach the material with a respect for, and a deep analysis of, the manifold texts and vibrant spirit of rabbinic literature. The authors accept the obligation to work within the established framework to reach additional understandings and to contribute to the continuity of the halakhic process, Jewish tradition, and the world of Orthodoxy.

This book should be seen in the historical context of Jewish women's learning. The first Bais Yaakov school was established in Cracow, Poland, by Sarah Schenirer (1883–1935), in response to a dramatically changing society. The argument she set forth before the outstanding rabbis of the day, including Rabbi Israel Meir Kagan (1839–1933), known by his great work the *Chafetz Chaim*, the Gerrer Rebbe, Rabbi Avraham Mordechai Alter (1866–1948), and the Belzer Rebbe, Rabbi Issachar Dov Rokeach (1854–1927), was that the world was changing quickly, and bringing new and enticing roles for women, which would surely lure young women away from Judaism. Sarah Schenirer convincingly articulated the danger to the Jewish family and to Judaism that would result and said that Jewish women must have more access to Jewish experiences and education. Greater knowledge would then surely lead to a strengthening of the Jewish woman's commitment to Jewish life and family. The rabbis gave their blessing. So right was Sarah Schenirer and so successful was this phenomenon that the school she opened in 1918 with twenty-five students grew, within twenty years, to a movement composed of hundreds of schools with over 35,000 female students worldwide.

Similarly, in 1954, Yeshiva University recognized a vacuum in women's Jewish education and, accordingly, opened Stern College for Women—whose objective was to require a Jewish studies as well as a secular degree program. In the 1970s, Yeshiva University established the first Beit Midrash for women and one of the first *shiurim*—in Talmud—was taught by Rabbi Joseph Ber Soloveitchik. One of the founders and moving forces in this modern movement was Rabbi David Mirsky. May their memories be blessed.

There has been an explosion of women's seminaries in Israel over the past two decades. Each seminary has its own emphasis, teaching women, both old and new approaches to Jewish texts and learning. Jerusalem is the center of women's learning and teaching, and their teachings have spread worldwide. On any given night in Jerusalem thousands of women gather to learn, to hear lectures, and attend *shiurim*.

And it all culminates here, with the publication of ***Jewish Legal Writings by Women***.

This volume had its genesis over a year ago with an idea initiated by our publisher, Tzvi Mauer: a book by observant women writing on Halakha. It was bold and innovative; nothing like it had ever been done, and we felt, the need for such a work was obvious.

A great and pleasant discovery was that when we sat down to compose a list of scholars we found that the roster of possible contributors, women who are doing serious research and writing in the field of Halakha, was well over a hundred. Halakhic scholarship is no longer a male-only bastion. Another surprise came when the responses started pouring in. Not only are women studying, teaching, and learning, they are also eager to write, and this was the perfect forum.

So abundant, eloquent, creative, and innovative were the articles we received, that it became clear that we had enough material for more than a single volume.

We determined to allow each author's voice to be heard, as much as possible, in her own style and language. The contributors come from a variety of backgrounds; they live in Israel, America, and Canada. Some are professors, while others are teachers and students in women's *yeshivot* and study programs, and still others learn in *chavruta*. All have achieved high honors as learned and respected members of their communities.

Traditionally, halakhic discourse is in Hebrew, and therefore it is fitting that we have included a Hebrew section in this work.

We hope that you will read and evaluate this work critically. Each article is a serious and well researched look at a halakhic issue, a valuable exploration of accepted thought, and a forging of a new presentation and understanding of accepted law. These articles are written by women, but they are as relevant for men as for women.

We would also like to express our gratitude to Noa Jeselsohn, Gloria Kanefsky, Zipporah Aviva Mirsky, Fern Seckbach, Rabbi Alan Yaniger, and Batya Yaniger for their helpful comments and contribution.

Please read, please learn, please become part of the dialogue... *kol mi she'osek betalmud Torah harei ze mit'ale*—Whoever is engaged in the study of Torah is exalted (*Pirkei Avot* 6:2).

Micah D. Halpern and Chana Safrai
Talpiyot, Jerusalem
Sivan 5758 / June 1998

I. THE BODY

Rabbinic literature has addressed attention to issues relating to the body for centuries. But the rabbis were not systematic in their analysis of this topic, even in the books or responsa dedicated to related subjects. The discourse and material for these contributions had to be culled and synthesized, and then analyzed.

Awareness of one's body is in vogue. Today's woman is far more conscious, educated, and aware of her body than she has ever been. This section is an attempt to place this heightened awareness in the context of Halakha.

The following five essays address this topic from this point of view. As is the case with almost every subject discussed by the rabbis over the centuries, their analyses range in approach and attitude. And, while the internal logic of the authors is consistent, their halakhic presentations are surprising in many ways.

Hair Distractions: Women and Worship in the Responsa of Rabbi Moshe Feinstein

Norma Baumel Joseph

And so, if women are on the upper level, even without a screen or curtain, or if they are below, but behind a substantial, high *mechitza*, so that there be no fear of levity, it is of no consequence if the women are visible.[1]

Worship space and women's presence invites an interesting analysis of the distractions of women's body parts, especially the uncovered hair of a married woman. The visibility of women and of their hair—especially during prayer—has been an issue of concern to Jewish legalists since the Talmud. But according to Rabbi Moshe Feinstein, prayer is not necessarily canceled or prohibited in the presence of visible women.

Hair Covering: Prohibitions and Confusions

In a series of responsa, Rabbi Moshe Feinstein, one of the great rabbinic decisors of the twentieth century, examines the prohibition involved in looking at women. His decisions reveal a distinction between the preferred and the adequate.[2] In authenticating a specific communal arrangement, he has permitted behavior that he would normally not allow but has justified it on the basis of current practice in "this country," the United States.[3] His decisions on uncovered hair fall into this category.

---

[1] Rabbi M. Feinstein, *The Sanctity of the Synagogue,* ed. Baruch Litvin (NY: Litvin, 1962) 123. Some of the points explored in this article appeared initially in my "*Mehitza*: Halakhic Decisions and Political Consequences," *Daughters of the King: Women and the Synagogue,* eds. S. Grossman and R. Haut (Philadelphia: JPS, 1992) 117–34.

[2] See Ira Robinson, "Because of Our Many Sins," *Judaism* 35 (1986): 35–46. Rabbi Feinstein's preferred standard is to avoid looking at women, *Iggerot Moshe* (IM), *Orach Chaim* (OC) 1:40.

[3] Thus in IM, *Yore De'a* (YD) 3:73, R. Feinstein justifies the hiring of female teachers. The telling title of that responsum is: "Concerning the practice in this country to hire female teachers and no one prevents this." For an elaboration of this theme in terms of female

The responsa in *Iggerot Moshe* (IM) reflect Rabbi Feinstein's very strong commitment to classical rabbinic Judaism as well as his pragmatic appreciation of life in the United States. His popularity emanated in part from the way in which he embraced and understood the modern world while maintaining a strict adherence to halakhic standards. American norms of work, marketplace and education often were integrated in his approach. For example, he determined: that men must travel the subway system to work, even if they will be in close proximity to women (IM, *Even ha'Ezer* (EH) 2:14); that a man may go to work without the traditional head covering and a widow may remove her hair covering for job advancement (IM, *Choshen Mishpat* (CM) 1:93; *Orach Chaim* (OC) 4:2; EH 1:57). As will become evident, every question and answer reflects the social reality of American Jewish life and Rabbi Feinstein's appreciation of and responsiveness to that life.

The Problem

The laws of *erva* (literally nakedness, the sexually forbidden) prohibit a man from looking at a woman if his intent is to receive pleasure; but intent is not the only determining characteristic (IM, OC 1:43; EH 1:56, 69). Equally important is the nature of the exposed area. Certain areas are never to be publicly exposed while other parts depend upon public dress codes. If the exposed area is usually covered, then it is prohibited for a man to look and he cannot pray under such circumstances. On the other hand, if women usually appear with this area uncovered and if it is not of the permanently covered parts, then it is not *erva* and prayer is not prevented.

Additionally, the Talmud warns that the hair of a woman contains an erotic element that requires covering.[4] It is noteworthy that not all women's tresses are distracting: an unmarried woman is never expected to cover her hair according to

---

education see my "Jewish Education for Women: Rabbi Moshe Feinstein's Map of America," *American Jewish History* 83 (1995): 205–22.

[4] *Berakhot* 24a; *Ketubbot* 72a; *Shulchan Arukh*, EH 21:2; OC 75:2.

Some of the complex halakhic arguments surrounding the requirement for a married woman to cover her hair is presented in: Rabbi Meyer Schiller, "The Obligation of Married Women to Cover Their Hair," *Journal of Halacha and Contemporary Society* 30 (1995): 81–108. See also Rabbi Michael Broyde's critique in the next issue of the same journal, 31 (1996): 123–28. Also Rabbi Broyde lists responsa that permit uncovered hair for married women in the discussion group on "Mail Jewish" 24.87 (1996).

the vast majority.[5] But all women must cover their shoulders and arms. For Rabbi Feinstein, as well as for a significant segment of Orthodox Jewry, these warnings have been translated into a specific dress code. A married woman must cover arms, shoulders and hair. Problems arise, however, in pinning down the legal consequences of these warnings.[6] Even though the law, as Rabbi Feinstein repeatedly asserts, requires married women to cover their hair at all times, especially in the synagogue (IM, OC 4:32), he rules that it is permissible to pray, to say the *Shema*, and hear the Torah read even if men can see the uncovered hair of married women (IM, OC 1:42).[7]

Significantly, this ruling is dependent upon the cultural norms of fashion and styles of clothing. There is a clear appreciation of the relationship between custom and sexual temptation. Since clothing styles change over time, prevention of distraction and seduction will have both a fixed and a relative component. If

---

[5] The problem of unmarried women's hair plagues many of the responsa. For Rabbi Feinstein the prohibition of hair is not of hair per se but of the hair that is prohibited, that of a married woman. See IM, OC 1:15. Further on I explore his reliance on the custom of unmarried women to be bareheaded.

[6] The issue is further complicated by the consideration of *dat yehudit* and *dat moshe*. Rabbi Schiller claims that hair covering is in the realm of *dat moshe*, but it appears that for some (the *Tur* and the *Shulchan Arukh*) it is *dat yehudit*. See Broyde, op. cit.

For Rabbi Feinstein it conceivably is *dat yehudit* and therefore, is amenable to social conditions. In support of this view see his ruling that a man cannot divorce his wife on the basis of an uncovered head; IM, EH 1:114 and 4:32.6. On the other hand, he certainly claims it is Torah law. Moreover, see the later discussion of a widow and divorcee, wherein he claims that they may remove the head covering because they are only obligated as *dat yehudit*.

[7] The distinction between *minhag* and law, as well as the weight given to social reality and public custom is at the heart of an interesting debate on the similarities between hair covering practices and *mechitza* requirements. Marc Shapiro, "Another Example of 'Minhag America,'" *Judaism* 39:2 (Spring, 1990): 148–54. Michael Broyde, "Further on Women's Hair Covering: An Exchange," *Judaism* 40:1 (Winter, 1991): 79–94. Leila Leah Bronner, "From Veil to Wig: Jewish Women's Hair Covering," *Judaism* 42:4 (Fall, 1993): 465–77. See also Schiller (n4 above).

For R. Feinstein the distinctions are clear: *erva* is a concept whose legal applicability is redefined in some instances by social custom. *Kalut rosh* has no such variability. Moreover, he is quite adamant that while he allows prayer to be said in the presence of married women's uncovered hair, he does not permit the women to go about bareheaded. They violate the law by their behavior. The only issue his rulings address are the consequences of that violation. The distinction between prohibition, permission and disapproval is quite important in this debate.

one is used to women's hair being covered, then an uncovered head is an unacceptable distraction or "indecency." If, on the other hand, women are seen daily with their hair uncovered, then the sight of hair in and of itself cannot annul religious services, even if Jewish law still requires women to cover their hair. Consequently, Rabbi Feinstein can adjust synagogue practice to a *minhag America* wherein many married women, even Orthodox women, appear in public with their heads uncovered. Thus, synagogue prayer is affected since some women attend services without the requisite hair covering. *Erva* for public prayer is culturally conditioned, according to Rabbi Feinstein, but the prohibition against uncovered hair of married women is not. Thus, an uncovered female head in synagogue is not condoned but her presence does not preclude prayer. *It is worth noting that he never condemns the women nor does he entertain banning them from the synagogue.*

This discussion is imbedded in and implicates the definition of the *mechitza*.[8] For Rabbi Feinstein the problem is not one of preventing visibility even though his preference is to avoid looking at women. His advice to those who are capable of the highest standard is to have a high *mechitza* that will prevent any and all visibility (IM, OC 1:40). Similarly, although he allows a little bit of hair to remain uncovered, he prefers that women cover all their hair (IM, EH 1:58). Nonetheless, he maintains a firm distinction between preferred and normative standards and will not tolerate the misapplication of those categories. "*The obligation of the* mechitzah *is due to frivolity and not gazing*" (IM, OC 1:40). Frivolity implies mingling; a forbidden levity arising in situations of social contact. Therefore, according to Rabbi Feinstein, a glass partition fulfills the legal requirements of *mechitza*—though perhaps not of *erva* (IM, OC 1:43, 3:23). In the latter text, he regretfully comments on the dress of contemporary women who do not cover their arms. That "uncovering" is certainly *erva* and would prevent prayer. Therefore, Rabbi Feinstein prefers a *mechitza* that is not glass. However, he permits it if women in the congregation are appropriately dressed. Accordingly, a balcony, which inherently prevents mingling, does not require a partition such as a curtain (IM, OC 1:41). Yet, if women's arms are exposed then a curtain that would block the view of the men might be required (IM, OC 1:42). His reasoning is quite consistent and rests, in part, on the talmudic discussion of

---

[8] For a discussion of his rulings on *mechitza* see my "*Mehitza*: Halakhic Decisions and Political Consequences," 117–34.

the arrangements in the Temple during Sukkot. At first the men were outside and the women were inside. That did not work. Then the men were inside and, according to Rabbi Feinstein, unable to see the women, but there was still a problem with levity that required the balcony. Public prayer requires a *mechitza* in order to prevent *kalut rosh*, frivolity, and not visibility. Moreover, Rabbi Feinstein contends that since it is not the custom of women today to cover their hair, it cannot be considered *erva* or nakedness. However, he maintains, shoulders and arms are of a different nature and require absolute coverage. Hence, the *mechitza* must be at least shoulder height, thereby covering the arm and shoulder areas that are still *erva*, but allowing for the visibility of hair.[9]

Nonetheless, Rabbi Moshe Feinstein's ruling is difficult to understand given the talmudic position on hair (*Ketubbot* 72a, *Berakhot* 24a) and the clarity of the prohibition in the *Shulchan Arukh* (OC 75:1–4). Rabbi Feinstein does not write a comprehensive responsum explaining his position vis a vis all these sources. But his position is developed in a variety of different texts. In *Iggerot Moshe* OC 4:112, he briefly discusses the issue, and in passing refers to the opinions of Rabbis Yosef Caro and Moshe Isserles in justifying that hair is not necessarily *erva*. Claiming the exigencies of the times, in several texts, he relies explicitly on the lenient rulings, as he labels them, of the *Rif* and the *Rambam* who assert that hair is not *erva* for the purposes of the requirements of *Shema* and Torah recitation. Rabbi Feinstein, uncharacteristically, also mentions the argument as presented by the *Arukh haShulchan* (OC 75:7) to support his claim that exposed hair, although forbidden, is not to be considered *erva*. This leniency is permitted in his view because of the social climate. Namely, "because of our many sins" we live in a place where the custom is one of bare heads creating a situation of *in extremis* which justifies a lenient position.

One of the most intricate arguments (IM, OC 1:42) uses a talmudic passage (*Berakhot* 24a) in which hair is clearly being placed in the category of *erva* especially in terms of the recitation of the *Shema*. Rabbi Feinstein develops his position from what is not said, a style of argument that though surprising falls well within classic talmudic discourse. He cites the biblical proof text used by Rav Sheshet to indicate that the hair of a woman is *erva* (*Berakhot* 24). Since the

---

[9] This distinction creates an interesting problem for R. Feinstein. A balcony does not require a *mechitza* since mingling cannot occur, but it does require a curtain if the women come to synagogue with bare arms because of the laws of *erva* (IM, OC 1:42).

text used is post-Mosaic scripture (from Song of Songs), Rabbi Feinstein argues that Rav Sheshet merely offers a rational argument to elucidate that hair (which is praised in the text) can be a source of temptation, as explained by *Rashi*. Rabbi Feinstein finds that by not relying on the Torah verse (dealing with *sota*), the ruling on hair cannot be placed in the category of unconditional *erva*. Uncovered hair is prohibited but Torah authority (Mosaic scripture) is not used. Therefore, it cannot be in the category of *makom mekhuse*, "those parts of the body that must always be covered." Augmenting the argument, he notes that it is not forbidden to recite the *Shema* in the presence of the hair of an unmarried girl according to the *Shulchan Arukh*, since they are accustomed to go about bareheaded. Consequently, just as there is no prohibition in terms of prayer in the presence of unmarried women because of their custom, so too there can be no prohibition regarding prayer when the custom of married women is to appear with uncovered heads. Therefore, according to Rabbi Feinstein, since married women today regularly appear in public with uncovered hair, even though it is forbidden to do so, it does not constitute *erva* for the purpose of prayer. Thus, prayer is permitted.

Hair Customs

Rabbi Feinstein's rulings on hair covering in general are intriguing. In accordance with the major decisors, he rules that all married women must keep their hair covered in all public encounters. He does not like the wig (*sheitel*) which has become common practice, but will allow it if women insist (IM, EH 2:12, 4:32).[10] Of consequence in his responsa, and consistent with traditional norms, is the practice wherein a woman follows the custom of her husband (IM, OC 1:158). If she is used to sephardic ritual, but he is ashkenazi, she must adapt to his pattern. Significantly, in some instances, such as her desire to follow the custom of her mother and wear a wig, Rabbi Feinstein allows her to do so despite the husbands disapproval and the rabbi's own qualms (IM, EH 2:12). On the other hand, he does not allow her to shave her hair if her husband disapproves since, according to Rabbi Feinstein, that specifically infringes on her husband's prerogative (IM,

---

[10] The wig itself has a long history of dispute. Many rabbinic authorities opposed it although the *Rama* permitted it (*Shulchan Arukh*, OC 75:2). Contra to R. Feinstein's position on both wigs and saying the *Shema*, Rabbi Jacob Emden went so far in his disapproval as to forbid a man's prayers in the presence of a woman whose head was covered by a wig only. See Leila Leah Bronner, *Judaism* 42.4, 472.

EH 1:59). He defends the consistency of these decisions in *Iggerot Moshe* EH 4:32 always insisting that these rulings are not indicators of inferiority or lack of respect.[11]

Covering and Uncovering

For Rabbi Feinstein, the critical factor is that a married woman's hair be totally covered, allowing only a little (of two fingers width) to be exposed (IM, EH 1:58). Yet, he permits certain women at certain times to go bareheaded. Even a married woman is allowed to go bareheaded at home (IM 1:58). He refuses to impose the standard set by Kimchit (*Yoma* 47a). Thus, although many responsa do require head covering even at home, Rabbi Feinstein specifically states that it is not necessary to cover her hair in the presence of a husband and that the requirement pertains only to the market place (IM, OC 5: 37.12).[12]

Notably, in *Iggerot Moshe* EH 1:57 he allows a widow to work in the public sector without covering her hair. In an unusual decision, Rabbi Feinstein states that he was once asked if a widow could be allowed to work in an office without covering her hair. She needed the job in order to support her children, and it appears to have been a condition of employment. He replied that in a case of great need it was permissible. In this case, he is persuaded that her employment and advancement is at risk if she does not dress like the others. A head covering is too conspicuous and, therefore, limiting in the expected conformity of the business world. Since she is the sole support of her family, and since for Rabbi Feinstein financial motives are acceptable, his leniency is understandable.

This ruling rests on a distinction between Torah law and rabbinic injunction. According to Rabbi Feinstein, Torah law forbids a married woman from appearing in public without the proper covering. That law is inviolate. Some rabbis extended it to widows but the extension is contained in the category of custom (*dat yehudit*).[13] He then explicates an ambiguous reference in *Rashi* on

---

[11] Rabbi Feinstein considers a wife subject to her husband in some respects. But the husband is also responsible to her or dependent on her in others. A description of his use of the term *meshu'abad* as denoting the disparate responsibility of husband to wife and vice versa requires another essay.

[12] See Rabbi M. Schiller, op. cit.

[13] See n6 above.

the lawlessness of the act. The interpretation of *Rashi*'s language leaves room for some confusion.[14] Rabbi Feinstein declares that in the case of a married woman the doubt raised imposes an outright prohibition that can not be mitigated by concerns of complete financial loss because the law directly emanates from Torah. The reverse applies in the case of the widow. Here the doubt leads to a lenient position as the violation incurs an abrogation of *dat yehudit* only. For Rabbi Feinstein the nuance of custom leaves room for leniency.

The important distinction is a complicated legal question as to whether hair covering for a widow involves a prohibition or an obligation. The former would brook no breach no matter what the difficulty. The latter would allow a leniency in the case of serious financial loss. He uses the distinctions in legal categories and linguistic ambiguities in an effort to accommodate the woman's needs. The law for a married woman is of a different order than for a widow. Different categories of law create room for different responses. He does not apply law in a vacuum. All married women must cover their hair. All formerly married women should cover their hair. The distinction in terminology reveals a different legal base that allows him to use his discretion in this ruling. Both the source of the law as well as the current social pattern affect his ruling.

In a similar case, Rabbi Feinstein is asked whether a divorced woman might be able to appear in public bareheaded. In this case (IM, EH 4:32.4), the young woman wants to be able to meet men for matrimonial purposes. She is afraid that a head covering will automatically indicate that she is currently married. Rabbi Feinstein is persuaded that her motive is legitimate and so allows her to remove her head covering. But, he warns, there are conditions. She must inform the man as soon as possible that she is divorced. He would not allow her to mislead a man, just to dispel incorrect first impressions so that she might eventually marry. She must also continue to cover her hair when not dating. This ruling ironically appears to contradict the basic premise of head coverings. If women must cover their hair so as to avert any sexual temptation, here we have a case in which she

---

[14] In IM EH 1:58, he even entertains that *paru'a* might mean disheveled. The discussion of the requirement for head covering is imbedded in a very complicated inference from the talmudic understanding of the text in *Sota*. See Schiller and Broyde, op. cit.

does not have to cover her hair specifically in those situations of possible sexual encounter and attraction.[15]

Again one could argue that she is not actually married at this point. Certainly, these two examples of his lenient position occur only with women whose marital status is ambiguous, or more accurately, formerly married. This legal distinction is a crucial factor in his responsum for the widow. Additionally, he looks to the particulars of motive—earning a living and future marriage—in order to permit women who ordinarily should cover their hair to appear uncovered. In fact, he insists that when they are removed from the particular circumstances permitting bareheadedness, they should again cover their heads. Thus, in his analysis, the laws requiring hair covering for married women are still operative for these two women. However, because of specific circumstances he will allow them to remove that covering temporarily. Although temporary, this unusual permission is significant and he does not use the formulary of *in extremis* or "because of our many sins."

This inquiry is further compounded by his position on the consequences of a married woman refusing to cover her hair. In a very interesting responsum (IM, EH 1:114), Rabbi Feinstein concludes that a man cannot divorce his wife for refusing to cover her hair. He reaffirms this judgment in *Iggerot Moshe* EH 4:32. His only given reason is that "nowadays," especially in America, the normative pattern is to be bareheaded.[16] Most women, even those who are observant, do not cover their hair. Under such circumstances, a woman's refusal to cover her hair cannot be categorized as lawlessness or rebellion.

The importance of this brief passage is the role given to social reality in determining legal policy. The behavior of women who do not cover their hair is unacceptable to him, but has no punitive consequences. He readily recognizes

---

[15] One further anomaly: Rabbi Feinstein rules that a wig without a hat on top of it is proper even though to all appearances it is uncovered hair. In one part of that responsum (IM, EH 2:12), he notes that even if the men do not recognize it as a wig the women will. This is indeed a strange comment given the purpose of female head covering is clearly to avoid all erotic thoughts in men not women.

[16] In this text, IM EH 4:32.6, Rabbi Feinstein notes that even in Europe they did not compel a divorce for infringement of custom. In America, he claims, it is not possible to permit a man to divorce his wife because she refuses to cover her hair. Moreover, if they do divorce, it is not a sufficient cause to diminish the value of her marriage contract.

changed social behavior and his responsa reflect his accommodation to practices of which he disapproves. The term "nowadays" is a powerful representation.

Interestingly, all his responsa on hair reflect this acceptance despite disapproval. He does not offer long explanations or legal arguments to permit, he merely acknowledges the prevailing custom and rules accordingly. He makes no apology for accepting the social environment.[17] Although he objects to the women's behavior, he will not allow the law to be misapplied in an effort to persuade them or control the objectionable behavior. Moral suasion is proper; inappropriate use of legal penalties or jurisdiction is not.

For Rabbi Feinstein this issue of intent and social purpose makes all the difference. Given motives that fit his vision, he can accept or accommodate the distinct and various needs of some. In the two cases previously mentioned, although the motives differ, Rabbi Feinstein is convinced that the women's intentions are proper. In *Iggerot Moshe* EH 1:57 he permits a widow to appear without any head covering for professional advancement. His ruling is predicated on an understanding of the difficult conditions of life for a widow and the realities of marketplace norms. He does not advise her to seek employment elsewhere, nor does he caution her about the slippery slope of immodesty. Her motives are clear, forthright and proper. In *Iggerot Moshe* EH 4:32.4, he permits a divorcee to uncover her hair in order to meet potential husbands. In the latter text he explores the similarities of these two cases. He sets the stage for a permissive ruling by first dealing with the ethical question of deception. He posits that it is not possible to deceive, as everyone in her community knows she was married and will tell the prospective groom once he starts asking questions. In addition, her previous marital state will become apparent via the registration at City Hall. Thus, he posits that her motives are clearly not improper. Rather, she merely wishes to have a chance to "find favor in someone's eyes" before they know about the divorce. Rabbi Feinstein concurs with her that her divorce status could be an impediment to future marital prospects. He then compares this case to *Iggerot Moshe* EH 1:57, in which he permitted a widow, the sole support of her children, to remove her head covering for financial and career reasons. Similarly, in this case, he permits the divorcee to be bareheaded in order to improve her marriage prospects. This concession to social reality is limited, however. When she is not in a social situation, she must cover her head. He also

---

[17] This fact enhances our understanding of his position on hair as *dat yehudit*.

clarifies his leniency in this area of law by claiming that the requirement for a divorcee to cover her head is only *dat yehudit*—custom, and not *de'oraita*—Torah law. This argument is identical to the responsum for the widow.[18] It is noteworthy that this text is very brief, referring only to his own earlier related decision.

His permissiveness in this area of head covering is consistent. He would wish that every married woman always covered all her hair. But he is quite aware of the social realities that face even observant Jews. Finances and marital prospects are both important enough to him to bring about a lenient decision. He is also quite aware of the prevailing American pattern. Women in the United States do not wear any head covering. It makes perfect sense to him that in order to advance financially one would have to look the part. Similarly, in order to attract a husband, a young woman must also look the part. Thus, his acknowledgment of American norms and styles of dress is an important factor in these responsa. It enables him to appreciate rather than disparage the motives of those involved. Furthermore, as noted above, in specific responsa on prayer and synagogue, he rules that it is permissible to pray in the presence of women whose heads are not properly covered (IM, OC 1:42). Again, his recognition of the custom of most Americans including Jewish women is apparent and operative.

Although Rabbi Feinstein would not accept any claims that mixed pews in the synagogue constitute an acceptable *minhag*, the above cited decisions indicate that there is an arena in which American custom plays a decisive role. In 1990, Marc Shapiro wrote of "Another Example of *Minhag America*."[19] In it he argues that the common practice amongst married women to leave their hair uncovered is an example of *minhag America* that is raised by Rabbi Feinstein. The debate this article sparked concerning *minhag* versus law is substantial. Rabbi Broyde's response that there is a halakhic, rather than just *minhag*, basis for the impact of social conditions on hair covering is vital.[20] But for the purpose of this inquiry the

---

[18] In both texts, Rabbi Feinstein does not cite the biblical source. Unlike his explicit argument for the Torah authority of *mechitza*, in our case he does not pinpoint the text through which head covering is established as Torah law. In *mechitza* he was arguing for a unique position (as is argued in my 1992 article). Here he assumes that all know and agree, even though some traditional sources appear to leave female head covering in the category of *dat yehudit*.

[19] *Judaism* 39:2 (Spring, 1990): 148–154.

[20] Rabbi M. Broyde, "Tradition, Modesty and America," *Judaism* 40 (1991): 79–87.

significant factor is the easy acceptance of the *erva* of hair as being subject to American social custom and standards. For Rabbi Feinstein the legal requirement for hair covering is marked by the concern for *erva* which, under certain circumstances, is culturally determined. *Minhag* does have a place in determining practice or rather in the above cases, the consequence of certain practices. Consequently, Rabbi Feinstein can adjust synagogue practice to a *minhag America* wherein many married women appear in public, despite the prohibition, even in the synagogue, with their heads uncovered.[21] It is surely a sign of Americanization when Rabbi Feinstein acknowledges that head covering can be a handicap in business for both men and women. He also understands that dating in America requires a different pattern of familiarity. Hence the divorcee can uncover her hair in order to meet a man. This pattern of meeting a man and getting to know him is not anathema to Rabbi Feinstein. He appears to accept the idea that men and women need to know each other before marriage and does not advise that they rely exclusively on a matchmaker.[22] The American norm of dating as a means to finding an appropriate marriage partner appears to be part of his cultural vocabulary.

Given these cases, plus his ruling on reciting the *Shema* in the presence of uncovered female hair, one must conclude that for Rabbi Feinstein hair covering is not automatically or absolutely *erva* despite the talmudic references. Social custom and public habit play a major role in these personal issues of modesty and morality.

Thus, the legal decisions in these cases are determined to a degree by public custom. However, in the decisions on *mechitza*, as with those on hair, public behavior and custom are not the only determining factors. Rabbi Feinstein is very careful to maintain an absolute fixed standard as well as insist on keeping distinct the categories of law. Looking at women and deriving pleasure from that act, involves a personal code of modesty and license and affects men and women

---

[21] However, he definitely cannot accept the claims for a *minhag* of mixed seating, as Broyde clearly states, ibid.

[22] It is worthwhile to compare the premise of this decision with R. Feinstein's permission to a bridegroom to read a marriage manual so that he would know what to do on the night of his wedding (IM, EH 1:102).

differently (IM, EH 1:69).[23] *Mechitza* applies to public behavior and to men and women equally (IM, OC 1:43). In fact, he is very careful to distinguish the laws of *mechitza* from other laws that appear similar, but are not. They are instead due to reasons of personal moral laxity such as those that fall into the category of *erva*, *hirhur* (lewd or distracting thoughts) or *yichud* (the prohibition that man and woman, other than husband and wife, not have the opportunity for intimacy). *Mechitza*, he insists, is not required to prevent men from seeing women.[24] It is not about intimacy; it is about frivolity in the presence of prayer. It focuses on public morals not private ones. Though he prefers that men never look at women, he rules that female visibility does not enter into the category of *kalut rosh* and that *erva* is not the reason for *mechitza* (IM, OC 1:40). Despite his preferences, Rabbi Feinstein will not allow anyone to confuse the issues or to argue for *mechitza* or head covering on the wrong halakhic grounds.

In Rabbi Feinstein's estimation, the principle of *mechitza* requiring separation for prayers affects males and females equally. The forbidden state of frivolity

---

[23] In IM EH 1:69, he discusses men's and women's thoughts and temptations in the framework of *hirhur*. There he explains that there is also a prohibition of *hirhur* for women though it differs from the concerns and regulations for men. Both men and women must refrain from thoughts that are promiscuous. However, with women there is no concern for viewing (*histaklut*) since there is no possibility of "wasting seed" which is the source of the prohibition for men. Thoughts do lead to acts and that is the context of these rulings. However, while in some circumstances such as prayer women must be restricted to protect the men, in others men must learn to control their thoughts. Thus, in IM EH 1:56 he does allow men to be in difficult environments for the sake of work.

There is an aspect that applies only to women in the added prohibition of *dat yehudit* forbidding women from *pritzut* (*Ketubbot* 72), degenerate acts. Interestingly, the regulations of *dat yehudit* apply only in cases of individual acts. However, if the custom of all the women in the city is to act (or dress) in a certain way, then it is not necessarily considered *pritzut*. Thus, as in the case of the *mechitza*, if married women do not cover their hair, that mode of dress becomes non-erotic. However, Rabbi Feinstein claims that although one cannot count this accepted pattern of dress as immoral, nonetheless it is preferable to stop it due to standards of additional modesty and *chassidut*. This decision (IM, EH 1:69) is congruous with his rulings and preferences concerning prayer and the visibility of women's hair. It is also consistent for him to use moral pressure to ensure an additional and uncompromising standard of modesty. Nonetheless, he does not refrain from including patterns of cultural custom in his reasoning and ruling accordingly.

[24] Those rabbinic authorities who rule that a *mechitza* must be high enough to prevent the men from seeing the women at all would not allow a *mechitza* whose top third is glass as Rabbi Feinstein does.

occurs when men and women socialize. Thus, preventing this state must affect both sexes in the same manner. This is a ruling dependent upon place and numbers rather than upon individual behavior.[25] Although many women feel that the *mechitza* itself reflects the inferior status of women and many Jews believe it exists to protect men from women, clearly Rabbi Feinstein does not agree. *Mechitza* protects men and women from frivolity which is forbidden during prayer and which effects them equally. Neither gender is more responsible than the other.

In conclusion, Rabbi Feinstein's permissiveness is noteworthy. Covering is only necessary in the marketplace and even a menstruant at home need not cover her hair. A wig is acceptable but shaving is not. A little can be exposed and even if hair is visible prayer can be uttered. Exposed hair is no cause for divorce and a widow or divorcee may uncover their hair in certain circumstances.

Nonetheless, these authorized standards reveal an apprehension. Women and their hair are distractions and men should not look. Worship may take place in their visible presence, but it is better to avoid this. Remarkably, the heads of all males are also to be covered during worship. But there is no parallel standard or concern that women will be distracted. The end result is an affirmation of separation: of male centrality and of the differentiation of women in the worship community.

---

[25] In a series of small decisions regarding *mechitza* in the volume published posthumously, Rabbi Feinstein noted that it happened sometimes that one or two women entered the *beit midrash* during prayers to say kaddish or collect charity. There was no *mechitza*. He rules that as long as the practice is irregular or accidental, then a *mechitza* is not absolutely required (IM, OC 5:12.2).

Marriage of Minor Girls in Jewish Law:
A Legal and Historical Overview

Tirzah Meacham (leBeit Yoreh)

This article will examine the biblical, talmudic, and geonic sources, and their codification by Maimonides, pertaining to the marriage of a Jewish girl in her minority. To achieve this goal we shall begin with an overview of marriage age norms as reflected in the above-mentioned talmudic literature. We must keep in mind that age of marriage is a sociological phenomenon, varying in time and place. The texts quoted here, however, are, for the most part, non-historical legal texts, hence idealized. A society's laws and the way that society conducts itself are not always identical. Occasionally, moral advice may be formulated in legal terms but will not have the force of law.

The other issue of critical importance in examining the issue of marriage of minors is the danger of reading the texts in an anachronistic manner. The Western world is now finally sensitized to issues of child abuse, particularly pedophelia. At the outset of this article I wish to state my personal bias; sexual relations between a child and an adult are not acceptable now, nor were they acceptable at any stage in history. Legal systems which allowed an adult to marry a child (and here we are speaking of an adult man marrying a minor girl) without prohibiting consummation of the marriage did not take into consideration the physical or emotional welfare of the child. Consent, understanding and freedom from coercion, which are necessary components in other legal acts, are missing in such a relationship. Most people today would consider the marriage of a prepubertal child a form of child abuse, particularly with our expectations of immediate consummation of a marriage. It is, however, cultural relativism which sanctions different practices, and each society creates its own norms.

There are so-called Third World countries today which have as a norm a very early marriage age. That fact is one of the distinctive points of difference between these and Western countries because early marriage in these societies usually leads to a higher rate of reproduction. It may not be clear that all child-brides considered their marriages abusive. What is clear, however, is the fact that this issue is hardly addressed in our texts. This may be because our texts were composed and redacted by males. The few places recorded in the Talmud in which the actual language of girls repudiating a marriage indicate deep scorn and anger on the part of the girl.[1] Perhaps everyone viewed early marriage as natural without serious consideration for the physical and emotional well-being of the child, or, perhaps, the options, which included the threat of no marriage at all, were too frightening to entertain. We do know that the expectation for early marriage was enveloped in positive language: fulfillment of the commandment of procreation at the earliest possible time, avoidance of sin, the blessing of seeing grandchildren, and the emotional and economic stability generated by a successful marriage.

Society has changed in its expectations about marriage age. These changes have been embodied in civil laws which establish a minimum age for marriage, usually requiring parental consent if the couple is below the age of legal majority. These laws tend to take into account the general physical and emotional welfare of the parties and societal goals, including population control. Medical care and social welfare systems have done much to extend fertility to later years and reduce the dangers of death in childbirth as well as alleviate the specter of permanent poverty for the unmarried woman. What may have passed in Antiquity and the Middle Ages as an appropriate marriage age no longer holds for contemporary reality and, as indicated, may never have been appropriate.

Initial Texts

Early marriage was considered a desideratum in Jewish communities from earliest times for several reasons. It discouraged promiscuity for both males and females and it may have allowed the maximum period possible for procreation thereby increasing the population size and its stability.[2] Moreover, the younger the bride in a system which appears to have been patrilocal, the

---

[1] *Yevamot* 107b.

[2] It must be noted that girls, even after menarche, generally do not begin to ovulate for a long period, from several months to two years. In that case, the early marriage immediately upon menarche or shortly thereafter, would not necessarily add to the procreative period.

more complete her training and integration into her husband's household could be. Marriage at puberty, of course, guaranteed maximum use of the procreative years, whereas marriage before puberty increased the likelihood that the girl would be a virgin at the time of marriage.

There are no specific directives for a precise age of marriage for boys. Mishna *Avot* 5:21 has in its list of appropriate actions for specific ages, "eighteen for marriage."[3] In light of the fact that the list almost exclusively refers to activities rabbinically designated for males: learning Torah, Mishna, and Halakha, and the age of thirteen for the obligation of fulfilling the commandments, we presume the age of marriage also refers to males. Some see this age as the minimum age for marriage for males while others believe that marriage at this age or by this age was the suggested norm. Later talmudic sources suggest that even earlier ages may be encouraged for marriage in order to prevent lustful thoughts and spilling of seed. For example, in *Kiddushin* 29b–30a, Rav Nachman mentions that he was married at sixteen. He maintained that it would have been better had he been married at fourteen for then he could have scorned the evil impulse altogether. This indicates that at approximately age fourteen, he had reached puberty, making ejaculation and nocturnal emissions possible. Boys tend to reach puberty a year or so after girls but there is much individual variation. It seems clear from the strong rabbinic statements against masturbation, or even accidental loss of seed, that early marriage age for males was connected to notions of sexual purity.

Other factors affecting marriage age for males are: (1) The expectation of learning Torah which is rabbinically considered a time-bound positive commandment incumbent only upon men. It is more easily accomplished without the financial and time burdens family life imposes unless the wife's family becomes the student's patron, as is common in some Jewish circles even today. (2) The legal requirement to procreate and support one's spouse and guarantee her *ketuba*. This generally means learning a profession, sometimes requiring lengthy apprenticeship.[4] Of course, wealthy families and

---

[3] This Mishna is considered a late addition and is not found in the excellent manuscripts. See Y.N. Epstein, *Mavo leNusach haMishna*, 2nd ed. (Jerusalem, 1964) 978.

[4] See *Kiddushin* 1:7, *Tosefta Kiddushin* 1:11 and *Kiddushin* 29a for a discussion of the obligation of the father to teach his son a profession.

some rabbinic families had more opportunity to support sons and thereby allow earlier marriage if such were considered desirable.

What was the normal age of marriage for girls? The *Wisdom of Ben Sira* 42:9–14 draws a rather depressing picture of a father's worries about his daughters: possible seduction as minors (making them unmarriageable or at the very least reducing their bride price significantly),[5] possible intentional fornication by a girl of marriageable age, and inability to find a husband for the fully mature woman. This reference seems to indicate that marriage prior to sexual maturity was certainly the norm, if only to prevent the fate of becoming 'an old maid' who would eventually be at a great disadvantage economically, especially in her old age.

Single mature women constituted a destabilizing factor in a patriarchal society. The system is constructed such that girls and women are under the dominion of their fathers or husbands. Divorce (and sometimes widowhood) required that the financial consolidation established at marriage be disrupted in order to pay the *ketuba*. As in most societies, even today, widows were often poverty-stricken, requiring special enactments concerning their welfare. The Torah repeatedly demands care of widows and orphans. Social mechanisms, such as home-based economics, like weaving, served as a preventative measure for female impoverishment.

The independent legal status of a mature woman must have been threatening to the Rabbis. Such a woman could buy and sell property and was legally responsible for her own actions without the mediation of a male. It also put her on a par with the man concerning the obligation to fulfill *mitzvot*; the argument in *Kiddushin* 30b to exempt women from the obligation of honoring one's parents held that the woman was first answerable to her husband, and only then to God. In short, the unmarried state was considered anomalous. Thus an unmarried status gave her more disruptive power than was the norm for women. As a result, she was also no longer as protected by the system as would have been the case had she married. Without a father (or another guardian) to arrange a marriage, and without a husband to mediate between her and the world, a woman who had far less training in commerce and real estate may have been disadvantaged and easily victimized. As well, given the strong

---

[5] The *ketubbot* of non-virgins were half the value of the *ketubbot* of virgins according to *Ketubbot* 1:2.

value placed on family and children, such a woman was considered to be outside the societal norms.

S.D. Goitein, basing his opinion on the lack of evidence in *geniza* documents, assumed that marriage of minors was a rare occurrence.[6] Moshe Herr[7] and Adiel Schremer[8] tend to see the marriage age norm as well after puberty. M.A. Freidman[9] holds an intermediate position while A. Grossman brings ample evidence from responsa that early marriage age, including of minor girls, was common and reached a peak in the twelfth and thirteenth centuries.[10]

The legal status of a girl in rabbinic law changed with her age: under the age of twelve years and a day she is considered a "minor," *ketana*; from twelve years and a day for the next six months she is a "marriageable girl," *na'ara*; after that period she was an "adult," a *bogeret*. Although there is some difference of opinion among the codifiers, the category of *na'ara* was dependent not only upon age but also on the appearance of two pubic hairs.[11] If after attaining the age of twelve years and a day, the girl grew two pubic hairs she was considered a *na'ara* according to all opinions. In the event that she grew pubic hair after attaining the age of eleven years and a day some Rabbis disqualify her from *me'un*, the right of a minor girl who was contracted in marriage by someone other than her father to repudiate the marriage, but do not give her the full status of *na'ara*. In the event that she did not grow pubic

---

[6] Avraham Grossman, in his article *"Nissu'ei Boser beChevra haYehudit bimei haBeinayim ad haMe'a haShlosh-Esrei,"* *Pa'amim* 45 (1991) 108–9 comments that Goittein's argument in *A Mediterranean Society*, vol. III: The Family (Berkely-Los Angeles-London, 1978) 76–79, is one of silence.

[7] M.D. Herr, *"Chayei Yom Yom shel haYehudim,"* *HaHistoria shel Eretz-Yisrael* (Jerusalem, 1985) 5:148.

[8] Adiel Schremer, "Jewish Marriage in Talmudic Babylonia," Doctoral dissertation (The Hebrew University, 1996) 25–41, 63–94.

[9] M.A. Friedman, "The Ethics of Medieval Jewish Marriage," ed. S.D. Goittein, *Religion in Religious Age* (Cambridge, Mass., 1974) 83–102, is aware of the weakness of the argument from silence but tends to accept Goittein's conclusions. See Grossman, ibid., 108–9 and n1.

[10] See A. Grossman, ibid., 108–25.

[11] See T. Meacham, *Sefer haBagrut veSefer haShanim* (Jerusalem: Yad haRav Nissim, 1998) Introduction, ch. 6 for a more complete discussion on the differences among the codifiers.

hairs for some time after completing her twelfth year, some Rabbis allowed *me'un* until the pubic hairs appeared unless she had had sexual intercourse after twelve years and a day.

Although there are a few negative rabbinic statements concerning women's autoeroticism or lesbianism (*mesolelot*),[12] we do not see expressions of concern about this type of behavior as a stimulus for early marriage. This is not the case for males. Concern over masturbation and spilling seed was certainly a major factor encouraging early marriage for them. It is possible that rabbinic views of female physiology which separates between sexual stimulation and what was considered female seed accounts for this difference. Elsewhere I have discussed at length the possibility that both biblically and rabbinically menstrual blood was considered female seed.[13] Texts which refer to a girl's marriage before menarche may be expressing concern for her potential loss of seed. The perceived danger for minor girls was fear of seduction while for older girls fornication and independence were feared. Both ideas encouraged early marriage. I now turn to a more detailed discussion of some of the central sources that stand behind the above statements regarding early marriage of girls.

Discussion of Sources

Let us begin with the critical biblical text concerning the right of a father to contract marriage for his daughter. Deuteronomy 23:13–21 describes a situation in which a man has married a woman, hated her and claimed that she was not a virgin when he married her. Her parents counterclaimed that she was a virgin and brought forth the tokens of her virginity. The man is then punished by lashes and a fine of one hundred silver coins is paid by him to the bride's father for having slandered a daughter of Israel. He was forced to remain married to her without the right of divorce. This was understood by the

---

[12] See e.g., *Yevamot* 76a. For a discussion of this issue see Reena Zeidman, "Marginal Discourse: Lesbianism in Jewish Law," *Women in Judaism: A Multidisciplinary Journal* (Internet based) 1-1 (Fall, 1997).

[13] See T. Meacham, *Mishna Nidda: A Critical Edition with notes on Commentary and Redaction and Chapters in Legal Development and Realia*, (Hebrew) Doctoral dissertation (The Hebrew University, 1989) 1:154–69.

Rabbis to mean that if the bride and her father consented she was to remain married to him. If, however, the claim was true, she was stoned.[14]

These verses demonstrate the extent of the father's power in the marriage process. A man betrothed, then married a woman, but it was her father, either with the groom himself or with his father acting as his agent, who arranged the marriage and its financial conditions. Perhaps the best example of biblical expectations in this regard is the story of Dinah and Shechem in which not only the specific individuals were discussed but also the exchange and taking of brides was expressed as the general expectation (Genesis 34:16): "We will give our daughters to you and we will take your daughters for ourselves..."[15] Deuteronomy 23:16 is very clear on the power of the father: "I gave my daughter to this man..." It is the father who gives her to her husband and it is the father who is compensated for his son-in-law's slander of his daughter. The father, of course, may have been held responsible for the behavior of his daughter, in which case he, too, was slandered. The *tannaic* legal Midrash *Sifre Devarim*, *Piska* 235 (Finkelstein ed., 269), defines his rights more clearly: "'I gave my daughter to this man' teaches that it is the father's right to contract marriage for his minor daughter." This right is echoed in Mishna *Ketubbot* 4:4:

> The father merits his daughter's marriage [money whether] by money, docu-
> ment, or sexual intercourse and merits the things she finds and [the value of]
> her handiwork, and [has the right to] cancel her vows and receives her *get* but
> does not have usufruct [use of the fruits] in her lifetime. [If] she marries—the
> husband has more [rights in that he], has usufruct in her lifetime, and he is ob-
> ligated in her maintenance, redemption, and her burial...

Again we ask, from what age is a girl considered marriageable? Mishna *Kiddushin* 1:1 delineates the three ways by which a woman is acquired in marriage: money, contract, and sexual intercourse. A man could arrange marriage for his daughter by money or contract from the day of her birth. We find reference to this right in several geonic works: *She'iltot* (59), *Hilkhot Re'u* (page 83), *Halakhot Gedolot* (Warsaw, 83c), and *Sefer haBagrut* (chap. 6).

---

[14] The rabbinic texts require a very stringent warning procedure and competent witnesses in order to inflict capital punishment, making it essentially impossible to execute anyone.

[15] All translations in this article are by the author.

Mishna *Nidda* 5:3 limits marriage from birth to those methods by excluding intercourse as a mode of acquisition until the girl is three years and a day old: "A girl of three years and a day may contract marriage by sexual intercourse." The reason given in *Nidda* 45a is that only from that age onwards is the hymen permanently removed by intercourse. Prior to that age, according to this source, it may regenerate.

Were girls actually married at such early ages or were these theoretical discussions? A point which speaks against them being merely theoretical discussions is that other topics refer to the same age issue. These include *me'un*, the right of an orphan girl to repudiate a marriage valid rabbinically but not under the Torah, as it was arranged for her by her mother, brother, or guardian (*Yevamot* 13:1–2); marriage prior to menarche (*Nidda* 10:1) in reference to potential menstrual impurity at first intercourse even when no signs of puberty have appeared; and discussion on who receives her writ of divorce, *get*, for her in her minority (*Gittin* 6:2–3, *Gittin* 65a). The discussion of *me'un* refers to actual cases (*Yevamot* 107b) and the various versions of a *get me'un*, as well as specific *Responsa*, make it unlikely that such early marriages were only theoretical.

Me'un, of course, may be a special case in which the girl is disadvantaged because she is an orphan. It is possible that because of that situation, which may have caused economic hardship, marriage was contracted for her at an earlier age than her father would have arranged had he lived. Such an early marriage might prevent her from living a life of poverty or prostitution, as well as allow her mother to remarry more easily. It may also have reflected the situation of the mother and sons. The girl no longer would have to be supported, maintaining as much of the estate for the sons as possible, and it would be easier for the mother to remarry.[16] However, texts such as those mentioned above, and others, indicate that the father did indeed marry off his daughters at extremely early ages. *Gittin* 6:2 states: "...Whoever is not capable of keeping her *get* [safely by herself] cannot be divorced." A *beraita* in *Gittin* 64b states this and then the obverse: "Our Rabbis taught: A *ketana* who is capable of

---

[16] See Miller, *Teshuvot Geonim* 105 which was brought by Grossman, ibid., 112 and n12. The marriage of two minor girls contracted for them by their mother seems to have been part of a package deal in which the mother's new husband's brother and nephew married the minor girls.

keeping her *get*—she can be divorced but if she is not capable of keeping her *get* she may not be divorced…" The ability to keep something safe is predicated on the ability to distinguish between things of value and worthless objects. *Gittin* 65a has the following:

> There are three qualities in a child: [If when given] a stone he throws it away, but [when given] a nut keeps it—he can purchase for himself but not for others. An [orphan] girl of corresponding ability can be betrothed in such a way that she must [actively] repudiate the marriage in order to be released. *Pe'utot* [young children from ages 6 to 10] can buy and sell moveables and a girl of corresponding [age] can be divorced [receive her own *get*, if an orphan] from a marriage contracted by her father…

The next stage in the *Gittin* 65a text is the period when vows are examined as to their validity, at the age of eleven years and a day for girls and twelve years and a day for boys. It is clear that the ages in this passage go up, meaning that marriage could be contracted for a girl of six by her mother or brothers, and she could be divorced from a marriage contracted by her father because she was mature enough to guard her *get*. Before that age, her father would receive her *get*.

We may assume that the undisputed right of the father to contract marriage for his minor daughter was actually used regularly, and, at least occasionally at a very young age. The norm, however, was more likely that the girl was betrothed near the time that the first signs of puberty appeared and in accordance with Mishna *Ketubbot* 5:2 was actually married twelve months later. That time period not only allowed her to prepare her trousseau but allowed her time to mature physically, although not necessarily to full puberty. The reality of the situation was that marriage post-puberty was less likely. This seems to indicate that the normal age for marriage was before puberty and possibly before twelve and a day, or at least that the first of the two stages of marriage, betrothal, was completed before her legal majority. It was to the father's advantage to betroth his daughter as a minor, *ketana*, or as a *na'ara*, because he received the money of the *kiddushin* and could use it to her advantage or to his own as compensation for the loss of her work. After she became a *bogeret*, the money was hers. One other factor contributed to her marriageability as a minor and a *na'ara*: her father had a right to revoke her vows, preventing her from assuming any obligations which would reduce her suitability as a bride.[17]

As puberty has remained very constant in the Middle East, with menarche around age fourteen according to Greek and Roman sources, it is likely that the first signs of puberty appeared before age twelve and a day.[18] As we have seen, *Nidda* 6:11 prohibits *me'un* at the appearance of two pubic hairs and obligates the girl in all the commandments of the Torah at that time. Two conditions were generally required for full legal majority in Jewish law: (1) age (twelve years and a day for girls, thirteen years and a day for a boy) and (2) the appearance of two pubic hairs. Several geonic works address the issue of the appearance of two pubic hairs before the legal age had been reached and the consequences on the girl in reference to consummation of marriage and her right of *me'un*.[19]

Such things as economic situation, maturity of the girl, and availability of a husband, undoubtedly influenced the age of marriage in each specific case. We do know from several talmudic statements that contracting marriage for a girl before she reached legal majority was certainly the most desirable situation. The statements encourage fathers to spend money to arrange suitable dowries if the girl was a *bogeret* and not yet betrothed, lest she remain unmarried. We find, for example, in *Pesachim* 113a: "Your daughter has matured, free your slave and give [him] to her [so that she can be married as soon as possible]."

Balance and Ambivalence

We must assume that the majority of fathers have their daughters' welfare in mind and want stable marriages for them. Such would be the natural protectiveness which we assume is appropriate, rather than a mere desire to avoid the possible shame of an illicit relationship. The sources encourage early marriage and yet genuine stability can be attained only if the bride also desires the

---

[17] See *Nedarim*, ch. 10–11.

[18] Solon and others refer to the age of menarche. See T. Meacham, *Sefer haBagrut*, Introduction, ch. 4.

[19] Most notably, Rav Amram Gaon forbids *me'un* if two pubic hairs have appeared from age eleven years and a day onwards. For a full discussion of the various geonic opinions, see T. Meacham, *Sefer haBagrut*, Introduction, chs. 5–7.

marriage and works for its success. We will examine a number of texts which show how the Rabbis related to the difficult balance of both encouraging early marriage and accepting the father's right to contract it while being cognizant of the daughter's role in its success. In *Kiddushin* 2:1 we find:

> A man contracts marriage [with a woman] by his own agency or through his agent. A woman [accepts a] contract of marriage by her own agency or through her agent. The man may contract marriage for his daughter while she is a *na'ara* through his own agency or through his agent...

Kiddushin 41a takes up this last point:

> The man may contract marriage for his daughter while she is a *na'ara*: While she is a *na'ara*—yes; while she is a minor *ketana*—no! This is supported by Rav: Rav Yehuda said in the name of Rav and [another version] says R. Elazar [said]: It is forbidden (*asur*) for a man to contract marriage for his daughter while she is a *ketana* until she grows up and says "I want so-and-so for a husband."

Although the right of the father to contract marriage for his minor daughter has been established, his right is limited by the prohibition, *asur*, until she has reached a stage where she can actively state her desire for a particular husband. The Babylonian Talmud grants him the right to contract marriage for her but seems to forbid him from using it. There is no larger context given for Rav's (or R. Elazar's) prohibition. Just prior to this point in the *sugya*, Rav forbids contracting a marriage through an agent lest the man, who has not seen the bride, find something unseemly in her and come to hate her. A woman is not prohibited from acting through an agent because according to Resh Lakish, it is better for her to be married to anyone than to be unmarried.

A number of geonic texts follow this line of reasoning. In the eighth century *She'iltot* (59) (and in the somewhat later *Halakhot Gedolot*, Warsaw 83c) we find:

> ...Even though from her minority to her majority she is under her father's authority, it is not desirable that her father contract marriage for her until she is mature, for Rav Yehuda said [in the name of] Rav: It is forbidden for a man to contract marriage for his daughter while she is a *ketana* until she grows up and says "I want so-and-so for a husband."

In the ninth century work *Hilkhot Re'u* (83) we find the same text with a significant change: "...Even though from her minority to her majority she is under her father's authority, she *cannot* be contracted in marriage until she matures, for Rav Yehuda in the name of Rav said..." (my emphasis)

According to this text, a marriage cannot even be contracted for her until she is able to consent.[20] *Rambam* (*Hilkhot Ishut* 3:19) also recognizes the right of the father but limits it in somewhat different language, in the language of "rabbinic commandment":

> ...Even though the father has the authority to contract marriage for his daugh-
> ter while she is a *ketana* and while she is a *na'ara* to whomever he pleases, it is
> not worthy of him to do so. Rather, it is a rabbinic commandment that he not
> contract marriage for his daughter while she is a *ketana* [but rather waits] until
> she matures and says I want [to be married] to so-and-so. So too [for] the man,
> it is not worthy for him to contract marriage to a *ketana*...

Rambam is most emphatic about the inappropriateness of contracting marriage with a minor both from the father's side and from the husband's side. The latter may be guilty of delaying procreation by marrying a girl incapable of reproduction due to her physical immaturity.[21]

Pregnancy in early adolescence is particularly dangerous. Some awareness of the possible physical hazards of pregnancy in a girl who has not fully matured is found in *Tosefta Nidda* 2:6. According to that text, the minor girl is one of the three women permitted to use a *moch*, a contraceptive absorbent. Such ideas must have been based on reality, another indication that marriage of minor girls and young adolescents was common.

There is one case in which the father is prohibited from contracting marriage for his minor daughter. If he has already contracted such a marriage and

---

[20] Grossman, ibid., 110 and n7 suggests that this significant change, which eliminates the possibility of minor girls being contracted in marriage, may in fact be an error in the translation, *Hilkhot Re'u* being a Hebrew translation of *Halakhot Pesukot*. The text in *Halakhot Pesukot* is similar to that in *She'iltot*.

[21] There are several discussions in the Babylonian Talmud about the questionable legitimacy of non-procreative sexual relations. In addition to *Tosefta Nidda* 2:6 which includes a *ketana* among those who should use a contraceptive absorbent, *moch*, lest she become pregnant and die, men who "sport" with minors are responsible for the delay of the messiah according to *Nidda* 13b.

it has ended in divorce or widowhood while his daughter was still a minor, her status in reference to him changes. According to *Yevamot* 13:6 she becomes an "orphan in her father's lifetime" which exempts her from his authority in that he can no longer contract marriage for her. It is not clear that this is a punishment for poor judgment on his part or whether the fact of her status as a married woman prevents her from returning to absolute minority. It does, however, prevent serial marriages arranged by the father for his minor daughter, something which apparently even in that period would have been considered child abuse. A similar attitude is found in Beit Shammai's reluctance to allow *me'un* more than once because "the daughters of Israel are not *hefker* [without protection]."

Conclusion

The absolute right of the father to betroth his minor daughter (at least once) is predicated not only on his presumed concern for her welfare (and possibly that without the framework of marriage she would act in a manner which would shame the family), but also on the model of limited *patria potestas*. Biblical and rabbinic law never gave the father absolute rights over the lives of his children to the extent that he could murder them or refuse to recognize his paternity without just cause. He was, however, entitled to far-reaching control over them, especially over his daughters in the matter of marriage. Part of this control was probably connected to his desire for control over financial resources: the money for her own marriage which accrued to him before her legal majority, and the amount of dowry he provided.

The possible parallel to the father's right to contract marriage for his minor daughter was essentially rejected in the case of his son. Although there are texts which mention the possibility of the father contracting marriage for his minor son, this idea was precluded.[22] The need for a legal act on the male's part in marriage meant that the son had to be acting as an adult in order to contract marriage. Even in the case where the boy had reached puberty before he came of legal age, married and fathered a child, he was obligated to do *kiddushin* again as an adult and could send the woman away without a *get* because the marriage was not entirely valid.

---

[22] See T. Meacham, *Sefer haBagrut*, Introduction, 60ff.

The passive aspect of 'being acquired' did not even include the daughter's consent as a *ketana* or as a *na'ara*. Although the sages expressed ambivalence at the lack of such a minimal requirement as her consent, they did not codify the prohibition in legal terms but stated it as a moral desideratum. The talmudic text which states "it is forbidden (*asur*) for a father to betroth his minor daughter" became in the codes and responsa "it is not worthy that a father should..." Never did the text have the power of a real prohibition, only a moral exhortation.[23] Fathers who transgressed this prohibition were not beaten and probably not chastised in any way.

The force of moral law is often weakened by economic realities, social ills, abuse of power, and willingness to do evil or gain illicitly at another's expense. According to Grossman, in the Middle Ages when Jews were forced by restrictions on their means of livelihood to seek other means of income, they took up long distance trading, resulting in extended travel.[24] A number of rabbinic decrees reflect that social reality. This resulted in making the marriage of minor girls more common, because it was considered to be ultimately for the welfare of the girls. Another suitable dowry might not be found when the girl was of the appropriate age, leaving her unmarried. This practice was also taken up by non-merchant Jews and thus became common.

The Torah was interpreted to mean that a father has absolute right to contract marriage of Torah validity for his minor daughter. In the event of his death, the mother and brothers, have more limited rights. They can contract rabbinically valid marriage for the minor girl. In that case, however, she had the possibility to repudiate that marriage. Whenever an unscrupulous father misuses his power and contracts halakhically binding marriage for his minor daughters as a means of gaining economic advantage, the Jewish world should react. Unfortunately, in the past few years this power has been used in a ploy for materialistic gain in divorce settlements.

By claiming to have betrothed his minor daughter and refusing to identify the groom unless his wife agrees to certain demands in the property settlement, such a father is reverting to practices of the Middle Ages, in which the father

---

[23] See the discussion by Yedidyah Dinari, "*Hishtalshalut Takenat haMe'un (Pa'alo shel R. Menachem meWirzburg),*" *Dinei Yisrael* (1981–83) 10–11:327–28.

[24] Grossman, ibid., 117–18. This may have been influenced by local non-Jewish custom, and was especially common among the royalty.

betrothed his minor daughter without informing his family.[25] By putting the threat of remaining an "anchored woman" (*aguna*) or marrying another and producing *mamzerim*, such a father has proven that he has no real concern for his daughter's welfare. These unscrupulous men are not only severely compromising the welfare of their daughters and breaking civil law, they are bringing shame upon the people of Israel. To prevent such abuse, a universal decree, *takana*, should be instituted at once by all halakhic bodies, revoking the right of a father to contract marriage for his minor daughter, and the authority of such betrothals should no longer be recognized in civil law nor be sanctioned in religious law.

---

[25] Consequently, if other marriage arrangements were made for the girls, there was a possibility that the original groom would interrupt the wedding. See Grossman, ibid., 121 for actual cases.

Beauty, Beautification, and Cosmetics:
Social Control and Halakha in Talmudic Times

Chana Safrai

"Three things gratify a man, a beautiful house, beautiful equipment,[1] and a beautiful[2] wife."[3] Appreciating and admiring physical beauty are not alien to rabbinic thinking.[4] One example in early rabbinic tradition is the famous debate over how to praise a bride. The school of Hillel argues that one should praise the bride by saying that she is righteous and beautiful (כלה נאה וחסודה), while the school of Shammai argues that one should praise her according to her qualities (כלה כמות שהיא).[5] It is an appropriate compliment to praise someone's beauty, even if it is not completely true in one's estimate.

The love story between Rabbi Akiva and his wife Rachel is legendary. After years of her suffering and sacrificing for his study, Rabbi Akiva presented his wife with a "Jerusalem of Gold" pendant, thus rewarding her devotion with a piece of expensive jewelry. This story suggests that giving frivolous adornments is an appropriate reward for inner beauty and faith. According to this source Rabbi Akiva's sons, Rabbis in their own right, were embarrassed by the extravagant behavior of their father, but he rejected their reservations, exercising his personal authority, and his preference for giving his wife gifts which embellished her beauty. In other words, he opposed the social norms and their explicit social control and critique. This seemingly minor event, together with the reactions it caused, reflects the subject of this paper, which is an attempt to apply, and contrast, a modern feminist awareness

---

[1] כלים, cloth or any type of goods.

[2] All three have the same adjective נאה and reflect a similar attitude to all three.

[3] *Berakhot* 57b.

[4] A.S. Hirshberg, "*Yofya veHityafuta shel ha'Isha biZman haTalmud,*" *Ha'Atid* 4 (Berlin, 1912) 1–53, esp. 4–8.

[5] *Ketubbot* 17a and *Kalla Rabati* 10:1.

of cosmetics and physical appearance to the halakhic decisions relevant to those times.[6]

In recent years philosophers and feminists have directed their attention to the common and evident pressures placed on individuals by society to ignore their personal preferences and to adopt, or conform to, socially accepted expectations. They draw attention to the amount of coercion, and even oppression, involved in the dictates of the modern norms of fashion and beauty. Proper dress and dress codes are seen as restricting personal growth and individual expression. Not conforming to social standards may cause someone to be ostracized. Furthermore, society is prejudiced against misfits and there is immense pressure to "fit in." As with the norms of fashion, so too with the norms concerning the body. The body has also become the target of supervision and control. As the awareness of the individual concerning his or her body and its appearance increases and the societal norm intensifies physical deformities and handicaps are highlighted. In brief, individual choice and behavior is guided—either by encouragement, or discouragement—by culture and society, including its changing values of beauty and appearance.

Jewish halakhic discourse has an interest in, and provides guidance concerning, the most minute actions of the individual. Likewise, Jewish law functions as a social structure for a community, and therefore, is also an agent of social control. The working assumption is that a "woman's body," its beauty and presentation, functions as a statement and as a conduit for direct social control.[7] Her appearance is an example of working through social control within the family, between husband and wife, father and daughter, and among females of her family. Participation and avoidance, obedience and reluctance are manifestations of social structures, the accepted Jewish way of life.

---

[6] M. Foucault, *Mikrophysik der Macht, Ueber Stafjustiz, Psychiatrie und Medizin* (Berlin, 1976). B.S. Turner, *The Body of Society: Explorations in Social Theory* (Oxford, 1984). N. Wolf, *Der Mythos Schoenheit* (Reinbek-Rowwohlt, 1991). K. Davies, *Reshaping the Female Body, The Dilemma of Cosmetic Surgery* (Routledge, 1995). F. Franckenstein, "Making up Cher," *The European Journal of Women's Studies* 4.1 (1997): 7–22.

[7] Women's bodies are more effected by social control than are the bodies of men. See the two previous contributions in this volume.

Social control is a modern term for an age-old phenomenon. Part of the study of modern social control is to identify a society's "controls"—the expressions and methods of imposed conformity, investigate them, and evaluate them. Social control is a tool to evaluate and appreciate life and its structures. Study of Social Control's advocating of "free" life and the breaking down of societal norms and their limitations, could be construed as antithetical to Halakha, which is the main foundation of Jewish life. But no! In the context of Halakha, social control is an important factor in the ever-changing nature of Jewish life.

How should the tradition respond to the new challenges and new notions of preference and behavioral codes, such as prevail in today's modern, non-conformist society? This presentation of sources of early rabbinic thinking and the variety of attitudes toward the conformity of beautification and women can help place in context the inner workings and struggles of a highly structured religious social order. The limitations—and the stretching of those limitations—are sociologically and historically far removed from our modern, open civilization, and yet, not completely divorced from it either.

The Norm in Talmudic Times

The Rabbinic sources from the *tannaic* period as well as from the *amoraic* times seem to reflect a common assumption that women are supposed to use cosmetics in an appropriate manner. Excessive use of cosmetics indicated "loose behavior."[8] Thus R. Shimon b. Yochai claims that one of the three obvious signs of a grown-up girl (בוגרת) is that she "makes up" her eyes (כוחל).[9] The *Amora* Rav Yehuda says: "Daughters of Israel, once they grow up and are not yet adults: the poor ones apply white washing paint, the rich ones apply fine flour, and the daughters of kings apply oil of Myrrh...."[10] R. Shimon b. Menasha seems to claim that the body and its presentation is part of the process of transforming a girl into a woman. God himself presented a

---

[8] A.L. Epstein, *Darkhei Ishut uMinhageha al pi Torat Yisrael* (Tel Aviv, 1960) 58–61.

[9] *Tosefta Nidda* 6:4.

[10] *Moed Katan* 9b, *Shabbat* 80b. *Pesachim* 42b–43a: Rav Yehuda in the name of Rav.

"made up" Eve to Adam.[11] Women are expected to be "made up" as part of the natural order and maintain an aura with their feminine behavior.

On the other hand, deviating women like the "fallen woman" (isha sota) are presented to the public without make-up. The Nazirite woman, however, is expected to maintain her appearance even during her Nazirite rites.[12] Likewise, in the *amoraic* tradition both in Israel and in Babylon, one encounters a discussion on the norm of eye make-up—the כחול. This substance serves both as medication and decoration. The question is whether one is permitted to apply it on the Shabbat. Substantively, the argument is whether women apply it to one eye or not. In the Babylonian tradition Rav Huna argues that modest women apply blue to one eye only. The discussion goes on to quote a contrasting tradition from the *tannaic* period and from Israel in the name of R. Shimon b. Elazar: "For medication one eye, and for decoration both eyes."[13]

In the parallel text in the *Yerushalmi* one sees a social judgment concerning cosmetics.

> R. Bun bar Chiya said: "A woman dyes one eye in blue and goes out to the market." R. Abun said: "Even the worst of prostitutes does not do this, but even a woman suffering in one eye dyes the other as well before going out to the market." R. Mana said: "...A woman dyes one of her eyes and covers the second and goes out to the market."[14]

R. Bun, supported by the school of Caesarea and R. Shimon b. Elazar, argues, from their social context, in support of a coquette—one dyed eye and a veil over the other; and for this they bring a biblical support from Song of Songs 4:9. The Babylonian tradition, and R. Abun, one of the *nachutei*,[15] promotes a different understanding. According to them, the Israelite conduct of the time is declared promiscuous and mischievous. Thus her behavior with regard to cosmetics is monitored by the Rabbis and her appearance positions

---

[11] *Shabbat* 95a; *Yalkut Shimoni* Gen. 23, exegesis on the words "and God built the rib."

[12] *Sifre*, Num. *Zuta* 6:18, 245; *Nazir* 45b.

[13] *Shabbat* 80b.

[14] *Yerushalmi Shabbat* 8:3 [11b].

[15] One of the Rabbis that commuted between the communities in Babylon and Israel.

her halakhically on the social moral hierarchy. But different customs show a different hierarchy.

Embellishment

Keeping the laws of the Torah and fulfilling the commandment is compared to a human king saying to his wife: Adorn yourself so as to be desirable (רצויה) to me.[16] A similar parallel is made in Ecclesiastes *Rabba* in the name of Bar Kapra and his son R. Isaac.[17] According to them, one should compare observance of the Torah to:

> The wife of a governor who used to embellish (מתקשטת) herself in front of her female neighbors. Her friends mocked her saying: "Your husband is not here for whom do you dress up (מתקשטת)?" She answered: "My husband is a sailor, with a favorable wind he will return and will find himself by my side. Better that he should see me in my adorned state than in neglect."[18]

Another comparison is between a man with professional skills and a married woman, "whether she is made up or not nobody looks at her, but if she is not [made up], it is a curse." On the other hand a woman with no husband—whether she is adorned or not—is looked at by everybody, and she is not cursed if she is not made up.[19]

The objective of embellishment is to attract one's husband, rather than attracting outside attention. A revealing text is found in the exegesis of R. Aba to the word "good" in Lamentations 3:17, where "good" is explained as "a ready-made bed and a woman that adorns herself for rabbinic scholars."[20] The Rabbis saw themselves as rewarded when they had a well-kept, attractive wife, who adhered to the customs and the norms of beauty.

Rav Yosef, a Babylonian Rabbi, claims that once a widow starts dying her eyes she abdicates her rights for her maintenance allowance from her hus-

---

[16] *Sifre* Deut. 31:68 and 43:102.

[17] Thus it is an approach reflected in many generations and not restricted to a single time, place, or person.

[18] Ecclesiastes *Rabba* 9:8.

[19] *Tosefta Kiddushin* 1:11.

[20] *Shabbat* 25b.

band's family. According to Rav Yosef, she has no need to apply make-up since she has no husband, and once she begins to apply cosmetics, she virtually declares that she is interested in leaving her late husband's household. In other words, her immediate society controls her cosmetic use.

The following anonymous short discussion is of interest.

> Some say: "if she becomes a prostitute [she has no rights of maintenance], let alone if she uses make-up." And others say: "if she uses make-up she has no right to maintenance, but if she prostituted she has the right!" Why? She was driven by her desire.[21]

This implies that sexual desire is understood and is not punished financially, but pure cosmetic beauty is socially frowned upon, and is liable to cause the widowed woman her livelihood. According to this debate, women do not use cosmetics out of self-interest but rather for the pleasure of their husbands, and to entice them. But her use of cosmetics is under tight control of his family, even after her husband's death.

Rav Huna also maintains that the application and wearing of cosmetics is an activity for young women and not for older women. Rav Chisda objected strongly: "He said to him: 'In the name of God! Even your mother [applies cosmetics], even the mother of your mother, and even when she is one step away from her grave...'"[22] Rav Huna, the disciple of Rav Yosef, reflects the teaching of his master on the subject, and underscores the social controls involved. Rav Chisda's objection does not necessarily oppose the strong ties between cosmetics and marriage, but it surely reflects the strong influence of the norm in women's lives. These norms are reflected in many matrimonial laws.

Divorce

Cosmetics plays a role in various laws of divorce. A famous debate between the schools of Hillel and Shammai concerns the accepted causes for divorce. According to the school of Hillel, incompatibility could be considered a cause

---

[21] *Ketubbot* 54a.

[22] *Moed Katan* 9b.

"even if he found one nicer[23] than [his wife]."[24] According to tradition, the ruling of Hillel became the accepted Halakha, and one is permitted to speculate on the social implication of this particular ruling. Any trivial reason could be a cause for divorce, including a woman's physical condition and her looks. Some of the implications of this ruling, in regard to cosmetics, follow in the sections below.

I. The Menstruating Woman

The menstruating women is described in the biblical text as feeling ill (דוה)[25] (Leviticus 12:33). In Rabbinic tradition a debate ensues: "The first Elders said: In her menstruation she should refrain from make up, i.e., blue to the eyes or rouge (אכיחול ופירקוס). And then R. Akiva came and taught [authoritatively]: This situation might cause hatred, and he might want to divorce her [therefore, she should not refrain from make-up]..."[26] In early Halakha then, menstruation regulation required one to refrain from elaborate cosmetics, which might cause a physical attraction between husband and wife. This may imply that it was noticeable when a woman was menstruating. She was without, or with less make-up. Her impurity is no longer a private affair, it is now public knowledge. This was certainly a form of social control.

R. Akiva attempted to change the old regulation on a different social basis. He argued that since neglect of appearance is a possible, if not plausible, cause for divorce, those regulations introducing neglect into the family must be revoked. And so women are encouraged to use cosmetics at all times in order to maintain the family structure. This deliberation does not refer to personal preference but rather to maintaining the social order.

Another text also refers to this issue: "All the days of her menstruation she should be ostracized. Thus they said[27]...she who neglects herself the Rabbis

---

[23] Once again נאה.

[24] Mishna *Gittin* 9:10 and parallels.

[25] Suffering pain, uncomfortable, feeling sick are the regular translations for the term. The Rabbinic tradition however picked up the discomforting element.

[26] *Sifra Metzora*, ch. *Zavim* 5. See also *Shabbat* 64b.

[27] מכאן אמרו could be *terminus technicus* for an early citation. J.N. Epstein, *Mavo leNosach haMishna* (Jerusalem, 1948) 733ff.

are satisfied with. And she who decorates (מקשטת) herself during her menstrual period the Rabbis are dissatisfied with her (אין רוח חכמים נוחה הימנה)."[28]
This text from *Avot DeRabbi Natan* reflects the early approach. (Although the
text is not earlier than the end of the *tannaic* period.[29]) Does it suggest a
parallel text of the elders prior to R. Akiva or does it suggest regression in
perspective? Is this a later negative response to the decree of R. Akiva? Here
one immediately recognizes a shift in social controls—less concern for divorce
and significantly more rigorous application of purity regulations. Could one
decide the chronological order?

Consider also the statement: "...the Rabbis are dissatisfied with her." It
implies that many were disobedient—to the point of even creating a norm as
such. The Rabbis decreed, but not all women complied. The term suggests that
the desire to enforce social control is stronger than the ability to actually do so.

II. Provisions

A husband is obligated, as part of the marriage contract, to provide for his
wife. Yet, in the marriage contract itself one does not read of any specific
obligation to buy cosmetics. Nonetheless, in the discussion concerning
provision we read that the bridegroom, in some cases, pledges to put ten
Dinarii (coins) in her perfumes' treasure.[30] The *Tosefta* adds: "A story about
the daughter of Nakdimon b. Gurion, for whom the Rabbis ruled that she
should be given the large sum of five hundred gold *Dinarii* for perfumes every
day...She cursed at them and said: 'Thus you should give your daughters?'"[31]
Cosmetics, even in abundance, are part of the rabbinic understanding of the

---

[28] *Avot deRabbi Natan*, version A 2:1 (Schechter, 8), in variant version B 3:1 (Schechter, 12).

[29] The date of this midrashic work is in scholarly debate. For a short summary see, S. Safrai, ed., *The Literature of the Sages*, part 1 (Assen/Maasatricht/Philadelphia: CRINT, 1989) 376–78.

[30] Mishna *Ketubbot* 6:4, See the qualifying discussion in the Talmud 66b. Similarly, if a husband left his wife with no provision, the court will confiscate his possessions for her cosmetics (תכשיט), since she should not be neglected! (*Ketubbot* 48a).

[31] *Tosefta Ketubbot* 5:9; *Yerushalmi Ketubbot* 5 [30c]; *Ketubbot* 66b; Ecclesiastes *Rabba* 1:8; *Psikta Rabati* 29:30, 140a.

marital agreement. Neglect of this appropriate provision is a legitimate cause for the wife to initiate divorce.

Women who married into the house of Avtinas entered into a special category within the Rabbinic tradition. The house of Avtinas supplied the incense (*ktoret*) materials for the Temple,[32] and the *Tosefta* reports that they refrained from using perfumes so as not to cause suspicion of misused sanctified materials.

> Their women never came out perfumed, and when a man from their family married a woman from another family he conditioned the relation with abstinence from perfume, so that again nobody would say that they misused the *ktoret* materials, as it is written "And you should be clean before God and Israel." (Num. 32:22)[33]

The Avtinas house, according to this *tannaic* tradition, assumed tight personal social control of their own families. Their social and professional life officially dictated their females' behavior and cosmetic usage. Women joining the family had to give up their personal preferences and the accepted social rights for perfume. The social requirement simply came first. A woman could choose not to agree, but in so doing the choice reflected social control assumptions and consequences.

III. Pledge Against Decoration

A third case is that of the husband who takes a pledge to prohibit his wife from using adornments (קישוטים),[34] or washing.[35] The Mishna considers this a full-fledged cause for divorce, equivalent to the denial of sex or provision of food by the husband. Tradition recognizes a relationship between social and economic levels and recognizes the more urgent needs of "wealthy women."[36]

---

[32] Mishna *Yoma* 3:11.

[33] *Tosefta, Yoma* 2:6, *Yerushalmi Yoma* 3:9 [41a], *Yerushalmi Shekalim* 5:2 [48b], *Yoma* 38a, *Shir haShirim Rabba* 3:5. For a halakhic discussion of this case see Yosef Dovid Epstein, *Sefer Mitzvot haBayit*, vol. 1 (New York, 1981) 359–62.

[34] A general term for either cosmetics or jewelry.

[35] *Yerushalmi Ketubbot* 7:3 [31a].

[36] Mishna *Ketubbot* 7:3.

And, the *Tosefta* tradition even adds some fashion considerations. A woman has the right to her own taste even when her husband finds it socially improper, as in the case of an older women wearing younger fashions and vice versa.[37] For the first time one can begin to see a recognition of personal preferences. However, here too, it may well be that the major interest was still to control the use of cosmetics and jewelry and dictate a general norm of compliance, and not simply to motivate the husband to comply with a personal norm.

Obligation to Maintain the Norm

Are there regulations that force women to legally adhere to some basic norms of personal physical appearance? While there are no fast norms for this, it seems that this control is placed in the hands of the husband. He has the right to comply with or to reject his wife's wishes and direct her behavior. Clearly, his wishes and preferences take precedence over her religious devotion in this instance.

Pledge to Refrain

In the case of a woman pledging either to use "adornment" or to refrain from using "adornment," the husband has the right to cancel her religious pledge, even if she took an oath in the name of God. The female dependence on male (father's or husband's) acceptance is scripturally based (Num. 30:2–17). The rabbinic activity lies in the details attached to the biblical ordinance, and in some cases, to the rationale given for the Halakha. Thus, women have no controlling personal choices regarding their adornment—either as to cosmetics or jewelry, and require male consent; the social control here is given to the males in the family. This becomes an additional area of the male's social control.

Nazirite

Once again, it is a biblical ordinance that gives the father/husband the right to eliminate the Nazirite pledge of a woman. The husband has an unlimited right

---

[37] *Tosefta, Ketubbot* 7:3.

to cancel any vow—though limited in time; the annulment (usually) has to immediately follow the vow. It is illuminating to take note of the rabbinically articulated rationale for enlarging the time period of annulment. At the very end of the Nazirite rituals, just before his wife is obligated to shave her hair, the husband gets the right of annulment "Since he might say: I cannot stand a neglected[38] wife."[39] The objection is not religious, though a vow is a religious act. But rather, this is the beauty preference of the husband, even if he refrained from using his prerogative at the earlier stage. This argument stresses the significance of her appearance, and turns it into a decisive factor overruling her own personal wishes and religious endeavors.

Cosmetics in Mourning

According to custom, physical neglect (עינוי)[40] is a part of the obligation of the mourner as they remain at home for a period of seven days and are visited by community members. During this period, a husband has no right to force his wife to maintain cosmetic appearances while she is in mourning for her parents. She is, however, *required* to refrain from using them when her husband is in mourning for his relatives.[41] The Babylonian Talmud adds to the custom, claiming: "The young woman[42] is not permitted (רשאה) to neglect herself in the mourning day over her father."[43] Sitting relatively exposed to visitors and the public eye, and being in the marriage market, the young women must maintain a certain standard. Her personal inclination to express mourning, as well as related mourning customs, are overruled by prominent social expectations and control. She should marry, and presumably, can do so "only" if she is presentable—even when in mourning.

---

[38] Whose hair is not made according to custom, or is shaven.

[39] Mishna *Nazir* 4:5.

[40] Refrain from washing, cosmetics, wearing shoes, using beds and chairs (sitting and sleeping on mattresses), and sexual intercourse.

[41] *Ketubbot* 4b; *Moed Katan* 20b; *Yerushalmi Moed Katan* 3:5 [83a].

[42] בוגרת, unmarried as yet. See also the previous article.

[43] *Ta'anit* 13b.

Rabbinic language clearly suggests that they conceive their role as directors and controllers of this social order, and that women are viewed as part of the social structure where their personal preference regarding cosmetics and beauty does not usually fall into the empowerment side of the halakhic considerations. Even in the case of the married woman mourning her close family members the halakhic discourse approaches the conduct from the point of view of the husband's rights. *Her* mourning is presented as a restriction of *his* rights.

Shabbat and Holidays

Another aspect of the cosmetic norm is reflected in the Halakha of the Shabbat and Holidays.

A major halakhic concern on Shabbat is refraining from the use of, or the moving of, any object pertaining to "weekday activities," which is a Rabbinic extension of the biblical ordinance not to work on the Shabbat. The Mishna devotes many chapters to this, and sections of chapter six of Mishna *Shabbat* are relevant here. The question they raised is: what are permissible paraphernalia to carry out of the house on that day? Or, when in public, what is considered part of regular dress and conduct and thus accepted or not accepted on this holy day? The formal objection is not to the appearance in public, but rather the permission of what to use and carry outside of the house. In fact, this law functions as a social control. The list for women includes specific clothing, jewelry, cosmetics, medicines, and amulets.[44]

The Mishna suggests that there is a noticeable difference in dress and appearance on the Shabbat affecting all members of the community, females in particular. Furthermore, concerning cosmetics, the Mishna reports a debate among Rabbis: "a woman should not go out with...bundled herb perfumes,...[nor] a dish of perfumed oils if she has to bring a sin offering. These are the words of R. Meir. The Rabbis[45] [on the other hand,] allow her [to go

---

[44] Mishna *Shabbat* 6:1,3.

[45] The *Tosefta* tradition reports an inner difference between R. Eliezer and the Rabbis. Each is permitting the use of one sort of perfume and does not permit the other. *Tosefta Shabbat* 4:11 and parallels.

out] in the case of bundled herb perfumes and a dish of perfumed oils."[46] Though it is a private action, the language is of formal punishment 'sin offering,' thus implying a watchful public eye, regular customs, and adherence to regulations, i.e., social control with minimal deviations. Again, the debate suggests that social control is very tight and that there are degrees of expectation in different circles, each probably exercising its particular control. The difference in habits would serve then as a social identity, confirming social strata and place as well as direct control.

Pessach and Sukkot both have *Chol haMo'ed*—semi-holy days, during which work is not permitted unless it is urgent. The definition of urgency is given in part to the individual's discretion but it is also partly dictated. One might assume that the Halakha and local customs rotate between the need to celebrate and the urge to accomplish as much as possible within the restricted week. In this dilemma one finds a debate pertaining to cosmetics. "A woman applies her cosmetics (תכשיטיה) during the intermediate days of the holiday. R. Yehuda says: She should not white wash[47] herself because it is ugly (ניוול) on her."[48] Regular make-up is permitted, thus expected, but more sophisticated activities involving longer, painstaking procedures should be avoided. Once more, make-up is deemed as necessary and regular—the accepted norm, and there is a rabbinic assumption of necessity regulating those activities.

Jerusalem and Cosmetics

The Jewish custom to mourn the destruction of Jerusalem and to always remember the city is reflected in our subject. The *Tosefta* reads: A woman performs her entire cosmetic ritual (כל תכשיטיה) but leaves a small part undone, in memory of Jerusalem, as it is written: "If I forget you Oh Jerusalem, let my right arm be forgotten" (Psalms 137:5).[49] Jerusalem is a core identity concept and women are required to subject their sense of beauty and perfection to the group sense of identity. The personal is sacrificed for the sake of the

---

[46] Mishna *Shabbat* 6:3.

[47] A method of shaving.

[48] Mishna *Moed Katan* 1:7.

[49] *Tosefta Bava Batra* 2:17.

group/social enterprise. Cosmetics are once again rendered and controlled by the social context.

Concluding Remarks

In a society where codes of fashion, beauty and behavior are continually changing, in a world where the general has been practically and ideologically replaced with the private and individual, the rabbinic Halakha with its long tradition can be seen as an enigma. This paper is an attempt to bring these two into a dialogue.

Cosmetics and body care are conceived of in modern thought as a private realm, and that regulations in this area infringe upon individual rights and freedom, threatening autonomy. Addressing the rabbinic tradition with these concerns is the aim of this paper.

There is no doubt that female cosmetics and personal grooming (תכשיטים וקישוטים) constitute a recurring theme in Halakha. It seems that social control is a governing motive for much of the above mentioned legislation of that time. Ultimately, the message was that women, and in particular wives, should pay special attention to their looks to meet societal expectations and requirements.

Social control does not stay indoors in Jewish law. Appearances in public require certain norms, and divergence is frowned upon and evokes repercussions. Neighbors, community, and the Halakha have the right to control, chastise, intervene, and even punish, in cases of "dangerous" diversions. In those cases, the personal preferences of both husband and wife are of lesser interest, and social standards have priority.

The more public arena of social control is primarily directed to maintain the family structure of the social order. In this arena, women do seem to have certain rights and are able to exercise their social power. In a highly controlled society they receive backing and protection from the legal system.

Though the rabbinic tradition presents itself as authoritative, one finds clues to a different reality. Yes, the Rabbis would like to regulate and control these intimate aspects of life, but even in talmudic times they already admit that women's inner, personal pressures and preferences are sometimes stronger than their centralist and conformist vision. They might not appreciate it, they reprimand it, but they admit its existence as part of tradition.

Duration of Breastfeeding in Jewish Law

Deena Rachel Zimmerman

Human milk is recognized as the ideal form of infant nutrition both by medical research and Halakha. To quote the most recent policy statement of the American Academy of Pediatrics (AAP):[1]

> Human milk is uniquely superior for infant feeding and is species-specific; all substitute feeding options differ markedly from it...Epidemiologic research shows that human milk and breastfeeding of infants provide advantages with regard to general health, growth and development, while significantly decreasing risk for a large number of acute and chronic conditions. Research in the United States and Canada, Europe and other developed countries, among predominately middle class populations provide strong evidence that human milk feeding decreases the incidence and/or severity of diarrhea, lower respiratory infection...

Chazal, from practical experience noted:

> "*Stam tinok mesukan etzel chalav.*"

> "The average infant is at danger from [lack of] milk." (*Yevamot* 114a)

According to modern science and Jewish law, how long (i.e., how many months/years) is breastfeeding an ideal?

The same AAP statement cited above also states:

> Exclusive breastfeeding is ideal nutrition and sufficient to support optimal growth and development for approximately the first 6 months after birth... Gradual introduction of iron enriched solid foods in the second half of the first year should complement the breast milk diet. It is recommended that breastfeeding continue for at least 12 months, and thereafter for as long as mutually desired.

---

[1] American Academy of Pediatrics, "Breastfeeding and the Use of Human Milk," *Pediatrics* 100 (1997): 1035–39.

The World Health Organization encourages breastfeeding until two years and beyond.[2] How do these recommendations fit with a halakhic approach? Are there halakhic implications to the duration of nursing?

The Obligation

Breastfeeding is the method of infant feeding that is assumed by Halakha and considered a marital obligation of a wife to her husband.[3] If the mother did not want or could not nurse her own infant the option was to hire another woman, a wetnurse. Circumstances existed that the husband would have to pay for this service such as if it were not her family custom to nurse. At other times, if the mother had sufficient funds, she could pay for it herself. However, for a woman who did not have the funds, the *Shulchan Arukh*[4] based on the Talmud[5] ruled that if a woman has vowed not to breastfeed her infant, she could be compelled to do so until the child was 24 months of age. Today, however, a large number of women unfortunately do not nurse. According to 1996 statistics, only 59.7% of American women initiated breastfeeding and only 21.6% continued until 6 months of age.[6] (In other countries the number are generally higher.) The *Nishmat Avraham* questions whether at present a woman can be halakhically compelled to nurse her infant since many women do not. He feels though that a number of months *are* perhaps indicated in light of the known medical benefits.[7]

The evidence of the medical benefits does have halakhic implications. Caring for one's health is a halakhic imperative.[8] With the known health benefits for the infant and mother it would thus seem that breastfeeding would

---

[2] M. Sugarman and Kendall-Tackett. "Weaning ages in a sample of American women who practice extended breastfeeding," *Clin Pediatr* 12 (1995): 642–49.

[3] *Ketubbot* 59b.

[4] EH 82:1.

[5] *Ketubbot* 59b.

[6] Ross Laboratories, *Mother's Infant Feeding Survey*, 1996

[7] EH 81:1.

[8] F. Levin, *Halacha, Medical Science and Technology* (Brooklyn: Maznaim, 1987) 3–38. See bibliography and sources there.

have halakhic import as well. However, since many *poskim* have not emphatically forbidden or condemned some practices today with clear medical evidence of harm, such as smoking,[9] it is certainly unlikely that they would forbid the use of substitute methods of infant feeding.

The Minimum

So great was the fear of harming the child from not nursing that the Rabbis decreed that a woman who is nursing at the time of her husband's death was not allowed to remarry during the nursing period (*Yevamot* 36b). Furthermore, she should not remarry during pregnancy as most pregnant women will become nursing women (*Yevamot* 42b), and it was thought that after three months of pregnancy there would no longer be sufficient milk for the older child.[10]

The standard "nursing period" in the Talmud is 24 months. On the citation on *Yevamot* 36b, *Rashi* states simply "A woman whose husband has died and she is pregnant or nursing is forbidden to remarry until the infant is 24 months old because that is how long an infant nurses." From the words in the Gemara it would appear that this rule does not apply to a nursing divorcee unless the child will not nurse from another woman. However, there are those who would forbid remarriage in these circumstances as well (see *Tosafot* on *Yevamot* 36b) This decree of "*meneket chavero*" is brought as Halakha in the *Shulchan Arukh*:[11]

> The sages decreed that a man should not marry or even betroth the pregnant [former] wife of his friend or the nursing [former] wife of his friend until the infant is 24 months old excluding the day the infant was born and the day that

---

[9] F. Rosner, "Cigarette Smoking and Jewish Law," *Halacha and Contemporary Society*, ed. A.S. Cohen (NY: Ktav, 1984). See also *Smoking and Damage to Health in the Halachah* by R. Menachem Slae (Jerusalem: Acharai Publications, 1990).

[10] This is not necessarily true today as many pregnant women can continue to nurse and in fact it is possible to "tandem nurse" to children of different ages. However, at the time of the Talmud, women in general had a poorer nutritional status than today, proving difficult at times to provide the additional calories needed for both nursing and pregnancy.

[11] EH 13:11.

they are betrothed regardless if she is a widow, divorcee, or prostitute whether she has weaned the child or given it to a wetnurse...

This decree is given such import because it involved the fear of harm to the infant and in general, unlike many other rabbinical enactments where the tendency is to be lenient, the trend with this decree is to be stringent.[12] The Jerusalem Talmud even finds a prooftext in the Tanach.[13] "Do not remove the boundaries which the ancestors have placed and in the fields of orphans do not come."[14] (The play on words here is that fields = "sadei" and breasts = "shadei"). Rav Yosef Caro, the author of the *Shulchan Arukh*, in the *Beit Yosef* (his commentary on the *Tur*), makes it clear how seriously this decree is to be taken:[15]

> A number of such circumstances have come before me and I have forbidden all of them...and anyone who tries to be lenient in this manner is breaking the fence (*poretz geder*) of the words of the sages.

Others were willing to be lenient in extraordinary circumstances such as Rav Mintz who allowed a nursing prostitute to marry because of the physical and spiritual benefits that would be accrued to her and the child by her being married.[16] Many attacked him for this action but the *Chatam Sofer* defended him, as the initial reason for the decree was the benefit of the infant.[17]

The *Chatam Sofer* also states that even at the time of the Talmud many infants nursed for shorter periods.[18] However, because of the fear of harming the child by not nursing, the decree of remarrying applies until 24 months of age due to concern for the minority of infants who need the full 24 months. Thus saying that today women often nurse for less does not lessen the import of the Rabbinic decree of *meneket chavero*. Rav Moshe Feinstein did take

---

[12] *Otzar haPoskim* 73a.

[13] *Sota* 4:3.

[14] *Mishle* 23.

[15] *Beit Yosef* on *Tur* 13:1.

[16] *Mahari Mintz* 5.

[17] *Chatam Sofer* 2:422 and 3:30.

[18] EH 30.

current trends into consideration as a reason for leniency. In general his feeling was that 21 months is sufficient taking into consideration that since it would take 3 months of pregnancy for the breastmilk to cease, even if the mother became pregnant immediately on remarrying the infant would have the benefit of 24 months of breastmilk. R. Moshe Feinstein also said there was basis for accepting an 18 months minimum as this example is given in the Talmud in a debate between *Beit Hillel* and *Beit Shammai*.[19] He also ruled in times of great need, for example an Israeli war widow whom someone was willing to marry now but not to wait, 12 months would be a sufficient wait prior to remarrying.[20]

When issues of remarrying are not involved, at least 18,[21] or 24 months is desirable. The *Pitchei Teshuva*, commenting on the *Shulchan Arukh*,[22] quotes a responsa of the *Adnei Paz* who states:[23]

> Those who feel that weaning an infant early is good for the child's Torah learning are in error...in fact it is forbidden to wean before 24 months unless there is a compelling reason.

The Maximum

The original source of discussion of a limitation of the duration of breastfeeding is found in the Talmud (*Ketubbot* 60a):

> An infant continues to nurse to 24 months [of age]. From this point on it is as if he is nursing from an unkosher insect (*sheketz*) according to Rabbi Eliezer. Rabbi Yehoshua states even to 4 or five years. If he stopped nursing after 24 months and returned [to breastfeed] it is comparable to nursing from an unkosher insect. From here [4–5 years] on it is comparable to nursing from an unkosher insect.

---

[19] *Nishmat Avraham*, EH 13:11.

[20] *Iggerot Moshe*, EH 49 and 50.

[21] *Tzemach Tzedek haChadash* 45 as quoted in A. Steinberg, *Encyclopedia Hilkhatit Refu'it* (Jerusalem, 1994) s.v. "*Hanaka.*"

[22] YD 81:7.16.

[23] *Siman* 17.

Interestingly, these ages are compatible with the duration an infant will generally nurse if allowed to continue to breastfeed until the child is ready to cease. For example, a study of weaning ages in American women who practice extended nursing and wait for child initiated cessation of breastfeeding shows that the modal age of weaning is 37 months.[24] Many traditional cultures today also practice breastfeeding until 2–4 years.[25]

What could possibly be the halakhic problem with breastfeeding as long as the child desired? Why need a maximum at all? In general kosher milk comes from kosher animals. Although human meat is not to be consumed, human milk is kosher. The rabbis however were afraid that if direct nursing from a woman was permitted even for an adult, people may incorrectly determine that milk from an unkosher animal is permitted and thus they proscribed direct nursing for "adults."[26] The debate in the Gemara is from what age this rabbinic degree applies to children.

The opinion of Rabbi Yehoshua that breastfeeding up to age 4–5 years old is permitted is accepted as Halakha. However, another requirement for permitting breastfeeding beyond 24 months is that the child has not stopped nursing for 3 consecutive days. The *Yerushalmi* adds the additional proviso that this three-day separation has to be by a healthy infant, not one who is sick.[27]

The Halakha as stated in the *Shulchan Arukh*:[28]

> An infant breastfeeds until 4 years for a healthy child and 5 years for a sickly child if he has not ceased; but if he is weaned for three whole days [= 72 hours] after 24 months he should not be returned to the breast. This is if he ceased while healthy, but if he ceased due to an illness and was unable to nurse, he can be returned. If there is a danger, he can be returned even after a number of

---

[24] M. Sugarman and Kendall-Tackett, ibid.

[25] K.A. Dettwyler, "A time to wean: the hominid blueprint for the natural age of weaning in modern human populations," *Breastfeeding Biocultural Perspectives,* eds. P.S. Macadam and K.A. Dettwyler (NY, 1995).

[26] *Taz,* YD 81:9.

[27] *Ketubbot* 5:6 [30a].

[28] YD 81:7.

days. Within 24 months of age even if he ceased in health for a month or more he can be returned and nurse until the end of 24 months.

There are a number of debates on exactly when restarting is permitted. Can a child who was in danger continue once the danger has passed?[29] Can a child who ceased for a prolonged period while less than 24 months return until 24 months exactly or as long as he/she wishes?[30] As in general, Halakha "errs" on the side of leniency and caution when a possible risk to health is involved,[31] why the hesitation to allow resumption of breastfeeding? One reason given is that a child can have the benefits of expressed breastmilk at any age thus there is less reason to permit continued direct breastfeeding.[32]

An issue not addressed in any printed responsa to date is what if the mother of a child over 24 months leaves the child for three days. One such example would be a mother who is hospitalized due to illness. From the general principle of *piku'ach nefesh* it would seem that this would be permissible. What if, however, she leaves for non-medical reasons, for example, on a business trip?

A possible answer to this question seems to be found in the *Haga'ot Maimoniyot*,[33] in his commentary on the *Rambam*. The *Rambam* states that the three-day separation is a reason not to restart only in a healthy child, not a sickly one. The *Hago'at Maimoniyot* points out that the source of this is the *Yerushalmi* and explains "*mitoch boryav*," that the child does not need to nurse but stopped of his or her own volition, and is no longer interested in nursing, "*katz bo*." It would thus seem that if the interruption was due to maternal reasons, restarting nursing would be permitted.

To summarize, it would appear that an "Halakhic Policy Statement" on the duration of breastfeeding would read as follows:

> Breastfeeding is the ideal form of infant nutrition and thus should be encouraged as part of a total plan of healthy behavior. It is recom-

---

[29] *Shakh,* YD 81:22. See also *Responsa Yabia Omer,* YD 5:11.

[30] *Lechem Mishna* on *Rambam, Hilkhot Ma'akhalot Asurot* 3:5.

[31] *Shulchan Arukh,* OC 428.

[32] See n28 above.

[33] Comment 7 on *Rambam,* ibid.

mended that breastfeeding continue for at least 18–24 months, and may continue thereafter until 4 years for a healthy child and 5 years for a sickly child as long as the child while healthy, has not initiated an interruption of 72 hours (once the child is over 24 months of age). In cases of interruption of this length, please consult a competent halakhic authority.

Establishing and Uprooting Menstruation
With the Pill

Devorah Zlochower

A non-contraceptive benefit of the Pill is the increase of regularity in a woman's menstrual cycle. Synthetic estrogen and progestin, the major components of oral contraceptives (the Pill), imitate the natural increases of estrogen and progestin which stimulate growth and maintenance of the endometrial lining of the uterus. As a result, menstruation does not take place when a woman is taking the Pill. Additionally, there is increased predictability on what day the woman will begin menstruating after she stops taking the oral contraceptive. Although some initial spotting or breakthrough bleeding may occur with today's lower estrogen Pill, menstrual predictability remains one of the benefits of taking the Pill.[1]

The ability to prevent the natural flow of the menses requires us to re-evaluate the *halakhot* of *vestot* (menses) for a woman who is taking the Pill.

Consider the following case:

A woman has her period every 26 days. She has maintained this pattern on at least three consecutive occasions and has thereby established a *veset kavu'a*, a fixed cycle. The Halakha requires this woman to refrain from sexual inter-course with her husband on the 26th day of her menstrual cycle. Additionally, she cannot resume sexual activity until she has examined herself internally to make sure that she is not menstruating. This woman now begins to take the Pill

---

[1] Robert Hatcher, et. al., *Contraceptive Technology*, 16th revised ed. (Irvington: Irvington Publishers, 1994) ch. 10, esp. page 254. "Spotting has increased with all the lower-dose pills in comparison with the higher dose pills of 30 years ago... Spotting and breakthrough bleeding tend to diminish dramatically over the first few months of pill use with all the combined pills." See also Richard Dickey, *Oral Contraceptive User Guide* (Oklahoma: Information Guides, 1987) 15–19 and table 2-2 on pages 22–23. The author describes how oral contraceptives block pregnancy by increasing the progestational, estrogenic and androgenic activities in the body; the breakdown of the endometrial lining in the uterus which is indicated by uterine bleeding only occurs when the estrogen and progestin quantities are reduced. As long as the woman has sufficient amounts of estrogen and progestin circulating in her body she will not menstruate.

and she menstruates 28 days after the onset of her last period, four days after she takes the last pill.

This case presents a number of questions:

1) How long must this woman wait before she can ignore her pre-existing *veset* of 26 days and its requisite laws?

2) Do we require the woman who is now taking the Pill to establish a fixed pattern over three consecutive occasions or can she establish this new *veset* immediately?

3) What type of *veset* does the woman establish while taking the Pill? Is it based on the number of days in her cycle, like the *veset* she had before she took the Pill, or is it based on the number of days after she stops taking the Pill that she begins to menstruate? For example, if the woman goes on vacation and, in order to delay the onset of menstruation, takes the Pill for 30 days instead of the usual 21 days, must she refrain from sexual activity 28 days after her last period or does she refrain on the fourth day after she stops taking the Pill?

4) If the woman stops taking the Pill does she return to her previous *veset* of 26 days, and if so, when?

These questions will be answered by a focused examination of the laws of *vestot*.

We will examine, in turn, the halakhic category of *mesuleket damim,* a women whose menstrual cycle is suspended; the typology of *vestot*; the application of *chazaka* to the laws of *vestot*; and the resumption of a *veset*.

Mesuleket Damim

We are introduced to the category of *mesuleket damim* in two passages in the Talmud. In a Mishna in *Nidda* 39a, Rabbi Meir rules that a woman who is hiding out of fear is considered a *mesuleket damim*, a woman who has had her period suspended. In *Nidda* 9a, the Talmud declares that a pregnant woman is also considered a *mesuleket damim* and has the same halakhic status as the woman who fears. There are two practical differences between the *mesuleket damim* and a menstruating woman. While a woman experiencing her normal menstrual cycle is required to refrain from sexual intercourse with her husband during her *veset*, a woman whose period has been suspended does not. Additionally, a woman who is experiencing her normal cycle cannot resume sexual activity once her *veset* has passed until she does a *bedika*, an internal examination; a *mesuleket damim* who forgets to do that examination may resume sexual activity.

While the Talmud makes no distinction between the cases of the pregnant woman and the woman who fears, most of the commentators see a practical difference, requiring *bedika lekhatchila* (*ab initio*) and cessation of sexual activity for the woman who fears but not for the pregnant woman.[2] This practical difference points to a definitional distinction for *Tur*[3] and *Rashba*.[4] They maintain that the pregnant woman has a long-term suspension of her menstrual cycle during her pregnancy while the woman hiding in fear only experiences a temporary suspension of her menstrual cycle. The Halakha requires the woman who fears to do *bedikot lekhatchila* and to refrain from sexual intercourse during her *veset* since her period may still arrive. In contrast, a pregnant woman who bleeds during her pregnancy does not have to be concerned for her previous *veset* during the following month; the bleeding is simply considered an anomaly.[5]

Other decisors who accept the practical distinction do not see a significant theoretical difference between the case of the pregnant woman and the case of the woman who fears. *Beit Yosef*,[6] *Perisha*,[7] and *Shakh*[8] do not view the case of the pregnant woman and the case of the woman who fears as essentially different. These decisors argue that different women might react differently to

---

[2] *Tur* (YD 184, page 42b); *Beit Yosef, ad loc.*; *Rama* (YD 184:8), *Shakh, ad loc.*; *Taz, ad loc.* For opposing view see *Rashba* (*Torat haBayit, Dinei Vestot*, page 12b) Note that *Beit Yosef* requires *bedika lekhatchila* even for the pregnant woman.

[3] YD 189, page 58b.

[4] *Torat haBayit, Dinei Vestot*, page 13b.

[5] *Shulchan Arukh* 184:7 and 189:33 point out that the pregnant woman referred to here is one whose first trimester is completed. See Rabbi Moshe Feinstein's responsum in Rabbi Shimon Eider's *Halachos of Nidda*, (Hebrew), vol. 1, page 5; Rabbi Mordechai Eliyahu, *Drakhei Tahara*, 83–84, and Rabbi Shmuel Wozner, *Shi'urei Shevet haLevi*, 30–31 for a discussion whether contemporary women, whose pregnancies can be detected at the earliest stages, are considered *mesuleket damim* during the first trimester of pregnancy.

[6] YD 184, s.v. "*ha'isha shehayta nichba'it.*"

[7] YD 184:16.

[8] YD 184:21.

fear and that total suspension of the menses for every woman is not certain. *Taz* believes that the suspension is total for both the pregnant woman and the woman hiding in fear. However, since the fear of the woman hiding could lift, even during her travail, and her normal cycle would resume, he does not consider such a woman a *mesuleket damim* throughout this entire experience as he does the pregnant woman.[9]

Is a woman taking the Pill a *mesuleket damim*? Is she like the woman who fears or is she like the pregnant woman? Since a pregnant woman experiences a total suspension of her period and a woman in fear does not, it would seem obvious that the Pill, which completely suspends menstruation, would be similar to pregnancy.[10] However, if a woman taking the Pill experiences breakthrough bleeding or spotting on a regular basis because the estrogen level in the oral contraceptive is too low for her, then she might not be a *mesuleket damim* at all. The bleeding might be considered anomalous like the periodic bleeding of a pregnant woman. Since the bleeding results from her body's reaction to the hormones, I think it raises serious concerns for her status as a *mesuleket damim* altogether. I have not seen any discussion in the literature on this issue.

Dayan Yitzchak Weiss[11] disagrees. He explains that our knowledge of the effectiveness of the contraceptive in suspending menstruation is based on the testimony of doctors, many of them not Jewish. Dayan Weiss rules that the testimony of these doctors is not acceptable halakhic proof. Therefore, we cannot demonstrate that the Pill suspends menstruation in any predictable fashion, and *bedikot bedi'avad* (*ex post facto*) and refraining from sexual intercourse on the day of the previous *veset* are required. It is important to note that Dayan Weiss was referring to a contraceptive in which dosages varied widely among women; oral contraceptives today have proven track records that demonstrate consistency.

---

[9] YD 184:11.

[10] One could argue that pregnancy suspends menstruation for 9 months while the Pill, in its normal usage, suspends menstruation for 3 weeks; perhaps the suspension caused by taking the Pill is not as permanent. I find this argument difficult since the Pill has the capacity to suspend menstruation for great lengths of time; menstruation only occurs because the woman normally stops taking the Pill for one week every month.

[11] *Minchat Yitzchak* 1:127.

Rabbi Eliezer Waldenberg,[12] basing his *pesak* on a responsum of Rabbi David Ben Zimra,[13] disagrees with Dayan Weiss. He points out that the Pill has been tested and has been proven effective in suspending menstruation for millions of women; testimony of doctors is not required. However, he is unwilling to pronounce the Pill a case of total suspension of the menses until the woman taking the Pill has established a *chazaka* that she does not menstruate on the day of her previously established *veset*. Once she has established a *chazakah* she need not do a *bedika*; prior to the establishment of a *chazaka*, *bedikot lekhatchila* and *perisha*, cessation of sexual activity, are required.[14] This formulation is modeled on the case of the woman who fears. Rabbi Shmuel Wozner,[15] Rabbi Shlomo Levi[16] and Rabbi Ovadia Yosef[17] consider the track record of the modern Pill to be sufficient and do not require a *chazaka* to define her as a *mesuleket damim*. They rule that her situation is analogous to that of a pregnant woman and do not require any *bedikot* for the prior *veset*.

Rabbi Moshe Sternbuch suggests that a woman taking the Pill may be even more certain than a pregnant woman that she will not experience uterine bleeding and need not observe her prior *vestot*.[18] However, in another responsum he states that he is uncomfortable ruling against Dayan Weiss and limits his lenient ruling to a bride.[19]

---

[12] *Tzitz Eliezer* 13:103.

[13] *Radvaz* 8:136.

[14] It is important to note that *Radvaz* (1480–1573) was dealing with an entirely different medication. Rabbi Waldenberg does not note this point but follows *Radvaz* without this consideration.

[15] *Shi'urei Shevet haLevi* (YD 184:8.2). He limits this ruling to brides and women who demonstrate a medical need for the Pill.

[16] "*Hashpa'at haShimush beGlulot al Dinei Vestot*," *Techumin*, vol. 3 (1982): 181.

[17] *Taharat haBayit* 2:18.

[18] *Teshuvot veHanhagot*, vol. 2 (Jerusalem, 1994) 433. Rabbi Sternbuch claims that a pregnant woman who previously had a regular menstrual cycle must observe her *vestot* during the first trimester since she still may experience sensations similar to those she experiences with her *veset*.

[19] *Teshuvot veHanhagot*, vol. 1 (Jerusalem, 1992) 491.

A Typology of *Vestot*

According to Rabbis Wozner, Levi, Yosef, and Waldenberg, our woman is no longer concerned with her *veset* for the 26th day of her cycle. When does she establish her new *veset*? What type of *veset* does she establish? To answer these questions we now turn to the definitions of the various *vestot*.

A *veset* is a predicted day when a woman can expect her period. Halakha presents us with a typology of *vestot*:

A *veset leyamim* is a calendrical *veset* based on the date of the woman's last period. There are two subcategories of *vestot leyamim*: 1. *Chodesh*[20]—the same date in the new month that a woman had her period in the last month. 2. *Haflaga*[21]—the same number of days that separated her last two periods is used to set a day this month when she can expect her period.[22]

A *veset haguf* is a physiological *veset* in which the woman has a physical sensation that signals the onset of her period. *Vestot haguf* are bodily sensations such as yawning, cramps, or feelings of heaviness.[23]

A *veset machmat ones* relies upon external causes to signal the beginning of menstrual bleeding. The *Tosefta* (*Nidda* 1:2) lists jumping, being hit or coughing as examples of this *veset*.[24]

A *veset* for a woman taking the Pill does not fit the *veset leyamim* model since it relies on a different set of causal operators. A *veset leyamim* is established according to the number of days in a woman's menstrual cycle.[25] Taking the Pill replaces the natural menstrual cycle with an artificial one based on taking or not taking the Pill. A woman has control over this artificial cycle and can choose the day on which her period will arrive. For example, if she

---

[20] *Shulchan Arukh*, YD 189:2.

[21] Ibid.

[22] The *ona beinonit* is a type of *haflaga*.

[23] *Shulchan Arukh* (YD 189:19) states that these sensations alone cannot indicate that her period will arrive on a particular day. However, once she has these sensations and we have proven by means of *chazaka* that her period will soon follow, she and her husband must refrain from sexual intercourse.

[24] The Zuckerman edition of the *Tosefta* substitutes "being sick" for "coughing."

[25] *Chodesh* might operate differently; it seems to operate on a lunar cycle rather than on the woman's menstrual cycle.

chooses to take the Pill 30 consecutive days rather than the usual 21 days, she will not menstruate those entire 30 days. Thus, if she usually sees blood four days after she stops taking the Pill she will now see blood on the 34th day rather than on the 25th day. Stating that she has a *veset leyamim* for the 25th day is inaccurate; she has a *veset* for the fourth day after she stops taking the Pill.

The *veset haguf* model is likewise irrelevant. Most *Rishonim* agree that *vestot haguf* are limited to sensations or pains that result from the arrival of the menses[26] as opposed to the cessation of the Pill which actively causes menstruation. Moreover, the *Shulchan Arukh,*[27] following the majority of *Rishonim,* limits *vestot haguf* to these physical sensations.[28] Accordingly, taking the Pill would clearly not operate as a *veset haguf.*

The category that seems most appropriate is *veset machmat ones.* In *Nidda* 11a, the Gemara discusses a woman who experiences menstrual bleeding after jumping. The Gemara presents two versions of the case. There is also a textual dispute in the second version of the case making a clear reading of this Gemara even more elusive. Consequently, *Rishonim* offer three interpretations of this Gemara. *Rambam*[29] and *Ramban*[30] state that the Halakha does not recognize the category of *veset machmat ones* and we do not view "jumping" as causative; the woman has a simple *veset leyamim.*

On the other hand, *Rashba* believes that the Gemara points to two possible scenarios.[31] In one scenario, jumping in combination with the arrival of her

---

[26] *Ravad, Ba'alei haNefesh, Sha'ar Tikkun haVestot,* page 52; *Raza, Sela haMachloket Lesha'ar Tikkun haVestot,* 25; *Rashba, Torat haBayit, Dinei Vestot,* 13a–b. The Mishna on *Nidda* 63a lists the following as symptoms of a *veset*: yawning, sneezing, feeling pain at the top of the stomach or the bottom of the bowels, discharging, or shivering. The Gemara on 63b includes feeling heaviness in the head or limbs and belching. These *Rishonim* view this list as the comprehensive list of *vestot haguf.* However, *Ramban, Hilkhot Nidda* 6:8,12,13 argues that *veset haguf* includes jumping and eating spicy foods; he does not recognize a separate *veset machmat ones.*

[27] YD 189:17,19.

[28] *Shulchan Arukh* does not mention a *veset* for eating spicy foods; *Rama* (YD 189:23) mentions it but does not rule what type of *veset* it comprises.

[29] *Hilkhot Issurei Bi'a* 8:5.

[30] *Maharshal* on *Nidda* 11a, s.v. *"ubeshabbat kaftza velo chaza."*

[31] *Rashba* on *Nidda* 11a, s.v. *"kigon dekafitz bechad beshabbat vechaza"*; *Maharshal, ad loc.*

veset leyamim cause her to experience menstrual bleeding. Menstruation, when caused by a combination of factors, creates a hybrid *veset* known as a *veset murkav*. In the second scenario, the jumping is non-causal and the woman's period simply arrives on the predicted day. According to *Rashba*, a *veset machmat ones* exists. However, because we cannot determine fully that it causes the onset of the menses, it can only operate in combination with a *veset leyamim*. *Shulchan Arukh*[32] adopts *Rashba*'s reading.[33]

Both *Rashi* and *Raza* offer readings of *Nidda* 11a that allow for a simple *veset machmat ones*. *Rashi*[34] states that once a woman has had a flow of uterine blood on three occasions after jumping she has a *chazaka* that she will see blood any time she jumps.[35] *Raza* explains that a *veset machmat ones* can exist as a *veset murkav*[36] (combined with *veset leyamim*) or as a simple *veset*.[37] *Tur*[38] following *Rashi* and *Raza* rules that there are both simple and hybrid *vestot machmat ones*. According to these decisors the act of stopping the Pill, an external act that brings about menstruation, may be a type of *veset machmat ones*.

If we treat the act of stopping the Pill as any other *veset machmat ones* then according to *Rashi*, *Raza*, and *Tur* we have an appropriate model for a *veset* for the Pill. However, *Rashi*, *Razah*, and *Tur* represent the minority opinion and rules of *pesak* dictate that we follow the majority of *Rishonim* and *Shulchan Arukh*. And according to the majority opinion, stopping the Pill only

---

[32] YD 189:18.

[33] *Shulchan Arukh* (YD 189:17) indicates clearly that the ruling follows the second version, the *lishna achrina* of *Nidda* 11a; he does not believe that the first version holds any halakhic weight. *Shulchan Arukh*'s ruling is patterned on *Rambam* (*Hilkhot Issurei Bi'a* 8:5). *Rashba*, however, uses the first version of *Nidda* 11a to prove a *veset leyamim ulekfitzot* exists. So do *Ravad* (*Ba'alei Hanefesh, Sha'ar Tikkun haVestot*, page 52) and *Tosafot* (*Nidda* 11a, s.v. "*ela lekfitzot*"). See *Shakh* (YD 189:49) for further analysis and sources.

[34] *Nidda* 11a, s.v. "*ela lekfitzot*."

[35] *Rashba* (*Torat haBayit, Dinei Vestot* 13a) reads this *Rashi* as *Rashi*'s final opinion regarding this matter. It could be argued that *Rashi* is stating this only as a *hava amina*.

[36] This is the *maskana* in *Nidda* 11a.

[37] *Raza, Sela haMachloket* on *Ba'ale haNefesh, Sha'ar Tikkun Vestot* 25.

[38] YD 189, page 55a.

creates a *veset* when it is combined with a *veset leyamim*. This would lead to the bizarre conclusion that our woman, when she takes the Pill for an extended period of time, would have a *veset* for the 25th day, even though she is still taking the Pill, and she would not have a *veset* for the fourth day after she stops taking the Pill, the day she normally menstruates.

Is the *veset* that is created by taking the Pill a *veset machmat ones*? Rabbi Shlomo Levi rules that the Pill is more powerful than a *veset machmat ones*. He believes the reason why a *veset machmat ones* cannot stand independently, according to most decisors, is that it cannot be demonstrated conclusively that *ones* causes a uterine flow. On the other hand, we can demonstrate conclusively that taking the Pill will block menstruation.[39]

In *Nidda* 63b, the Gemara presents another type of *veset* in which a woman who eats spicy foods has her period as a result. The *Rishonim* discuss whether this *veset* called *veset akhilat shum* is a new *veset* or whether it fits into the categories of *veset haguf* or *veset machmat ones*. *Rama* lists the opinions but does not suggest an interpretation of his own.[40] According to *Rama*, *Rosh* and *Mordechai* suggest that a *veset* based on eating spicy foods is a new *veset*. *Tosafot*[41] emphasize that eating spicy foods is not an example of *veset machmat ones*. According to *Rama*, *Tosafot* group eating spicy foods with *vestot haguf. Rashba* groups eating spicy foods with *vestot machmat ones*.[42]

Rabbis Forst and Levi use *veset akhilat shum* as a model for the Pill. According to Rabbi Forst, stopping the Pill is similar to eating spicy foods because the resulting menstruation is "caused by outside intervention but it replicates the body's natural process";[43] it is different from eating spicy foods because causation can be demonstrated with the Pill but not with eating spicy foods. Rabbi Levi uses *Tosafot*'s *veset akhilat shum*, a type of *veset haguf*, as his model[44] since such a *veset* does not need an accompanying *veset leyamim*.[45]

---

[39] *Techumin* 182.

[40] YD 189:23.

[41] *Nidda* 63b, s.v. "*akhla shum vera'ata.*"

[42] *Rashba, Torat haBayit, Sha'ar haVestot* 8b.

[43] *The Laws of Nidda* (NY: Mesorah, 1997) 366.

[44] *Techumin* 184–5.

The statements of Rabbis Levi and Forst indicate that our woman would have her *veset* on the fourth day after she stops taking the Pill.

Chazaka

According to Rabbis Shlomo Levi, Ovadiah Yosef, Shmuel Wozner and Moshe Stern,[46] whether they adopt a Talmudic model or not, a simple *veset* for the particular day a woman has her period after she stops taking the Pill exists. Our woman has a *veset* for the fourth day after she stops taking the Pill. How often must she have experienced the beginning of her menses on this day before this *veset* is established? In order to answer this question we need to explore the nature of *chazaka*.

Halakha distinguishes between an established *veset* (*veset kavu'a*) and an unestablished *veset* (*veset she'aina kavu'a*). *Kevi'ut* is a measure of the reliability of the *veset*. When a woman has a *veset kavu'a*, which occurs once her menses have begun on the predicted day three occasions in a row, she can expect the onset of her period on that day.[47] Once a woman has a *veset kavu'a*, her *veset* is uprooted only if she does not replace it with another *chazaka*.[48]

Thus, a reliable pattern is said to exist when it has been demonstrated three consecutive times. Why do we require a triple occurrence to establish a pattern? The Gemara explains that a triple occurrence is a *chazaka*.[49] The method of establishing *kevi'ut* for a menstrual cycle is no different than the method for establishing any type of pattern. *Chazaka* is needed to infer a causal relationship between two events. The function of *chazaka*, according to this explanation, is to reduce the uncertainty regarding the link between two events; the more times that these two events are linked the more likely that

---

[45] This is true for *vestot haguf* in general.

[46] *Techumin* 181; Rabbi Ovadia Yosef, *Taharat haBayit* 2:18; *Shi'urei Shevet haLevi* 184:8,2; *Be'er Moshe* 6:137.

[47] *Shulchan Arukh*, YD 189:2,4.

[48] *Shulchan Arukh*, YD 189:2.

[49] *Yevamot* 64b. Three occurrences creates a *chazaka* in the opinion of Rabban Shimon ben Gamliel; Rebbi only requires two occurrences. The scope of this paper does not allow exploration of this issue in any great depth. For further information, see "*chazaka*,"*Encyclopedia Talmudit*, vol. 13 (Jerusalem, 1992).

they are causally related.[50] To establish the link between the beginning of menses and a particular day of a woman's menstrual cycle, we require those two events to appear together three times. However, if we had some alternative method of demonstrating a strong causal connection between a particular day of a woman's cycle and the onset of her menses, perhaps we would not need to rely on *chazaka* to demonstrate that link.[51]

When a woman is taking oral contraceptives, an artificial hormonal cycle regulating uterine activity is created. By maintaining levels of estrogen and progestin in her body, the uterine lining is continuously told to grow and maintain itself; no menstruation or collapse of this lining will occur as long as the woman takes in these hormones.[52] A woman taking the Pill will not menstruate, and her period will arrive in a predictable fashion during the week she is not taking the hormones. Based on this physiological reality, Rabbi Shlomo Levi rules that a woman taking the Pill does not need a *chazaka* to establish her *veset*. The *veset* is established immediately since medical studies demonstrate the high predictability of the Pill.[53] On the other hand, Dayan Weiss[54] and Rabbi Waldenberg[55] require *chazaka*. Dayan Weiss reasons that the evidence is not conclusive and therefore the need for *chazaka* remains. Rabbi Waldenberg indicates that the evidence is sufficient and yet he requires a *chazaka*! Perhaps his requirement for *chazakah* is a formal one; no *vestot* are established without *chazaka* and a *veset* for the Pill is no exception.[56]

---

[50] In classic yeshiva parlance, the *chakira* of *chazaka* is whether *chazaka* is a *birur*, a discovery of a causal link, or a *chalot shem*, a formal change of status. I am using the *birur* explanation here.

[51] *Nidda* 63b gives a clear example of a *veset* that does not require establishment by *chazaka*. This *veset* is the *veset haguf*. Thus, there is precedent for theorizing that other methods than *chazaka* can establish a *veset*. Note, however, that a *veset haguf* alone cannot establish a *veset*; it must be accompanied by a *veset leyamim*.

[52] Richard Dickey, 14–19.

[53] *Techumin* 180–82.

[54] *Minchat Yitzchak* 1:127.

[55] *Tzitz Eliezer* 13:103.

[56] Note, however, that *Nidda* 63b presents the case of *veset haguf* in which a *veset* is established without a *chazaka*.

Going off the Pill

Our woman now wishes to stop taking the Pill altogether. Does she re-adopt her *veset kavu'a* for the 26th day of her cycle which she established before starting the Pill, or does she begin anew with a *veset she'aina kavu'a*?

Shulchan Arukh[57] rules that a woman who has completed her pregnancy resumes her prior *veset*; *Tur*[58] presents an alternative ruling in which a woman who has completed a pregnancy must have her period once after the pregnancy and on the day of her prior *veset* before that *veset* is resumed. However, *Tur* rules that the prior *veset* is resumed immediately after the pregnancy.[59] Rabbi Shlomo Levi[60] and Rabbi Mordechai Eliyahu[61] rule that a woman who goes off the Pill resumes her prior *veset* immediately.[62] Their ruling assumes that a woman who is taking the Pill is a *mesuleket damim*; and just as a pregnant woman resumes her prior *veset* once her pregnancy ends a woman who goes off the Pill completely resumes her prior *veset*.[63]

Conclusion

I began with four questions about the Pill's status regarding the laws of *vestot*:

1) How long must a woman who started taking the Pill wait before she can ignore her pre-existing *veset*?

---

[57] YD 189:34.

[58] YD 189, 59a.

[59] *Tur ad loc.* adds that Ramban requires the woman to have her period once before the *veset* is resumed. *Beit Yosef* (YD 189, s.v. *vehaRamban katav*) posits that the prior *veset* cannot be resumed until the state of *mesuleket damim* is removed; once the woman has her period once she returns to her prior *veset*.

[60] *Techumin* 185.

[61] *Drakhei Tahara* (NY: American Friends of Sucath David, 1984) 87.

[62] *Beit Yosef* (YD 189, page 59a) states that *Tur*, who believes that a *veset machmat ones* does not need to combine with a *veset leyamim*, would rule that a woman with such a *veset* would resume her prior *veset* immediately. A woman who goes off the Pill would then resume her prior *veset* immediately.

[63] *Rashba, Torat haBayit, Dinei Vestot*, page 13a, reasons that the suspension of the menses during pregnancy is due to the pregnancy; once the pregnancy is over the body resumes its normal operation.

2)   Do we require a woman who is now taking the Pill to establish a fixed pattern over three consecutive occasions or can she establish this new *veset* immediately?

3)   What type of *veset* does a woman establish while taking the Pill? Is it based on the number of days in her cycle, like the *veset* she had before she took the Pill, or is it based on the number of days after she stops taking the Pill that she begins to menstruate?

4)   If the woman stops taking the Pill does she return to her previous *veset* and if so, when?

According to Rabbi Shlomo Levi, Rabbi Shmuel Wozner and Rabbi Ovadia Yosef, a woman taking the pill, like a pregnant woman, is a *mesuleket damim*.[64] Just as a woman experiencing a normal pregnancy maintains the lining of the uterus, so to a woman while taking the Pill cannot menstruate. As a *mesuleket damim*, she need not be concerned with her prior *vestot* at all during the duration of the suspension.[65] However, since the *mesuleket damim* only suspends her natural cycle, once she goes off the Pill and her natural cycle resumes, her previous *veset* is re-instated.[66]

Although the Pill does not fit into the models of *veset leyamim* or *veset machmat ones*, many decisors believe that there is a *veset* for the Pill. Some halakhists place the Pill in the category of *veset akhilat shum*, looking for a *veset* that exists in the Talmud on which to base this new phenomenon. Others are willing to treat it as a new *veset*. Regardless of the Talmudic model, according to these decisors, a *veset* for the Pill would be based on the number of days after ceasing the Pill that a woman begins to menstruate.

---

[64] Dayan Weiss would disagree. Perhaps with today's pills, which demonstrate uniform effectiveness for millions of women, he would have taken a different position.

[65] Once the status of *mesuleket damim* has been established, the woman need not concern herself with her *veset*. There is a major debate among contemporary halakhists whether a pregnant woman need wait the three months mandated in the Talmud before considering herself a *mesuleket damim*, since we can now determine pregnancy much earlier. One of the aspects of the debate is whether the three months acts as a *chazaka* or whether it is simply the time when a woman would begin to show visible signs of pregnancy. If one considers the three months a *chazaka*, it would stand to reason that a woman taking the Pill might also require a *chazaka* before she can ignore her old *veset*. See *Tzitz Eliezer* 13:103.

[66] *Shulchan Arukh*, YD 189:34.

The need for a *chazaka* to establish a *veset* for the Pill is disputable. While Rabbis Shlomo Levi, Shmuel Wozner, Ovadia Yosef and Mordechai Eliyahu state that a *chazaka* is not necessary since the Pill is an extremely reliable and accurate predictor of the onset of the menses, Rabbi Waldenberg, adopting the responsum of David ben Zimra, believes that such a *chazaka* is necessary. Although the Pill seems unquestionably reliable in giving a woman currently taking the Pill the status of a *mesuleket damim*, it is reasonable to doubt that the Pill immediately confers an equivalent predictability for the day a woman on the Pill will menstruate.

II. THE SOUL

Contributions in this section probe the history and development of prayer and learning. Whether it be *tzitzit*, *tefillin*, or kaddish, the contributors attempt to resolve the apparent conflict between a woman's active spiritual devotion and the established Jewish practice. Rabbis over the years have dealt with the issues raised here and, continuing in their tradition, our authors' halakhic analyses are precedent setting.

Two central foci of Jewish life are prayer and learning. This section is largely dedicated to furthering our understanding of the role of women in these crucial components of Judaism.

The final essay in this section has everything and also nothing to do with women. It is dedicated to illuminating the role of *kavana*—intention in prayer and in the fulfillment of *mitzvot*. Many of the essays in this book are about issues relating to women while several explore questions equally applicable to women and men.

Wrapped Attention:
May Women Wear *Tefillin*?[1]

Aliza Berger

Until the current generation, there have been only isolated instances attested of women wearing *tefillin*.[2] Even today, *tefillin* constitute a sort of last frontier of

[*] I thank Rabbi Saul Berman for his permission to use material from his lectures on this topic (lecture to Orthodox Roundtable at Lincoln Square Synagogue, New York, February 1994, and series of classes, at Lincoln Square Synagogue, Fall, 1993). I also thank Rabbi Uri Cohen for directing me to several sources, my sister Shulamith Berger and Gitelle Rapoport for logistic help, and my husband, Dov Cooper, for his ideas, comments, and moral support. Any errors are mine.

[1] *Tefillin* (phylacteries) are two black leather boxes containing scriptural passages written on parchment. The four scriptural passages contained in the *tefillin* are the four passages relating to *tefillin* in the Bible: Ex. 13:1–10, 11–16; Deut. 6:4–9 and 11:13–21. One box is bound to the left arm (or the right arm, if one is left-handed) and the other to the forehead with strips of black-colored leather. *Tefillin* are typically worn during the weekday morning prayer service.

[2] The case of Michal—the daughter of a Kushite (*Eruvin* 96a and *Mekhilta deRabi Ishmael, Bo, Masekhta dePascha* 17), or the daughter of King Saul, according to the Jerusalem Talmud *Eruvin* 10:1 [26a]—will be addressed at length in this paper. In more recent history: First, at least two unidentified women in Siena, during the Italian Renaissance (The American Academy for Jewish Research, *Sefer haYovel Likhvod Levi Ginzburg*, NY, 1946, 294). Second, in Morocco, the daughter of HaNagid Rav Moshe ben Attar who married Rav Hayim ibn Attar (1696–1743, known as the *Or haChaim*) (J.M. Toledano, *Ner haMaarav*, Jerusalem: The Sephardic Library-Machon Bnei Issachar, 1989, 217). Third, perhaps other Italian women of rabbinic families of the eighteenth century (S. Zolty, *And All Your Children Shall be Learned: Women and the Study of Torah in Jewish Law and History*, NJ: Aronson, 1993, 47 n120); and, fourth, Hannah Rachel Webermacher, the "Maiden of Ludomir," a Hasidic leader in nineteenth-century Poland (ibid., 250). However, the only reliably documented instance is the last one (D. Golinkin, "Are Women Permitted to Wear *Tefillin*?" *Asufot* 11 (1998): 183–96, in Hebrew).

There is no proof for the popular legend that *Rashi*'s daughters wore *tefillin*. However, it is interesting to speculate on why this association arose; it probably has to do with the fact that *Rashi*'s daughters were known to be exceptional in that they were educated.

See Y. Mirsky, "Women, Tefillin, and the Stories of the Law," *Kerem* 5 (1997): 36–45, for a midrash-based study of Michal's wearing of *tefillin*.

the "positive time-bound commandments" from which women are exempt.[3]
Consider the list: reciting the *Shema*, counting the *omer*, sitting in the *sukka*,
taking the *lulav*, hearing the shofar, wearing *tzitzit*, and wearing *tefillin*.[4] With
the exception of wearing *tzitzit* and *tefillin*, these commandments are performed regularly and without controversy by huge numbers of Orthodox
women today. *Tzitzit*, while rarely worn by women, have still been worn more
often than *tefillin* by exceptional women throughout Jewish history.[5] *Tzitzit* are
also worn more commonly than *tefillin* by Orthodox women today. Halakhic
issues will be the main consideration of this paper; however, we shall set the
scene by first mentioning several other factors that have likely contributed to
the rarity of women wearing *tefillin*.

One factor, that of "impurity" (*tuma*), is actually quasi-halakhic. This factor
is the same one that resulted in the past custom in certain communities for
women who were menstruating to avoid attending synagogue,[6] and in the
misconception still current among many people that a menstruant can defile a
Torah scroll by touching it. When I was thirteen years old, attending a
coeducational Orthodox school, a girl in my class picked up a boy's set of
tefillin, in its velvet bag, to ask if someone had forgotten it. The (female)
teacher yelled at the girl, horrified. She did not say why what the girl had done
was wrong, but, perhaps even then on some level, it was "obvious." This was a
strong, irrational and ignorant reaction to a woman who did not even touch
tefillin.

A second factor is that *tefillin* are mysterious. Wearing *tefillin* looks and
feels strange. Wrapping a holy article so intimately around oneself, and having
to do so precisely, can be a frightening prospect for anyone, male or female.
Tefillin can be inaccessible and inconvenient: they are expensive and more
difficult to learn how to put on than *tzitzit*, and, in the synagogue, cannot be
hidden as *tzitzit* can.

---

[3] A commandment to perform a certain action which can only be performed at certain
times.

[4] This is one version of the list (*Rambam*, *Sefer haMitzvot*, after the list of positive
commandments).

[5] See, e.g., biographies of women in M. Kaufman, *The Woman in Jewish Law and
Tradition* (NJ: Aronson, 1995) 84–85.

[6] See e.g., *Rama*'s gloss to *Shulchan Arukh*, *Orach Chaim* 88:1.

Another factor, which applies to a certain extent to *tzitzit* as well, is fear of the unknown. It simply has not been customary for women to wear *tefillin*, while it has been customary for them to perform other commandments from which they are exempt. For this reason, *tefillin* are still ingrained in the consciousnesses of most Orthodox Jews, both men and women, as something associated solely with men.

These extra-halakhic factors often lurk in the background, coloring discussions about the issue of whether women may wear *tefillin*. Having mentioned these factors, we will now—hopefully rationally—examine the halakhic development of this issue. We shall begin with the Bible and cover the entire development chronologically through contemporary times.

I. Bible and Talmud

The Bible tells us that the purpose of *tefillin* is to serve as a tangible reminder of God's Torah and commandments: "Impress these words of Mine upon your heart and soul: bind them as a sign on your hand and let them serve as frontlets between your eyes, and teach them to your children....."[7]

According to Jewish tradition, women are not obligated to wear *tefillin*. The Mishna (*Berakhot* 3:3) states: "Women, slaves, and minors are exempt from the recitation of *Shema*, and from *tefillin*, and are obligated in prayer..." The Talmud supports this idea by an analysis of the above verse from the Torah. First, this verse supports the idea that only men are obligated to learn Torah, but not women, because it uses a Hebrew word (translated above as "children") which literally means "sons."[8] Then, since this same verse which exempts women from Torah study also discusses *tefillin*, stating that the purpose of *tefillin* is to remind one of the Torah, women's exemption is extended to *tefillin*.[9]

---

[7] Deut. 11:18–29. This is part of the *Shema* prayer. Translation based on that of the Jewish Publication Society of America (Philadelphia, 1962). The same idea is contained in Deut. 6:6–8, which is also recited as part of the *Shema*.

[8] *Kiddushin* 29b; *Sifre Devarim*, ch. 46.

[9] See *Kiddushin* 33b–34a for a more extensive discussion. See also *Mekhilta Bo, Masekhta dePascha*, ch. 17, Jerusalem Talmud *Berakhot* 2:3 and *Pesikta Rabbati*, ch. 22.

Tefillin are categorized as a "positive time-bound commandment," in other words, a commandment to perform an action which can only be done at certain times. In the case of *tefillin*, the time limitation is that they are not worn on Shabbat and holidays.[10] Women's exemption from wearing *tefillin* is extended, by association, to other positive time-bound commandments.[11] Thus, *tefillin* serve as a paradigm of women's exemption from positive time-bound commandments.

If women are exempt from wearing *tefillin*, may they wear them as an option? More generally, what is the implication of exemption from a commandment? Is one permitted to perform it at all? The Talmud addresses this issue directly in its discussion of whether a woman is permitted to ritually lay her hands upon a sacrifice which she brings to the Temple (i.e., *semikha*, an action which demonstrates ownership of the sacrifice). This action is obligatory for men. R. Yossi is of the opinion that women are permitted to perform it, but R. Yehuda holds that women may not.[12] A rationale for the latter opinion is that it is based on the Torah's injunction "Do not add to them [i.e., the commandments] and do not subtract from them."[13]

Like *tefillin* being the paradigmatic example of women being exempt from time-bound commandments, ritual laying of hands on a sacrifice serves as the paradigm for the rule for women's performance of commandments from which they are exempt (sometimes referred to as "optional commandments"). According to the view that women are permitted to ritually lay hands on a sacrifice, they are similarly permitted to perform all commandments from which they are exempt; according to the view that women are not permitted to

---

[10] *Tefillin* are not worn on these special days because these days are referred to in the Torah as a "sign" between God and the people of Israel, as are *tefillin* (Exodus 31:17; *Menachot* 36b). Since we already have one of these "signs" on Shabbat and holidays, we do not need another, so *tefillin* are not worn.

[11] *Kiddushin* 33b ff.

[12] *Rosh haShana* 33a, where Scriptural support is found for the opinion that women may not ritually lay hands on sacrifices, using reasoning similar to that which we saw for women's exemption from studying Torah. The Bible states, introducing the laws of sacrifices: "Speak unto the children [literally: 'sons'] of Israel" (Lev. 1:2). This language supports the idea that men ritually lay hands on sacrifices, but not women. Cf. also *Chagiga* 16b and *Sifra, Vayikra*, ch. 2.

[13] Deut. 13:1. *Rashi* to *Rosh haShana* 33a and *Rashi* to *Eruvin* 96a.

ritually lay hands on a sacrifice, then they may not perform any commandments from which they are exempt.

The principle of women's exemption from optional commandments is
applied to the issue of women wearing *tefillin* in the following passage from
the Talmud:[14]

> It was taught in a *tannaic* source: Michal the daughter of the Kushite[15] wore
> *tefillin* and the Sages did not protest her action... Since the Sages did not pro-
> test it is clearly evident that they hold the view that it is a positive command-
> ment the performance of which is not time-bound. But is not another possibil-
> ity that he [the author of this source] holds the same view as R. Yossi who
> ruled: "It is optional for women to lay their hands on a sacrifice"?[16]

Let us examine this text. After presenting a case in which the Sages "did
not protest" Michal's wearing of *tefillin*, this passage brings two different
views about how the commandment to wear *tefillin* applies to women. The
first view assumes the position of R. Yehuda, which implies that women may
not perform optional commandments. The reasoning for the first view goes as
follows: We know that Michal wore *tefillin*. But how can that be, if she is not
allowed to perform optional commandments? This seeming contradiction is
resolved by the clarification that *tefillin* are a "regular" positive commandment. This implies that women are obligated to wear *tefillin*. The second view,
presented in the last sentence of the text, is that *tefillin* are a positive
time-bound commandment, which women have the option of performing. As
the Talmud says explicitly, this follows the opinion of R. Yossi.

Another version of the anecdote about Michal and the Sages is found in the
Jerusalem Talmud.[17] Here, after reporting as in the Babylonian Talmud that
the Sages did not protest Michal's wearing *tefillin*, a second version is reported
in which the Sages did protest her act.[18] The protest is consistent with R.

---

[14] *Eruvin* 96a–b. See also *Mekhilta Bo Masechta dePascha*, ch. 17.

[15] I.e., King Saul (*Moed Katan* 16b, based on Psalms 7:1).

[16] Translation based on that of Soncino.

[17] *Berakhot* 2:3. See also Jerusalem Talmud *Eruvin* 10:1 [26a–b].

[18] The term "did not protest" or "protested" is used only occasionally in halakhic
literature. The use of this term begs attention because it appears to imply a value judgment

Yehuda's view that women may not perform optional commandments.[19] (Note that this is a different solution than the first view we saw in the Babylonian Talmud, which was also consistent with R. Yehuda's view.[20])

---

on the part of the Sages regarding Michal's action. This possibility is worth further exploration.

The meaning of the term "to protest" is addressed directly in another passage. *Tosefta Pischa* 3:1 (cf. also *Pesachim* 55b–56a, which records only the second half) lists six acts performed by the inhabitants of Jericho, three "in accord with the wishes of the Sages" and three "not in accord with the wishes of the Sages." R. Yehuda (note that he appears in our discussion as well) said of the first three acts: "If it is in accord with the wishes of the Sages, let everyone do these things!" In other words, R. Yehuda is asking how the term "in accord with the wishes of the Sages" is to be understood. The six acts are then listed again, but with a change in language. This time, the Sages "do not protest" the first three acts and "protest" the last three. This clarification indicates that all six of the acts, whether protested or not, were disapproved of by the Sages, and ideally, they would not have been performed. Applying this import of "protesting" to our case leads to the conclusion that whether or not the Sages protested, they disapproved of Michal's action. This is in fact the interpretation of *Ramban* (*Chidushei haRamban, Kiddushin* 31a). (But *Ramban*'s actual ruling is probably different; cf. n36 below.)

Other commentators on the Talmud ascribe all the weight to the version of the Babylonian Talmud, which says that Michal's wearing *tefillin* was not protested, and totally discount the part of the Jerusalem Talmud's version which says that this was protested; it is standard practice for commentators and halakhic authorities to follow the Babylonian Talmud over the Jerusalem Talmud. According to *Rashba* (*Teshuvot haRashba*, Jerusalem: *Makhon Tiferet haTorah*, 1989, responsum 123), Michal "acted in accord with the wishes of the Sages." *Ritva* specifies (*Chidushei haRitva* to *Eruvin* 96a, s.v. "*midilo michu bahen*") that Michal's case is different from that of the people of Jericho; according to *Ritva*, it is clear that Michal acted in accord with the wishes of the Sages from the fact that they did not protest her action.

Thus, it appears that a negative value judgment of Michal could very well be indicated in the Talmud. However, for the actual halakhic ruling, this is overridden by the weight accorded to the Babylonian Talmud over the Jerusalem Talmud, to the point where Michal's act is viewed with approval.

[19] This explanation of the debate is the "plain sense" of the Talmud. Later we will encounter commentators who interpret the subject of the debate differently.

[20] While the talmudic presentation is fresh in the reader's mind, a point will be interpolated which will become significant only later on. Since the talmudic discussions are closely tied to the anecdote about Michal and do not say anything explicitly about women in general wearing *tefillin*, the question arises here as to whether the opinions expressed in the Talmud could be referring only to Michal and not to other women. In other words, perhaps it is acceptable for Michal to wear *tefillin*, but not for other women. But this does

Summary: We have seen three talmudic opinions about whether women may wear *tefillin*: (1) women are obligated; (2) women are exempt but may wear them; and (3) it should be "protested" just as the performance of other optional commandments should be protested. The Talmud established fairly early on that *tefillin* is a time-bound commandment, which eliminates the view that women are obligated to wear *tefillin*. Thus the situation at the end of the talmudic period was that the answer to the question of whether women may wear *tefillin* is solely dependent on which side one takes in the debate over whether women are permitted to perform commandments from which they are exempt.

II. Geonic Period[21]

Our talmudic sources are not elaborated on in this period. However, other relevant developments did occur; these are listed here.

1) The only reference I found in geonic literature to women and *tefillin* is a mention in passing that ordinary people tried to avoid having menstruating women touch *tefillin*.[22] However, elsewhere, the Babylonian *Geonim* reject the idea that holy objects such as Torah scrolls and *tefillin* can be defiled by being touched, e.g., by a man who experienced a seminal emission. By extension this applies to menstruants as well.[23]

---

not seem likely. Really, it is the other way around: the Talmud here applies general principles about women's performance of commandments to the specific case of Michal. This point is made here because later authorities do attempt to distinguish what was permitted to Michal and what is permitted to women in general. However, this does not appear to be the straightforward sense of the passage.

[21] The geonic period lasted from about 700 CE to 1000 CE. The time and place of the editing of *Pesikta* and of *Targum Yonatan* was pointed out by Rabbi S. Berman. Of course, even though these sources were edited during the geonic period, both of them contain earlier material, so it is not possible to know how ancient a particular passage is in these sources.

[22] *Teshuvot haGeonim haChadashot* (Jerusalem: Ofek Institute, 1995) responsum 161, 233–37. Cf. also *Berakhot* 22a.

[23] Ibid., 235 n22.

2) *Pesikta Rabbati*,[24] edited in Palestine early in the geonic period, repeats the version of the anecdote about Michal of the Jerusalem Talmud, which recorded both protest and non-protest of Michal's wearing *tefillin*. Thus there is evidence of continuation of the tradition of the Jerusalem Talmud in its geographic area.

3) Based on the talmudic sources, we had concluded that whether or not women may wear *tefillin* depends only on the issue of whether or not women may perform commandments from which they are exempt. However, later sources complicate the issue by introducing various factors specific to *tefillin* that might make women's performance of this particular commandment problematic, while still permitting women to perform optional commandments in general.

The earliest source to introduce such a factor is *Targum Yonatan* translation of the Torah (*Targum Yerushalmi*). *Targum Yonatan* interprets the biblical prohibition for a woman to put on men's apparel[25] as meaning that women should not wear *tzitzit* and *tefillin*. However, *Targum Yonatan* is not considered to be a halakhic source, and no halakhic sources of the talmudic or geonic periods refer to its interpretation. It will come up in a later period.

Summary: Halakhic authorities usually follow the Babylonian Talmud and it may even be assumed that they do so unless they state otherwise. Since the geonic literature is silent on the question of whether women may wear *tefillin*, it may be assumed that, in this period, the opinion of the Babylonian Talmud that women may wear *tefillin* was accepted—irrespective of whether women actually wore or even touched *tefillin* during the geonic period.

III. Period of the *Rishonim*: Permission

As in the geonic period, the vast majority of authorities in this period follow the scheme we laid out for the end of the talmudic period: that whether women are permitted to wear *tefillin* is simply dependent on the general question of whether they are permitted to optionally perform commandments. In this

---

[24] Ch. 22.

[25] Deut. 22:5.

period, it is established that women are in fact permitted to optionally perform commandments; permission to wear *tefillin* follows along from this.

Several minority opinions, each expressed by one, or at most two authoritites, deviate from this pattern. One authority holds that women may not optionally perform commandments. Three others, like *Targum Yonatan* which we saw in the geonic period, introduce factors specific to *tefillin* which distinguish it from other optional commandments.

Majority View: Women May Perform Commandments From Which They Are Exempt

This debate was resolved in favor of permitting women to perform optional commandments.[26] It is also apparent that far from permission being granted grudgingly, performance of optional commandments is generally viewed as worthwhile and desirable. For example, a reason given already in the Talmud for permission for women to optionally lay their hands on sacrifices is to afford them spiritual satisfaction.[27] The Talmud states that "One who is commanded to perform a commandment is greater than one who is not commanded and performs it."[28] In other words, someone who is exempt from a commandment does receive a reward for performing it, although this reward is smaller than that received by someone who is commanded. According to *Ritva*, the reason one who is not commanded receives a reward it that "Out of the goodness of one's heart one put oneself in the category of performing God's commandment."[29] *Nimukei Yosef* also expresses a positive reason for permitting optional performance of commandments: "For all [the Torah's] ways are pleasant, and all her paths are peaceful."[30]

---

[26] See, for example, *Tosafot* to *Eruvin* 96a, s.v. "*dilma savar lakh kerabi yossi de'amar nashim somkhot reshut.*"

[27] *Chagiga* 16b; *Sifra Vayikra*, ch. 2.

[28] *Kiddushin* 31a.

[29] *Chidushei haRitva* to *Kiddushin* 31a, s.v. "*de'amar Rabbi Chanina, gadol hametzuve ve'ose memi she'aino metzuve ve'ose.*"

[30] Proverbs 3:17. *Nimukei Yosef* to *Kiddushin* 31a, s.v. "*avdina yoma tuva,*" in *Shitat haKadmonim* (NY, 1970).

Tefillin are included in women's permission to perform optional commandments. In fact, the general principle that women may perform optional time-bound commandments is based in part upon Michal's optional wearing of *tefillin*.[31] The *Sar* of Coucy[32] (c. 1200) agrees with this view that women may perform commandments from which they are exempt, specifically including *tefillin* on his list of optional commandments which women may perform. *Sefer haChinukh* (c. 1250–1300) explicitly permits women to wear *tefillin*, noting that Michal did so.[33] *Rashba* (c. 1300) also permits, even interpreting the ambiguous wording of the Talmud that the Sages "did not protest" Michal's wearing of *tefillin* as meaning that Michal "acted in accord with the wishes of the Sages."[34] *Rosh* (1250–1327), in his discussion of women's exemption from *tefillin*, does not mention any problems with their wearing *tefillin*.[35]

---

[31] Rabbenu Tam (1100–1171), in *Tosafot* to *Eruvin* 96a s.v. *"dilma savar la kerabi yossi de'amar nashim somkhot reshut"* and *Rosh haShana* 33a s.v. *"ha rabi yehuda ha rabi yossi."*

Additionally, Rabbenu Tam reasons that if Michal wore *tefillin*, presumably she blessed upon them as well. He infers from this that women may make blessings on optional commandments. This became the prevalent opinion in Ashkenaz, while the opinion in Sepharad (less unanimously) was that women should not make the blessings. Note that the ashkenazic and sephardic opinions agree that women may *perform* the commandments, which is our main concern. The issue of whether or not women may make the blessings on *tefillin* is treated only tangentially in this paper since there is little which distinguishes this issue from the general debate over whether women may make blessings on positive time-bound commandments.

According to Rabbenu Tam, what was protested in the Jerusalem Talmud about Michal's wearing of *tefillin* was not women's performance of commandments from which they are exempt—as we had explained as the plain sense of the Talmud—but rather women's making blessings on these commandments. Note that according to this explanation of the debate, ashkenazi women would be permitted to wear *tefillin* even according to the opinion that Michal's act was protested.

[32] Cited in *Hagahot Maimoniyot*, note *mem*, to Rambam's *Mishne Torah*, *Hilkhot Tzitzit* 3:9.

[33] Jerusalem, 1961, Chavel edition, Positive Commandment 421.

[34] *Teshuvot haRashba* (Jerusalem: *Makhon Tiferet haTorah*, 1989) responsum 123.

[35] *Halakhot Ketanot, Hilkhot Tefillin* (end of tractate *Menachot* 122b) par. 29.

Other authorities do not single out *tefillin* for any special attention, indicating that they hold that women may wear *tefillin*. For example, *Rif* (1013–1103) simply cites the Mishna (cited above) which states that *Shema* and *tefillin* are optional for women. *Rashi* (1040–1105) is cited as ruling that women should not recite blessings on optional commandments; it may be inferred from this that he did, nonetheless, permit women to perform them. *Rambam*[36] (1135–1204), *Sefer Aguda*[37] (c. 1348), and others simply rule that women may perform positive time-bound commandments. *Ramban*'s (1194–1270) final opinion is not clear from what he writes, but the commentator *Nimukei Yosef* (c. 1400) interprets *Ramban* as permitting women to perform optional commandments.[38]

Minority View: Women May Not Perform Commandments From Which They Are Exempt

Ravad (1120–1197) is the sole dissenting voice during the period of the early *Rishonim* who rules that women should not perform optional commandments. Recall that we had attributed the opinion that women may not optionally lay their hands on sacrifices to this violating the prohibition of "adding on to the commandments." *Ravad*, however, has a different approach to this issue. He groups together three opinions from the Talmud: (1) that women cannot optionally lay hands on sacrifices; (2) that the Sages protested Michal's action; and (3) that teaching women Torah is equivalent to foolishness.[39] *Ravad* generalizes from the reason for not teaching women Torah, applying it to *all* optional commandments. According to *Ravad*, if women were to perform an optional commandment, they might not treat it with the requisite respect. Having a mindset that is not respectful enough might, in turn, lead to one's not being careful to perform the commandment properly. This would constitute a serious problem because commandments are supposed to be performed exactly

---

[36] *Mishne Torah, Hilkhot Tzitzit* 3:9; *Rambam* states that women are exempt from *tefillin* in *Sefer haMitzvot*, Positive Commandments 12 and 13.

[37] To *Eruvin* 97–98.

[38] To *Kiddushin* 31a. Cf. R. Klapper, letter to *HaMevaser* (Yeshiva University newspaper), NY, October 1993: 15. Cf. n30 above for citation of *Nimukei Yosef*.

[39] *Sota* 20.

in the prescribed manner. *Ravad* also adds that women performing optional commandments could lead to immodest behavior.[40]

However, *Ravad* rules that there are exceptions to women not being permitted to perform optional commandments. According to him, women *are* permitted to perform optional commandments for which there is no chance of encountering the problems that he raised. He includes in this category commandments that are not prone to error such as taking the *lulav* and sitting in the *sukka*.

While *Ravad*'s opinion that women may not perform optional commandments is not accepted, his reasons that such performance is undesirable are utilized by some later authorities in connection with women's wearing of *tefillin*.

Majority View—But *Tefillin* Are an Exception

Tosafot (12th century) are the second source we encounter (the first was *Targum Yonatan*) which considers the question of whether women may wear *tefillin* to hinge on a factor specific to *tefillin* rather than on performance of optional commandments in general. Specifically, *Tosafot* explain that the talmudic debate over Michal's wearing *tefillin* does not stem (as we had explained) from the debate over whether women may perform optional commandments. While both sides agree that women may perform optional commandments, Michal's wearing *tefillin* was protested because "*tefillin* require [one to have] a clean body [in order to wear them], but women are not diligent about being careful." According to the other opinion that Michal's wearing of *tefillin* was not protested, one need not be concerned about this "clean body" factor.[41]

---

[40] To *Sifra Vayikra*, ch. 2.

Ravad does not explain why this would be, but the problem may be that these three commandments—Torah study, *tefillin*, and laying hands on sacrifices—could involve mixing with men. (See also section below, "A woman shall not put on men's apparel.")

[41] *Eruvin* 96a, s.v. "*Michal bat kushi hayta manachat tefillin.*" *Tosafot*'s re-interpretation of the reason for the debate is motivated by a contradiction between two texts: R. Yehuda, who rules that women may not optionally lay their hands on a sacrifice, elsewhere reports without negative comment an anecdote about a woman performing an optional commandment: he recounts that Queen Helene sat in the *sukka* (*Sukka* 2b).

While *Tosafot*'s actual opinion follows that of the Babylonian Talmud that Michal's wearing of *tefillin* was not protested, and hence they hold that women may wear *tefillin*, their interpretation of the rejected opinion is significant because later authorities apply this "clean body" issue, which *Tosafot* raises only theoretically, to rule for practical purposes that women's wearing *tefillin* should be protested. In fact, "clean body" is the concept most central to the halakhic development of our issue.

"Clean body" (*guf naki*) is a halakhic concept which is applied by the Talmud solely to the wearing of *tefillin* (but not particularly to women). The passage in which the concept of bodily cleanliness is introduced goes as follows: The Talmud first reports a statement by R. Yannai that "*tefillin* require a clean body like Elisha, the Possessor of Wings." It is then reported that Abaye interprets "clean body" to mean that one should not flatulate while wearing *tefillin*, while Rava interprets it to mean that one should not sleep while wearing *tefillin*.[42] A story is then related to explain the meaning of the name Elisha the Possessor of Wings. Elisha was a person who wore *tefillin* in the marketplace even during a time of persecution when there was a Roman decree that anyone caught wearing *tefillin* on their head would have their brains pierced. When he saw a Roman officer approaching, Elisha took off his *tefillin* and hid them in his hand. The officer asked, "What is that in your hand?" Elisha answered, "The wings of a dove." He opened his hand and there were dove's wings in it—hence his name[43].

This passage appears to contradict itself regarding the meaning of the term "clean body." That Elisha was worthy of having a miracle happen to him implies that he was an especially righteous person. This, in turn, would imply that "clean body" is a spiritual state which an ordinary person could not attain. R. Yannai's statement seems to imply a spiritual dimension as well. Yet if, as the passage also states, bodily cleanliness has to do with flatulence and/or sleeping, then "clean body" is merely a physical state that most anyone can easily achieve. Why did Abaye and Rava interpret the term in a way that

---

[42] Both these opinions are accepted; the reason for not sleeping is commonly understood to be in order to avoid inadvertent flatulence.

[43] *Shabbat* 49a and 130a; Jerusalem Talmud *Berakhot* 2:3 [46] which contains the blunter statement, "R. Yannai said: Anyone who is not like Elisha, the Possessor of Wings, should not wear *tefillin*."

seems to fly in the face of the point of the story about Elisha? It seems reasonable to hypothesize that Abaye and Rava were fully aware that their definitions contradicted the original sense of "clean body." However, they formed physical definitions anyway in order to avoid a more consequential contradiction: a conflict between the Torah commandment to wear *tefillin* and an impossible requirement that one be as righteous as Elisha in order to be able to wear them. The physical definitions avoid an untenable situation in which people would neglect a Torah commandment.[44]

With this understanding of the concept of "clean body," let us now return to *Tosafot*. *Tosafot* state that, according to the (rejected) opinion in the Jerusalem Talmud that Michal's wearing of *tefillin* was protested, women are not diligent about maintaining the bodily cleanliness requirements. This wording (as opposed to saying, e.g., "women are incapable of being diligent") implies that a woman could, however, in theory, fulfill the requirements. That women are capable of fulfilling the requirements implies in turn that the definition of bodily cleanliness for women, like that for men, must be physical and not spiritual (since a spiritual requirement is essentially impossible to fulfill). We mention this now in order to set in place in advance a defense against later authorities who will argue that the definition of bodily cleanliness is in fact spiritual for women, since it was defined physically for men only because of a particular necessity (men's obligation) which does not apply to women.[45]

---

[44] Spiritual definitions of "clean body" did persist in the minority, however, even into the period of the *Rishonim*. See for example, *Beit haBechira* to *Berakhot* 14b and *Shabbat* 49a (based on Jerusalem Talmud *Berakhot* 2:3).

[45] There is actually one source contemporaneous with, or even earlier than, *Tosafot* which appears to rule for practical purposes—not just as an explanation of a rejected opinion as in *Tosafot*—that women's wearing of *tefillin* should be protested on grounds of women being unable to maintain a clean body. This is *Sefer haEshkol* (mid-12th century). However, this citation appears only in one of two editions of the book; it appears in the less reliable (Auerbach) edition and is left out of the more reliable one (Albeck). There being no other evidence of such an opinion in the time and place of *Sefer haEshkol* also counts against its reliability (S. Berman, lecture to Orthodox Roundtable, February 1994). Information on the relative reliability of the editions of *Sefer haEshkol* is from ibid. and from "Abraham ben Isaac of Narbonne," *Encyclopaedia Judaica* 2:146–47.

Maharam's View

After *Tosafot*, several *Rishonim* explicitly mention the issue of clean body and reject it as a problem.[46] The first authority to actually rule that women's wearing of *tefillin* should be protested due to the issue of bodily cleanliness is the *Maharam* of Rothenburg (c. 1215–1293). *Maharam*'s rulings in this matter (as is the case for many of his rulings) were written by his disciples rather than by *Maharam* himself. One of *Maharam*'s disciples, *Tashbetz*, cites him as ruling that "They should not wear *tefillin* because they do not know how to keep themselves in a state of purity (*tahara*)."[47] The anonymous *Kol Bo* cites *Maharam*'s ruling as "If they wish to wear *tefillin*, one does not listen to them,[48] because they do not know how to maintain a state of cleanliness (*nekiyut*)."[49]

These terse citations of *Maharam* leave at least two questions unanswered. Do "cleanliness" and "purity" refer to the same thing? Also, *Maharam* does not make explicit whether he believes it is impossible for women to keep themselves in the proper state, or whether he believes that women simply do not do so, but could if they wanted to. Because many later authorities use *Maharam*'s ruling as a reference point, it is important to understand his ruling fully, so we shall treat these questions in detail.

Cleanliness vs. Purity: *Kol Bo*'s wording of *Maharam*'s ruling clearly shows that the issue involved is that of bodily cleanliness. However, does "purity" in the *Tashbetz*'s version refer to physical, bodily cleanliness as well, or could it possibly refer to a matter of purity that is specific to women, namely, ritual impurity due to menstruation? This is a tempting interpretation, because it would explain why women would have trouble maintaining bodily cleanliness while men do not, and thus would explain a difference between men and

---

[46] *Ramban* and *Ritva* to *Kiddushin* 31a. *Ramban* states the rejected opinion bluntly as "women are frivolous (*nashim da'atan kalot*), while *tefillin* require a clean body."

[47] *Tashbetz*, Paragraph 270.

[48] This phrase can be taken to mean the same thing as the Jerusalem Talmud's "the Sages protested."

[49] *Kol Bo*, Paragraph 21. For a list of sources regarding the relative reliability of the *Tashbetz*' and *Kol Bo*'s citations, see D. Golinkin, n64. See also n59 below.

women in permission to wear *tefillin*. There are also some historical hints that could lead to interpreting women's problem with wearing *tefillin* as due to menstrual impurity. We have mentioned a practice from the geonic period that women did not touch *tefillin* during their period of menstrual impurity. In addition, a source from after *Maharam*'s time attests that the custom in some communities in Ashkenaz was for menstruants to refrain from attending synagogue and from touching Torah scrolls. *Maharam* could be referring to something along these lines, especially since he lived in Ashkenaz.

However, it seems doubtful that *Maharam*'s concern is menstrual impurity. First, *Maharam* is as lenient as other authorities regarding the ritual purity required for wearing *tefillin* in general. Like them, he holds that Torah scrolls and *tefillin* cannot be defiled through coming in physical contact with impurity such as that from a seminal emission.[50] Consistent with this is that women's not touching Torah scrolls was merely a custom and not a law. So there is no reason to expect *Maharam* to be exceptionally strict when it comes to women's ritual impurity and *tefillin*. Second, other sources discussing *tefillin* use the word "purity" in contexts which make it clear that the word refers merely to the physical definition of bodily cleanliness.[51] The *Tashbetz* may also be using the word "purity" in this sense. Thus, the two terms cited in *Maharam*'s name would be equivalent, both referring to bodily cleanliness.

In addition, it is worth noting that later authorities who cite *Maharam*'s opinion invariably use *Kol Bo*'s version which has the word "cleanliness," adding support to the idea that this was *Maharam*'s concern rather than ritual impurity. (Although, of course, it could also be that *Kol Bo* was the only version available to them.) Also, *Maharam*'s phraseology "They *do not know how to be careful to keep themselves* in a state of purity"—as opposed to something along the lines of "Women are sometimes not in a state of purity"— seems to referring to some factor that could be under a woman's control. Yet menstruation is obviously not controllable. Also, it would be odd to say "do

---

[50] *She'elot uTeshuvot Maharam bar Baruch,* vol. 2 (Jerusalem, 1986–7), Lvov ms., responsum 223. Actually, this responsum is a quotation from R. Yehudah b. Barzilai. Cf. also *Rambam* (*Mishne Torah, Hilkhot Sefer Torah* 10:8) who mentions specifically that menstruants may touch a Torah scroll.

[51] See e.g., *Shulchan Arukh,* OC 37:3 where "purity" is used to refer to a minor boy's wearing *tefillin* and is defined as refraining from sleeping and flatulence.

not know" to refer to one of the few things that, in the time of the *Maharam*, women *were* trusted to know: the intricate laws of family purity, including checking for blood, counting days, and preparing for ritual immersion.

A plausible interpretation of *Maharam* which we shall follow in this paper is that the term "purity" is used loosely to refer to a physical factor related to women's ritual purity, namely, a woman's being physically dirty from blood during her menstrual period.[52] Similar to the suggestion regarding ritual impurity from menstruation, this interpretation is attractive because it involves a physical difference between men and women. It provides a rationale for why women would not "know how" to keep the requirements of bodily cleanliness while men would: either no women bothered to figure out how to keep clean enough since they did not wear *tefillin* anyway, or hygienic conditions were poor, making it impossible to keep clean enough. Consistent with this interpretation is that even in cases where menstruants refrained from attending synagogue and touching Torah scrolls, they kept this custom only during their actual menstrual period, while ritual impurity lasts for an additional week after the bleeding is over. That *Maharam* is referring to uncleanness from menstrual blood is supported by the fact that when *Maharam* permits a man who experienced a seminal emission to wear *tefillin*, he describes the situation as one in which the man is capable of keeping himself physically clean from the emission. It seems reasonable that if refraining from having semen on one's body is included in the definition of bodily cleanliness in addition to flatulence and sleeping, then so too would be refraining from having menstrual blood on one's body.[53]

---

[52] This interpretation is the one used by S. Berman, ibid.

[53] There are other instances of post-talmudic additions to the bodily cleanliness require-ments. Most notably, one is also required to pay attention to the *tefillin* (e.g., *Shulchan Arukh*, OC 37:9). This was interpreted by some as merely meaning to refrain from levity and idle talk (e.g., *Tur*, OC 44). Since *Maharam* shows unusual strictness on the question of women wearing *tefillin*, it is also worthwhile to check whether he is unusually strict for men as well. He is not. *Maharam* uses a lenient definition offered by other authorities as well: He states that during a time of persecution, only people who are as righteous as Elisha the Possessor of Wings should wear *tefillin*, since only they can count on a miracle to save them. However, in ordinary times, merely the physical definition is required and all men should wear *tefillin*.

Maintaining Bodily Cleanliness: Possible or Impossible? Our second question was whether *Maharam* believes that women cannot attain appropriate bodily cleanliness,[54] or that women do not maintain bodily cleanliness because they are not accustomed to doing so—but if they wanted to, they could.[55] Either meaning is possible, but his wording ("they do not *know how* to") seems closer to the latter meaning. This interpretation is similar to our understanding of *Tosafot*'s wording that women are "not diligent about being careful." A third, related possibility is that the wording "they do not know" implies an educational concern: Since women were uneducated about laws that seem not to have directly concerned them, it was assumed that they did not know the rules of bodily cleanliness for *tefillin*.

In sum, we are left with three possibilities for why *Maharam* believes that women do not know how to maintain bodily cleanliness: either (1) the women of his time were unable to maintain bodily cleanliness; (2) women were not accustomed to maintaining it; or (3) women were not educated about how to maintain it.

Turning for a moment to a brief preview of a practical ruling for today, it is apparent that an attempt to apply *any* of these three possible reasons to women of today would not succeed. First, today's hygienic conditions—e.g., the advent of sanitary napkins and tampons—provide women with the ability to keep their bodies clean of menstrual blood. In terms of the third possibility, education, it is reasonable to suppose that before a woman would wear *tefillin*, she would first learn all the rules of *tefillin* including the requirements of bodily cleanliness, as does (or should) a Bar Mitzvah boy. In terms of the

---

[54] This interpretation of *Maharam* is given by *Eliya Rabba* (n2 to *Shulchan Arukh*, OC 38), who explains that while the wearing of *tefillin* by women in the time of the Talmud was indeed not protested, *Maharam* observed that women in his own time were less careful about maintaining the appropriate bodily cleanliness.

[55] *Maharam* is interpreted in this manner by *Magen Avraham* (to *Shulchan Arukh*, OC 38:3), who uses *Tosafot*'s phraseology "women are not diligent about being careful" to explain *Maharam*'s opinion. *Magen Avraham* reasons that if women were obligated to wear *tefillin*, they would have to, like men, take the risk and try to be careful to maintain bodily cleanliness. This comment is further evidence that according to this interpretation, women are in theory capable of maintaining the requisite bodily cleanliness. (But see *Arukh haShulchan* below for an opposing interpretation.) Similarly, *Magen haGiborim* (*Shiltei haGiborim* 38:2) interprets *Maharam* as meaning that women usually do not give any thought to trying to maintain the requirements of bodily cleanliness.

second possibility, becoming accustomed to maintaining bodily cleanliness, it is also reasonable to suppose that the woman would acquire this habit once she is educated about its necessity.

Two Other Minority Views

Maharam's opinion is the only restrictive one followed by later authorities, and we shall return to it in the next section. However, we shall first mention two other restrictive views which surface briefly in the period of the *Rishonim*.

Modesty: *Or Zaru'a* (who intriguingly, was a teacher of *Maharam*) (late 1100s–mid-1200s) raises the possibility that a woman wearing *tefillin* involves some problem related to the halakhic understanding that "a woman's hair is nakedness."[56] It is not clear whether he has in mind a woman's hair showing due to her wearing *tefillin*, or to *tefillin* coming in contact with "nakedness." However, this is almost immaterial, because *Or Zaru'a* does not actually rule that this is a problem.

Rebellion: R. Yeshaya of Trani Acharon (*Riaz*) (1235–1300) states that women should not wear *tefillin* because "it appears like the ways of dissenters who transgress the words of the Sages and do not wish to interpret the sources as they do."[57] This is a reference to the Sages protesting Michal's wearing of *tefillin* (in one talmudic version).

Reactions to *Maharam*: Disagreement, Then Agreement

The developments of the latter part of the period of the *Rishonim* involve reactions to the *Maharam*'s ruling. Of course, the absence of reaction is also highly significant. Of the three main disciples of the *Maharam*—*Hagahot Maimoniyot* (d. 1298), the *Mordechai* (1240–1298), and the *Rosh* (1250–1327)—none even mentions his ruling,[58] implying that they follow the majority view that women may wear *tefillin*. (Recall that *Maharam*'s rulings are known chiefly through the writings of his disciples.) *Tur* (c. 1275–c. 1340)

---

[56] *Berakhot* 24a; *Or Zaru'a*, part 2, *Hilkhot Rosh haShana* (Zhitomir, 1862) 62a.

[57] *Piskei Rid/Piskei Riaz*, vol. 3 (Jerusalem: *Makhon haTalmud haYerushalmi*, 1971) *Rosh haShana* 4:3, col. 84. Also cited in *Shiltei haGiborim* to *Rif* (*Rosh haShana* 33a).

[58] S. Berman, ibid.

chiefly through the writings of his disciples.) *Tur* (c. 1275–c. 1340) makes no mention of the issue, implying permission for women to wear *tefillin*.

Those authorities who do react to *Maharam* disagree with his ruling. *Orchot Chaim* (c. 1325) questions *Maharam*'s ruling on two counts. First, he notes that the Sages did not protest Michal's wearing *tefillin*. Second, he cites *Rashba*'s permission for women to perform all positive commandments.[59] R. Yosef Caro (1488–1575), in the *Beit Yosef*,[60] explains that *Maharam* rules as he does because he takes into account the view expressed in the Jerusalem Talmud that the Sages did protest Michal's action. In the *Shulchan Arukh*, R. Caro merely states that women are exempt from *tefillin* because it is a time-bound commandment.[61] So it is clear that R. Caro disagrees with *Maharam* and rules that women may wear *tefillin*.

Despite the fact that the overwhelming majority of *Rishonim* permit women to wear *tefillin*, the three major ashkenazic authorities of the later and "transition generation" of *Rishonim*—i.e., the generation between the *Rishonim* and *Achronim*—rule that the wearing of *tefillin* by women should be "protested," following the language of the Jerusalem Talmud. In doing so, all these figures, who are from Ashkenaz, follow a ruling already present in Ashkenaz, that of *Maharam*. These are the *Rama* (1530–1572), the *Maharshal* (1510–1573), and the *Levush* (1535–1612); *Levush* was a student of the *Rama* and the *Maharshal*. Let us examine their rulings.

Rama, who adds ashkenazic glosses to the *Shulchan Arukh*, states in the name of the *Kol Bo* (one of our sources for *Maharam*'s ruling) that "If women wish to be strict upon themselves [and wear *tefillin*], we protest this."[62] *Levush* also states that women's wearing *tefillin* should be protested, and adds that the

---

[59] It is possible that the *Orchot Chaim* was also the author of the anonymous *Kol Bo*, who originally cited *Maharam*. The *Orchot Chaim* is either a later, enlarged version of the *Kol Bo* or the *Kol Bo* is a later digest of the *Orchot Chaim*; but it is not clear if they were written by the same person. For more information on the relationship between the *Kol Bo* and the *Orchot Chaim*, see sources cited in D. Golinkin n51.

[60] To *Tur* 38:3.

[61] *Shulchan Arukh*, OC 38:3.

[62] *Rama* to *Shulchan Arukh*, OC 38:2.

reason is a concern about bodily cleanliness.[63] While *Rama* does not state his reason, we may assume that he also has in mind bodily cleanliness, since that is the reason given by the *Kol Bo*, his source.

Maharshal also agrees with the *Maharam*'s ruling. In addition, he introduces two crucial new elements into the debate, both weighing against allowing women to wear *tefillin*.[64]

Maharshal re-interprets the passage in the Babylonian Talmud about Michal wearing *tefillin*. In our analysis of this text, we had concluded that the Talmud's discussion, including permission to wear *tefillin*, referred to all women, not just to Michal.[65] However, *Maharshal* interprets the passage differently. According to *Maharshal*, the Sages did not protest the fact that Michal wore *tefillin*, but they *would* protest any other woman wearing *tefillin*, because of the problem of maintaining bodily cleanliness. The only reason the Sages did not protest Michal's wearing *tefillin* was that she was a special case: she was, according *Maharshal*, the daughter of the king, did not have children, and was a completely righteous person. For these three reasons, Michal was able to maintain the requirements of bodily cleanliness.

The first new element *Maharshal* introduces is partly a methodological one. Prior to *Maharshal*'s ruling, the opinion that women's wearing *tefillin* should be protested was methodologically unattractive because it involved following the Jerusalem Talmud over the Babylonian.[66] However, *Maharshal*, by reading the opinion of the *Maharam* into the Babylonian Talmud,[67] brings into the mainstream the opinion that women's wearing *tefillin* should be protested. This development is likely part of what causes later authorities to be somewhat more inclined to rule that women's wearing *tefillin* should be protested. Additionally, evidence of the attraction of *Maharshal*'s interpreta-

---

[63] Note 3 to *Shulchan Arukh*, OC 38. *Levush* also *may* be the first halakhic authority to apply to women's wearing of *tefillin* the idea from *Targum Yonatan/Yerushalmi* that this involves the problem of a woman's wearing men's apparel. What is not clear is whether he applies this problem only to *tzitzit*, or to *tefillin* as well. See also n82 below.

[64] *Yam Shel Shlomo, Kiddushin* 1:64.

[65] See discussion above, n20.

[66] See, for example, *Beit Yosef* above, to *Tur* 38:3.

[67] S. Berman, ibid.

tion that "Michal was special" is that this theme appears in later rulings,[68] with variations as to what it was that made Michal exceptional.[69]

The second factor *Maharshal* introduces—or rather, re-introduces from the Talmud—is the idea that the requirements of bodily cleanliness include a spiritual aspect. According to Maharshal, part of Michal's being able to maintain bodily cleanliness was that she was "completely righteous." Such a requirement, as *Maharshal* correctly implies, is impossible for other women to fulfill.[70]

However, *Maharshal*'s definition of bodily cleanliness as spiritual does not seem warranted. First, our analysis of *Tosafot*, who were the first to relate the issues of bodily cleanliness and women wearing *tefillin*, showed that they definitely interpreted bodily cleanliness as physical. Second, in general (i.e., not specific to women), a tradition of lenient, easily attainable bodily cleanli-

---

[68] Cf. R. Klapper, ibid.

[69] For example, *Ma'ase Rokeach* (to *Shulchan Arukh*, OC 38), says that Michal's *tefillin*-wearing was not protested because she thought she was obligated to wear *tefillin*. According to *Magen haGiborim* (*Shiltei haGiborim* 38:2), it was not protested because Michal said that she would be careful to keep the clean body requirements. According to *Levush*, Michal was exceptional in that because everyone recognized her, she was not subject to suspicion of attempting to mix with men. (See section below on "A Woman Shall Not Put on Men's Apparel.") For additional reasons given for Michal's uniqueness, see the sections on "Kabbalistic Reasons" and *Arukh haShulchan* below.

[70] *Maharshal* does not explain whether his other reasons that Michal was able to maintain bodily cleanliness—that she was the daughter of a king and that she did not have children—are also spiritual aspects of bodily cleanliness, or physical ones. Either is possible.

In terms of physical bodily cleanliness, the significance of being the daughter of a king would be that Michal had access to better hygienic conditions than other women, as well as leisure time. The physical advantages of her not having children would be her being able to avoid problematic situations that a mother might encounter such as becoming physically dirty from bleeding due to childbirth, not being able to predict when she might get dirt or worse on her body from a child, and/or child care taking up so much of her time such that she would not be able to concentrate on *tefillin*.

Alternatively, *Maharshal*'s mentioning that Michal had no children may reflect a kabbalistic understanding which infers from this biographical fact that Michal had the soul of a man (cited in e.g., *Kaf haChaim*, OC 38:9). This is obviously a spiritual characteristic, and as such would be unattainable by other women. It is less obvious how her being the king's daughter could be explained as a spiritual characteristic.

ness requirements for wearing *tefillin* began in the Talmud (i.e., the interpretations made by Abaye and Rava) and continued throughout the periods of the *Geonim* and *Rishonim*.[71] Thus, there seems to be little if any foundation for

---

[71] E. Kanarfogel, "Not Just Another Contemporary Jewish Problem: A Historical Discussion of Phylacteries," *Gesher* 5 (1976): 106–21.

The motivation for increasingly lenient definitions of bodily cleanliness is in itself a fascinating topic. Of most relevance to us is the surprising lenience of some of these definitions (one of which, as mentioned above, is even used by *Maharam*), which widens even more the discrepancy between the easily attainable definitions for men and *Maharshal*'s "spiritual" definition for women.

Historically, in response to a decline in wearing of *tefillin*, halakhic authorities in the periods of the Geonim and *Rishonim* made efforts to encourage performance of this commandment. (See ibid. for a detailed discussion of why the decline occurred.) One method of encouragement was to make the requirement of *tefillin* seem easier by de-emphasizing the ideal of wearing *tefillin* all day. (The original requirement for *tefillin* was to wear them all day; see M. Kasher, *Torah Shlema*, vol. 12, 240–47 for a discussion of whether the Bible itself requires one to wear *tefillin* all day, or whether this was a Rabbinic addition to a biblical commandment to just wear them for a short time each weekday.) This was done by varying the requirement of bodily cleanliness depending on whether *tefillin* were to be worn all day or just during prayer. For example, one version of the bodily cleanliness requirement was that in order to wear *tefillin* all day one needs to be as righteous as Elisha. (Note that Elisha himself, in the talmudic anecdote, wore *tefillin* all day.) But to wear *tefillin* just during prayer, the physical requirements are sufficient. R. Yehudai Gaon supports this version of the requirement through an *a fortiori* argument based on the fact that we read from the Torah scroll during prayer. A Torah scroll is obviously more holy than *tefillin* since it contains the entire Torah, while *tefillin* contain only four passages from the Torah. Thus, the fact that there are no special bodily cleanliness requirements which a person must meet in order to be able to read from the Torah during prayer proves that people certainly have enough bodily cleanliness for *tefillin* during prayer time (B. Levin, ed., *Otsar haGe'onim*, Haifa, 1928, *Berakhot* 87, page 39.) *Sefer Mitzvot Gadol* (Positive Commandments, 3) directly challenges the idea of any spiritual requirement at all for *tefillin* during prayer, saying that "there is no such thing as a person who is so evil that they are unworthy of *tefillin* during prayer."

A related means of encouragement, similar to that employed by Abaye and Rava in the Talmud itself, was to assert that there is never any spiritual requirement whatsoever for wearing *tefillin*. For example, *Sefer haChinukh* (ed. Chavel, Positive Commandment 421; translation based on that of Feldheim, 1988) refers to, and disagrees with, those authorities "who are stringent about the holiness of this precept, and by their words dissuade the masses from occupying themselves with it." According to *Sefer haChinukh*, rather than needing special righteousness in order to wear *tefillin*, it works the other way around: *tefillin* keep one from one's evil inclinations. Perhaps as a result of wearing *tefillin*, which remind one of worshipping God, an evil person will repent and become purified (Cf. also

Maharshal's position that there exists such a basic difference between the prerequisites for men's and women's performance of the same act.

Summary: All three major ashkenazic halakhic authorities of the latter part of this period follow the *Maharam* over the decided majority opinion of permission recorded in the earlier *Rishonim*, ruling that the wearing of *tefillin* by women should be protested. In addition, *Maharshal* introduces two new aspects to the debate which open the door to further restrictive opinions. As a result of these developments, subsequent authorities have a new picture to deal with:[72] a tradition of permission followed by a trend to restrict. Faced with this pattern, it will no longer be possible for an ashkenazic authority to permit women to wear *tefillin* without addressing the restrictive views.

IV. Period of the *Achronim*: Mixed Opinions

The majority opinion during most of the period of the *Rishonim* permitting women to wear *tefillin*, which was followed by a trend of ashkenazic opinion to protest this practice, gives way to a mixed picture in the period of the *Achronim*. On the restrictive side, some authorities discuss *Maharam* and indicate agreement with him,[73] and others put forth views similar to that of *Maharshal*.[74]

However, there is also indication of permission. This comes about in part due to a crucial element of the restrictive views up to this point in time, namely, that none of them expressly *prohibits* the wearing of *tefillin* by women. Rather, the decisors carefully preserve the Jerusalem Talmud's

---

Chavel, ed., *Kad haKemach*, in *Kitvei Rabbenu Bachya* (Jerusalem: Mossad haRav Kook, 1970) 444–46 and Responsa *Rama miPano*, 39).

Another set of sources, rather than comparing physical and spiritual aspects of clean body, assumes that the requirement is solely physical and emphasizes that the physical requirements are easy to achieve. *Tosafot* (to *Pesachim* 113b, s.v. "*v'eyn lo banim*") stress that it is a simple matter to maintain bodily cleanliness during the recitation of *Shema*. *Rosh* comments, "Today, when we are accustomed to wearing *tefillin* only during prayer, it is a simple matter for a person to be careful during that time" (*Halakhot Ketanot, Hilkhot Tefillin, Menachot* 122b).

[72] S. Berman, ibid.

[73] For example, the sources discussed in nn54 and 55 above.

[74] For example, the sources discussed in n69 above.

language of "protest," which is a categorization a degree less severe than prohibition. As a result of this circumstance, while *Achronim* do have to use the existing restrictive views as a point of reference, at the same time, the absence of outright prohibition in these opinions affords the *Achronim* some maneuverability to permit.[75]

Also, in addition to the issue of bodily cleanliness, new objections to women wearing *tefillin* are raised during this period.

Other Values Overrule Requirement of Bodily Cleanliness

Maset Binyamin (c. 1550–c. 1620) permits women to wear *tefillin*, which is very significant in view of the fact that this decisor was a student of both *Rama* and *Maharshal* and thus a direct heir to the ashkenazic trend to protest the practice of women wearing *tefillin*. As we mentioned, granting permission in the face of such a tradition was possible because these authorities did not outright prohibit women from wearing *tefillin*. *Maset Binyamin* states that while it might seem inappropriate for women to wear *tefillin* because of the problem of bodily cleanliness, it is nonetheless permitted because this problem is overridden by other important values. First, *tefillin* serve as a symbol of taking upon oneself the "yoke of Heaven," i.e., God's commandments. Second, *tefillin* provide spiritual satisfaction to the wearer.[76]

The line of reasoning of *Maset Binyamin* recalls both the general positive attitude of the Talmud and *Rishonim* about people taking on optional commandments, and calls on the same specific reason we saw that permission was given for women to ritually lay their hands on sacrifices.

Minor Problems in Addition to Bodily Cleanliness

Besides the issue of bodily cleanliness, various other issues are raised during the period of the *Achronim*. We shall treat these briefly. However, none of

---

[75] S. Berman, ibid.

[76] *Maset Binyamin*, responsum 62. I was directed to this source by S. Berman, ibid. This responsum is also of poignant interest. *Maset Binyamin* addresses the question of whether a blind person may be called to the Torah; the issue arose because he himself had gone blind. In the responsum, he mentions his sad feelings about missing out on the experience of being called to the Torah.

them is considered to be as serious a halakhic problem as bodily cleanliness, because they are each mentioned by at most a few authorities.

"A woman shall not put on men's apparel.":[77] We had mentioned in the section on the geonic period that according to *Targum Yonatan* (a non-halakhic source), this means that women should not wear *tzitzit* and *tefillin*. However, it took many hundreds of years for any halakhic authority to make use of this idea. While *Ravad*, whom we saw, may indirectly have done so with reference to optional commandments in general, the first to refer to this idea explicitly and specifically with reference to *tefillin* is *Bet Hillel* (1615–1690).[78] *Bet Hillel* cites the *Targum* and rules that women should not wear *tzitzit* or *tefillin* because it will lead them to prostitution or adultery. The connection between *tefillin* and these sexual transgressions stems from the general attitude of the Talmud toward "cross-dressing." According to the Talmud, the reason the Torah considers cross-dressing to be an abomination is that it allows a person to mix freely with members of the opposite sex, which in turn can lead to sexual transgressions.

However, most *Achronim* explicitly reject[79] or do not mention that women wearing *tefillin* involves the prohibition of cross-dressing. This is primarily because they follow the opinion that cross-dressing is only prohibited when it is done for the purpose of making oneself appear more beautiful.[80] A woman wearing *tefillin* does not fit this criterion; Michal did not wear *tefillin* in order to appear beautiful but rather to perform a commandment.

Excessive Pride ("*yohara*"): *Maharam Schick* (1807–1879) forbids women to wear *tefillin* because he believes it involves the sin of excessive pride.[81] Although *Maharam Schick* does not say so explicitly, apparently the problem

---

[77] Deut. 22:5.

[78] To YD 182:1.

[79] E.g., *Responsa Maharam Schick*, OC, responsum 173; *Sdei Chemed, Ma'arekhet Lamed*, rule 116; *Iggerot Moshe*, part 4, OC, responsum 49.

[80] E.g., *Maharam Schick*, ibid.

[81] Ibid., OC, responsum 16.

is that the woman may (or appears to) believe that she, unlike other women, is capable of maintaining the appropriate level of bodily cleanliness.[82]

Additionally, according to *Maharam Schick*, another problem with women wearing *tefillin* is that even if a particular woman does maintain the bodily cleanliness requirements, this situation could lead to other women also wearing *tefillin* even though they are not careful about the requirements.

Eve's Curse: *Shevut Ya'akov*[83] (d. 1734) combines two ideas to determine that women's wearing *tefillin* should be protested. First, one of Eve's curses was that her head is "wrapped up like a mourner."[84] Second, there is a halakhic opinion that mourners (through the day of the burial) cannot wear *tefillin* because they might not be able to concentrate properly on them. These two ideas together lead to the conclusion that women, being "perpetual mourners," can never concentrate properly on *tefillin*. Therefore, one should protest their wearing *tefillin*.

Kabbalistic Reasons: Various kabbalistic understandings of the nature of *tefillin* suggest that it is inappropriate for women to wear them.

One understanding, which follows the opinion that *tefillin* are men's apparel, is that *tefillin* are a "secret of the male world," and therefore women should not wear them.[85] Another kabbalistic understanding is that the head-*tefillin* are representative of the male and the arm-*tefillin* of the female;[86]

---

[82] *Levush*'s discussion of women wearing *tzitzit* (*Hilkhot Tzitzit*, to OC 17:2) *may* also raise the problem of *yohara* for wearing of *tefillin*. *Levush*—somewhat inexplicably—states that Michal wore *tzitzit*, while making no mention of her wearing *tefillin*. According to Levush, since (1) for a woman to wear *tzitzit might* involve a transgression of the prohibition for her to wear men's apparel, and (2) it has not been customary for women to wear *tzitzit*, a woman who wears *tzitzit* is guilty of the sin of excessive pride; her sin lies in her intimation that she is above suspicion of licentious activities. This same reasoning might apply to *tefillin*—but only if *tefillin* are considered "men's apparel." Cf. n63 above. See next article.

[83] 2:11.

[84] *Eruvin* 100b.

[85] *Shomer Emunim* (d. 1830) to Deut. 22:5.

[86] *Yafe laLev* (R. Nissim Yitzchak ben Chaim Palaggi) vol. 3 (part 6), OC 38, and A. Kaplan, *Tefillin* (NY, 1975) 56–57. *Yafe laLev* says that the arm-*tefillin* are female because

this implies that women should not wear the head-*tefillin*. R. Aryeh Kaplan, making use of the fact that the *tefillin* boxes are referred to in Hebrew by a word (*bayit*), that also means "house," suggests that it is unnecessary for women to wear *tefillin* because women resemble God through the home, while a man accomplishes this through the *tefillin*. None of these ideas, however, are mentioned in non-kabbalistic halakhic works, and may therefore be discounted for our purposes.

Modesty: *Hagahot Maimoniyot*[87] (d. 1298) cites—but does not rule according to—an opinion (likely that of *Or Zaru'a*, above) that women should not wear *tefillin* because "a woman's hair is nakedness." While this is not cited by any authorities as a halakhic problem for women's wearing of *tefilliln*, it *is* a reminder that keeping one's hair covered—as many married Orthodox women do—while wearing *tefillin* poses logistic problems. However, the problems are far from insurmountable. We shall consider this issue on a practical level.

First, to address a related issue, it is perfectly acceptable to cover the arm-*tefillin* (e.g., with one's sleeve), in order to keep the arm covered for purposes of modesty. *Rama*,[88] citing the *Mordechai*, rules that one need not be particular about whether the arm-*tefillin* are covered or visible. According to the *Mishna Berura*, it is even preferable that the arm-*tefillin* be covered up.[89]

It is apparent from common sense that there are two alternatives for covering one's head while wearing *tefillin*: wearing the covering under the *tefillin* and wearing it over the *tefillin*. Either of these alternatives could pose a halakhic problem. With regard to wearing the covering under the *tefillin*, nothing is supposed to separate the head-*tefillin* box and straps from the head. Putting a head covering over the *tefillin* might also be a problem if it leaves some hair exposed.

---

they are worn on the weaker arm; according to Kaplan, the arm-*tefillin* represent a woman's womb.

[87] To *Rambam Hilkhot Tzitzit* 3:9, note *lamed*. *Hagahot Maimoniyot* is actually a *Rishon*, but is included in this section because this view is a minority opinion.

[88] To *Shulchan Arukh*, OC 27:11.

[89] *Mishna Berura* ad loc., n47.

Shulchan Arukh states that it is best for the head-*tefillin* to be visible.[90] Elsewhere, he rules that while wearing *tefillin*, it is permissible to wear on your head what you usually wear there; he gives the example of wearing a hat but not a shawl.[91] Presumably *Shulchan Arukh* assumes that these articles are leaving the *tefillin* and straps exposed. In fact, men do wear *kipot* or hats pushed back on the head while wearing *tefillin*. This type of arrangement solves the difficulty for a woman who is not concerned with covering up every last bit of her hair; a hat, kerchief, or some similar covering could cover most of the hair while still leaving the head-*tefillin* showing. Covering up all of one's hair while leaving the *tefillin* exposed would be harder, but probably is still possible through use of some imaginative type of head covering.

Another solution to this logistic problem could be found based on the ruling that while the head-*tefillin* should *a priori* be visible, if it was covered, the commandment to wear *tefillin* is still fulfilled *post facto*.[92] It is possible that a halakhic authority faced with this question would decide that the requirement for the woman to cover her head would take priority and she should cover the *tefillin*.

Mishna Berura cites the *Machatzit haShekel* as ruling that long hair could be problematic for wearing *tefillin* because it might constitute a separation between the *tefillin* and the head. Also, long hair could make it impossible to keep the head-*tefillin* box in its correct spot.[93] This issue can probably be dealt with as logistics demand.

V. The Twentieth Century: Still Mixed Opinions

From the start of the twentieth century through to today, halakhic opinion is divided about whether women may wear *tefillin*. Two of the most prominent ashkenazic halakhic authorities of the early twentieth century, *Arukh haShulchan* (1829–1908) and *Chafetz Chaim* (1838–1933, author of the *Mishna Berura* and the *Be'ur Halakha*) both rule that women's wearing of *tefillin* should be protested. However, *Chafetz Chaim*'s ruling may be somewhat

---

[90] OC 27:11.

[91] OC 41:1.

[92] *Mishna Berura* to *Shulchan Arukh, OC* 41:4.

[93] *Mishna Berura* note 14 to *Shulchan Arukh, OC* 27:4.

mitigated by another statement of his. Due to the weight which ashkenazim ascribe to views of these authorities, and because these authorities introduce new elements into our debate, we treat their views at length. In addition, we shall see several views which permit.

Arukh haShulchan: Severe Restriction

Arukh haShulchan's[94] position that one should protest women's wearing *tefillin* is based on restrictive elements from previous opinions, particularly that of *Maharshal*. We shall first summarize *Arukh haShulchan*'s discussion and then comment on his arguments.

First, *Arukh haShulchan* notes that *tefillin* is different from the commandments of *sukka* and *lulav*, which women are permitted to perform even though they are exempt from them. What is different about *tefillin* is that they "require an extremely high degree of care in order to maintain the requirements of bodily cleanliness." To support this idea, *Arukh haShulchan* cites the statement of the Babylonian Talmud that "*tefillin* require one to have a clean body like Elisha the Possessor of Wings" and the Jerusalem Talmud's statement that "anyone who is not like Elisha the Possessor of Wings should not wear *tefillin*." In view of this strict requirement, says *Arukh haShulchan*, the only reason men are permitted to wear *tefillin* is that they are *obligated* to be careful to maintain the requirements of bodily cleanliness during the recitation of *Shema* and *Shemone Esrei* (the "eighteen benedictions" prayer, which forms the central part of the prayer service). Historically, even men went from wearing *tefillin* all day to wearing them for only a short time because of the difficulty of maintaining these requirements. Similarly, minors stopped wearing *tefillin* because they are not obligated to do so. Based on this reasoning, there is no justification for women, who have no obligation to do so, to put themselves into the danger of transgressing the requirements of bodily cleanliness. "For women, the time of *Shema* and *Shemone Esrei* is like all day with regard to men." *Arukh haShulchan* ends by noting—like *Maharshal*—that Michal was permitted to wear *tefillin* because she was a purely righteous woman and knew how to be careful to maintain the requirements of bodily cleanliness. However, he says, other women do not meet these standards.

---

[94] OC 38.

The two main arguments upon which *Arukh haShulchan* bases his position are that people should wear *tefillin* only when obligated to do so, and that the bodily cleanliness requirements are in part spiritual.

(1) People should wear *tefillin* only when obligated to do so: According to *Arukh haShulchan*, it is so hard to maintain the bodily cleanliness requirements for wearing *tefillin* that only under conditions of obligation may one risk possibly not being able to maintain the requirements. Since women will never become obligated to wear *tefillin*, *Arukh haShulchan* is thus the first authority to provide an explanation *which is applicable to any time and place* of why the rules of bodily cleanliness should apply differently to women than to men.[95] (Recall, in contrast, that we showed that *Maharam*'s ruling may not apply to women today.)

To partially respond to this argument of *Arukh haShulchan*, we shall show that the times when males wear *tefillin* are not exactly equivalent to those times when they are obligated to do so. This will demonstrate empirically that one may wear *tefillin* when one is not strictly obligated to do so.

Once it became accepted that *tefillin* were not worn all day, the requirement to wear them was limited to *Shema* and *Shemone Esrei*[96] of the morning prayer service. Yet, even today, men invariably wear *tefillin* during the entire morning service. This can last more than thirty minutes in the synagogue, with *Shema* and *Shemone Esrei* taking perhaps ten minutes of that time. Thus, it seems ingenuous to argue that men wear *tefillin* only when obligated.[97]

Similarly, *Arukh haShulchan*'s argument is also weakened in view of the ruling that someone who is experiencing stomach problems and feels that they

---

[95] S. Berman, ibid. However, it is likely that *Arukh haShulchan* reads *Magen Avraham* as a precedent for his opinion.

[96] See e.g., *Shulchan Arukh, OC* 37:2; *Chaye Adam* rule 14, *Hilkhot Tefillin* 18. The halakhic sources say that *tefillin* should be worn during "*tefilla*." This word literally means prayer and in modern Hebrew is used to refer to the entire prayer service, but in these sources it refers to the *Shemone Esrei* only.

[97] In fact, even today there are a few pious men who study Torah all day while wearing *tefillin* and quite a number who wear them for a short while after the morning prayers while studying Torah (*Mishna Berura* note 7 to *Shulchan Arukh, OC* 37:2, states that there is a custom to do this). However, since such pious behavior is rare and sometimes frowned upon, we shall consider only the usual occurrence of wearing *tefillin* during the entire morning prayer service.

cannot maintain bodily cleanliness during the entire prayer service, but can do so for a short while, should put on *tefillin* and recite the blessings on them just before *Shema.*[98] But if maintaining bodily cleanliness is as difficult and risky as *Arukh haShulchan* claims, then a true minimal length of time for wearing *tefillin* ought to have been determined—perhaps, during *Shema* and *Shemone Esrei*—and everyone should follow this practice every day. An examination of actual practice shows that people regularly "run the risk" of wearing *tefillin* when they are not strictly obligated to do so.

The second argument which *Arukh haShulchan* uses to demonstrate that people only wear *tefillin* when obligated is that while minors used to begin wearing *tefillin* as soon as they were mature enough to control their bodily cleanliness,[99] at some point in history, minors stopped wearing *tefillin*.[100]

However, despite what *Arukh haShulchan* says, minors actually do wear *tefillin*. A prevalent ashkenazic practice today is for boys to begin wearing *tefillin* and reciting the blessings on them a month or so before their Bar Mitzva in order to practice (*chinukh*). A contemporary ruling which is even more at variance with *Arukh haShulchan*'s idea is that of the sephardic authority Rabbi Ovadia Yosef, who rules that *tefillin* may be worn beginning a few years prior to majority.[101] We may argue that this is similar to the case just discussed of wearing *tefillin* for a minimal time during prayers; if maintanence of bodily cleanliness can only be done under conditions of obligation, as *Arukh haShulchan* claims, then one would expect that there be elaborate rules for minors to practice putting on *tefillin*. For example, perhaps they could practice different parts of the task, but never perform it entirely until the day of their Bar Mitzva, similar to the way a prospective convert to Judaism has to always be sure to break a law of Shabbat until they actually convert. Or they could remove the *tefillin* immediately after donning them, rather then wearing them during the prayer service as is the current practice. The absence of such

---

[98] E.g., *Shulchan Arukh*, OC 38:2.

[99] This is the ruling in *Shulchan Arukh*, OC 37:3, based on *Sukka* 42a.

[100] This is the ruling of the *Rama* ad loc., based on a minority opinion among *Rishonim* expressed by *Sefer ha'Itur*.

[101] *Yechave Da'at* 2:4. This ruling follows that of *Shulchan Arukh*. But it is not clear whether this would mitigate the argument of the *Arukh haShulchan*, who was ashkenazic.

concern is another example *tefillin* being worn without a condition of obligation.

Another contention which we tentatively put forth is that minors stopped wearing *tefillin* due to some factor other than problems with maintaining bodily cleanliness. Historically, during the period of the *Rishonim*, people wore *tefillin* less because—in addition to their being worried about being able to maintain bodily cleanliness—they were generally confused about the laws of *tefillin*.[102] Although this is not attested in any halakhic sources, we speculatively offer the suggestion that minors stopped wearing *tefillin* because people in general were wearing *tefillin* less; this in turn occurred due to general confusion about the laws of *tefillin* at that time. If this is true, then the *Arukh haShulchan*'s argument that the reason minors do not wear *tefillin* is due to a problem with maintenance of bodily cleanliness does not necessarily follow from the observation that minors do not wear *tefillin*.

Nonetheless, even if one accepts our above presentation against *Arukh haShulchan*'s claim that people wear *tefillin* only under conditions of obligations, an implicit part of *Arukh haShulchan*'s claim on this point still remains valid. The examples of a minor wearing *tefillin* and a man wearing *tefillin* for a longer period of time than required are both cases in which the individual *is* obligated to wear *tefillin*, just not at that particular time. In contrast, a woman is *at no time* obligated to wear *tefillin*. It may be that while an individual who is obligated to wear *tefillin* at some other time can extend this "permission" to times when they are not obligated, a woman has no such option.

However, note that accepting this line of reasoning involves accepting *Arukh haShulchan*'s minority definition of bodily cleanliness as spiritual as well as physical (see next section). Understanding the requirements as physical, as do almost all authorities, means that there is no "danger" involved in exempted individuals attempting to meet them. Using a physical understanding, there is no reason to distinguish between an exempt person wearing

---

[102] E. Kanarfogel, ibid. It is also interesting to note that this is the same period in which the validity of women wearing *tefillin* first begins to be questioned. Thus, for women as well as minors, the real issue *may* be the general confusion about the laws of *tefillin*. In other words, if men do not know the laws, how could women possibly know them? Note that *Maharam*'s rulings are worded in terms of women's lack of knowledge.

tefillin and an obligated person wearing *tefillin* at optional times. The distinction is only operative if one defines bodily cleanliness as spiritual.

(2) The requirement of bodily cleanliness is spiritual: The argument of the *Arukh haShulchan* that one should protest the wearing of *tefillin* by women is based in part on the idea that wearing *tefillin* requires one to possess an "extremely high level of bodily cleanliness." That the type of bodily cleanliness required is spiritual in addition to physical is evident both from the *Arukh haShulchan*'s citations of the talmudic statements that one needs to be like Elisha the Possessor of Wings in order to wear *tefillin*, and from his citation of *Maharshal*'s view that part of Michal's maintenance of bodily cleanliness involved her being fully righteous. The same line of reasoning which we used above to oppose *Maharshal*'s view applies here as well.

In addition, *Arukh haShulchan*'s definition of bodily cleanliness implies that men meet a spiritual requirement. Although *Arukh haShulchan* does not state this idea explicitly, it is a necessary implication of his defining bodily cleanliness as spiritual, yet still permitting men to wear *tefillin*. This contrasts with the strong tradition in halakhic history to define bodily cleanliness as physical in order to allow men to attain it.

Chafetz Chaim: Moderate Restriction

The *Chafetz Chaim* agrees with *Rama*'s ruling that the wearing of *tefillin* by women should be protested, explaining this by paraphrasing *Tosafot*: "[Tefillin] require bodily cleanliness, while women are not diligent about being careful."[103] However, while *Chafetz Chaim* surely does not recommend that women wear *tefillin*, he indicates elsewhere that this is theoretically possible. He mentions, in the context of another ruling, that a woman who has taken upon herself the obligation of wearing *tefillin* may not serve as a ritual scribe for *tefillin* because her obligation is on a lower level than that of someone who was commanded to wear *tefillin*. Implicit in this is the assumption that she *may* wear *tefillin*.[104] The reason *Chafetz Chaim* can entertain this possibility is that

---

[103] *Mishna Berura*, note 13 to *Shulchan Arukh*, OC 38:3.

[104] *Chafetz Chaim*'s statement also raises the question of whether a woman who begins to wear *tefillin* would then be obligated to continue doing so. However, the issue of levels of obligation, including self-obligation, is beyond the scope of this paper.

he categorizes *Rama*'s opinion as "merely a stringency" to account for the opinion mentioned in the Jerusalem Talmud that Michal's wearing *tefillin* was protested.[105] It is interesting to note that the assumption that women could in theory take on the obligation of wearing *tefillin*, which underlies this ruling, lies in direct opposition to *Arukh haShulchan*'s assumption that there is no way women can take on the obligation.

Permission

Bodily Cleanliness Also Required for Prayer: The opinion that women's wearing of *tefillin* should be protested actually engenders several inconsistencies which we shall discuss here. Those commentators who point out the inconsistencies suggest resolving them by being more lenient regarding women wearing *tefillin*.

An inconsistency in *Rama*'s position raised by *Tehilla leDavid*[106] (d. 1910) is that the view that women cannot wear *tefillin* due to a problem with maintaining the requirements of bodily cleanliness conflicts with the requirement for women to recite the *Shemone Esrei*. This conflict arises because the bodily cleanliness requirement is used by halakhic authorities not only as a prerequisite for wearing *tefillin*, but also as a prerequisite for the recitation of *Shema* and the *Shemone Esrei*.[107] Since women are obligated to pray the *Shemone Esrei*,[108] argues *Tehilla leDavid*, one must assume that women are considered capable of maintaining bodily cleanliness for the amount of time it takes to recite it (say, about five minutes). Similarly, says *Tehilla leDavid*, we must assume that women could be able to keep their attention focused on the *tefillin* during this time, since focused attention is also a prerequisite for prayer.[109] While *Tehilla leDavid* does not go so far as to rule against *Rama*, he

---

[105] *Be'ur Halakha* to *Shulchan Arukh*, OC 39, s.v. *"kasher likhtov tefillin."*

[106] *Tehilla leDavid*, (Jerusalem, 1993) OC 38:1.

[107] E.g., *Shulchan Arukh*, OC 80:1.

[108] That women are required to pray the *Shemone Esrei* is not a unanimous opinion among halakhic authorities, but it is the most common opinion (*Mishna Berura* note 4 to *Shulchan Arukh*, OC 106:1).

[109] E.g., *Magen Avraham* to *Shulchan Arukh*, OC 44:2.

states that the idea that one should protest women who wish to wear *tefillin* during the *Shemone Esrei* "requires further investigation."[110]

A similar point to that raised by *Tehilla leDavid* arises from the fact that women are exempt from reciting the *Shema*.[111] The position that women are not capable of maintaining bodily cleanliness leads to the conclusion that women would not be permitted to recite the *Shema* at all. Yet no halakhic decisor even mentions the possibility that women's reciting *Shema* should be protested. In fact, it is recommended that women recite the first two sentences of the *Shema*[112] in order to take upon themselves the yoke of Heaven.[113]

---

[110] *Tehilla leDavid* notes that a previous opinion exists which is opposite to his own suggestion: that of *Eshel Avraham* (to *Magen Avraham*, cited in n55 above). *Eshel Avraham*, apparently anticipating an argument like that of *Tehilla leDavid*, specifies that women's wearing *tefillin* even during *Shema* and *Shemone Esrei* should be protested. However, it is not clear—nor, apparently, was it clear to *Tehilla leDavid*—how this is implied by either *Magen Avraham* or by the citations of *Maharam*.

[111] See beginning of paper and *Shulchan Arukh*, OC 70:1.

[112] See e.g., *Shulchan Arukh* OC 70:1 and *Rama*'s gloss ad loc.

[113] We shall suggest an alternative resolution to the contradiction raised by *Tehilla leDavid*, in which women's wearing *tefillin* would be protested while still allowing women to optionally recite the *Shema* and obligating them to recite *Shemone Esrei*. However, ultimately it does not seem that this suggestion solves the contradiction.

One might suggest that wearing *tefillin* requires some type of "higher level" of bodily cleanliness than that which is required for prayer, and that women are accustomed to attaining the level required for prayer, but not that required for *tefillin*. Something along these lines may be inferred from the debate over whether someone who is ill with serious stomach problems—who all authorities agree cannot wear *tefillin*—can pray. *Shulchan Arukh* (*Orach Chaim* 80:1) rules that such a person cannot pray either. However, *Be'er Heitev* (ibid., n1) qualifies this, saying that this is only the ruling for someone who has stomach problems due to something that one ate, which will pass in a day or so. However, if one has a chronic stomach problem, this rule would imply that one should give up praying altogether. Since this is an undesirable state of affairs, the compromise position of *Be'er Heitev* is that if one has chronic stomach problems, one should not give up praying. Rather, one should pray, but without *tefillin*. This distinction probably indicates a technical difference between praying and wearing *tefillin*: one can interrupt one's prayers if the illness comes on, but one cannot rip the *tefillin* off in time. In this logistic sense, then, *tefillin do* require a higher level of bodily cleanliness than prayer. Perhaps this logistic difference is applied to women as well, allowing them to pray and recite the *Shema* but not to wear *tefillin*. But, still, it is not clear why this would apply differently to men and women.

Along similar lines to *Tehilla leDavid*, the anonymous *Mishne Halakha*[114] (late 20th century) notes that the *Chafetz Chaim*[115] writes that one who wears *tefillin* for as short a time as one minute has performed the commandment. *Mishne Halakha* comments that anyone, even a woman, is capable of being careful for such a short time. He suggests—although he says that this needs further study due to a possible problem with the prohibition for women to wear men's apparel—that if women want to wear *tefillin* for a minute, one should not protest.

Resolution of these inconsistencies could involve permitting women to wear *tefillin* for some very limited time period, and explaining that *Rama* meant to include this possibility.[116] Or, more daringly, one could interpret

---

The opposite idea, that prayer requires a higher level of bodily cleanliness than wearing *tefillin*, is reflected in another ruling. This ruling focuses upon the attention required while wearing *tefillin* as well as on the bodily cleanliness requirements. *Rama* of Fano (1548–1620) (*Responsa Rama miPano*, 39) states that if one is not in the proper frame of mind, one should not be praying in the first place, let alone wearing *tefillin*, "because prayer requires bodily cleanliness and purity of place and mind much more than *tefillin*." His proof for this is a talmudic statement (*Shabbat* 10): the Talmud states that in the "outer room" of the bathhouse, where everyone is clothed, one may recite both the *Shemone Esrei* and wear *tefillin*. In the "middle room" of the bathhouse, where some people are naked and some are clothed, one may not recite the *Shemone Esrei*. Regarding *tefillin*, in the middle room, one does not need to remove them if they are already on, but one may not put them on either. In the "inner room," where everyone is naked, one must remove one's *tefillin*. According to *Rama* of Fano, the rules regarding the middle room imply that the bodily cleanliness required for recitation of the *Shemone Esrei* is greater than that required for wearing *tefillin*. The same may be inferred from *Mishne Torah*, *Hilkhot Tefilla* 4:8 and *Hilkhot Tefillin* 4:22.

In sum, this set of examples is inconclusive as to whether the requirements of bodily cleanliness are greater for the recitation of *Shemone Esrei* or for the wearing of *tefillin*, since there is evidence both ways.

[114] First ed., Jerusalem, 1986; second ed., Jerusalem, 1989.

[115] *Be'ur Halakha*, to *Shulchan Arukh*, OC 37, s.v. *"mitzvatan."*

[116] *Tehilla leDavid*'s tentative solution to the apparent contradiction between his line of thought and the *Rama*'s saying to protest women wearing *tefillin* is that although *Rama* did not say so explicitly, he was protesting women wearing *tefillin* all day, but would permit them to wear *tefillin* for a shorter time.

Support for this solution is that there are, in fact, other instances of ambiguity as to whether sources discussing the wearing of *tefillin* are referring to all day or to part of the day. See for example *Mishna Berura* note 19 to OC 40:8, who finds such an ambiguity in

Rama's entire position as "a mere stringency" (to use *Chafetz Chaim*'s language). Support for this is *Rama*'s statement elsewhere that women may perform all time-bound commandments and recite the blessings on them.[117]

Tefillin Keep One From Sinning: *Ravaz* (1866–1930), a prominent halakhic decisor in early twentieth-century Romania, addresses those authorities who suggested that wearing *tefillin* could be a problem because of the prohibition for a woman to wear men's clothing; we saw that these authorities had said that this could lead to sexual transgressions. According to *Ravaz*, it does not make any sense to suggest that wearing *tefillin* could lead to sexual transgression. Rather, he says, the opposite is true: the act of wearing *tefillin* prevents one from sinning.[118] *Ravaz* cites earlier sources to support this idea.. For example, a story is related in the Talmud[119] about Rava, who upon observing that Abaye seemed overly merry, quoted to him the verse "*And rejoice with trembling*,"[120] as a hint that Abaye should limit his merriness. Abaye an-

---

the *Shulchan Arukh*, and *Be'ur Halakha* to OC 37:3 regarding *Rama*'s ruling that minors should not wear *tefillin*.

However, contrary to the suggestion of *Tehilla leDavid*, evidence indicates that Rama equally protests women wearing *tefillin* for a short time and all day. Other statements by *Rama* (not specific to women) indicate that while he has in mind a theoretical possibility of wearing *tefillin* all day, he is well aware that this is not the usual practice. For example, regarding the *Shulchan Arukh*'s (OC 25:12) discussion of whether one is required to make the blessing on *tefillin* more than once a day if one puts them on and takes them off more than once a day, *Rama* does not remark that this would be an unusual situation. This indicates that wearing *tefillin* all day is a possibility for *Rama*. However, in his comment to *Shulchan Arukh* OC 27:1, where he disagrees with the *Shulchan Arukh* about whether one needs to cover up the head-*tefillin* out of respect in front of one's teacher, *Rama* specifies that "today, when we wear them only during the recital of *Shema* and the *Shemone Esrei*, this [i.e., covering up the head-*tefillin*] is not necessary." Thus the pattern seems to be that *Rama* mentions the distinction between *tefillin* being worn only during prayer rather than all day when the difference affects a ruling. It follows from this that if *Rama* thought that women could wear *tefillin* for a short time, just not all day, he would have mentioned this explicitly. But he makes no such distinction. We may therefore assume that it makes no difference to him: for the whole day or for part of the day, one should protest women wearing *tefillin*.

[117] Gloss to *Shulchan Arukh*, OC 589:6.

[118] *Responsa Ravaz* 73.

[119] *Berakhot* 30b.

[120] Psalms 2:2.

swered, "I am wearing *tefillin*." In other words, wearing *tefillin* engenders a proper state of mind. Another support cited by *Ravaz* is that according to *Rambam*, "as long as *tefillin* are on someone's head and arm, they are modest and God-fearing, are not attracted by levity and idle talk, and do not have improper thoughts. Rather, their mind is devoted to truth and justice."[121] Although it is a bit hard to tell since he discusses the issue of women and *tefillin* only in the course of responding to a different question, the wording used by *Ravaz* almost certainly indicates that he would permit women to wear *tefillin*.

VI. The Situation Today: Still Mixed

Restriction

Two prominent late twentieth-century halakhic decisors, R. Moshe Feinstein[122] and R. Yehuda Herzl Henkin,[123] both rule that women should not wear *tefillin*, based on *Rama*'s position. R. Feinstein, like *Arukh haShulchan*, mentions that a high degree of bodily cleanliness is required for *tefillin* and that even men only wear *tefillin* for a short time each day.

Permission

The following opinions by Orthodox rabbis sanction women to wear *tefillin*: first, R. Saul Berman mentions in passing in an article on the general topic of women and Halakha that some Orthodox women have begun wearing *tefillin*.[124] Second, R. Eliezer Berkovits ruled that women are permitted to wear *tefillin*, based in large part on his view that today, women are capable of maintaining the physical requirements of bodily cleanliness.[125]

Although most Orthodox synagogue rabbis have not had to address the issue of whether women may wear *tefillin* in their synagogue, some prelimi-

---

[121] *Mishne Torah, Hilkhot Tefillin* 4:25.

[122] *Iggerot Moshe,* part 4, OC, responsum 49.

[123] *Bnei Banim*, vol. 2, responsum 3.

[124] S. Berman, "The Status of Women in Halakhic Judaism," *Tradition* 14.4 (Fall, 1974): 5–28.

[125] *Jewish Women in Time and Torah* (Ktav, 1990) 73.

nary trends may be discerned from synagogues where this question has already arisen. One New York City synagogue rabbi, ruled that it was in theory permissible, but in terms of actual practice decided not to permit women to wear *tefillin* in his synagogue.[126] His reasons were, first, that several of the synagogue members had expressed objection; the rabbi said that he did not want to violate the dictum that a decision should be "agreeable to the congregation." His second reason was that no "great halakhic decisor" subsequent to *Rama* had explicitly permitted women to wear *tefillin*. He advised women who wish to wear *tefillin* to do so in another synagogue or at home. On the other hand, some Orthodox rabbis have permitted women to wear *tefillin* in their synagogues.[127]

From this small sample, we may generalize and say that in a very small number of Orthodox synagogues it would currently be a natural step to allow women to wear *tefillin*, while in many others there would be objections on the part of the members of the congregation, both for halakhic and extra-halakhic reasons, such as fear of appearing non-Orthodox. Also, some rabbis would still hesitate to rule that women may wear *tefillin* in their synagogues so long as no contemporary halakhic authority who they consider prominent enough has paved the way with a ruling.[128]

VII. Summary

The Talmud does not single out *tefillin* as more problematic for women to perform than any other positive time-bound commandment. Accepting this situation, the Geonim and the majority of *Rishonim* rule that women are permitted to wear *tefillin* just as they are permitted to optionally perform other positive time-bound commandments.

---

[126] Rabbi Allen Schwartz, Ohab Zedek Synagogue, lecture, 1996.

[127] For example, Rabbi Haskel Lookstein, Kehilath Jeshurun, Manhattan, New York.

[128] One prominent Israeli Orthodox rabbi, who neither publicizes nor enforces this ruling, has told individuals that he believes that women today are obligated to wear both *tzitzit* and *tefillin*. He bases this on the understanding that the reason women were exempted from time-bound commandments was that their time was not their own, but rather their husbands'. (David Avudraham (c. 1300), in *Avudraham haShalem* (Jerusalem, 1963) 25.) Today, he says, however, most women would be considered "free" according to this criterion; for all of these women, this exemption no longer applies.

At the end of the period of the *Rishonim* and in the period of the *Achronim*, various objections to women wearing *tefillin* were raised. The main objection is that women do not maintain bodily cleanliness, which is a prerequisite for the wearing of *tefillin*. A highly significant observation is that through the period of the *Rishonim*, and even in the period of the transition generation between the *Rishonim* and *Achronim*, in which several restrictive opinions are expressed, almost no authority rules that it is *forbidden* for women to wear *tefillin*. Rather, restriction is invariably expressed more weakly in the precise terminology used in the Jerusalem Talmud, namely, that the wearing of *tefillin* by women should be "protested."[129] This affords *Achronim* the freedom to revert to the opinion that women have no problem maintaining the appropriate level of bodily cleanliness, even after earlier authorities had restricted the wearing of *tefillin* on these grounds.

The twentieth century saw a mixed picture, with some authorities permitting and most others maintaining that women should not wear *tefillin*. We attempted to show that permitting women to wear *tefillin*, rather than restricting them, is consistent with halakhic rulings about men's wearing of *tefillin* and regarding women's obligation in prayer.

Decision: Based on the presentation in this paper, a contemporary halakhic authority faced with deciding whether women may wear *tefillin* would have the following choices:

1) The wearing of *tefillin* by women should be protested based on the *Rama*'s ruling and subsequent decisors who follow his ruling such as R. Moshe Feinstein.

2) Same as (1), but permitting women to wear *tefillin* during *Shema* and *Shemone Esrei*, or for a minute.

3) The wearing of *tefillin* by women should be protested, based on the *Arukh haShulchan*'s following *Rama* and his further understanding that *tefillin* should be worn only under conditions of obligation.

---

[129] S. Berman, ibid.

Three authorities rule that women are forbidden to wear *tefillin*: *Riaz* (also cited by *Shiltei haGiborim* to *Rif*), the Vilna Gaon, who is the only one to forbid on the grounds of bodily cleanliness (*Bei'urei haGra* to *Shulchan Arukh*, OC 38:3), and *Maharam Schick*.

4)   Women may wear *tefillin*, based on *Maset Binyamin, Ravaz*, and the majority of *Rishonim*.

Some factors that should be noted before ruling are the following: First, Ruling (4) is directly based on existing rulings and does *not* involve any attempts to show that the reasons for previous halakhic rulings no longer apply based on changes in the world that have occurred during the current century. In contrast, in order to reject Ruling (1), one *would* have to involve consideration whether a ruling might no longer apply given a changed set of circumstances, specifically, better hygienic conditions, and perhaps also better educational conditions for women. Third, in this paper we argued that Ruling (3) is inconsistent with the normative halakhic understanding of the requirements necessary for a person to wear *tefillin*; it is stricter. Whether one agrees with this argument will in part determine one's opinion about Ruling (3). Fourth, for a woman who prays regularly and considers this an obligation, Ruling (2) may be preferable over Ruling (1).

VIII. Conclusion

The wearing of *tefillin* by women was mostly a theoretical issue until this generation. The issue has become practical in large part due to the increased amount of education common among Orthodox women, particularly education in primary halakhic sources. In this context we may consider whether the *Ravad*'s objection to women wearing *tefillin*—which even in his time was a minority opinion—still applies. According to *Ravad*, since women are not obligated to wear *tefillin*, they will not take it seriously. He arrives at this conclusion through application of the reason some objected to women learning Torah, which was essentially that "women are frivolous (*nashim da'atan kalot*)." However, in today's reality, in which women are being educated in Torah and Halakha, I believe that it can, conversely, be assumed that they would take the commandment of *tefillin* seriously. Empirical observation of Orthodox women who wear *tefillin* bears out this assumption.

In ruling that women should not wear *tefillin*, R. Yehuda Herzl Henkin suggests that women concentrate instead on increasing their connection to Judaism in other ways. Similarly, others have suggested in different contexts that Orthodox women ought to find expression of their belief through intensive learning of Torah rather than through changes in ritual. These are helpful suggestions given that one is ruling to restrict. However, an advantage results from ruling positively: the more options there are available for expressing a connection to religion, the more individuals can choose to concentrate on options that offer them particular spiritual satisfaction and for which they may have a special talent. Studying Torah may not be suitable, or not be enough, for everyone. Performing charitable work might be a strong point of some, learning a strong point for others, and prayer a strong point for yet other women. If *tefillin* offers a halakhically legitimate avenue for religious expression and satisfaction, there is no reason to cut it off as an option for Orthodox women.

Ask most people to picture an Orthodox Jew at prayer, and they will picture someone wearing *tefillin*. The person they will picture will likely be a man, but that is beside the point. The point is that *tefillin* is an accessory unique to, and intimately associated with, Jewish prayer. As we have shown in this article, there is little halakhic reason to deny to Jewish women the particular expression of Jewish belief represented by *tefillin*.

Surely it is reasonable to be concerned, as are some of the restrictive decisors, that if an individual is not obligated to do something, their mindset might be such that they would tend to be less consistent or less punctilious about performing it. However, the talmudic Sages already recognized this factor— yet still allowed optional performance of commandments. They saw as a sufficient "penalty" for non-obligation the idea that one who is not obligated to perform a commandment and performs it receives a smaller reward than one who is obligated and performs it (perhaps because of the greater worry about correct performance on the part of one who is obligated[130]). Thus, the Sages put the religious satisfaction that would result from performance above concerns about whether the commandment would be performed punctiliously.[131]

Perhaps the Sages were not worried about possible incorrect performance because they trusted that someone who would go out of their way to perform a commandment would also make sure to perform it correctly. This attitude certainly characterizes Orthodox women who wear *tefillin* today. With this assurance, the alternative which brings the most honor to the Torah is reviving

---

[130] *Tosafot* to *Kiddushin* 31a.

[131] See for example, *Ritva*, *Nimukei Yosef* and *Maset Binyamin*, ibid.

the encouraging, trusting attitude that the Sages express in general about performance of optional commandments: "For all [the Torah's] ways are pleasant, and all her paths are peaceful."[132]

---

[132] Proverbs 3:17. Nimukei Yosef, ibid.

Fringe Benefits: Women and *Tzitzit*

Aviva Cayam

The biblical law to tie fringes (*tzitzit*) on the four corners of one's garment is found in two places in the Torah. In Numbers (15:38–40) it says:

> Speak to the children of Israel and tell them they should make fringes on the corners of their garments for generations; and they should place on the corner fringes, a twisted thread of blue. It will be to you as fringes and when you see it, you will remember all the commandments of God and you will do them; and you will not follow after your heart and after your eyes by which you are seduced. In order that you remember and do all my commandments and be holy to your God.[1]

In Deuteronomy (22:12), the law of fringes follows immediately after the prohibition of mixing wool and linen (*shatnez*), where it then says:

> Tassels (*gedilim*) you shall make for yourself on the four corners of your clothing with which you cover yourself.

The Hebrew terms *tzitzit* and *gedilim*, as well as defining what constitutes a garment, are discussed in great detail in Rabbinic literature.[2]

The most important rabbinic discussion relating to women and their traditional exemption from the commandment of fringes can be found in a Midrash

---

[1] Translations from the Hebrew texts are by the author.

[2] The biblical commandment refers to a type of outer clothing, *tallit*, whose four corners would require fringes. The talmudic discussion mostly revolves around this kind of garment, except for one story of a man who was "saved" from his near sin with a prostitute by his *tzitzit* (*Menachot* 44a). Here, the *arba kanfot* seem to refer to an undergarment. The rabbinic legislation of wearing a *tallit katan* in order to fulfill the law at all times was later codified as standard practice by the *Rishonim*. For one possible historical explanation, see Vallentine's *Jewish Encyclopedia* (London, 1938) 48: "It may be assumed that the *arba kanfot* originates from the times of persecution when Jews were afraid to exhibit the *tallit gadol*." Although the terms are often used interchangeably when discussing *tzitzit*, there are separate blessings for each garment.

Halakha, expounding on the verse in Numbers[3] which sets the parameters for obligation:

> God said to Moses, and they shall make for themselves fringes. Even the women are implied. Rabbi Shimon exempts women from *tzitzit* because women are exempt from positive commandments limited by time. This is the rule: Rabbi Shimon says: [regarding] all positive commandments which are limited by time, women are exempt; these laws apply to men, not to women; to those fit [to observe the law], not to those unfit [to observe the law]. Rabbi Yehuda ben Bava says, specifically the Rabbis exempted the veil of a woman from fringes and only obligated a *tallit* (shawl) because there are times when her husband covers himself with it.

This passage raises at least two major concepts which define the nature of the commandment of *tzitzit:* the question of time and the question of person. Seemingly, women would be included in the command given by God to Moses, but Rabbi Shimon learns that the law of *tzitzit* does not include women. Furthermore, a garment meant exclusively for women is exempt, while "unisex" clothing requires fringes.

The Babylonian Talmud (*Menachot* 40–43) expands the discussion to include many other aspects of the law. When is the blessing made on the *tzitzit*: when you attach the fringes to your garment or when you wear them? What if the clothing is owned but never worn and stays folded in your drawer? What about borrowed garments? What if the garment is owned by two people? Is the law still valid if we do not have the blue dye required in the Biblical passage? What if a garment has more than four corners? What type of material requires *tzitzit*? Textual interpretation of the law's proximity to the prohibition of *shatnez* teaches us that the law of fringes supersedes the law of mixed materials, meaning one could put wool fringes on a linen garment.[4] A completely different textual inference interprets *tzitzit* (and *tefillin*) to be exclu-

---

[3] *Sifre* 115, in Horovitz' critical edition; *Sifre* 61, in edition printed with Malbim; *Shalach*, Section 8, in *Sifre* edition printed with the Gaon of Vilna (*Gra*) and Naphtali Berlin (*Netziv*).

[4] This applied to the biblical law of *tekhelet*, the special blue-dyed thread included in the fringes. Since today we cannot identify that dye with certainty, attaching *tzitzit* to clothing which would constitute *shatnez* is prohibited.

sively male clothing,[5] although this did not become normative rabbinic thinking.[6] Regarding who exactly is included in the law of *tzitzit* and who is not,

> the rabbis taught: all are obligated in [the law of] fringe: priests, Levites, and Israelites, converts, women and slaves. Rabbi Shimon exempts women because it is a positive commandment limited by time and [from] all positive commandments limited by time, women are exempt... What is the reasoning of Rabbi Shimon? It has been taught [in a *beraita*] regarding "and when you see it" (Numbers 15:39), this excludes clothing worn at night.[7]

The rationale of Rabbi Shimon is that since fringes are required only on clothing worn during the daytime, when they can actually be seen, *tzitzit* must be a time-limited commandment. Since women abide by the legal principle which exempts them from the obligation to observe positive laws which are limited by time,[8] mandating *tzitzit* on the corners of one's garment cannot be required of females.

---

[5] *Targum Yonatan*, Deuteronomy 22:5.

[6] Perhaps because fringes themselves appear as the non-gendered object of a commandment, not an ordinary garment. Perhaps also, because the Rabbis reject the position that simply wearing each other's garments without the intent of looking like the opposite gender is an "abomination." See *Nazir* 59a. *Rambam* places the law of cross-dressing as part of the prohibition against idol worship and R. Caro applies the law to larger practices of sexual immorality. Neither halakhic source associates *tzitzit* with gender-related clothing.

[7] *Menachot* 43a.

[8] A fuller discussion of the principle of women's exemption from most positive commandments which are limited by time, and their inclusion in almost all the negative commandments, can be found in *Kiddushin* 34–36. The *beraita* quoted in *Kiddushin* 33b asks: "What are the commandments which are time limited? *Sukka, lulav,* shofar, *tzitzit* and *tefillin*." The rule and its exceptions are discussed at length, addressing the previously mentioned commandments, although not elaborating on *tzitzit*. The status of women's obligation is analyzed by focusing on such laws as studying Torah, affixing a *mezuza* on the doorpost, rejoicing on the festivals, assembling in the Temple every seven years, eating matzah on Pesach, bearing children, redeeming the firstborn and fearing one's parents. See also *Berakhot* 20b for a shorter debate. The law of *tzitzit* is not mentioned in that context.

The question of time is essential to women's exemption from *tzitzit*. In at least two other citations,[9] a *beraita* is quoted stating clearly that the law of fringes is meant to be observed only "when you see it" (Numbers 15:39), meaning, during the daylight hours. This statement was implemented with the ruling that a blind person's garment requires *tzitzit*, because other people can see the fringed clothing, even if the blind cannot. The Jerusalem Talmud[10] lists *tzitzit* as a commandment which is *not* limited by time, but explains that

> Rabbi Shimon exempts women since [he considers] fringes a positive commandment limited by time since a night garment does not need fringes. Rabbi Laya said: the reasoning of the Rabbis [that *tzitzit* are not time limited] is that certainly if one had a garment meant for both day and night, it would require fringes.

Sifre offers this conclusion (without mentioning the disagreement over time raised in reference to women): "A garment meant for both day and night is obligated in *tzitzit*."[11] Rabbi Yehuda also saw the law of *tzitzit* as a commandment not limited by time. "Rabbi Yehuda attached (blue-dyed) fringes to the aprons of the women of his household"[12] and "Rabbi Amram the Pious would

---

[9] See *Shabbat* 27b and *Zevachim* 18b.

[10] *Yerushalmi Berakhot* 3:3 [6b].

[11] The Netziv explains that in the *Sifre* cited earlier, Yehuda ben Bava's point that a garment shared by men and women requires *tzitzit* is based on the model of a garment worn for both day and night. In fact, the halakhic resolution defines the law of *tzitzit* as limited by the type of garment worn during daylight: if one wears pajamas during the day, even garments with four corners, they do not require fringes. There are conflicting opinions about day clothes worn at night.

[12] *Menachot* 43a. Rabbi Yehuda used to recite the blessing each morning and the Talmud addresses the question of how he could include women, since by saying the blessing in the mornings, he was indicating that the law was indeed limited by time. The Chatam Sofer explains that Rabbi Yehuda's inclusion of women could be learned from a different source: the juxtaposition of *tzitzit* to remembering the Exodus. "The *Beit Yosef* brings a Midrash that at the time of the splitting of the Red Sea, the angel Gavriel decreed that the waters should part in front of them on the merit of the fringes they [would] wear in front, and the waters behind them on merit of the fringes they [would] wear in the back. And if so, since women were present at the same miracle, they would be obligated in *tzitzit* even though the night is free from the obligation." See *Responsa of Chatam Sofer*, part 1, OC 195.

hang (blue-dyed) fringes on the aprons of the women of his household,"[13] Yet, the view of Rabbi Shimon was dominant and is the one used as the basis for the later halakhic exemption of women.[14]

Almost all sources acknowledge the non-obligatory status of women when it comes to laws limited by time. In his counting of the 613 commandments, *Rambam* lists sixty specific positive precepts which he feels are operational at all times and in all places for the average adult Jewish male. Of those, women are obligated to keep forty-six laws and exempt from observing fourteen specific ones. *Tzitzit* is listed as one of the fourteen exemptions for females.[15] What does the status of exemption mean? Are those people who are not obligated, nevertheless permitted to perform the precepts? Despite the differential in the reward factor, does the law allow for optional performance?[16] Are there negatives consequences which might limit the possibility of women to perform those laws from which they are exempt?

Rambam[17] codifies the law, first answering several issues about the time for the required fringes and the timing of the blessing:

---

[13] *Sukka* 11a. Rabbi Amram attached the *tzitzit* but did not cut them until he determined which act (attaching or cutting) was essential to the commandment, thereby providing a model for the law of *sukka* covering.

[14] See *Sefer Halakhot Gedolot, Hilkhot Tzitzit*, end of chapter, where Rabbi Shimon's exemption for women is stated as law without debate. (However, the issue of a minor performing the precepts is presented with multiple opinions.)

[15] Maimonides, *Sefer haMitzvot*, Positive Laws, last paragraphs.

[16] See *Kiddushin* 31a, *Avoda Zara* 3a and *Bava Kamma* 17a and 38a for Rabbi Chanina's principle: "Just like someone who was not obligated receives a reward for observing the law, how much more so for the person who is obligated to keep the law and observes it. For Rabbi Chanina said, greater is the person who is commanded and does it, than one who is not commanded and does it." The rationale behind this statement is both theological and psychological. The person who is doing God's will is on a "higher" plane than one who is observing the law for any other reason, no matter how spiritual. *Tosafot* say that a person will exercise greater care in fulfilling the law if it is the word of God. Furthermore, it is human nature to rebel when ordered to do something, so the person who overcomes his natural tendency to reject commands is rewarded for controlling his instincts. In the eyes of the rabbis, directing one's ego to serve God is a task worthy of greater reward.

[17] Maimonides, *Mishne Torah, Hilkhot Tzitzit* 3:7,8.

The obligation of *tzitzit* is during the day and not at night, as it says: "and when you see it"—during the time of visibility. A blind person is obligated in *tzitzit* even though he cannot see, since others see his garment [with the fringes]. A person is permitted to wear *tzitzit* at night, whether on a weekday or on Shabbat, even though it is not the [required] time, provided that he does not recite the blessing. From when in the morning should the blessing be recited? When one can recognize the difference between the blue [fringe] in it and the white in it. And how does one bless on it? "Blessed are you God, our Lord, King of the Universe, who has commanded us to wrap in fringes." Each time he wears it during the day, he recites a blessing before he wears it. He does not bless the *tzitzit* during the time he is making them, because the endpoint of the commandment is to wrap oneself in it.

Determining who is included in the law of *tzitzit*, *Rambam* states:[18]

For every person who is obligated to perform this commandment; if he wears a garment that requires fringes, he should put *tzitzit* [on the garment] and then wear it. If he wears it without the fringes, he has violated a positive commandment. However, clothing that requires *tzitzit*, as long as no one wears it, but it remains folded and set aside, is exempt from *tzitzit*, since the obligation is not on the garment, but rather on the person who owns the *tallit*.

One paragraph earlier, *Rambam* addresses the question of women:

Women, slaves and minors are exempt from the biblical law of fringes. According to the Rabbis, any child who knows how to dress himself, is obligated in *tzitzit*, in order to educate him in the commandments. Women and slaves who want to wear *tzitzit*, wrap themselves [in it] without a blessing. And this is the case with other positive commandments from which women are exempt. If they want to perform them without a blessing, they are not prevented.

Ravad[19] comments on *Rambam*'s assertion that women and slaves could voluntarily perform the precepts without a blessing.

---

[18] Ibid., 3:10.

[19] Avraham Ben David of Posquieres, on *Rambam, Mishne Torah, Hilkhot Tzitzit* 3:9. His actual statement opens with the line "specifically for fringes that are not from prohibited mixed materials." Since the law of *shatnez* is a biblical prohibition, it can only be overridden by another biblical commandment, not by the rabbinic optional performance of

...And there are those who disagree and say [that these laws can be done] even with a blessing and they say that even the recitation of the blessing is voluntarily possible. And they bring support for their words from the first chapter of *Kiddushin*[20] from the words of Rabbi Yosef who said: At first, I used to say that whoever would tell me the law was in agreement with Rabbi Yehuda, who said that a blind person is exempt from the commandments, I would celebrate [make a party for the rabbis], because I am not obligated and I perform the laws. And if the law says that someone who is not obligated is not eligible to say the blessing, then he would have violated a prohibition, because he himself recited blessings, and if he could not recite the blessing, what reason would there be to celebrate?[21]

Thus, *Rambam*'s option of voluntary performance is expanded by *Ravad* to include the possibility of reciting the blessing.[22]

---

a law. (See note 4.) For a different perspective on *Ravad*'s meaning see R. Yisrael Gustman *Collection of Lessons on Tractate Kiddushin* (Hebrew) (1970; reprinted in Jerusalem, 1991) lesson 20 (end).

[20] *Kiddushin* 31a.

[21] Rabbi Yosef was blind and used to perform the commandments. At first, he heard that Rabbi Yehuda had declared all blind people exempt from the laws, and he wanted to celebrate because he thought it was better to voluntarily observe the laws. *Ravad* infers that if Rabbi Yosef could not make the blessings to go along with those voluntary actions, why would he want to celebrate? It must be that he was allowed to recite the blessings as he performed the commandments and that was something worthy of celebration. (Rabbi Yosef later learned that one who is obligated indeed gets a greater reward, whereby he wanted to celebrate if anyone had told him the law was *not* according to Rabbi Yehuda.) See also *Bava Kamma* 87a.

[22] See also the *Hagahot Maimoniyot* on *Hilkhot Tzitzit* 3:40. There he cites *Rashi*'s agreement with *Rambam* (performance without the blessings) and quotes the view of Rabbenu Tam (performance with the blessings). He concludes with the following statement: "And the Sar of Couzy [R. Shimshon, brother-in-law of the *Smag*] also wrote according to the words of Rabbenu Tam, that women can recite the blessing for *lulav, tefillin* and other [precepts]. And that is what Rabbenu Simcha wrote regarding blowing the shofar, that a woman who blows for herself should recite the blessing and we do not prevent her." The permissibility to recite blessings for the optional performance of laws focuses on at least two important issues. How can a person who is not commanded say the words: "Blessed are you, God... who has sanctified us with His commandments and commanded us to..." prior to voluntarily undertaking an action? Also, would the optional recitation constitute a violation of the Biblical law against using God's name in vain? The

Twelfth century *Tosafists* have a strong tradition of affording women the opportunity to perform commandments from which they are exempt.[23] Rabbenu Tam bases his claim that blessings are permitted for voluntary performance on the examples of Michal who wore *tefillin* (and recited the blessing), the wife of Yonah the prophet who went up to Jerusalem for the pilgrimage festivals, and the women who were granted permission to lay their hands on a sacrificial animal in order to "give the women spiritual satisfaction."[24] "And women are permitted to recite blessings on the positive commandments which are limited by time, even though they are exempt from that specific commandment."[25] In *Tosafot* we find the wording even stronger than *Ravad*'s:

> why would Rabbi Yosef celebrate if he was losing out on the blessings of *tzitzit, lulav, tefillin, Megilla, chanukka* lights, *sukka,* and *havdala, kiddush* of the [Shabbat] day, and the blessings of *Shema* for *shacharit* and *arvit,* as well as all the blessings? As we learn in chapter *HaMeine'ach,* if one wants to be pious, he should observe all the blessings.[26]

Yet, Rabbenu Tam says that we cannot equate the status of a blind person or a minor performing optional commandments with women's performance of the laws, because both blind men and young boys are still part of the same large

---

poskim (codifiers) are divided, usually along the lines of the *Rishonim* cited above. This topic is addressed in some of the recent books on women and Halakha. See Rachel Biale, *Women and Jewish Law* (Schocken, 1984) 41–43; Eliezer Berkovits, *Jewish Women in Time and Torah* (Ktav, 1990) ch. 4; Avraham Weiss, *Women at Prayer* (Ktav, 1990) ch. 6, nn16, 17. Also see Blu Greenberg, *On Women and Judaism* (JPS, 1981) 39–104 for an overview of the status of women in Judaism. See the sources cited in Getsel Ellinson, *Serving the Creator* (WZO, 1986) ch. 4 (also available in Hebrew).

[23] For the detailed reasoning behind the inclusion and exemption of women in such laws as Chanukka, *Megilla* and *pessach,* plus their obligation in *birkat hamazon* and prayer, see the *Tosafot* on the following citations in *Berakhot* 20b, *Megilla* 4a, *Sukka* 38a, *Arachin* 3a and *Eruvin* 96b.

[24] *Eruvin* 96a–b. See discussion in the previous article.

[25] *Rosh haShana* 33a, *Tosafot.* See also the *Tosafot* in *Kiddushin* 31a which makes a similar statement.

[26] *Bava Kamma* 30a. Other ways to be pious are also mentioned there: being careful about all the laws of *nezikin* (damages) or keeping all the tractate of *Avot* (ethics). *Tosafot* in *Rosh haShana* cites the third option, reciting blessings.

group which has an obligation, males. Instead, *Tosafot* acknowledge that although females are exempt from time limited commandments, there are other laws women are obligated to perform. *Tosafot* also refer to the possibility of a woman being one of the seven called up to the Torah and permitted to recite the blessing.[27] Thus, the optional performance of any commandment plus the recitation of blessings is still rewarded by God.[28]

The *Rif*, R. Yitzchak Alfasi[29] codifies the opinion of Rabbi Shimon: "Everyone is obligated in *tzitzit*... Rabbi Shimon exempts women because it is a positive commandment which is limited by time and women are exempt, and the law is as Rabbi Shimon." The *Rosh*[30] there also cites the *Sifre* (after a lengthy analysis of Rabbenu Tam) and concludes "therefore, it appears that fringes [even] of mixed material is permitted on a man's shawl, whether on a man or a woman, either in the day or in the night even though it is considered a positive law limited by time." *Sefer Yeraim*[31] and *Sefer Mitzvot Gadol*[32] both document the exemption of Rabbi Shimon as accepted practice, and the *Smag*

---

[27] *Megilla* 23a continues "however, a woman is not called to the Torah out of respect for the congregation (*kevod hatzibur*)." In the *Tosafot* cited above, Rabbenu Tam rejects this example, as well as women's requirement to say the grace after meals (*birkat hamazon*) as proof of their equal status regarding the optional performance of laws.

[28] Whether or not one may make a vow and/or permanently obligate oneself in a commandment is a debate among the *poskim*. See the *Magen Avraham*, *Orach Chaim* 289:1 on women and counting the *omer* where he states that although women are not obligated: "they have taken it upon themselves as an obligation." *Abudarham* says that women are exempt from positive laws limited by time because "a wife is in service to her husband to fulfill his needs. If she was obligated in these laws, it is possible that in the midst of performing a precept, her husband would ask her to perform a service for him; and if she is fulfilling the commands of the Creator, 'woe to her' from her husband. If she would act on her husband's orders and leave the commands of her Creator, 'woe to her' from her Maker. Therefore, the Creator freed her from His commandments in order that she be at peace with her husband." See *Sefer Abudraham*, ch. 3. A similar claim by the *Levush* is addressed by Akiva Eiger when he comments on "women today who are strict and careful and eager in their observance of most positive laws limited by time." See *Responsa of R. Akiva Eiger*, sec. 1.

[29] Yitzchak Alfasi (*Rif*), *Halakhot Ketanot*, *Hilkhot Tzitzit*, opening lines.

[30] Asher ben Yechiel, *Piskei haRosh*, *Hilkhot Tzitzit* (s.v. "excluding").

[31] Eliezer of Metz, *Tzitzit*, sec. 401.

[32] Moshe of Couzy (*Smag*), Positive Commandment 26.

adds the opinion of Rabbenu Tam who permits women to recite blessings.[33] *Sefer haChinukh*[34] says that the law of *tzitzit* applies to males, in every place and at all times, but not to females. "And if the women want to wear a *tallit*, they may wear it without reciting the blessing according to the opinion of some of the commentators, and a few have said, even with a blessing." The overall tenor of the early Rabbinic opinion clearly exempts women from the law of fringes, but permits women who want to wear *tzitzit* to do so, even with the option of reciting the blessing.

The *Tur*[35] obligates the blind to have fringes and exempts women, citing the *Rambam*'s option of wearing *tzitzit* without reciting the blessing. "And he [*Rambam*] follows the view that explains that women may not bless something from which they are exempt. But Rabbenu Tam wrote that they could recite the blessing even if they are exempt, and it is better if they do not recite the blessing."[36] R. Yosef Caro[37] comments on the *Tur* with a review of Rabbi Shimon and the views of Rabbenu Tam, *Rif* and *Rosh*. He takes the *Rambam* one step further by explaining *Rambam*'s rationale for permitting the wearing of *tzitzit* without the blessing:

---

[33] See the *Ran* (Rabbenu Nissim) to the *Rif* on *Rosh haShana*, ch. 4 and the *Ritva* (Yomtov ben Avraham Ashvili) on *Kiddushin* 31a. Both sources discuss women doing optional commandments, saying the blessings and getting a reward. The *Ritva*, in a discussion of the reasons why a person who is obligated gets a greater reward than one who volunteers, comments that even the person opting to keep a law gets some reward. "After all, from a goodness of heart and piety he placed himself in service of God's command. And specifically for a law that God commanded of others, he has the will to do. However, when a person, on his own, takes on a law which was never commanded in the Torah whatsoever, that is what is said about one who was never commanded and performs it, [he] is called a fool."

[34] Attributed to Aharon haLevi of Barcelona, Commandment 386.

[35] Yaakov Baal haTurim (*Tur*), OC 17.

[36] The *Bach* (R. Yoel Sirkes) and the *Derisha* (R. Yehoshua Falk Katz) both address the discrepency between the *Tur*'s permission for women to recite the optional blessing over the shofar and his preference that women not recite the blessing for *tzitzit*. The *Bach* explains that women have already been accustomed to hearing the shofar and reciting the blessing, so there are "opinions on which to rely" if they continue to do so. However, if women were to ask for permission prior to saying the blessing, in cases like these which involve rabbinic dispute, they should be discouraged.

[37] *Beit Yosef, Orach Chaim* 17.

Regarding the law, we maintain it is like the *Rambam*, that when in doubt about reciting a blessing, we are lenient [and do not bless]. The *Igur* has written in the name of the *Maharil* about women who wear *tzitzit*, that it is silly and appears arrogant, and there was one woman in our neighborhood who wore it.

The *Maharil's* responsum[38] quoted by Caro raises several interesting points. He discusses the idea of women reciting optional blessings and addresses the issue of wearing fringes as possibly violating other prohibitions. Based on the *Hagahot Maimoniyot*,[39] the larger concerns which might pose a problem are wearing *shatnez* (which would also apply to men) and carrying "the extraneous" fringes on Shabbat, since *tzitzit* are not required of women.

The *Maharil* then explains that the law of *tzitzit* is not like other commandments since it is a "requirement of the garment," not of the person. This means that one is not obligated to go out and purchase a four-cornered garment to attach fringes, but only if one already owns such a garment does he have to put on *tzitzit*.[40] The only reason a man wears fringes is to

enter himself into the obligation as we learned from Moses. Did he [Moses] need to eat from the fruits or satisfy himself from the good of the land? Rather, Moses said "Many commandments were given to the children of Israel that cannot be observed except in the land of Israel. I will enter the land in order to fulfill all of them myself." These words apply to men. But women, what [meaning] does it have for them, because after all, they are not obligated. It

---

[38] Yaakov ben Moshe haLevi Moellin of Mainz, *New Responsa* 7.

[39] *Hagahot Maimoniyot, Hilkhot Tzitzit* 3:30. He explains the contrasting views of the *Bavli* and *Yerushalmi* Talmuds about whether the rabbis protested or not when Michal wore *tefillin* and the wife of Yonah went (up) to Jerusalem. "I found [an explanation] in the name of a great person that whenever there was the possibility of bringing non-sanctified meat into the Temple or showing the nudity of a woman's hair when wearing *tefillin* or carrying a shofar on Rosh Hashanah, the rabbis prevented her. However, when there is no 'whiff of a sin,' like with *sukka* and *lulav*, even though she is biblically exempt, the rabbis did not prevent her from doing it." The *Maharil* touches on why the law of *tzitzit* is not mentioned directly in this list (although the entire passage appears in the chapter on fringes).

[40] One might argue that if men are not required to go out and purchase *tzitzit*, since it is dependent on the garment, not the person, then men too should not be permitted to wear *tzitzit* on Shabbat. Indeed, there are those *poskim* who consider wearing a *tallit katan* to be carrying on the Shabbat.

also seems to me that the essence of the law of *tzitzit* is to remember all the commandments of God... and women are not included in the 613 commandments... they are a "people unto themselves."[41] Therefore, based on all the reasons mentioned, even though I have seen women wearing four cornered garments with fringes, and still today there is one woman in our neighborhood, it seems to me astonishing and is considered arrogant of them and they are called fools.[42]

Several aspects of the *Maharil's* comments shed light on new developments in the halakhic attitude toward females and fringes: a few women wearing *tzitzit* must have become more visible, there seems to be a rabbinic attempt to diminish women's inclusion in the 613 laws, and the issue of arrogance is introduced into the voluntary pursuit of commandments by women.[43] This shift is evident in the *Levush's*[44] strong wording that despite the legal permission granted women to wear *tzitzit*, even with the blessing and even though they receive a reward,

> ...it is still foolish and arrogant if they do so. Despite the fact that with other positive time-limited commandments women have been accustomed to observing them and reciting the blessing, what they are used to doing, they do; what they are not used to doing, they do not do. And with *tzitzit*, we do not find it done, except for one in a thousand, like Michal the daughter of Saul and others; therefore, they should not wear fringes.[45]

The notion of *yohara* (arrogance or pride) is mentioned in the halakhic literature in several cases of excessive piety where the rabbis debate its implications. A groom on his wedding night who claims he is able to concen-

---

[41] *Shabbat* 62a.

[42] In the *Maharil's* book of customs, he mentions that the reason why he did not stop Rabbanit Bruna from wearing her *tzitzit* was because he thought she would not listen.

[43] See *Megilla* 14b where "Rabbi Nachman said: Arrogance is not becoming in women." His examples are two of the prophetesses, Devorah and Chuldah.

[44] Mordechai Yaffe, *Sefer Levush Malchut, Hilkhot Tzitzit* 17:2.

[45] Several later authorities take issue with the Levush's assumption that Michal wore *tzitzit*, since the texts only mention her wearing *tefillin*. (See *Eliya Rabba* 17:2 and the *Sdei Chemed*, ch. 9, sec. 15.) The Levush continues with a discussion of male garments on females and concludes that the law "does not apply to the daughter and wife of a king."

trate and recite the *Shema* might be seen as arrogant, as well as a person who refrains from work on the ninth of *Av*. A person who prays with the *tefillin* of Rabbenu Tam or who continues to wear mourner's clothes out of sadness for Jerusalem would be considered arrogant. However, a person who insists on eating in the *sukka* those things that can be eaten outside the *sukka* and a person who takes on the extra fast days of a *talmid chakham* do not demonstrate *yohara*. There are talmudic rabbis who feel that only those acts done publicly constitute arrogance, while actions done in private do not display "extreme pride." The social environment, common practice, and tone of the times all factor into the rabbinic determination of arrogant religious behavior.[46]

R. Yosef Caro codifies the exemption of women (and slaves) in the *Shulchan Arukh*[47] by explaining tersely "that it [*tzitzit*] is a positive commandment limited by time." R. Isserles[48] comments on the female prerogative, picking up on the exhibitionist nature of their observance:

> In any case, if they want to wear [*tzitzit*] and recite the blessing, the option is theirs, like with other positive commandments that are limited by time. Yet, it appears arrogant and therefore women should not wear *tzitzit*, since it is not an obligation of the person, meaning a man is not obligated to buy a cloak for himself in order to observe the law of fringes.[49]

The *Taz*[50] comments that the concept of "obligation of the person" in the law of fringes differs from the "obligation of the object" in the law of *lulav*, where

---

[46] There may also be a halakhic distinction between arrogance (*yohara*) and *appearing arrogant* (*michzei keyohara*). For an analysis of the parameters of excessive stringency in religious behavior, see Sara Weinstein *Piety and Fanaticism* (Aronson, 1997), especially ch. 7 on *yohara*. She quotes the *Sdei Chemed* who cites R. Israel Bruna's responsum on wearing *tzitzit* on top of one's clothing. R. Bruna considers it arrogant for students (in contrast to the rabbis) of that time to dress in such a manner. Ibid., 201 n13. See also *Otzar haGaonim* 1:35–36 (ed. B. Levin, Haifa, 1928) where Rav Natrunai (some say Rav Hai) felt that holding one's *tzitzit* during the recitation of the *Shema* was "*derekh yehirot*." Yet, it is a common practice observed today.

[47] OC 17:2.

[48] Moshe Isserles (*Rama*), OC 17.

[49] See *Shulchan Arukh*, OC 19 where *tzitzit* are codified as "*chovat gavra*," the obligation of the person.

[50] David haLevi (*Turei Zahav, Taz*), OC 17.

women do recite the blessing even though *lulav* is also a positive law which is time-limited. Here, even a man has no biblical requirement to go out and purchase a garment with four corners, but rather if he wears such clothing, then he must attach *tzitzit*. On the other hand, a man *is* required to go out and buy a *lulav* to fulfill the commandment.

The *Magen Avraham*[51] agrees that people who voluntarily wear fringes can recite the blessing even though they are exempt because a person who optionally fulfills a commandment still receives a reward. "And they are able to recite [the blessing] 'who has commanded us' because since males are obligated, others also get a reward." This view of female observance as a subset of male obligation is also addressed by the *Pri Megadim,*[52] who hints at the deeper issue of gender relationships. Beyond the issue of a woman's ability to recite the blessing, she is not violating the prohibition of "adding to the law,"[53] since when the men are obligated, so are the women, since a "woman from a man was taken."[54] Therefore, as a result of their connection through the original act of Creation, they share in the larger framework of Divine service. The *Machatzit haShekel*[55] expands the spiritual dimension:

> ...if women would not be rewarded, they certainly would not be able to say a blessing and give praise for this law... Even though we do not serve God in order to get the reward, nonetheless, a precept that is rewarded helps us to acknowledge the great value of the act and to praise the Almighty who brought us toward this observance, allowing us to be sanctified through His commandments.

The *Arukh haShulchan*[56] summarizes the earlier sources and presents halakhic proof that women may indeed wear *tzitzit* and recite the blessing. However, he challenges that conclusion based largely on the *Rama* and actual practice.

---

[51] Avraham Gumbiner, OC 17.

[52] *Eshel Avraham, Yosef Te'omim*, OC 17.

[53] Deut. 13:1. This prohibition forbids someone from adding to the laws of the Torah.

[54] Based on Genesis 2:23.

[55] Shmuel haLevi Kallin, OC 17.

[56] Yechiel Epstein, OC 17:2–3.

Yet, in reality, we have not heard of this and we do not permit her to wear a *tallit*, even more so to say the blessing. This is not like *sukka* and *lulav* which happen once a year and is a precept for that moment. But the law of *tzitzit* lasts all year and it is not nice for women. Furthermore, all the [other] commandments are obligations for men too, therefore women may also observe them. But *tzitzit* is not an [actual] obligation as it says in [*Orach Chaim*] section 19, and we do not let women observe it. That is the meaning of what our teacher the *Rama* wrote that "in any case, if women want... it appears arrogant and therefore women should not wear *tzitzit*, since it is not an obligation of the person"; as if to say that it appears arrogant because it is done with regularity, and since it is not obligatory upon men unless they have a four-cornered garment, we do not allow this practice [for women]; this is the custom and it should not be changed.

R. Epstein's conclusion raises the whole question of custom, *minhag*, and what constitutes those practices which have changed over time and place. As we saw earlier, the *Maharil* witnessed several women who did wear *tzitzit*, yet the *Arukh haShulchan* wrote that he had not heard of this practice. The notion of precedent as a factor in establishing acceptable practice, is an issue which is debated in all areas of halakhic literature. Synagogue protocol, communal structure, holiday customs, even marriage laws[57] have evolved from a delicate balance between law and custom. Custom often has the power of law[58] and the fact that in various communities women related to the commandments so differently, is also a reflection of the cultural fluctuations which have existed in the status of women.[59]

---

[57] See *Rambam, Hilkhot Ishut*, 13–15 where the standards used to determine a husband's exact obligation of providing for his wife were dependent on "local custom."

[58] See Aryeh Kaplan's detailed chapter on custom, where he cites hundreds of sources on this topic in his book *The Handbook of Jewish Thought* (Maznaim, 1979) 1:13.

[59] In addition to custom, the laws of women have their own gauge of acceptable religious behavior known generally as *dat yehudit*. This amorphous concept regulates traditional practices by setting a standard of commonly recognized activity which is in keeping with the subtleties of an observant lifestyle. Maimonides defines *dat yehudit* to mean "the customs of modesty practiced by the daughters of Israel." See *Mishne Torah, Hilkhot Ishut* 24:12. See the discussion in the previous article.

The *Chaye Adam*[60] draws a distinction between *tzitzit* and *tefillin*, acknowledging that women are exempt from the law of fringes because it is a positive law limited by time.

> In any case, if they want to wear *tzitzit* and bless [on them], they may recite the blessing. That is the law with regard to all time-limited positive commandments, like *lulav* and *sukka* and others, except for *tefillin*, where if they want to be strict with themselves [to wear *tefillin*] we prevent them.

The *Mishna Berura*[61] explains that *Shulchan Arukh*'s exemption for women and slaves is based on the principle that all positive laws limited by time are learned from *tefillin*, which in turn is derived from the female exemption from the commandment to study Torah.[62] He concurs with the earlier reasoning that *lulav* differs from *tzitzit* because of the nature of the obligation placed on the person, not the object, although *Mishna Berura* points out that in practice, "we consider the law of fringes to be both an obligation of the person and an obligation not required of the person, and they are both considered a leniency."[63] Commenting on the *Rama*'s assertion that women who are not obligated may recite the blessing, *Mishna Berura* states that "even one who is not commanded and performs the law receives a reward. And they are able to say 'who has commanded us' [in the blessing] because since the men are commanded, they [those exempted] also receive a reward."

The *Kaf haChaim*[64] surveys the halakhic opinions which permit and forbid the recitation of blessings for the optional law of *tzitzit* and extends the ruling to blessings for other commandments done voluntarily. He concludes with an

---

[60] Avraham Danzig, *Hilkhot Tzitzit* 11:43.

[61] Yisrael Meir Hacohen (*Chafetz Chaim*), *Hilkhot Tzitzit* 17.

[62] See *Pesikta deRav Kehana* 22:5.

[63] A ruling that it is an obligation of the person enables someone to leave his four-cornered garment in the drawer without requiring it to have *tzitzit*, until he actually wears the clothing. A ruling that it is an obligation of the garment frees the person from being required to go out and purchase four-cornered clothing, rather he must attach *tzitzit* only if he already owns such clothing.

[64] *Yaakov Chaim Sofer*, OC 17:4.

intriguing source, a quote from the *Chida*[65] who wrote how originally he [the *Chida*] had been upset when he came to Israel and saw the women there reciting the blessing on the *lulav*, so he asked many learned rabbis of his time and they agreed that the women were wrong to do so.

> After a while, I came across a collection of writings by our teacher, Yaakov of Marvege who asked directly of Heaven and was answered.[66] He asked this question and was told that if they [women] come to bless the *lulav* and shofar, they are permitted to do so... and since that time, I have been accustomed to tell the women to bless the *lulav* like their ancient custom. And if our master [R. Yosef Caro] who decreed that women should not bless, would see the responsum mentioned above, he certainly would have decided yes.

Rabbi Moshe Feinstein[67] issued a responsum on the subject of religious women who have incorporated some of the struggles of the feminist movement into aspects of Jewish life, such as "women who observe the Torah and pray with a *tallit*."[68] He reviews the role of women and the reasons why females are exempt from some laws, as well as the belief that Torah, both the written and the oral, were given by God at Sinai and cannot be changed, not toward greater leniency or strictness. Even if the rabbis have the power to issue a ruling (*takana*), its use is only short term and for a particular case. Furthermore, the fact that God exempted women from positive commandments which are time-limited must stem from a rationale unrevealed to us and not even known by great Torah scholars. Of course, for some aspects of God's ways, the reasoning is known.

> Ordinary women in the world are not wealthy and it is placed on them [the job of] raising boys and girls which is the more important work for God and the Torah. Therefore, God created nature such that for all living things, the female

---

[65] Found in two places in the responsa of Chaim Yosef David Azulai (Chida): See the *Birchei Yosef* 654:2 and *Yosef Ometz* 92.

[66] Yaakov of Marvege was a *Tosafist* who authored *She'alot u'Teshuvot Min ha-Shamayim*, a collection of responsa that were conveyed to him in dreams.

[67] IM, OC 4:49.

[68] The wording of the question addressed to Feinstein implies a bias on the part of the questioner. Most "women who observe the Torah" might take on practices like *tallit* specifically because they are precepts in the Torah and not out of a feminist agenda.

raises the offspring. Human beings are no exception to the rule that the nature of the woman is more capable of raising children, so in this their lot is lightened by not obligating them in the study of Torah and in the positive time-limited laws. Even if the natural order of things are changed in the world, for all females and for all wealthy women for all time, and even when the child-care can be left to other people, like in our country, the law of Torah and even the law of the rabbis will not change. No battles will help because there is no power which can change anything even with the approval of the whole world, and the women who are stubborn and want to fight and change things, they are essentially denying the Torah...

R. Feinstein continues:

it is clear that every woman has the right to perform even those commandments that the Torah did not require of her and they are fulfilling a precept and receive a reward for doing it. Even according to the opinion of *Tosafot*, they are permitted to recite the blessing, and it is our custom that women observe the law of shofar and *lulav* and also say the blessing. Therefore, even *tzitzit* are allowed for a woman who wants to wear a garment which is distinguishable from men's clothing, yet has four corners on which she is able to attach fringes and fulfill the commandment[69]... However, clearly this only applies when the woman desires in her soul to observe the law although she was not commanded; yet, when it is not due to this intention, but rather stems from her resentment toward God and His Torah, then it is not a precept. On the contrary, it is a forbidden act of denial when she thinks that there will be any change in the laws of Torah which she took on.

R. Feinstein explains that women's exemption from those laws is no indication of the female's diminished sanctity.

In the area of sanctity, women are equal to men... for whenever we find [in the Torah] mention of the sanctity of Israel, it is also speaking of women; which is why women can recite the blessings with the formula 'who has sanctified us with his commandments' just like men even though the Torah does not obligate them. It is just a leniency due to whatever reasoning of God's, to make it easier for women as mentioned above, and not due to her inferiority, heaven forbid.

---

[69] However, R. Feinstein says that a woman wearing *tefillin* should be prevented.

Yet, R. Feinstein advises the rabbi who posed the question to firmly protest against "those women who persist in their foolish and stubborn belief, since none of Israel's holy customs can be changed."

Over the past two decades several books have been written which address the topic of women and commandments, including the wearing of *tzitzit*. R. Moshe Meiselman[70] was one of the first to deal with the whole range of women's issues in light of the Halakha and after citing the classic sources, he acknowledges that while women may perform most optional laws from which they are exempt, Judaism assigns men a public role and women a private one. Regarding *tzitzit*, Meiselman relies on the *Rama*'s concept of *yohara* to discourage women from voluntarily taking on "a doubly optional activity" and warns that "the *mitzvot* are not meant to be tools for ego trips." Menachem Brayer[71] authored a two-volume work on "the psycho-social and psycho-historical perspectives" of the role of women in Rabbinic literature. Commenting on *tzitzit* and *tefillin* and other commandments based on time from which women are exempt, Brayer formulates that the halakhic exemption was meant to encourage "women to assume the role of devoted wife and mother" which may be "the true way to find fulfillment and happiness."

In 1990, several books were published which broadened the discourse over women's halakhic participation, both works quoting extensively from sources which are inclusive of women's religious roles. R. Eliezer Berkovits[72] focuses on *tefillin* as the paradigm of optional observance for women and reviews the laws regarding specific rituals, blessings and prayer groups, concluding that "the status of women has fundamentally changed in comparison to previous generations." Therefore, contemporary women need to embrace spiritual outlets which increase their connection to Judaism, especially when the Halakha affords them that opportunity. R. Avi Weiss[73] analyzes the whole topic of women and prayer and by extension, clarifies the halakhic positions on women's roles. Particularly responding to the growth of Orthodox women's

---

[70] *Jewish Woman in Jewish Law* (Ktav and Yeshiva University, 1978). See ch. 22 on *tallit*.

[71] *The Jewish Woman in Rabbinic Literature* (Ktav, 1986). See vol. 2, ch. 11.

[72] *Jewish Women in Time and Torah* (Ktav, 1990). See ch. 4.

[73] *Women at Prayer* (Ktav, 1990). See chs. 1 and 8.

prayer groups, he touches on many of the options available, including the question of *tzitzit*. R. Weiss discusses the permissibility of making changes in custom and law for women when done "not to diminish the Torah, but to enhance their Jewish commitment and halakhic observance." Two years later, an anthology on women and the synagogue entitled *Daughters of the King*[74] (with articles written primarily by women) included a personal vignette on wearing *tallit* and *tefillin*, as well as perspectives on observance from both the Orthodox and Conservative communities.

Michael Kaufman[75] in his book, briefly cites the halakhic sources on *tzitzit* and acknowledges *Rambam*'s permissive view, yet concludes with several restrictive opinions based on the *Rama*. Joel Wolowelsky[76] in his recent publication, calls for greater understanding and acceptance of women's strivings for "broader participation in religious life." Despite the reality that "the image of a woman in *shul* wearing a *tallit* probably evokes little sympathy even in the Modern Orthodox community," Wolowelsky builds on Feinstein's responsum and challenges the halakhic world to refrain from seeing every woman wearing a *tallit* in synagogue as "making some sort of demonstration in the women's section." He concedes that most observant Jews "have little association with specially designed women's *tallitot*" and perhaps,

> ...these creative tallitot enable a woman to perform an optional *mitzva*, encourage *tzeni'ut* in dress, and work against the style-consciousness prevalent in many synagogues... When we hear a new proposal, we must make sure of what we are hearing... We also need not shy away from admitting that our discussions assume a changed perspective on the position of women within our religious community.

Aside from the halakhic responsa and rabbinic articles which address male and female roles and women's relationship to optional commandments, the

---

[74] Edited by Susan Grossman and Rivka Haut (JPS, 1992). See "On Wearing *Tallit* and *Tefillin*" by Dvora Weisberg. See also Judith Hauptman's discussion of *tzitzit* in "Women and the Conservative Synagogue."

[75] *The Woman in Jewish Law and Tradition* (Aronson, 1993). See ch. 14.

[76] *Women, Jewish Law and Modernity* (Ktav, 1997). See Introduction.

Hebrew literature has few references to women and *tzitzit*. R. Getsel Ellinson[77] compiled a three volume series of annotated textual sources relating to women, including the topic of *tzitzit,* which he places in the chapter entitled "commandments which women are not permitted to observe." The series *Techumin*[78] carried an article by R. Eliav Shochatman[79] analyzing the legal position expressed by the Rabbinate in response to women's prayer groups requesting to pray at the Wall. He addresses several aspects of the question, including women wearing *tallitot* and he includes a few of the classic sources, ranging from the *Rambam* to the *Arukh haShulchan.* He quotes from Meiselman's restrictive view and then refers to Feinstein's responsum on women, calling Feinstein's granting of permission "a single opinion among the scholars of our generation." Shochatman includes the opinions of the former Chief Rabbis who both express the view that women should not wear *tzitzit,* despite their apparent halakhic ability to do so. That position is challenged in separate articles by Shmuel Shilo and Rivkah Luvitz,[80] who both cite numerous rabbinic sources which allow women to wear *tzitzit,* and offer dissenting opinions on other aspects of women's prayer, as well.

It is clear from the halakhic texts that women are legally exempt from the commandment to wear *tzitzit,* but it is equally obvious that the majority of *poskim* enable women to observe this law by choice. This is part of the larger question of the voluntary performance by females of those laws from which they have traditionally been exempt. The sources cited in this article focus on a woman wearing *tzitzit,* while a derivative of the law is the actual making of the fringes and attaching them to one's clothing. The majority of codifiers (including some who feel women should not voluntarily take on this commandment), with a few notable exceptions, permit women to *make* or *tie* the *tzitzit,* in contrast to Gentiles who are prohibited.[81] The *Menorat haMa'or*[82]

---

[77] *Ha'Isha vehaMitzvot* (WZO, 1974). See vol. 1, ch. 5. Two of the three volumes have been translated into English.

[78] Published by Zomet (Alon Shevut, Israel).

[79] *Techumin,* vol. 15 (1995).

[80] *Techumin,* vol. 17 (1997).

[81] Some authorities make a distinction between the various processes of spinning the threads, twisting them and tying them onto the garment. See *Shulchan Arukh,* OC 14:1

promises reward for those women who do make *tzitzit*, expressing what seems to be the normative view in this area:

> And even the women, who are exempt from the law of fringes, receive merit when they are occupied with them; as we have learned in *Bava Batra* [74a] that in the sea there is a hidden chest [covered with precious stones] reserved for the wife of Rabbi Chanina ben Dosa, where the *tekhelet* is kept for the righteous in the world-to-come.

The *Menorat haMa'or* and others[83] write of the sanctity and power contained within the *tzitzit*, and the special aura surrounding those who wear them. The Talmud[84] equates the wearing of fringes to keeping all the laws of the Torah and the person who wears *tzitzit* is worthy to receive the face of the Divine Presence (*Shekhina*). The Talmud describes how the Jewish people are constantly surrounded by God's laws: *tefillin* on their head and arms, *tzitzit* on their clothing and *mezuzot* on their doorposts. The Midrash[85] elaborates: "There is nothing for which God did not give Israel a commandment," explaining that the acts of plowing, planting and harvesting the field all have specific laws. There are rules for kneading bread and preparing food, for taking a baby bird from its nest, and covering the blood of slaughtered animals. Regulations exist for shaving one's head, building a house and burying the dead. So too, "when we cover ourselves with clothing, we were told to attach fringes." The functional rationale for the fringes is to deter us from yielding to the pervasive temptations we encounter, creating a physical barrier to sin. *Tzitzit* are a constant reminder of our relationship with God, visibly hanging from our garments to serve as testimony and protection.[86] The

---

which states that women are fit to make *tzitzit*, although the *Rama* thinks it is not preferable. See *Tosafot* to *Gittin* 45b (s.v. "all") and *Mishna Berura* (and the *Be'ur Halakha*) 14:3–4.

[82] *Yitzchak Abohav*, light 3, sec. 3, part 4, 1:3.

[83] See *Sifre*, Numbers 15; *Zohar, Shelach* 174; Maharal of Prague (*Chidushei Agadot*), *Sota* 17a; Nachman of Bratslav (*Likutei Moharan*) 7:4.

[84] *Menachot* 43b.

[85] *Tanchuma, Shelach*.

[86] See *Sefer haChinukh* 386; Eliyahu Vidash, *Reisheet Chokhma*, section on Holiness, ch. 6; *Chofetz Chaim on the Torah, Shelach*.

spiritual significance is alluded to (in the use of the blue thread) by symbolizing heaven itself,[87] bringing us closer to the love and fear of our Creator. *Bachye*[88] says that one who wears fringes should be especially cautious not to sin, because the word *tzitzit* is derived from the Hebrew word *metzitz*, which means "looking," implying that God is watching us, as well.

Halakha both reflects history and creates history. Although the study of Torah texts is timeless, the halakhic codes that emerge from those texts are rooted in specific places and times. That is the paradox of rabbinic interpretation: it concretizes the massive body of oral law that has been transmitted since Sinai by actualizing traditional solutions to contemporary situations. Synthesizing all prior Jewish wisdom into its current application, the ancient and the modern merge to form halakhic practice. Historically, women have often observed precepts from which they were officially exempt, with little record of their "unofficial" practices.[89]

The fact that Torah study for women is burgeoning today, whereas relatively few observant women have opted to wear *tzitzit*, may have more to do with the centuries-old image that *tzitzit* are masculine than a literal reflection of the written word. Like hearing the shofar, blessing the *lulav* and counting the *omer*, which were not biblically mandated for females but are now routinely done, perhaps the wearing of fringes is yet to be claimed by women "who desire in their souls to observe the law although they were not commanded."[90] If passion for the commandments is not motivation enough, we are told[91] that "anyone who is careful in the observance of *tzitzit* will merit being served by 2800 servants, as it says in Zecharia (8:23): 'So says God, the Lord of hosts, in the end of days ten people from each of the world's nations will grab onto the corner [of clothing] of every Jew, saying, we will follow you

---

[87] *Menachot* 43b.

[88] Bachye ben Asher, *Kad haKemach*, *Tzitzit*.

[89] See Shlomo Ashkenazi, *Ha'Isha be'Aspaklarit haYahadut*, vol. 1 (1979) where he lists Jewish women throughout the ages who practiced various laws.

[90] R. Feinstein cited earlier.

[91] *Shabbat* 32b.

because we have heard that God is with you.'"[92] If the Gentiles of the world will cling to *tzitzit* in order to embrace the Creator, who knows what *tzitzit* might do for Jewish women today?

---

[92] Rav Nissim Gaon explains that since there are 70 nations of the world and ten people will hang onto each of the four corners of a Jew's *tallit*, that is 700 multiplied by four which equals 2800.

Women and the Study of Torah in the Thought of the Lubavitcher Rebbe

Susan Handelman

"If your Torah had not been my delight (שעשעי), I would have perished in my poverty." Psalms 119:92

Introduction

Anyone who has tasted the joy of deep immersion in Torah study, knows well the meaning of that verse. Many women have yearned for that delight, and many have merited, especially in our generation, to experience it. This volume itself testifies to the great advances women have made in Torah study. These have not, of course, always come easily. Nor are the arguments about the permissibility and scope of Torah study for women resolved. If one would query a range of observant Jewish women about their obligation in Torah study, the answers would vary from, "women have no *mitzva* to engage in Torah study," to "women are obligated to know the practical laws that relate to them such as *kashrut*, Shabbat, *nidda*, but only men have an obligation to study Torah for its own sake and continuously" to "women can and should engage in the highest levels of Torah learning." The halakhic history is long and complex, and the struggles of contemporary Jewish women have

---

* I dedicate this essay to the remarkable women who have made it possible for me and so many other women to search the depths of Torah, who have founded the Torah institutions in Jerusalem where I have studied, and who have taught me their Torah and helped me make it my own: Malkah Binah, the founder of Mattan, Chanah Henkin, the founder of Nishmat, and my female teachers at these *yeshivot* who have also become dear friends: Bryna Levy, Simi Peters, Aviva Zornberg. And to my *chavruta*, Gilla Rosen, with whom I have had the privilege to share many moments of Torah as a wondrous *shashua*, pleasure.

I also thank the Jerusalem Fellows program of the Center for Advanced Professional Educators in Jerusalem in which I participated in 1997–98 for the time and support needed to write this essay. And R. Shlomo Gestetner, founder of the Ma'ayanot Institute of Jewish Studies in Jerusalem, for his assistance in researching the Chabad sources.

re-opened them. But this, too, is part of the very delight of Torah—its continuous renewal.

With so many opportunities to pursue serious Torah study now available to women, one might wonder what need there is for another essay on this subject. But in the service of Torah, and as part of its delight, I hope to add here a new facet to the subject. The text I want to examine in depth is part of the legacy of the late Lubavitcher Rebbe, R. Menachem M. Schneerson (1901–1994) whose general position on Torah study for women has become fairly well known: he endorsed teaching Oral Torah and Talmud to women, stressed the importance of their seriously learning Jewish philosophy and *chassidut*, and supported the establishment of many schools for women.

The essay which I introduce is untranslated and known mostly only to scholars of Chabad. The material comes from part of two extensive public talks in the years 1970 and 1971 during traditional large chassidic gatherings connected to the holiday of Shavuot. His oral discourses at these gatherings were then transcribed, edited, and published.[1] This analysis, unlike his more popularly known other statements on the subject, is carried out strictly within the framework and technical internal logic of the halakhic system. It does not appeal to sociology, psychology, philosophy, politics, history, or polemics. It engages the classical rabbinic sources, and centers on a rigorous discussion of the way his predecessor, the first Lubavitcher Rebbe and founder of the Chabad movement, R. Schneur Zalman (1745–1813) codified the *halakhot* of *talmud Torah* in his own well-known and authoritative Code of Jewish Law, the *Shulchan Arukh haRav*. R. Schneerson will argue *that despite the differing sources of the obligation to learn Torah, women's Torah study is not halakhically secondary; it attains its own independent status and identity as intrinsic Torah study, and connects to the same essence of Torah as does men's study, with all the same spiritual effects and deep connection to God that such study entails; the difference is the* halakhic *catalyst by which they each reach talmud Torah. Moreover, her obligation to study is continuous, just as a man's.* I

---

[1] This text is found in Rabbi Menachem M. Schneerson, *Likkutei Sichot*, vol. 14 (Brookyln, NY: Kehot Pub. Society, 1978) 37–44 and then was reprinted with extensive footnotes and sources in his *Chiddushim uViurim leShas*, vol. 1 (Brooklyn, NY: Kehot Pub. Society, 1979) 217–23. There are many intricate arguments in the footnotes. I only include a few of them here. I refer the reader to the original for the fullest understanding of the argument in the footnotes and sources.

assume that the readers of this essay will vary widely in background and
familiarity with halakhic texts. Nevertheless, I have decided to closely follow
the intricacies in reasoning of the original and not to pre-digest or simplify the
material. For one thing, simplifications in presenting halakhic issues are often
very misleading. For another, I find the fascination of halakhic thought to be
its intellectual depth, its subtle and flexible modes of reasoning, its sharp inner
debates, its surprising conclusions. I have, however, eased the reader's way
somewhat by presenting the final results and conclusions of R. Schneerson's
analysis at the beginning of the major sections. The halakhic process, of
course, works the opposite way, beginning not with a thesis but rather through
the presentation of questions, counter-questions, examination of sources,
logical analysis, proofs and counter-proofs until a conclusion can be reached.

In writing this paper, I have chosen to blend my voice more or less into the
style and tone of classic halakhic commentary—a different rhetorical genre
than Midrash or Bible commentary, or philosophical hermeneutics, but no less
creative in its own intricate way.[2] It has required me to work within the
constraints of the internal logic of the halakhic system, a system to which I am
also personally fully committed. Yet the boundaries are vast; from the
discourse of the Sages of the Talmud, to the halakhic codifiers and commentators from medieval to modern Europe, from Spain to France to Poland. And
finally it leads to a contemporary theological and historical understanding of
women's intensive participation in Torah study as part of a redemp-
tive-messianic process.

For all contemporary women in search of their connection to Torah, I hope
to show how the way forward begins first with the way back, back into the
sources. The subtlety of this analysis will require the reader's patience, but this
forbearance, will be rewarded, I hope, since R. Schneerson makes some
striking innovations in understanding the nature and scope of Torah study for
women. One must labor to work one's way through the material, but this labor
is also the source of the ultimate pleasure of Torah study. And only through

---

[2] For my philosophic reflections on rabbinic methods of analysis and commentary, see
my *The Slayers of Moses: The Emergence of Rabbinic Interpretation in Modern Literary
Theory* (Albany: State Univ. of New York Press, 1982) and *Fragments of Redemption:
Jewish Thought and Literary Theory in Scholem, Benjamin, and Levinas* (Bloomington:
Indiana Univ. Press, 1991).

this labor, does one make the Torah her own, as in the talmudic midrash from *Avoda Zara* 19a:

> "But only in the Torah of God is his desire, and in his Torah he meditates day and night" (Psalms 1:2). Rava said that at the beginning of this verse, the Torah was called after the name of the Holy One blessed be He ("Torah of God"). But at the end of the verse, it is called "his Torah" i.e., after the name of the student who has studied it.

I. The Issue

We start at the beginning, with one of key classical rabbinic sources on the issue of the nature of women's obligation in Torah study, the Talmud, *Kiddushin* 29b. The larger context is a discussion of the obligation of parents towards their children, and children towards their parents.

> How do we know that she [the mother] is not obligated to teach her children? Because it is written [Deut. 11:19] *velimadetem* ["and you shall teach"], which also can be read *ulemadetem* ["and you shall study"]: hence whoever is commanded to study is also commanded to teach; whoever is not commanded to study, is not commanded to teach.
> And how do we know that she is not obligated to teach herself? Because it is written, "*velimadetem* (and you shall teach)," "*ulemadetem* (and you shall study)": the one whom others are commanded to teach is commanded to teach himself; and the one whom others are not commanded to teach, is not commanded to teach himself. How then do we know that others are not commanded to teach her? As it is written in Scripture "And you shall teach them to your sons [*velimadetem et baneikhem*]"—your sons but not your daughters [*benoteikhem*].

A contemporary woman reading this statement without much knowledge of the talmudic and halakhic processes, might well be taken aback. Firstly, it is critical to remember that the text is speaking here about the *legal* nature of religious obligations and their consequences. As is well known, there are other sources in the Talmud and Halakha which probe the question of whether this is a *prohibition*, or only an *exemption*, and if the latter, to what extent women may indeed be obligated or voluntarily take upon themselves to learn Torah The history of halakhic codification and interpretation takes its own interesting course, which in the interests of space and coherence, I relegate mostly to the footnotes.

Since his analysis will be strictly halakhic, R. Schneerson begins by citing parts of his predecessor, R. Schneur Zalman's codification of the *halakhot* in the section of the "Laws of Torah Study" in his *Shulchan Arukh haRav, Yore De'a,* (1:14) which begins with the sentence,

> *Isha eiyna bemitzvat talmud Torah, shene'emar velimadetem et beneikhem velo et benoteikhem.*
>
> .אשה אינה במצות תלמוד תורה שנאמר ולמדתם אותם את בניכם ולא את בנותיכם

I pause here to note the difficulty in translating the beginning of this sentence from Hebrew. Literally, it would read: "*A woman is not in* [i.e., *does not have*] *the mitzva of talmud Torah, as it says,* "*you shall teach them to your sons...*" *and not to your daughters.*'"

First, if this sentence were intended to mean that women are completely *exempt* from the study of Torah, he could have simply and clearly phrased it that way, based on the classic precedent of Maimonides' ruling (12th c.) at the beginning of his own codification of Laws of *talmud Torah* in his authoritative *Mishne Torah* (1:1): "Women, slaves, and children are exempt (פטורים) from *talmud Torah.*"

Here, the word *patur* unequivocally denotes "exempt." But again, exemption does not mean prohibition, and Maimonides goes on to say that a woman who chooses to study on her own is rewarded, and makes a further distinction between the prohibition of a man's teaching his daughter the Oral Torah and the permissibility of teaching her the Written Torah.[3]

---

[3] See *Hilkhot Talmud Torah* of the *Rambam* 1:13 where he writes: "A woman who studies Torah is rewarded, but not to the same degree as a man, for she is not commanded and anyone who does that which he is not commanded to do does not receive the same reward as one who is commanded, but only a lesser reward. However, even though she is rewarded, the Sages commanded that a man must not teach his daughter Torah. This is because the mind of most women is not disposed to study, and they will turn the words of Torah into words of nonsense according to their limited understanding." He then refers to the well known statement of R. Eliezer in the Talmud (*Sota* 21b): "anyone who teaches his daughter is as if he taught her trivial things (*tiflut*). What were they referring to? The Oral Torah. However the Written Torah should not be taught before the fact (*lekhatchila*)" but he continues, "if he has taught her [the Written Torah], it is not considered as if he had taught her *tiflut.*"

The ambiguous syntax of R. Schneur Zalman's *isha eiyna bemitzvat talmud Torah* will become extremely significant later on. It will support R. Schneerson's contention that women are *not* exempt from *talmud Torah*, but indeed *obligated* in it; their obligation, however, is not rooted in the *mitzva of talmud Torah* per se but in their obligation in *other mitzvot*. This distinction, which seems at this point rather subtle, is extensively developed by R. Schneerson

---

For further explanations of this—as a reference to a young daughter or to one who has not shown wisdom—as well as a list of many women through the ages who have been very learned in Torah (usually the products of great rabbinic households), see R. Katriel Tchorsh "*Zekhuyot haNashim le'Or haTorah*" (esp. pages 145–46) and R. Moshe Dov Willner "*Arikhat Chidonei Tanach veHishtatfut baHem*" (esp. pages 194–99) both in *BeTzomet haTorah vehaMedina*, ed. R. Yehudah Shaviv, vol. 2 (Alon Shvut: *Makhon Zomet*, 1991).

One of the ideas behind the greater reward for one who is commanded and performs the *mitzva* is that one's inner negative impulses fight more strongly against what one is commanded to do than against what one voluntarily takes upon oneself, and also that one is more careful about what one is commanded.

For further analysis of Maimonides' views and later sources, see *Gidrei Chiyuv Ktanim veNashim beMitzvat Talmud Torah* by R. Binyamin Rakover, in *BeShemen Ra'anan: Sefer Zikaron leRav Shalom Natan Ranan Kook*, ed. R. Ben Zion Shapiro, vol. 2 (Jerusalem: HaRav Kook, 1991) 478–99. Warren Zev Harvey also notes that in Maimonides' *Hilkhot Yesodei haTorah*, women are not exempt from the commandments involved in *Pardes*, the knowledge of God and His unity, and the love and fear of God. The *Pardes* for Maimonides also includes physics and metaphysics. The prerequisite for studying these realms, Maimonides says, is to first "fill one's belly with bread and meat," i.e., the knowledge of what is permitted and forbidden, and talmudic arguments such as the debates of Abaye and Rava. Maimonides concludes by saying that this prerequisite knowledge is available to all, "man and woman" alike (*Hilkhot Yesodei haTorah* 4:13). This implies a very large scope of Torah study for women and their ability to grasp it.

Harvey resolves the apparent contradiction between this statement and what Maimonides writes in the Laws of Torah Study by interpreting Maimonides to mean that women *do* have an obligation of Talmud and Torah study, "even though this obligation is not within the framework of the commandment of *talmud Torah*." "Women are in *one* sense required to study the Written and Oral Torah, but in *another* sense they are not required to study them." He speculates, based on Rav Soloveitchik's distinction between *mussar avikha* ("the instruction of your father") and *torat imekha* ("the teaching of your mother") (Proverbs 1:8), that Maimonides does not require women to study Written and Oral Torah for the purpose of carrying on the legal tradition of Halakha, but rather for the purpose of attaining *chokhma*—to enter the *Pardes* of knowledge, love, and awe of God. Her study comes via the commandments of *Pardes*, rather than through the commandment of *talmud Torah*. Warren Zev Harvey, "The Obligation of Talmud on Women According to Maimonides" *Tradition* 19.2 (Summer, 1981): 122–30.

and has profound ramifications. For now, suffice it to say that halakhic distinctions in the nature of men and women's obligation in Torah study have historically been interpreted in many ways: some have led to women's near exclusion from this realm; others have relegated their learning to minimal practical information, and discouraged or prohibited women from advanced study except in special cases; and others have sought to explore and develop the scope of their study. R. Schneerson's analysis falls into the latter category.

Let's return to the continuation of the wording and order of R. Schneur Zalman's *Shulchan Arukh*. R. Schneerson cites the following part of it:

> And just as she does not have a *mitzva* of *talmud Torah* for herself, so also does she not have a *mitzva* of teaching Torah to her children, and she is exempt from having to pay for their tuition... Nevertheless, if she assists her son or husband personally or materially to engage in Torah study, she divides the reward with them, and her reward is great since they are commanded and accomplish it through her.

At the end of the paragraph, R. Schneur Zalman (*Hilkhot Talmud Torah* 1:14) concludes:

> ומכל מקום גם הנשים חייבות ללמוד הלכות הצריכות להן לידע אותן כמו דיני נדה וטבילה
> ומליחה ואיסור יחוד וכיוצא בהם וכל מצות עשה שאין הזמן גרמה וכל מצות לא תעשה של
> תורה ושל דברי סופרים שהן מוזהרות בהן כאנשים.

> In any case, women are also obligated to learn the laws that pertain to them, to know them, such as the laws of *nidda, tevilah, melicha*, forbidden intimacy, and so forth, and the positive mitzvot not dependent on specific time, and all the negative *mitzvot* of the Torah and of the words of the Scribes, in which they are prohibited just as men.

This last statement about women's obligation to learn the "laws that pertain to them" is not new to R. Schneur Zalman. It has a long, important and interesting halakhic history, which I again summarize in the footnotes for the sake of holding onto the thread of R. Schneerson's argument.[4] Before I summarize the

---

[4] It's important to clarify that this description of which *mitzvot* women are obligated to study encompasses most of the 613 *mitzvot* of the Torah: all the 365 negative *mitzvot*, and all but a handful of the 248 positive *mitzvot* excluding only those which are called "time-dependent." These are *mitzvot* such as sitting in the *sukka*, waving the *lulav*, hearing the shofar, wearing *tzitzit*, laying *tefillin*, from which women are exempt (*Kiddushin* 29a;

key questions R. Schneerson asks about the internal order, logic, and verbal formulations of R. Schneur Zalman's text some important prefatory comments are necessary: the methodology that R. Schneerson will use may seem strange to readers unfamiliar with rabbinic methods of interpretation and commentary. Suffice it to say briefly that—as with all literary and legal writings—the text is assumed to be pregnant with meaning which requires deep searching out and analysis to be revealed. Apparent surface meanings are often only that—just the surface. Meaning is a result of ongoing questioning and interpretation through logic, dialectic, comparison with other sources, attention to nuance and seeming contradictions, dialogue with the history of other interpreters, and application to new situations. That holds true for biblical commentary as well,

---

33b). Many women have customarily taken upon themselves several of these, and (according to ashkenazi tradition) they are permitted to make a blessing (Blessed are You... who has sactified and commanded us to...") when they perform them.

In this chapter of his *Hilkhot Talmud Torah* 1:14, among the sources R. Schneur Zalman cites are the *Agur* (*Hilkhot Tefilla* 2:5), and the introduction to the *Smak* (*Sefer Mitzvot Katan* of R. Yitzchak of Corbeille, 13th c.) and the *Sefer Chasidim* 313. See also the *Smag* (*Sefer Mitzvot Gadol* by R. Moshe of Coucy, 13th c.) Positive *Mitzvot* 12, and *Beit Yosef*, OC 47; *Rama* on YD 246:6 et al.

R. Yosef Caro (16th c.) in his *Shulchan Arukh*, YD 246:6 quotes Maimonides on the issue but the *Rama* (R. Moshe Isserles, 16th c.) *adds* in his gloss on this passage "Nevertheless, a woman is obligated to learn the laws that apply specifically to women." Earlier sources for this Halakha are in the *Sefer Chasidim* and the *Sefer Mitzvot Katan* in the introduction, written by his students.

According to the *Sefer Chasidim* 313, a man is obligated to teach his daughters the *mitzvot* as basic *piskei halakhot*, i.e., digested *halakhot*. R. Eliezer's statement that whoever teaches his daughter is as if he taught her *tiflut*, refers to the depth of the Talmud, the rationale of the *mitzvot*, etc. But the *Sefer Chasidim* maintains the father does indeed need to instruct her in the laws of *mitzvot*: "For if she does not know the laws of Shabbat, how could she possibly be able to observe it; and the same holds true for the rest of the *mitzvot* in order for her to be able to fulfill and be scrupulous about them."

This is the meaning, the *Sefer Chasidim* continues, of Deut. 31:12 "Assemble all the people, the men, the women, and the children... that they may *hear* and that they may *learn* [to observe the Torah]": the women come to learn digests of the laws in order to know how to observe them. This is also the interpretation of R. Eliezer in *Chagiga* 3a, cited by the *Tosafot* on *Sota* 21b "Ben Azai *omer*." See also *Sota* 3 in the Jerusalem Talmud: R. Eliezer interprets the verse from Deuteronomy to mean that the men came to "study" and the women to "hear" in order to know how to perform their *mitzvot*, yet this does not constitute any type of Torah study that brings them the merit of Torah study per se.

of course, and that indeed is part of the delight of Torah study and the obligation to find new insights, *chiddushim*, in Torah.

R. Schneur Zalman also followed certain other rules in composing his *Shulchan Arukh*, which itself is a specific genre of halakhic writing. Since it was intended to be an updated collective codification of authoritative Jewish law for the broad community, he did not seek to impose his own innovative insights in Halakha. Any innovation, moreover, is valid only if it has support in precedents. So his novel understandings of Halakha are not explicitly stated here; but subtle nuances of phrasing or organization of material hint at these new ideas. One needs to examine the text carefully to extract them; their subtle and indirect expression does not impose them upon everyone. In a different rhetorical situation, by contrast, in *she'elot uteshuvot*, when directly asked for his opinion on halakhic issues, he writes openly what his personal opinion and innovations in Halakha might be.

R. Schneerson proceeds to scrutinize these indirect subtleties in order to reveal and develop these halakhic innovations. R. Schneerson's own novel interpretations are also subtly woven into the complexities of *his* own argument. In other non-halakhic analyses, he speaks far more directly and sweepingly, in the historical and theological senses, about the nature of women's learning, statements which I will examine at the end of this essay. Both these approaches, the subtle and the overt, the halakhic and theological, are necessary and complement each other.

II. The Questions

The Order of the Text

R. Schneerson begins with a very close look at the wording of R. Schneur Zalman's text and his ordering of the three sections.[5]

---

[5] It is interesting and significant that R. Schneerson, in analyzing the text of R. Schneur Zalman, omits entirely the middle passage of the paragraph in which R. Schneur Zalman refers to Maimonides' ruling that if a woman does learn, she is rewarded, but still a father should not teach her because women's mind are not disposed to study and they turn the words of Torah into nonsense. R. Schneerson does address this issue directly in the discourse of 1990 which I discuss at the end of this piece, where he declares that this characterization of women's minds is no longer historically accurate. Also in a discussion with the Belzer Rebbe, in a transcript in Yiddish from 4 Adar, 5741 (1981) R. Schneerson

1) "A woman is not in/does not have the *mitzva* of *talmud Torah*."
2) "Nevertheless, if she assists her son or her husband personally or materially to engage in Torah study, she divides the reward with them, and her reward is great since they are commanded and accomplish it through her."
3) "In any case, women are also obligated to learn the laws that pertain to them and to know them."

Logically speaking, he says, it seems that R. Schneur Zalman should have reversed his order of the different aspects of women's Torah study: he should have put #3, the most inclusive and universal obligation—i.e., that women are obligated to learn the laws relevant to them, to know them—*before* #2 the more limited case of those women who assist their husbands or children in Torah study and share the reward with them. For the last sentence, "women are obligated to learn the laws that pertain to them" constitutes he maintains, *talmud Torah itself* for women, and applies to *every* single woman.

By contrast, the woman who helps her son or husband is not in the category of "study" but rather "assistance"; and her connection is to the *reward* of the Torah study of her *son or husband*. This category is further limited by applying only to those women who have sons or husbands, and only to those who are in need of their wives' or mothers' assistance. Nor do these attributes of helping and being rewarded constitute any Halakha unique to women; women simply are included here in the larger category of *anyone* who gives assistance to those obligated in Torah study. In fact, in R. Yosef Caro's (16th c.) authoritative *Shulchan Arukh, Yore De'a*, "Laws of Torah Study" (246:6), the order indeed is reversed: (1) "Nevertheless, a woman is obligated to study the laws that apply specifically to her" is placed *before* the statement (2) "But if she assists her husband or children in Torah study, she divides the reward with them."

The Relation of the Morning Blessing over the Torah to the Obligation to Study

---

argues that in recent generations the situation has changed, women have had the opportunity to make great intellectual strides, are learned in secular studies, and now all women are able to study Oral Torah and should be taught in an intellectually challenging way, including Talmud; if one keeps their learning on a minimal level, *that* is teaching them *tiflut*, trivia.

There is a further important piece of halakhic information about women's relation to Torah study. In the set order of daily prayers, among the morning blessings which women recite are those over the Torah, including the words... "Who has sanctified us with his commandments and commanded us to engage in the words of Torah (*la'asok bedivrei Torah*)." What do these mean? R. Schneur Zalman in his *Shulchan Arukh, Orach Chaim* "Laws of the Morning Blessings" (47:10) writes: "Women make the blessings over the Torah because women are obligated to study the *mitzvot* that pertain to them, to know how to perform them...".[6] And then he adds some additional reasons.

From the fact that women say the blessings on *the Torah* over their study, we have a proof, maintains R. Schneerson, that their study of the laws pertaining to them is itself a matter of learning *Torah* and not simply a preparation for the *mitzvot* (*hekhsher mitzva*) they perform. This is a *critical* distinction. In halakhic terminology, *hekhsher mitzva*, is any act which is a

---

[6] The *Beit Yosef*, (R. Yosef Caro's commentary on the *Tur*) OC 47 on the "Laws of Morning Blessings" cites the *Agur* who writes in the name of the *Maharil* (R. Yakov haLevi Molin, early 15th c.) that women *do* say the blessing over the study of Torah in the morning ("Bless be You, Lord our God and God of Our Fathers Who has sanctified us with His commandments and commanded us to engage in Torah—*la'asok bedivrei Torah*") even though they are *not* obligated in Torah study and even though there is the talmudic opinion that one who teaches his daughter Torah is as if he taught her *tiflut*. This prohibition must then apply only to teaching her Oral Torah, but not to Written Torah... even though the text of the blessing "who has commanded to us to engage (*la'asok*) in Torah" implies the deep study that characterizes Oral Torah. "One nevertheless doesn't change the text of the blessing" he concludes.

The *Beit Yosef* adds a secondary justification from the *Maharil* for women's saying the blessing over the Torah: in the liturgy of the morning prayers, women, like men, recite passages that contain portions of the Torah dealing with the order of the Temple Sacrifices, and this entitles them to recite the *birkat haTorah*. And there is a general principle that the prayers were established to correspond to, and substitute for, the Temple Sacrifices. Women are obligated in prayer, and are therefore obligated in the reading of these portions of the Written Torah dealing with the sacrifices. He adds, "Even stronger are the words of the *Smag* who wrote that women are obligated to learn the laws connected to them."

R. Schneur Zalman, in his codification of the Laws of Morning Blessings, also adds as his *second* reason the above rationale of the *Beit Yosef*: that women say this blessing over Torah study due to their reading the portions in the prayer book taken from the Torah having to do with the Temple sacrifices. His *first and primary* reason, however, is that women are obligated to study the specific *mitzvot* that pertain to them, to know how to perform them. For those who oppose this line of reasoning, see n8 below.

prerequisite to the fulfillment of a *mitzva*, but does *not* constitute the *mitzva* itself. For instance, one needs to *build* a *sukka* in order to perform the *mitzva* of *sitting* in it, but we do not say a blessing on building the *sukka*; the blessing is said when the *sukka* is completed and we sit in it, and is formulated "Who has command us to sit (*leishev*) in the *sukka*." (There is, however, an interesting debate about this issue, and the extent to which certain kinds of preparations to perform *mitzvot do* indeed become part of the *mitzvot* themselves, which R. Schneerson will apply to the issue of whether a woman's obligation in learning is only a preparation to perform her *mitzvot*, but not actual Torah study itself, or becomes independent study.)

In other words, the issue here is the exact nature of the blessings women say in the morning liturgy over Torah study: exactly which portions of Torah are they making these blessings over, (Written or Oral); and is this blessing *obligatory* or only *permitted*? For being *obligated* to make the blessing would also imply that women also have an *obligation* to study Torah. And if so, does this obligation entail only the *mitzvot* that apply to them, or to something more, and also what manner and scope of study? For R. Schneerson, if women are saying the blessing over learning Torah, it means that their learning is itself *Torah study* and not just a preparation to perform the practical *mitzvot* that pertain to them such as *kashrut* or Shabbat. He will attempt further halakhic proof later on.

But now, if this is the case, if R. Schneerson wants to argue that women are indeed saying a blessing over their obligation and engagement in independent Torah study, he must first contend with other fundamental sources which appear to contradict this idea. He now raises the counter-arguments.

Contradictory Sources

1) Where is the source in the Gemara itself that women's study of the laws pertaining to them is something independent, a matter of *Torah study* and not just a preparation to fulfill the *mitzvot* in which they are obligated? The clear and simple meaning of "teach your sons, and not your daughters" seems to be that women do *not* have a category of independent Torah study—as R. Schneur Zalman himself writes at the beginning of the paragraph on the Laws of Torah Study in his *Shulchan Arukh* "A woman is not in/does not have a *mitzva* of *talmud Torah*."

2) This interpretation also appears to contradict the well known saying of the Rabbis in the Gemara *Berakhot* 17a and *Sota* 21a: "How do women *attain merit*? By bringing their sons to study Torah in school and sending their husbands' to study in the *beit midrash* and waiting for them until they return home";—that is, *not* by their own Torah study, but by facilitating and fostering the study of their sons and husbands. If their obligation to learn the laws pertaining to them were a matter of a *mitzva* for its own sake, of *talmud Torah*, then they would acquire merit from that endeavor, and the Gemara would have included it in the answer. What, then is the meaning of the question "How do they attain merit?"

3) Furthermore, in the tractate *Sota* (21a), there is the famous discussion about the nature of women's Torah study in the context of the *sota*, the suspected adulteress who proclaims her innocence. Following biblical law, she must endure a test of drinking the special bitter waters the priest gives her (Numbers 5:11–31). If she is innocent, the waters do not harm her, but if she is guilty, they cause her a painful death. The Mishna (*Sota* 3:14) explains, however, that in certain cases, even when she is guilty but has certain "merits," the lethal effect of the waters can be "suspended" for up to three years.[7]

On the phrase, "If she has merit, it [the punishment] is suspended for her," the Gemara asks: "What kind of merit? If you say, 'the merit of Torah' she is not commanded and rewarded [in the study Torah]..."; it then follows up with a statement similar to *Berakhot* (17a) citing the merit a woman does have when causing her children to study, and waiting for her husband to return from his learning, and thus dividing the reward with them.

---

[7] This Mishna then quotes the famous dispute between Ben Azzai and R. Eliezer over the merit of women learning Torah: "Hence, said Ben Azzai, 'A man should teach his daughter Torah so that if she must drink she may know that the merit will suspend her punishment.' R. Eliezer says 'If a man teaches his daughter Torah, it as though he taught her *tiflut*.'" Here *Rashi* understand *tiflut* to mean immorality; i.e., if she is taught Torah, she will acquire clever wisdom and know how to conduct immoral affairs without discovery.

See the interesting interpretation of this *sugya* by Lea Rosenthal in the journal *Pardes Revisited*, of the Pardes Institute in Jerusalem (Summer, 1995) that beyond the specific issue of women, these two positions also represent two ways of understanding the general intellectual and moral advantages and disadvantages of acquiring advanced knowledge. On the one hand, advanced knowledge can help one to negotiate the dangers of the world, but there is also always a cost and danger to gaining sophistication—that of losing one's innocence and moral integrity, becoming cunning instead of wise.

4) Women's obligation to study the laws relevant to them is, in the phrase-ology of R. Schneur Zalman, in order to *"know them," "to know how to perform them."* If so, it would seem that a woman who has already become expert in her knowledge of all these laws would *not* have any further obliga-tion of study. And in that case, she would also *no longer* be obligated to say the morning blessing over Torah study. There are, indeed, some great halakhic commentators who argue precisely that way.[8]

If that is so, why does R. Schneur Zalman cite women's obligation to study the *mitzvot* relevant to them, to know how to perform them, as the *first and primary reason* for women making the morning blessing over the Torah? For this condition is not relevant to *all* women. (In any case, he could have cited it as additional or supplementary, but not the primary reason.)

III. The Explanation

This section attempts to resolve these difficulties by proving that women's study of Torah does indeed acquire its own independent status. The halakhic catalyst for their reaching the same essence of Torah study as men is different,

---

[8] See the *Birkhei Yosef* of the *Chida* (R. Yosef Chaim David Azuli, 18th c.) on OC 47:7: who says that women's obligation to learn is *not* by virtue of the *mitzva* of *talmud Torah*, for women are exempt, but they are obligated "for the sake of knowledge of their practical laws, and if they have attained expertise in these laws, they have no further obligation at all to study."

This returns us to the debate over the nature of the blessing women say over the Torah. Another line of thinking maintains that this blessing is neither *obligatory*, nor does it imply that women's study of their relevant laws constitutes independent Torah study. Among these who argue this way are the Vilna Gaon (18th c.) and the *Beit haLevi* (19th c.). The Vilna Gaon interprets women's blessing over the Torah to be merely permitted, not obligatory, just as women are permitted to say blessings when they choose to perform any of the *mitzvot* from which they are exempt, the category of "positive *mitzvot* dependent on specific times" (*mitzvot asei shehazman grama*).

See also the opinion of the *Beit haLevi, She'elot uTeshuvot* 1:6 Men have a positive *mitzva* to *study*, including those subjects that are not immediately relevant to them. Women's obligation, is only to "know" the *mitzvot* which apply to them, but this does not constitute *study*. Women's study is just a means to acquire the knowledge; and women are not commanded to *study their mitzvot*. Consequently, if a woman would acquire expertise in her *halakhot*, she would no longer be obligated to study them at all.

but the effect is the same. The case is made through a series of examples, analogies, and halakhic proofs.

#1: The Case of the Torah Study of the non-Jew

The first analogy is to someone else who also does not have a direct *mitzva* of *talmud Torah*, but nevertheless is obligated to study: the non-Jew. About a non-Jew who studies Torah, the Gemara says:

> R. Meir said: "From where do we know that even a non-Jew who engages in Torah is like a High Priest?" As it is written in Scripture [Lev. 18:5]: "[you shall therefore keep my laws and judgments] which if a *person* [*adam*] shall do them, he shall live in them." It does not say "priests, Levites, Israelites" who will do them but "a person." This teaches that even a non-Jew who engages in Torah is like a High Priest, referring to the seven *mitzvot* in which non-Jews are specifically commanded. (*Sanhedrin* 59a; cf. *Bava Kamma* 38a; *Avoda Zara* 3a)

Notes R. Schneerson, the status of being "like a High Priest" which the non-Jew who studies Torah acquires, is attained specifically by virtue of his or her learning *Torah*. As the *Tosafot* in the Gemara (*Bava Kamma* 38a; *Avoda Zara* 3a) comment on the striking use of the term "High Priest":

> As it is written, 'More precious is it than pearls' (*yekara mepninim*) (Proverbs 3:15) and this is explicated (*Horayot* 13a): 'More than the High Priest who enters into the inner sanctuary (*mekohen gadol hanikhnas lifnai velifnim*).

This is a word play on the similarity of the Hebrew words for "pearls" *pninim* and "deeply inside" *lifnai velifnim*—for entering before God into the "inner of inners," the Holy of Holies, the province of the High Priest. The image is striking indeed: it implies this learning elevates the non-Jew to one of the highest levels of closeness and intimacy with God—the level attained by the High Priest in the Temple on Yom Kippur, the holiest day of the year, when the High Priest entered the holiest of places.

On the other hand, there is a possible contradiction, for the same source in *Sanhedrin* 59a also cites the opinion of R. Yochanan that "A non-Jew who studies Torah is liable to the death penalty." The Gemara helps resolve it by saying that although the Torah is given as an inheritance to Israel alone, non-Jews *are* permitted to study it because they are commanded to fulfill their special seven *mitzvot* (the prohibitions against theft, murder, illicit sexual relations, idolatry, blasphemy, eating a limb cut from a live animal, and the commandment to observe and set up courts of justice). Consequently, they need to study these laws *in order* to know how to perform these *mitzvot*.

But this still would not be enough to explain the talmudic statement that through his or her Torah learning the non-Jew becomes like the High Priest. For that implies they acquire the distinctive spiritual elevation of *engaging in Torah*, and that is quite different from practical performance of *mitzvot*. A Jew who performs *mitzvot*, for example, is never compared to the High Priest. We can infer, then, that the non-Jew's Torah study of the seven *mitzvot* is not *originally* (*lekhatchila*) learning for its own sake, but rather is done for another purpose, that of fulfilling the seven *mitzvot*; however since this learning is a *necessary and essential* preparation (and kind of training), it attains its own *independent* status, is *independent Torah study of its own* (*limud haTorah mitzad atzmo*). And that is indeed why the Gemara cited above can say that the non-Jew who studies Torah becomes "like the high Priest."

#2: The Case of Bringing a Sacrifice

The next example also comes from the realm of the Temple, from the *halakhot* of sacrifices. The Mishna and Talmud in *Zevachim* (1:4; 13a) discusses the four steps involved in carrying out a sacrifice: slaughtering, receiving the blood, carrying of the blood, and sprinkling the blood on the altar. R. Shimon holds that one could perform the sacrifice without the carrying of the blood to the altar: one could, for example, slaughter it directly at the side of the altar and sprinkle the blood there without the intermediate act of carrying. R. Eliezer, however, holds that an incorrect thought or intention one has while in the process of carrying the blood to the altar invalidates the entire sacrifice (for example, that he would eat of the sacrifice after three days instead of immediately). Maimonides codifies R. Eliezer's opinion as the Halakha in his *Hilkhot Pesulei haMukdashin* 13:4.

How can this possibly apply to women and Torah study? R. Schneerson cites the explanation of this Halakha by the Rogatchover Gaon (R. Yosef Rosen, 20th c.): even though carrying the blood to the altar is a preliminary step, taken *in order for* the act of sprinkling the blood that follows, it acquires its own distinctive and independent significance, to the extent that an incorrect thought at this stage invalidates the entire sacrifice. The carrying becomes its own critical, independent act. The principle: *something which is a necessary means/cause to accomplish a certain result, attains its own independent identity and essence.*[9]

Now here R. Schneerson makes his critical and intriguing innovation in understanding the nature of women's Torah learning. *The same principle, he maintains, applies to women's Torah learning: their obligation to learn the laws relevant to them is for the sake of "knowing how to perform them" and not due to the mitzva of talmud Torah for its own sake. But this type of study is nevertheless a* necessary *means/condition* for *fulfilling their practical mitzvot. And thus, their learning attains its own independent significance and reality.*

So when women recite the daily morning blessings over Torah study, they are doing so over the *Torah itself.* R. Schneerson here stands clearly in opposition to the opinion of the Gaon of Vilna and *Beit haLevi* who argue that women are *not* obligated to say this blessing since they are exempt from the *mitzva* of Torah study; and that women's study of the laws pertaining to them does *not* constitute independently significant Torah study. In the strong words of the Gaon of Vilna commenting on the *Shulchan Arukh, Orach Chaim* (47:14): "The Torah shouts to us 'And you shall teach your sons' and not your daughters.' So how could women possibly say the blessing 'Who has commanded us [to engage in Torah] and 'Who has given us the Torah'?"

For R. Schneerson, however, women are fully entitled and *obligated* to say the entire blessing. And there is a further step: since their learning the *halakhot* of their special *mitzvot* attains its own independent significance, becomes its own goal of independent Torah study, this learning is therefore *not limited only* to the time that "she needs to know how to perform them" in practice. So a woman who already knows all the laws relevant to her and "how to perform them" still has a connection to study of Torah and is able to make the blessing.

---

[9] The source is the Rogatchover Gaon's *Tzafnat Paneach* on the Torah, beginning of *Parshat Masei* vol 2, 51:3; see also his commentary on Maimonides' *More Nevuchim* 1:72 and his commentary on *Devarim*, 372. In the commentary on the *More Nevuchim*, he uses the phrase: "even though this is a cause, nevertheless, it is necessary and becomes like an *etzem* [essence, independent existence]." See also R. Schneerson's further analysis of the way preparation for a certain action acquires a certain independent status in Halakha in his *Likkutei Sichot*, 17:187–89.

Deeper Analysis of the Blessings over the Torah

In another essay, taken from the same series of discourses of Shavu'ot, 1970, R. Schneerson extensively analyzes the halakhic nature of the *birkhot haTorah*, blessings over the Torah. Here, too, one finds a novel understanding of women's obligation in Torah study. The essential point of his complex argument there is the following concept. The Torah blessings are different from the blessings said over performing a *mitzva*. When one makes a blessing over a *mitzva*, one must make no temporal interruption whatsoever between the moment of making blessing and the subsequent action of performing the *mitzva*. However, the halakhic obligation upon a man to learn Torah is *continuous* and *constant* throughout the day and night, and if he interrupts between the blessing and his actual study, it is not accounted as a complete cessation—*hefsek* (with certain exceptions halakhically defined as complete "removal of one's mind," such as regular nightly sleep) because even during the time one interrupts (such as to attend to one's bodily needs, or engage in business), one is still under the obligation to study, and one's mind is directed to returning to one's study (assuming one has set times for learning). *From the obligation to engage in Torah study constantly, and the way in which interruptions are not counted as disconnections, R. Schneerson infers that a man has a connection to Torah even at the time he is not engaging in it. The essence of the obligation to engage in Torah study constantly connects a person to the mitzva. Therefore, his halakhic obligation is to make the blessing over Torah study only* once *during the day, not each and every time he begins to study during the day or night.*[10]

---

[10] See the talk by R. Joseph Soloveitchik, "On the Love of Torah: Impromptu Remarks at a Siyum." He notes that one's consciousness of the *mitzva* of *talmud Torah* is connected to the fact that is is continuously obligatory the whole day. He defines this as a "latent awareness... present even when one is engaged in other matters" and makes the analogy to the continuous consciousness a mother has of her child: "even when the mother works at a job or is distracted by some other activity, there is a natural, latent awareness of her child's existence. This awareness remains throughout her lifetime and can never be extinguished" and flows from her devotion and feeling that she and the child are one, and the child is at the center of her life. The same, he says, is true for Torah; even when engaged in other necessary activities, the latent awareness of it never ceases. For it is the center of our lives and desires And that is why the text of the blessing is: *la'asok bedivrei Torah* and not *lilmod Torah*—to "engage in the words of Torah" as all encompassing involvement, rather than the phrase "to study Torah." For the blessing refers not only to the cognitive act, but to

But what does this have to do with women, who do not have a direct mitz-vah of *talmud Torah* day and night? In fact, says R. Schneerson, it helps us explain R. Schneur Zalman's specifically writing that women recite the blessing over the Torah because they are obligated in their practical *mitzvot*, to know how to perform them. Had he not specified this as the reason, we might have inferred that unlike men, women would indeed need to make the blessing *each time* that they begin to study during the day or night, and not just *once* a day. That they are also required to make the blessing only *once* a day thus implies that there is a similar *constancy of obligation* in women's Torah study. How is this so? Just as men bless the Torah only once a day due to their *continuous and constant obligation in Torah study*, so too, the *mitzvot* which women are halakhically obligated to learn are *mitzvot* in which women are *obligated the entire day*. Consequently, they too have an obligation to learn the entire day. And so they too make this blessing only once a day.[11]

---

this continuous latent awareness and deep commitment and connection to Torah. *Shiurei haRav: A Conspectus of the Public Lectures of Rabbi Joseph B. Soloveitchik*, ed. Joseph Epstein (NJ: Ktav, 1994) 181–85. I thank R. Jeffrey Saks for this reference , and other insightful remarks on this topic.

[11] See also the *Bayit Chadash* (*Bach*, R. Yoel Sirkes, 17th c.) ch. 47 on the issue in the *Tur*, YD 246:7 about the problem of women making the blessing on the Torah even though R. Eliezer says one who teaches his daughter Torah is as if he teaches her *tiflut*. He cites the *Maharshal* that "Women have a connection [*sheychut*] to the words of Torah when they study the laws that apply to them."

R. Schneerson's extensive analysis of the halakhic nature of the blessing over the Torah was published in the same volume of *Likkutei Sichot*, vol. 14, 148–55, and then later in *Chiddushim uVe'urim leShas* Chapter 2, "*Birkhat haTorah*," 3–11. The analysis deserves its own full exposition, but here is only one further key point among the many supporting arguments.

The blessings over the Torah, although included in blessings over *mitzvot*, are distin-guished from them. A blessing over *mitzvot* falls into the halakhic category of "blessings of gratitude" (*birkhot shevach*) to God for "sanctifying us with His *mitzvot*" whereas the blessing over the Torah is a blessing over "the essence of Torah study," (besides the fulfilling of the *mitzvot* which this learning includes). R. Schneur Zalman in his *Shulchan Arukh*, OC 47:1 writes: "A person should ensure that the precious vessel of God in which He delights every day [*mishtashe'a*] should be so important to him that he makes the blessing over it with a joy greater than over all the pleasures of the world." This formula-tion indicates that this blessing is *like* (but even more than) the category of "blessings of enjoyment" (*birkhot nehenin*). For one makes the blessing even if he does not understand... it is not limited to the pleasure of understanding the Torah, but is over the joy over the

This subtle reasoning leads to quite an extraordinary conclusion: both men *and women* have an obligation to study Torah the entire day. For men the obligation comes through the direct *mitzva of talmud Torah*. That is the way it is codified in the *Shulchan Arukh* of R. Yosef Caro, *Yore De'a*, "Laws of Torah Study" 246:1: "Every man is obligated to fix times for his Torah study in the day and the evening as it is written "And you should meditate in it day and night [Joshua 1:8]." For women, this obligation of continuous study comes via the halakhic channel of the *mitzvot* she is commanded to perform.

Now this perhaps explains why R. Schneur Zalman in his codification of the laws of Torah study in his version of the *Shulchan Arukh* did not write that "women are *exempt* from *talmud Torah*" but rather that "Women are not in/do not have the *mitzva of talmud Torah*." And also why he specifically wrote that women make the blessing over Torah due to their obligation to study their

---

essence of the Torah itself and God's gift of it to Israel.

As to the other halakhic reason for making the blessing over the Torah only once a day—that it is like all the morning blessings in general which are said only once a day—this still supports the idea of women's continuous obligation to study. R. Schneur Zalman writes in ch. 46 of his *Shulchan Arukh*, OC, that the Sages established all these morning blessings according to the order of the world; even though the creatures enjoy and benefit from these pleasures (such as sight, walking, bodily strength, the earth and heavens) *continuously* the entire day, they bless God only the *first time* that they experience these things each day.

R. Bakshi Doron, the Chief Sephardic Rabbi of Israel writes in a recent article that the son of the *Beit haLevi*, R. Chaim of Brisk, has an interesting way of understanding the issue. R. Yitzchak haLevi, the grandson of the *Beit haLevi* quotes his father R. Chaim (the *Beit haLevi*'s son) to say that the blessing over the Torah is not a blessing over the *mitzva* of *talmud Torah*, but rather the essence of Torah itself requires a blessing. Women have no direct *mitzva* of *talmud Torah* but they have what is called in halakhic terminology, the *cheftza*, the "object" of Torah, and so they make a blessing over it as well. The blessing is over the essence of Torah learning and not over the *mitzva* of *talmud Torah*.

In this light, R. Doron, says, we can better understand the relation of the blessing over Torah study to the morning prayers and how Maimonides deals with it in chapter 7 of his *Laws of Prayer*. He points out that the blessing over the Torah is not a blessing over a *mitzva*, otherwise Maimonides woud have placed it in his section on the Laws of Bessings; rather it is part of the *mitzva* of prayer, of serving God with all one's heart. The morning blessings are also part of fulfilling the *mitzva* to love and stand in awe of God and serve Him, which is the purpose of prayer. So too, the blessing over the Torah is said before study of Torah, which itelf is the way in which one attains love and awe of God. "*Bein Birkhot haShachar VeChiyuv Me'a Berakhot Bekhol Yom*" in *Melilot: Mechkarim Toraniyim* (Kiryat Arba: Makhon leRabbanei Yishuvim, 1997) 327–28.

relevant *mitzvot* as his *first* and primary reason: for through this learning women indeed do have a connection to Torah study *in its essence* and of itself. Their learning of Torah to keep the *mitzvot* of Shabbat, for example, is not just part of the *mitzva* of keeping Shabbat, but intrinsic Torah study of its own.

To sum up the subtle distinctions: there is (1) *talmud Torah*, and there is (2) *mitzvat talmud Torah*. Or, there is (1) the obligation of *talmud Torah*, and (2) the obligation of *mitzvat talmud Torah*. Women have the obligation of *talmud Torah* (but they "are not *in the mitzva* of *talmud Torah*"); nevertheless, their study attains its own independent status as Torah and bestows on them all the distinctiveness and elevation of intrinsic Torah study. *Their not having the direct mitzva of Torah study does* not *remove them from connection to the essence of Torah study.*

Again: *The key principle is that something which is a necessary means/cause to accomplish a certain result, attains its own independent identity and essence.* All of which leads to a remarkable transformation in understanding the nature and result of women's halakhic obligation to study Torah: although the halakhic rationale is based on her need to know the *mitzvot* that pertain practically to her, she must *study Torah* to accomplish this goal; and her study, therefore, is not just a secondary category of preparation to do a *mitzva* but—as an essential and necessary cause—it attains its own independent status and identity as Torah study. In sum for both men and women, there are two channels to the same end, which is connection to the essence of Torah study: for men the halakhic rationale is the direct *mitzva of talmud Torah*; for women the halakhic rationale is the obligation to *know how to perform mitzvot* that pertain to her. Though the pathways, or "halakhic catalysts" are different, both arrive at the same place. A woman's *talmud Torah* has all the same qualities of spiritual greatness and preciousness as a man's; it is not merely an accessory or secondary form of study.[12]

---

[12] There are many interesting practical ramifications to this question about the nature of women's blessings on the Torah and her obligation in Torah study, and whether her learning is only a *hekhsher mitzva* or Torah study itself. For example, were women not obligated in *talmud Torah*, they would not be obligated in the *mitzva* of writing their own Torah, which is for the purpose of study. Also the question of whether a person who is not related must tear *kri'a* (symbolic tearing of the clothes) at the bedside of a woman who has died. One tears *kri'a* because a person who dies is compared to a sefer Torah that has been burned, in which case all who are present are obligated to tear as a sin of mourning. See

IV. Further Questions and their Resolution

But we can't rest here. This contention still needs to address some of the questions raised in sections two and three, and other difficulties which now arise, especially concerning the issue of the reward for study.

Question #1: The Issue of Reward. "One Who is Commanded and Performs" Versus "One Who is *Not* Commanded and Performs"

One could argue that even if women's study of their *halakhot* does entail essential Torah learning, it is still ultimately the effect of their obligation in their relevant *mitzvot*. Women do not have the direct *mitzva of* Torah study per se, and so one can not say that they would receive the reward of someone who is in the halakhic category of one who is "commanded and performs the *mitzva* (*kemetzuve ve'ose*)" of *talmud Torah*.

Explanation: In fact, this distinction now will help answer question#2 in section II above where we asked why the Gemara does not specifically say that women acquire merit by virtue of their learning the laws relevant to them. It will also help us understand that Gemara in a new way. The Gemara in *Sota* (21a) had said that a woman does not have the merit of Torah study to protect her from the bitter waters because she is "not commanded" in Torah study. We can now *re-understand* this statement to mean not that one can't find *any obligation of Torah study for women*, but rather to be about *zekhut Torah*, "the merit of Torah." In other words, it is speaking about the *reward* for the one who is commanded in the *mitzva* of learning Torah; one who is in the halakhic category of "one who is commanded and does." It is specifically that kind of reward (the merit of the *mitzva of talmud Torah*) that suffices for full protection. When she assists her husband and children in learning, concludes, the

---

Radbaz on *Moed Katan* 25a. If a woman is exempt from the *mitzva* of *talmud Torah*, she would not be considered as a sefer Torah. Other ramifications have to do with a woman's obligation to hear the reading of the portion of the week in synagogue. See R. Moshe Weinberger "Teaching Torah to Women" *Journal of Halacha and Contemporary Society* 9 (Spring, 1985) 32–33, n30. See also pages 36–37 about the difference it would make in a case where extra money originally designated for a men's yeshiva could be transferred to the account of a local women's yeshiva.

Gemara, and divides the reward with them, then she indeed has the specific merit of Torah, which fully protects from the bitter waters.

A woman does acquire the special elevation and preciousness of Torah in learning her relevant *halakhot*, but since she is not in the category of "one who is commanded and does," she does not acquire the special merit of Torah studied as a result of a directly commanded *mitzva. The* difference in reward, *though, does not disconnect her either from her obligation to study, or from the essence of Torah itself, and the spiritual elevation of those who engage in it.*

Question #2: Dividing the Reward

R. Schneerson will now proceed to also re-connect her to the reward of those who are in the category of "one who is commanded and does." When we examine carefully the end of the Gemara in *Sota* 21a, and then R. Schneur Zalman's Laws of Torah Study, we note his phrasing "if she assists her son or her husband personally or materially to engage in Torah study, she divides the reward with them, and her reward is great since they are commanded and accomplish it through her." This statement raises another question: why, in fact, *should* she divide the reward with them for *their Torah study* simply because she helps them?

If we compare it to the case of someone who gives money to a poor person, which the poor person then uses to fulfill a *mitzva* (for example, she or he buys food for Shabbat with the money), we don't find in any place that the giver of the charity then has a *part in the mitzva* the poor person fulfills with the donated money. The donor only has the reward of fulfilling the *mitzva* of giving charity.

Explanation: When someone gives charity in this situation, the money then becomes the property of the poor person. So when the beneficiary afterwards does a *mitzva* with this money, he or she is performing his or her *own mitzva*. But in our case, the woman assists her son or husband *from the very beginning* (*milekhatchila*) in fulfilling the *mitzva* of Torah study. She performs such actions as to be a partner in this *mitzva,* assists in the *essence* of the *mitzva*, and so *divides* the reward with them; that is, she receives a portion of the reward of the husband and son.[13]

Parallel Example in the *Mitzva* of Having Children

Lest one think this is an over-reading of the text, there is halakhic illustration of this idea in the obligation to have children: The *Ran* (R. Nissim 1310–1375) in his commentary on the Talmud writes that even though a woman is not directly commanded (*metzuve*) to have children (*Yevamot* 65b) "nevertheless she has a *mitzva* because she assists her husband to fulfill *his mitzva*" (*Kiddushin* 2b). The rationale: the husband is only able to fulfill his *mitzva* in partnership with his wife, as it is written in Genesis 2:24 "and he should cling to his wife and they will become one flesh." Since her assistance is critical in the *mitzva*, "she also has a *mitzva*."

R. Schneerson now applies this explanation to women's assisting her husband or son in Torah study, to clarify why she "divides" the reward with them: when their *mitzva* of Torah study is accomplished due to her participation she, too, also has a *mitzva*.

Possible Objection: What Share of Which *Mitzva*?

But the *Ran*'s phrase "She has a *mitzva*" is somewhat ambiguous. We could read it in two possible ways:

1) "She has a *mitzva* (*stam*)": in the plain sense of a regular *mitzva*. That is, she has in fact no commandment to fulfill the obligation to have children, but since she helps her husband to fulfill *his mitzva*, she also has *a mitzva*. Yet she does not attain "the great *mitzva* (*mitzva rabba*) of be fruitful and multiply," of procreation (*Tosafot, Shabbat* 4a; *Gittin* 41b).

2) "She has a *mitzva*": this would mean she has a share in the *mitzva* itself of *procreation*.

This ambiguity casts doubt on the exact nature of her reward for helping her son or husband fulfill the *mitzva* of Torah study. To resolve the issue, we

---

[13] This is in accord with the Halakha in R. Yosef Caro's *Shulchan Arukh, Yore De'a* 246:1 (and also in the Laws of Torah Study in R. Schneur Zalman's *Shulchan Arukh*, Laws of Torah Study 3:4) that someone who is unable to study Torah can stipulate with his friend to learn Torah and assist him and it will be accounted as if "*he learns himself*" and "*he will divide the reward with him.*"

return to the source in the Gemara *Sota* (21a), and we now understand its specific wording in a new way. The Talmud says פלגאן בהדייהו "she *divides* with him" the reward, and R. Schneur Zalman writes similarly in his *Shulchan Arukh*: "...*sheya'asok beTorah, choleket skhar imahem.*" This precise language, *choleket,* "she divides" and not the more commonly used phrase, *notelet,* "she *takes* reward"—proves that it is the second sense that she has a part in actual *mitzva of talmud Torah.* As explained before: since the husband or son, *are commanded* (*metzuvim*) in the *mitzva* of *talmud Torah* and accomplish it with her aid, she has a portion in the fulfilling of this *mitzva,* that is, a portion in the *mitzva* of *Torah study.* And therefore "she *divides*" the *reward with them.* This indeed means, says R. Schneerson, that she is sharing the reward as one who *is* in the category of "being commanded and does [*metzuve ve'ose*]."

In other words, the text in *Sota* is doing two things according to R. Schneerson's reading: (1) *not* disconnecting women from the obligation to study Torah, but only speaking of the *difference in reward* between her form of study and that of men; and (2) on the other hand, giving her access to the same reward through the path of assisting her husband and children in their study.

He has now strikingly re-read this Gemara to mean that women *do* indeed have a connection to the *mitzva* of *talmud Torah,* and a reward similar to that of men. Again, the halakhic channel is different, but she can share in that form of reward, as well as the spiritual elevation and benefit of her own independent Torah study.

Possible Objection #2

But we are now faced with another question about the rationale R. Schneur Zalman gives for women saying the blessings over the Torah. If she indeed has a *portion* in the *mitzva of the talmud Torah* of her husband and son, and she *divides* the reward with them in the highest category of "one who is commanded and does" why didn't he then cite this in his *Shulchan Arukh* section on "Laws of the Blessings over the Torah," at least as an additional reason for why women make the blessing over the Torah?

Let's return to the analogy of a woman sharing in the *mitzva* of procreation. The critical difference is that her assisting her husband to fulfill that *mitzva* is entirely *voluntary.* If she desires, she can choose to marry, help him and so acquire a portion in fulfilling this *mitzva*. But she herself is not halakhically *commanded* [*metzuve*] to marry and procreate. She would only actually have a share in this *mitzva* if she decides to do so in practice. Similarly, assisting her husband and son in the study of Torah is also a *voluntary* action on her part. If she so desires, she *can* in this way participate in the *mitzva of talmud Torah* as "one who is commanded and fulfills" but she has no obligation to do so.

And *that* is why R. Schneur Zalman does *not* cite this as an additional reason for a woman's saying the blessing for Torah study. For a woman has no obligation to do so. If she did voluntarily assist them and connected to Torah study that way, her blessing over the Torah could fall in the category of the *optional* blessings women are allowed to make over *mitzvot* from which are exempt, but choose to perform. And one could not use that as a basis for why all women should be *obligated* to make the blessing over Torah study.

Now we can finally explain R. Schneur Zalman's precise wording and logical organization of his "Laws of *Torah Study*." The order was:

1)   "A woman is not in/does not have the *mitzva* of *talmud Torah*."
2)   "Nevertheless, if she assists her son or her husband personally or materially to engage in Torah study, she divides the reward with them, and her reward is great since they are commanded and accomplish it through her."
3)   "In any case, women are also obligated to learn the laws that pertain to them and to know them."

R. Schneerson had asked at the very beginning of his analysis, why the order of #3 and #2 was not reversed, since a woman's obligation to learn all the laws that pertain to her seems more universally applicable. We have now also seen that a woman's learning also acquires its own independent identity and precious value as Torah study per se; it is not just a preparation to perform *mitzvot*. But though she connects to Torah study that way, she does not *directly* connect to the *mitzva of Torah study*; instead the connection ultimately stems from her practical *mitzvot*. And *that* is why the order is not reversed—for the order goes according to her connection to the *mitzva of talmud Torah* in the category "one who is commanded and does." Yet though she is not "in the *mitzva* of *talmud Torah*," she still *can* connect to that very *mitzva of talmud Torah* and all parts of Torah as "one who is commanded and does" and divides the reward, through reason #2 assisting her husband or son in their learning.

So in the end, R. Schneerson has analyzed the text to imply that women can have it both ways: (1) independent Torah study of the same spiritual quality and level as men, and (2) reward for Torah study as "one who is commanded and does." We have come a long way from the initial surface understanding of the Gemara's statement "you shall teach your sons and not your daughters."

The Inner Meaning of *Talmud Torah*

In the concluding paragraphs of R. Schneerson's original text, he placed his halakhic analysis in the broader framework of what he calls *pnimiyut ha'inyan*, the "inner meaning." By this, he means chassidic philosophy's understanding of the ultimate spiritual and theological goals and effects of Torah study. Ultimately, for R. Schneerson, one cannot separate the various parts of the Torah—all are part of *Torah achat* "One Torah." His methodology, however, assumes that each part of Torah has its own separate principles of interpretation, its own rules. One does not confuse these realms with one another, nor apply the analytical principles of one to the other (for example, the rules of midrashic interpretation to the rules of halakhic reasoning, or the principles for interpreting Maimonides with those for *chassidut*). One first must exhaust the analysis of a given part of the Torah on its own terms, which he has done here so far for Halakha. Only afterwards, does he then show the unity of the parts and how each reflects the other.

Moreover, I would add, that Halakha cannot and should not be discussed without reference to these ultimate inner meanings. For "Halakha," in the end, is meant to be the "path" on which we walk in this life; the word itself is derived from the Hebrew verb *halakh*, "to walk." Without the broader context, halakhic discourse might seem almost "too close" to the ground on which we are trying to walk. But when seen in context, it is indeed what enables us to move gracefully across the complicated and confusing terrain of this difficult world. So what, in the end, is this entire intricate analysis of the *mitzva* of *talmud Torah* for women all about on an "inner spiritual level"? R. Schneerson interprets as follows:

> God and Israel are often metaphorically called "husband and wife" in the midrashic and prophetic literature (the entire biblical book, the Songs of Songs is based on the metaphor of God and Israel as a pair of lovers). The ultimate purpose of the creation in the command given to the first man and woman, Adam and Eve, is to "fill the earth and conquer it" (Genesis 1:28). The Hebrew word for "world" *olam*, is associated with the word *helem*, "concealment." In

other words, the world is, by definition, a place where God is concealed. To fill and conquer the "earth" means then, on a deeper level, to draw down into nature, the highest divine light, which can penetrate this concealment, and illuminate it.[14]

The classical interpretation of the word "conquer" in the Talmud (*Yevamot* 25b) is that "it is the way of the man to conquer, not the way of the woman" (and the *mitzva* or procreation falls only upon the man). R. Schneerson, however, now reads this metaphorically to mean that the infinite, higher power of God ("the man") is needed to accomplish this transformative task ("conquer") because finite creatures cannot change and elevate the world solely by their own natural powers; they need the power of a light higher than nature— and that is given to them through the Torah. For the Torah, as a supernal divine light, remains higher than the world even after it "descends" into the world.

That is the deeper meaning of the verse: "wisdom is better than pearls (*peninim*) and all things that are desired do not compare to it" (Proverbs 8:11). The rabbis have said that this "wisdom" refers to Torah, to which nothing can compare, even "the things of Heaven" (*Moed Katan* 9). "Things of Heaven" refers to the *mitzvot*, which are holiness enclothed in physical objects and actions, i.e., the leather straps of *tefillin*, the parchment and ink of a *mezuza*, the giving of charity with coins, even the verbal articulation of Torah study. But, concludes R. Schneerson, even after the Torah is "enclothed" in physicality, it still transcends it, as in the famous verse: "Is not my word like fire" (Jeremiah 23:29; *Berakhot* 22a). Torah is the category of "Heaven" itself. And through study of Torah, the Jews unite with Torah and so become the "masters of the world," i.e., able to bring this divine light into nature and transform the world.

Underlying R. Schneerson's reference to this union with Torah is the classical Chabad-chassidic understanding of the meaning of Torah study. Although Chabad literature is full of discussions of this subject, the basic source is R. Schneur Zalman's famous spiritual-theological guidebook, the *Tanya*, chapter five. The key idea put forth there is that when one grasps a concept intellectually, one "encompasses" it; the concept in turn is "encompassed by,

---

[14] *Likkutei Sichot*, 14:43.

enveloped, enclothed in" one's intellect; and at the same time one's mind is also "enclothed" in the concept. When one studies and grasps any Halakha in Torah, which is "the wisdom and will of God," the same union occurs. Writes R. Schneur Zalman in that chapter:

> One has thus comprehended, grasped, and encompassed with one's intellect, the will and wisdom of the Holy One, blessed be He, whom no thought can grasp, nor His will or wisdom, except when they are clothed in the *halakhot* that have been set out for us. At the same time, one's intellect is also enclothed in them. *This is a wonderful union (yichud nifla) to which no other union can compare, and to which there is no parallel at all in the material world—to become one and united from every side and angle.* [italics added]

And this, adds R. Schneur Zalman, defines the infinitely great superiority of the commandment to know and comprehend the Torah (*yedi'at haTorah*) over all the *mitzvot* involving action, "even the *mitzva* to study the Torah which is fulfilled by speech." In all these *mitzvot* of action or speech, one is encompassed by the divine light; with knowledge of the Torah, however, one encompasses within oneself the wisdom of God—to the extent that one grasps as much as one is able to of the knowledge of Torah, each according to their intellect and capacities. This knowledge is absorbed within, as the "bread and food" of the soul, which like physical nourishment, becomes transformed into one's very self.

R. Schneerson concludes his essay by saying that it is this union of the Jews with Torah via their study that gives them the power to change the nature of world, transform, and elevate ("to conquer") it. And thus *Benei Yisra'el* as the "woman" who "assists" her "husband" (God) in this work and this "*mitzva*"—becomes a "partner with God" (*Shabbat* 119b) in fulfilling the purpose of creation.

There are two final critical points here: First, R. Schneerson has once again taken a classical interpretation which, on the surface, seems to relegate "the woman" to a secondary role ("the way of the man is to conquer") and subtly re-read it so that "woman," (now signifying the service and strength of the entire Jewish people in their intimate relation with God), shares the position of the "man" in "conquering the world." This is the chassidic understanding of his previous halakhic analysis of the nature of woman's participation in and reward for helping a man in his *mitzva* of procreation.

Second, regardless of the halakhic channel through which one reaches the essence of Torah study, (be it through the man's direct *mitzva* of *talmud Torah* or the woman's study of her necessary *mitzvot*), the highest level is union with God through knowledge of Torah, a level higher even than the level of "*mitzva.*" *It is not a question of quantification, but the transformative connection to the very essence of talmud Torah.* A woman's study involves this same "wonderful union (*yichud nifla*)." *And this, I would emphasize, ought to be the ultimate center of all our contemporary discussions of women's (and men's) Torah study, whether one is able to study only a few verses of the Bible a day, or master an entire tractate of Talmud.*

What I find striking about the path R. Schneerson has taken us on is his reading of these texts to affirm the deep connection of women to the essence of *talmud Torah*, and the assertion of their constant halakhic obligation to engage in it. I mentioned at the beginning that his conclusions are reached without recourse to historical, psychological, or sociological explanations. His argument so far has not been based on any assumptions about "women's nature" or the quality of women's minds, or educational needs of the present time in the face of feminist challenges, but on the use of acute logic. On the one hand, I find this an affirmation of the integrity of the halakhic process itself. Other halakhic commentators indeed have analyzed these texts differently. One needs to decide, finally, whose logic is most compelling. But logic itself is also compelled by and compels other considerations, is part of a larger worldview and understanding of human nature, history, and theology. So we need now to ask what are the historical, psychological, sociological and cultural implications of this reading?

Implications—Philosophical and Cultural

This radical understanding of women's relation to Torah study also needs to find expression in the actual lives of women, the way they are taught, the way they perceive their relation to Torah, the way men perceive women's relation to Torah study, and the life of their communities. R. Schneerson spoke about these issues in a non-halakhic framework in an extensive talk on the role of women in Jewish education given in 1990, on the holiday of Lag Ba'omer. In this talk, he refers again to the basic talmudic and halakhic sources about women's Torah study, but in a predominantly sociological, theological, and cultural context. He draws out the practical implications, exhorts women to increase their study and teaching, and asks for the community at large to support this endeavor.[15] What is said subtly in the framework of technical halakhic analysis is proclaimed loudly in a different rhetorical situation.

A Woman's Involvement in the Education of Her Family: Enabler as Participant

Based on our first source from the Talmud (*Kiddushin* 29a), the Halakha specifies the father as the one upon whom is incumbent the *mitzva*, the formal legal obligation, to teach his children Torah. In actual practice, R. Schneerson notes, it is the mother who to a large degree, directs and guides the education and behavior of the children; he then proceeds to re-read in an innovative way, the other classical source in *Sota* (21a) about women's acquiring merit through assisting their husband's and son's learning.

At first glance, the woman's role in these sources seems quite passive; the Gemara in *Berakhot* (17a) describes it as "bringing their sons to study Torah in school, sending their husbands to study in the *beit midrash* and waiting for them until they return home." According to *Rashi*, the classic and most famous talmudic commentator (12th c.), this also means women giving their husbands permission to study in another city. On the same description in the source in *Sota* (21a), *Rashi* comments that "she does not engage in study; she takes pains that her children and husband study..."

R. Schneerson expands the definition of assistance and "taking pains" to include the *many different ways* in which women encourage and strengthen their children's study—among which are a woman's interest and involvement in the *learning of* her children (from primary school to yeshiva). Learning "of the children" becomes "learning with the children." For example, when she inquires about and asks them to review their lessons for her, she engages in a kind of learning *with* them. And, he adds, her mode of learning is often different—having more warmth and feeling than that of the father who tends more to "examine" the children. That feminine style he defines as adding a special "liveliness and enthusiasm," and as the type of education most needed and proven most successful in our generation—one emanating from "soft

---

[15] *Likkutei Sichot, Parshat Emor, Erev Lag ba'Omer*, 5750 (1990), "On the Obligation of Jewish Women in Education and Study of Torah," 171–75.

language" and a feeling of closeness and love rather than a hierarchical, more confrontational style.

There is also a reciprocal effect: through a woman's learning with her children, she increases *her own* study, including the parts of Torah that that she is not halakhically obligated to learn. As we saw before, she also receives a reward for that type of optional study as well, and is permitted to make the blessing of the Torah over it. But even the material she is obligated to learn, the laws necessary and relevant to her, in reality comprise such an abundance of material R. Schneerson adds, that "Would that all men were expert in all of this material women are obligated to learn."[16] In a footnote, he adds: "Since we are closer and closer to the time of final Redemption, and as Maimonides says, one must await the coming of the Messiah every day, also many of the laws of the Temple Sacrifices, etc." Also essential for her are *pnimiyut haTorah*, i.e., chassidic philosophy, and its explanations of the meaning of faith, love, awe, and the Unity of God, for women, too, are commanded "to know the God of your fathers and serve him with a complete heart." In sum, this reading of the sources has subtly redefined women's role from passive observer to active participant and model pedagogue.

Re-reading *Tiflut*

Yet what about the rest of the text in *Sota* (21a), R. Eliezer's famous opinion that the majority of women's minds are not disposed to Torah study, and that to teach them is to teach them *tiflut*. Here R. Schneerson's rejoinder is historical: in Jewish history there were many righteous woman who were expert and learned in Oral Torah from the time of *tannaim* on through succeeding generations. Many of these women debated matters of Halakha with and also edited the books of their scholarly husbands. As R. Yosef Yitzchak Schneerson (1880–1950), R. Schneerson's father-in-law and immediate predecessor as the head of the Chabad movement reports in his memoirs, the women in R. Schneur Zalman's own family were very learned, and R. Yosef Yitzchak himself educated his daughters in that manner.[17] In the

---

[16] See also n4 above.

[17] *Iggerot Kodesh* of R. Yosef Yitzchak Schneersohn (*RaYaTZ*) Vol 5, p. 336; *Sefer Zichronot*, Vol 2, ch. 80. R. Schneerson's wife was one of the daughters of R. Yosef

recent generations, women have been able to made great intellectual advances, and the generalization that "most women's minds are not disposed to Torah study" no longer applies. It is now permissible not only to teach the select few fit for advanced study, but all Jewish women.[18]

As to the curriculum: in addition to learning their practical *mitzvot*, women are not only *permitted* to study Oral Torah, but they *must* do so, for they are also now exposed to many external kinds of study and influence. Their curriculum should not just consist of digests of the laws but also include the reasons for the laws, and the intellectual debates surrounding them. Interestingly, R. Schneerson does not make any distinction between the forms of women and men's intellectual pleasure: "For the nature of a person, male or female, is to delight in and enjoy analytical study more; and through that form of study women develop their talents and abilities (*armumiyut*—cleverness) in the spirit of the holiness of Torah." This last comment is also a creative re-reading of *Rashi*'s interpretation of R. Eliezer's use of the word *tiflut* in the context of the discussion of the merits women can acquire to suspend the punishment of the bitter waters in the case of suspected adultery. *Tiflut, Rashi* says, means *armumiyut*, i.e., "craftiness, cleverness, cunning." That is, if a

---

Yitzchak. In Vol. 4 of *Iggerot Kodesh*, there is an interesting letter from R. Yosef Yitzchak to Chaya Sima Michaelover, a young woman in the Chabad *Achot haTemimim* group in Riga around 1938. In answer to her query on her spiritual situation, he gives a long excursus on the importance and methods of intense, analytical Torah study. I thank R. Naftali Loewenthal for this reference.

[18] There is a much earlier halakhic source for the development of this view. See the *Prisha* (R. Yehoshua Falk, 17th c.) on the *Tur, Yore De'a* 246 [115] who wrote that if a woman taught herself and studies properly she is no longer included in the category of "most women whose minds are not adapted to be taught. There would then be no prohibition on teaching her. "

For the further development of this view by others in the modern period, and for an exhaustive review of the entire halakhic history of woman and Talmud Torah, see R. Moshe Weinberger, "Teaching Torah to Women" in the *Journal of Halacha and Contemporary Society* 9 (Spring, 1985): 19–52. See also Shoshana Zolty, "*And All Your Children Shall Be Learned*": *Women and the Study of Torah in Jewish Law and History* (NJ: Aronson, 1993). For an excellent anthology in Hebrew of all the talmudic and halakhic sources, and *she'elot uteshuvot* on the topic, see the collection edited by R. Chanan Schlesinger, *Lelo Nechama* (in memory of Nechama Leibowitz z"tzl), published in 1997 by Nishmat, the Jerusalem Center for Advanced Torah Study for Women. I am also grateful to R. Schlesinger who was one of my own Talmud teachers, for his encouragement and support of women's study of Talmud.

woman is taught Oral Torah with all its forms of intricate logic and dialectic she will acquire the "cunning" to conduct immoral affairs without discovery. But R. Schneerson now reinterprets this word to mean the opposite: that by learning Torah women instead will advance in holiness; he adds the well known saying from *Berakhot* (17a): "A person should always be clever (ערום) [i.e., deliberate] in the awe of God."[19] In sum, women should be taught not just the *halakhot* practically relevant to them, but other parts of Torah—and in an ever expanding way. An additional benefit is that a woman can even further assist her husband and children's learning by her own intellectual participation.

These are the general guidelines he gave, but beyond that he did not seek to impose any fixed curriculum, or mandate for any and every school what women should be taught. He left it to each community to create a curriculum commensurate with the needs and character of its students. One could say that he set a goal and a vision, and left it to those responsible for each school to freely realize it using their own intelligence and talents. But at the end of the talk, he gives a very strong impetus for such action.

Theological Paradoxes: The Lowest and the Highest
From Sinai to the Final Redemption

This conclusion moves beyond the historical, psychological, and sociological realms to the metaphysical and messianic. Why is it, he asks, that specifically in these later generations this increase in Torah learning for women has occurred? There is a dual reason: on the one hand, theologically, there is the traditional idea that each generation further from Sinai is "lower" and so there is an increasingly greater need to bolster it. But even if we would say that the permission and need for later generations to study Oral Torah is due to their lower status, the result, says R. Schneerson, has been a great good, an increase

---

[19] Ibid., 175. See also the transcript of the meeting between R. Schneerson and the Belzer Rebbe (especially pages 7–11) in which the same issue is discussed, and R. Schneerson again maintains women should study Oral Torah and Talmud—that NOT to teach them in an advanced way is to "trivialize" their Torah and teach them *tiflut* (the other way *tiflut* had been interpreted by Maimonides as triviality). Also, see nn3 and 5 above.

in Torah study; and this is one of the *"positive innovations* of the later generations."[20]

If we look at the other side of the coin, each generation further away from Sinai is also closer to the final Redemption and Messianic Era. We could also then say that the reason we have merited the increase in Torah study for women in these latter generations is precisely because of that proximity. It is part of the preparation for—and already a taste of—redemption. A defining characteristic of that era is a great increase in knowledge and wisdom; and we now already have a "taste" of it, just as there is a Halakha that before Shabbat one is to taste each of the special dishes to be enjoyed at the Shabbat meal.[21]

But there is an even deeper connection of women to the Messianic era in the kabbalistic and chassidic understanding of the role of the feminine in the Era of Redemption and the World to Come: then all the "feminine" aspects of the world will rise to the highest stature, emerge from their concealment and diminution in the unredeemed world.[22] And that is the deeper reason, adds R. Schneerson, that the innovations and increase in Torah study of recent generations connects to and is emphasized more in relation to women. The effect of their study is also great: as the Talmud famously says (*Sota* 11b), "in the merit of the righteous women of that generation were the Jews redeemed from Egypt" and so he concludes, should it also be for us: in the merit of the

---

[20] Ibid., 174.

[21] See the discourse of R. Schneerson on the nature of chassidic philosophy and its innovations entitled *Inyana shel Torat haChassidut* (and the appendix printed there, a discourse given on the Last Day of Pesach, 1970) on the relation of the timing of revealing new insights and aspects of Torah. This latter discourse was given the same year and just a few months before the analysis of women's obligaton in Torah study. It is translated into English in the volume, *On the Essence of Chassidus* (Brooklyn: Kehot Pub. Soc., 1978).

[22] That is the deeper meaning of the famous verse from Proverbs (12:4) "A woman of valor is the crown of her husband" and from Jeremiah (31:21) "the woman will encircle the man." The crown, symbolizing the highest kabbalistic *sefira*, or divine attribute of *"keter,"* sits on top of and encircles the head. Similarly, the woman encircling the man signifies the highest level of divine revelation, in the mode of a *circle* (*makkif*). In a circle, all points are also equidistant from the center, rather than the hierarchical structure of a line. A circle also symbolizes what encompasses and can't be contained and delimited. There are hints to this in the wedding ceremony where the bride indeed encircles the groom, and in the language of the wedding blessings. See further the chassidic discourse of R. Schneur Zalman in his *Torah Ohr*, end of *parshat Vayigash*.

righteous women of our generation, may the full and complete redemption come.

I conclude with some personal remarks: As I was about to finish this essay, a building contractor wearing a *kippa*, and kissing the *mezuza* at the entrance of my Jerusalem apartment, entered to give an estimate for a job. He saw an Aramaic dictionary on a table and asked what it was for. I replied that I had been doing research for an article on the *mitzva* of *talmud Torah* for women. Jerusalem repairman are never shy about offering their opinions on Torah. "Ah," he smiled, "but there isn't any!" "Ah," I answered, "you would be surprised. Yes, there is; it's not so simple." I hope that this essay will ultimately have some effect in changing this popular attitude. I hope, too, that I have reinforced the faith of those who believe in the halakhic system, and somewhat illumined those less convinced—made them aware of its depth and creative flexibility.

The greatest advances women can make in all areas of contemporary Jewish life will come, I believe, first and foremost through *derekh halimud*, the way of serious learning—through their deeply engaging and mastering the wellsprings of all parts of Torah. Any progressive contemporary theology and politics for Jewish women must, finally, rest on a vision of the unity of Torah—on faith in and engagement with all its facets, Halakha, Kabbalah, philosophy, Midrash, Bible, Talmud. In *partnership* with God, we renew the revelation of the Torah daily, and labor to repair and redeem the world. We take delight in God's Torah... and God takes delight in ours.[23]

---

[23] See the famous midrashim describing God's *shashua* with the Torah; Midrash *Tehillim* 90:4 interpreting the line from Proverbs 8:30 "then I was before Him as a nursling, delighting (*shashuim*) every day, playing before him always"; *Bereishit Rabba*, 88:2; *Tanchuma* "*Vayeshev*" 4; Zohar 2:151a. And the chassidic-kabbalistic commentary on the meaning of this pleasure by R. Schneur Zalman in his *Likkutei Torah*, *Bamidbar* 18:3. Thus too, his addition of the word *shashua* in his formulation of the blessing over the Torah.

The Female Voice of Kaddish

Rochelle L. Millen

While women reciting the mourner's kaddish has rarely been a widespread custom, responsa literature, historical sources, and contemporary testimony point to it as a practice that has always been part of the communal behavior of the Jewish community. From seventeenth century Amsterdam to the post-Shoah period, women would say kaddish during *shiva* at home and frequently attend daily services to express their grief and pay proper tribute to a loved one through the public recitation of kaddish. Saying kaddish at the grave, during the funeral, was also a customary practice among devout women in certain communities.

When Rav Menachem Mendel Auerbach, a member of the *beit din* of Boston, died in 1952, his widow, Esther, said kaddish for her husband, although there were sons to do so. Mrs. Auerbach, scion of a rabbinical family from Kovno, recited kaddish in her home during the *shiva*, as well as for the remainder of the required thirty days in shul. She attended the services of the Bostoner Rebbe, then located in Dorchester, every day.[1]

This acceptance of the presence of Mrs. Auerbach at daily *minyan* stands in sharp contrast to testimonies about the responses of some rabbis and other members of the male Jewish community as evidenced in more recent decades. When the father of a longtime member of a Young Israel congregation in the New York area died, she recited kaddish during *shiva* and came to shul three times a day for the next three weeks. At the conclusion of the thirty days, she continued to come to recite kaddish, intending to do so for the required eleven months. To her surprise, she was confronted by her rabbi who said, "I've been very nice until now. We have to have a meeting about this." The "meeting" he requested became the occasion for him to yell at the woman, saying "there are bigger *tzedkaniyot* [righteous women] than you and they stay home and learn

---

[1] Related to me in December, 1997, by Ada Greenwald Jacobowitz in the presence of her mother, aged 93, Dorothy Auerbach Greenwald. They are, respectively, the granddaughter and daughter of Rav Auerbach.

Chumash." This brusque, insensitive, statement of disapproval notwithstanding, the woman correctly did not regard the rabbi's statement as a *pesak*, and simply continued coming, despite the hostile ambiance created by his harsh words. This occurred in 1979.[2]

These two incidents serve as paradigms, it seems to me, of the diverse attitudes evidenced in Halakha. Clearly, there are groups on the religious right where perhaps the very idea of a woman reciting kaddish is anathema, as there are certain groups in which it is considered inappropriate for a woman even to drive a car. This article is not about those groups within Judaism where women may be so restricted, although such groups are surely influenced by the more conservative responsa. Rather, the aim of this essay is to trace the development of the responsa literature regarding women and kaddish, analyzing the grounds and lines of argumentation.[3] I am especially interested in the divergent directions manifested in the halakhic literature of the last decade in response to this issue. The increasingly restrictive attitudes, often coupled with attacks on those legal authorities who arrive at more lenient conclusions, testify in my view to an underlying fear of the influences of feminism upon halakhic Judaism. The tension expressed in the responsa literature strongly resembles that which appeared in regard to the Bat Mitzvah controversy several decades ago.[4] That which was once a point of contention and dispute within the halakhic community—should a twelve year old girl celebrate her Bat Mitzvah in any fashion—is now *de rigeur*, even within many chassidic communities.

The life-cycle events, together with Shabbat and the *chagim*, form the bases from which Jewish identity and community emanate. Surely, then, the discussion of women as mourners, women confronting the finality of the death of a loved one, needs careful examination and analysis.

While women, according to Jewish law, are duty-bound in all the *halakhot* of *avelut*, or mourning, such as the rending of one's garment, the meal of

---

[2] The woman to whom this incident occurred prefers to remain anonymous.

[3] This article is an updated and expanded version of my "Women and Kaddish: Reflections on Responsa," *Modern Judaism* 10 (1990): 191–203.

[4] R. Moshe Feinstein, IM, OC 1:104, 2:97, 4:36, and 2:30; R. Ovadia Yosef, *Yechave Daat* 2:29 and *Yabia Omer* 6:29; R. Yechiel Weinberg, *Sredi Esh* 3:93. See analyses of Norma Baumel Joseph and Erica Brown in this volume.

condolence, the prohibitions of bathing or sexual intimacy during *shiva*, the one act often discouraged is the public declaration of the doxology of kaddish.

The earliest known responsum in which the issue of women and kaddish is discussed appears in the late seventeenth century work of R. Yair Bachrach, known as the *Chavot Yair*. Based on a particular set of circumstances in Amsterdam, R. Bachrach's responsum became known simply as "the Amsterdam case." It is referred to in nearly all subsequent discussions of women and kaddish. While rabbinic authorities agreed that the answer given in the Amsterdam case was the right one for that specific situation, other related questions arose in other cases. As we shall see, the responsa literature manifests two trends: one that restricts the premises and conclusion of the Amsterdam case, and a second one that expands upon them.

Kaddish has come to serve not only as a memorial prayer, but also as a cathartic connection to the community in the working through of grief. The question is: did the oft-times unavailability of kaddish to women have to do with the general exclusion of women from participation in public prayer, or were women able to—and did they in fact—recite kaddish? In examining the halakhic parameters of this query, theological, philosophical, and sociological factors come into play. As in all decision-making processes, the personality of those in positions of leadership also plays a crucial role. When I said kaddish for my mother, may her memory be blessed, I had to fight to have the lights turned on in the women's section. The rabbi refused to have the *tzedaka* box passed to me, proclaiming this action "immodest" and no member of the *minyan* spoke to me, certainly not words of comfort. While reciting kaddish for my father, may his memory be blessed, I was warmly welcomed; *mishnayot* were regularly learned in my father's memory immediately following davening. Regularly ensconced in the midst of a community which recognized my grief, its frozen glaze gradually became less brittle. Both experiences occurred in Young Israel synagogues in the 1980s. In each case, the rabbi set the tone. Thus, while the nuances of Halakha as expressed in its underlying philosophy and theology need to be scrutinized, an important aspect of the sociological factor would also include an examination of the positions of the religious leadership. We need to investigate the origin of kaddish in order to clarify these issues.

The kaddish prayer, which has four forms, was originally not part of the synagogue service. It had no connection to the prayer service for the dead. The

Talmud *Sota* (49a) notes that it was the concluding prayer with which the teacher or preacher indicated the end of his public discourse; it was formulated in Aramaic, as was the discourse itself. The first reference to kaddish as part of the synagogue service—indeed the first instance in which this doxology is termed kaddish—is in the tractate *Soferim* (16:12, 19:1, 21:6). This tractate, written in the sixth century after the closing of the Talmudic canon, also records the use of kaddish at funerals, the first reference we have to what seems to have become accepted custom. Addressed to all assembled, it was spoken in the Babylonian vernacular, i.e., Aramaic. A further association of kaddish with the dead noted in *Soferim* is that it was recited at the end of the seven day period of mourning as part of a concluding ceremony, of which learning and expounding texts was a part.

Originally the recitation of kaddish at the end of *shiva*, or the seven days, was reserved for those of scholarly accomplishment. Later, however, in order not to put anyone to shame, it became the accepted practice for everyone. An additional reference in *Soferim* to the connection between kaddish and mourning is given in 19:12. The text reads, "The reader after *musaf* goes behind the synagogue door, or in front of the synagogue where he finds the mourners and their relatives. He comforts them with the *berakha*[5] and then he recites the kaddish." During these centuries the kaddish was understood to be and recited as a doxology and a justification of God's ways.

In a geonic source, however, the *Ottiyot de Rabbi Akiva*, a new purpose is ascribed to kaddish: it is said to have the power of redeeming the dead from the sufferings of Gehenna.[6] Two references are given. In one, Akiva is said to meet a spirit in the guise of a man carrying wood. The wood, the man relates, is for the fire in which he is burned daily as punishment for his mistreatment of the poor. He would be released from this suffering, however, if he had a son to recite *barekhu*[7] and kaddish before a congregation that would respond with the

---

[5] This refers to the words of comfort extended to the mourners.

[6] This term originally referred to the Valley of Ben-Hinnom, south of the walls of Jerusalem.

During the monarchy, the valley was the site of the cult of Moloch, where children were burned. It then came to refer to the place of torment and punishment reserved for the wicked after death.

[7] The recitation in the prayer service of *barekhu*, or "Bless the Lord who is blessed,"

praise of God's name. Upon discovering that the man had neglected his son, Akiva cares for and studies with the young man until one day the son stands before a congregation, recites *barekhu* and kaddish, and releases his father from Gehenna. The idea that a son, by virtue of his piety, may exert a redeeming influence on behalf of a parent who has died is mentioned in other sources as well, contemporaneous with or later than the *Ottiyot de Rabbi Akiva*. An example is in the collection of midrashim known as *Tanna debe Eliyahu Zuta*, where R. Yochanan ben Zakkai, not R. Akiva, is the central figure.[8]

Mishnaic and talmudic sources state that the torture of Gehenna lasted twelve months,[9] hence originally kaddish was recited for that length of time. Later, however, it was deemed inappropriate for progeny to suppose the soul of a parent in Gehenna; the obligatory period of time for the recitation of kaddish was then reduced to eleven months. The practice of regular recitation of the kaddish by mourners seems to have become firmly established during the early thirteenth century, in response to the severe persecutions in Germany resulting from the Crusades. Kaddish is also recited on the *yahrtzeit*, or anniversary of death.

Once kaddish entered into the halakhic structure as a memorial prayer for the dead, how were women affected? First, as part of the liturgy requiring a *minyan*, or ten men, in order to be said, women were excluded as non-members of the male representative group. Second, in Henrietta Szold's famous response,[10] the recitation of kaddish, it is implied, is a *mitzvat ase shehazman graman*, a positive time-specified commandment—albeit one of

---

requires a *minyan*, or the presence of ten men, who then respond, "Blessed be the Lord who is blessed forever and ever" (Birnbaum translation). The ten men, in Jewish law, constitute a congregation.

[8] See also, however, *Sanhedrin* 104a. "A son confers privileges on his father, but a father confers no privilege on a son" (Soncino translation).

[9] See Mishna *Eduyot* 2:10; *Rosh haShana* 17a.

[10] "I believe that the elimination of women from such duties (reciting kaddish) was never by our law and custom—women were freed from positive duties when they could not perform them, but not when they could. It was never intended that... their performance of them should not be considered as valuable and valid as when one of the male sex performed them. And of the kaddish, I feel this is particularly true." Baum, Hyman and Michel, *The Jewish Woman in America* (NY, 1975) 45.

rabbinic origin—which, according to mishnaic sources, women are excused from performing.[11] Significantly, however, in all the responsa literature on kaddish, *mitzvat ase shehazman graman* is never cited as a reason for women's non-obligation to say kaddish. However, since kaddish became closely allied with public prayer, perhaps the association was implicit rather than explicit. Or perhaps kaddish was not regarded at all as a *mitzva derabanan*, a rabbinic enactment, but rather as a *minhag*, a custom, which gained the strength of social expectation, an expectation which did not devolve upon women.

Before examining some of the responsa literature, it is important to note the following. First, the Midrash cited earlier regarding R. Akiva speaks about son and father. As in many sources, the male—and male relationships—are considered paradigmatic; *ben*, being both the neuter and masculine in Hebrew, is also always translated as "son" rather than "child" or "offspring." The problems caused by language are known; they are complex, profound and difficult, and affect the innermost perceptions of ourselves, and ourselves in relation to others—especially others of the opposite sex. In an intricate system of jurisprudence such as that of Jewish law, the repercussions—need it be said?—are serious indeed. Critical feminist thinkers from Simone de Beauvoir to Judith Plaskow have addressed the issue. The Midrash mentions only *ben*, in every translation and interpretation understood as "son," and *av*, as "father." The other six relatives for whom one would also be required to say kaddish are not enumerated (i.e., mother, spouse, brother, sister, son, daughter). But there is a saving specification here. If son and father are paradigmatic, then clearly others are not excluded, but merely not mentioned. That is, as a son would say kaddish for a mother, a daughter might say kaddish for a father *or* a mother. While this is true theoretically, it should be noted that in eastern European culture a son was often called "my little kaddish" or "*kaddishle*," a name once applied by my late father, born in Poland, to my son, then seven years old. It is also interesting to note that the geonic and early post-geonic discussions of kaddish deal almost exclusively with the child (or son) saying kaddish for a parent, an eleven month proposition. But what about the relatives for whom traditional mourning takes place? For them—sibling or spouse, for instance—kaddish is said only for thirty days. Is there any relationship between the thirty-day recitation and release from Gehenna? No source that I know of

---

[11] *Kiddushin* 34a.

makes this connection. The parent-child relationship here receives decided emphasis.

Second, once kaddish became an established part of the observance of mourning, it came to serve important psychological functions. It compels the mourner to reaffirm connection with the community through daily prayer precisely when despair and alienation are most profound. As part of the community, the mourner testifies to his/her continuation within the tradition of which the deceased was a part. This is in accordance with the talmudic dictum in *Sanhedrin* 104a: "A child can endow a parent."[12] And in its most abstract sense, kaddish serves as a statement of the unknowability, though justification of God's ways. Kaddish becomes a significant component—a cathartic yet simultaneously self-affirming exercise—of the bereavement process. While the other laws of mourning were clearly designed with a psychological aspect in mind, that kaddish would also serve this purpose seems not to have been the motivation for requiring its recitation; benefit accruing to the soul of the departed—specifically the parent—was the original intent. Yet its psychological effects have long been acknowledged.

A third and last point to keep in mind: after the Holocaust, women all over Europe said kaddish. It was accepted, perhaps even expected and encouraged. So we have behavior that contravenes much of the halakhic literature. The problem seems to be this: women are unilaterally included in all requirements of mourning, of which kaddish is one. It was recognized that saying kaddish is consonant with a woman's identity as mourner, human being, Jew. But kaddish operates within the arena of public prayer from which women were proscribed as participants equal with men. Hence the dilemma. The responsa, as we shall see, straddle the fence, equivocate, seem inconsistent at times and in the end fail, I feel, to state adequately the case for women within the tradition. For even within the bounds of the traditional categories within which woman's status in Jewish law operates, there is much flexibility and adaptability. Unfortunately, while this openness may be used on an individual basis, it rarely appears in the halakhic literature as a precedent for others. As we shall see, the tendency in the responsa literature to restrict the ruling in the Amsterdam case is predominant, although there is also present a trend which expands upon it.

---

[12] See n8 above.

Let us now examine some of the responsa. That only sons said kaddish seems to have been the norm, a practice supported by both sociological and religious factors. However, in the *Chavot Yair*, R. Yair Bachrach, writing in the late seventeenth century, brings an important precedent. He says:

> An unusual and well-known event occurred in Amsterdam. A man died without a son, and before his death commanded that ten should study in his home every day for twelve months, and after the learning his daughter should say kaddish. And the scholars and lay officials of the community did not prevent her from doing so. Even though there is no proof to contradict the matter, being that a woman is also commanded in *kiddush HaShem*, and even though there is a quorum (*minyan*) of males called *bnei Yisrael*, and even though the incident of R. Akiva, which is the source of mourner's kaddish, refers only to a son, it *is* nonetheless logical that a daughter's kaddish is also purposeful, for it comforts the soul of the deceased, since she is also his progeny. However, one must be concerned for the fact that should this become prevalent, it might lead to a general weakening of the customs of our people, which are like Torah itself; then everyone would be erecting his own pulpit according to his own logic and deriding rabbinic enactments, which they would come to scorn.[13]

In the Responsum, R. Bachrach analyzes why the rabbinic authorities and lay officials in Amsterdam permitted the daughter of the man in question to say kaddish, obviously an unusual occurrence. He begins by stating that there is no "proof to contradict the matter," i.e., there are no compelling reasons that would contravene the decision. From a halakhic perspective, he is saying, a woman's saying kaddish is acceptable, permissible, and in the case under discussion, desirable. How is this so, given that the very existence of the responsum demonstrates that saying kaddish was not customary for women? That may be, R. Bachrach asserts, because the source for kaddish, i.e., the incident with R. Akiva, clearly refers, according to him, to a son (he understands *ben* in its masculine, not neuter sense). But there is halakhic precedent that overrides this consideration of *ben* as son only. That is that a woman is commanded in the *mitzva* of *kiddush HaShem*, which in some instances requires the presence of ten men, i.e., a *minyan*. As she can perform the *mitzva*

---

[13] My free translation from Responsum 222, *Responsa of the Chavot Yair* (Jerusalem, 1972).

of *kiddush HaShem* in the presence of ten men, she can likewise say the mourner's kaddish in the presence of ten men.

Kiddush HaShem, or sanctification of God's name, has three aspects in Jewish law. It can refer to martyrdom, to ethical perfection beyond the minimum standards set by rabbinic law, or to liturgical formulations which emphasize sanctifying God's name. This last type of *kiddush HaShem* pertains especially to the two formal prayers of *kedusha*[14] and kaddish. In kaddish, the congregational response of "May God's great name be blessed forever and to all eternity"[15] is considered a *kiddush HaShem*. Since, that is, a woman has an obligation to perform the *mitzva* of *kiddush HaShem* should the opportunity arise, she certainly can say kaddish,[16] which is an essential manifestation of this *mitzva*.

Other observations to be gleaned from this responsum are:

1) Kaddish was said by the woman in the home and not in the synagogue.

2) Despite the efficacy of the daughter's kaddish, and the solace it brings both her and her deceased father, there is caution in the face of the new. What if this change from the established practice leads to other, less palatable, perhaps less legitimate, although valid (according to the Halakha) practices? The custom until the time of the Amsterdam case was obviously that women did not recite kaddish. Despite the halakhic permissibility of women doing so, R. Bachrach discerns the overlap of religious law and social or cultural behavior, and is concerned about a general loosening of, or change within, the dominant modes of religious behavior.

3) The elders of the Amsterdam community consented to the dying man's request in the absence of a son, or sons, to say kaddish. Their decision may otherwise have been different.

---

[14] *Kedusha* is the third blessing of the *Amida* prayer. Known also as *kedushat HaShem*, it is inserted at the beginning of the third benediction when the reader repeats the *Amida* during public worship.

[15] My translation.

[16] Note that R. Bachrach's reasoning goes from "obligation" in *kiddush HaShem* to "can," "may," or "is permitted to" say kaddish and not from "obligation" in *kiddush HaShem* to "is therefore obligated to" say kaddish.

4) The responsum refers to what appears to be an unmarried girl (*na'ara*). Their decision may otherwise have been different in a circumstance involving a married daughter.

5) And lastly, why did the father request that the ten men study in his home and then have his daughter recite kaddish there? Some possibilities are:

a. women usually didn't attend synagogue, certainly not daily services

b. going to and from the synagogue may have been difficult or unusual or dangerous or simply impractical for an unaccompanied single Jewish woman.

c. saying the kaddish in a home after learning would be less controversial than at the prescribed intervals during the daily morning prayers.

d. the structure of the synagogue would not allow the woman to be heard from the women's section.

Whether the reasons were practical or sociological, kaddish at home was requested and accepted. Interestingly, and not surprisingly, this became a precedent in subsequent responsa. An example is that of R. Yaacov Risher, who wrote and published the *Shevut Yaacov*, a halakhic compendium in Lemberg in 1880. He cites the *Chavot Yair* in his decision that women may certainly say kaddish, in the presence of a *minyan*, at home.

The *Be'er Heitev* commentary[17] on the *Shulchan Arukh* cites the *Knesset Yechezkel*,[18] who comes to a similar conclusion. He says; "a daughter doesn't say kaddish at all in the synagogue. But if they [the male community] wish to make a *minyan* for her at home they certainly can." From not choosing the synagogue in the Amsterdam case, women here seem to be excluded from the synagogue, although their right to say kaddish is not questioned.

The *Gesher haChaim*[19] takes what seems to have been based on practical considerations—a woman saying kaddish at home rather than at the syna-gogue—and adds a completely new, and, in my opinion, untenable, dimension. Quoting R. Akiva, he states that the essential function of kaddish is carried out by a son. But a daughter may, of course, say kaddish. If she is under twelve years of age, she may say it in the synagogue; some, however, would prohibit

---

[17] Written by R. Yehuda Ashkenazi of mid-eighteenth century Frankfurt.

[18] Responsa of R. Ezekiel Katzenellenbogen, Hamburg and Altona, 1670–1749.

[19] Responsa of R. Yechiel Aaron Tukachinsky, written in 1947.

her doing so. If, however, she is twelve or over, she is not permitted to say kaddish in the synagogue. In either age group, kaddish may be said at home. The *Gesher haChaim* is adding a sexual element, puberty, where there is no indication that it is relevant.

The late R. Uziel, former Sephardi Chief Rabbi of Israel, states that kaddish is a male obligation only. But his reasoning does not hold up to careful scrutiny. This is what he says:

> Only a son can take his father's place sanctifying God's name in the community. In regard to a daughter, her good deeds work for the elevation of the souls of her parents who have died. But it is not her function to take their place in the community. The proof for this is that she is not part of the *minyan*.[20]

A daughter's good deeds elevate the souls of both mother and father, but she is precluded from taking "their place in the community," even, that is, the mother's place. When a son says kaddish for his mother, then, is *he* taking her place in the community? Is a daughter's not being part of a *minyan* proof that she does not take her mother's place in the community? What has happened here is that the son's recitation of kaddish is being understood not only as a means of elevation of the soul of the parent, but also a continuation of the father's *public* role in prayer. Both daughter and mother, in that case, remain ancillary. R Uziel's attempt to explain what he understands as their peripheral status in regard to kaddish is thus confusing and unconvincing.

The former Chief Rabbi of Tel Aviv-Yaffo, R. Chaim David haLevi, writes an astounding responsa. After discussing when *ben* and *banim* refer to the masculine or the neuter and analyzing some of the earlier decisions in an unorthodox fashion, he renders a decision that a woman is prohibited from reciting kaddish even at the cemetery because it may cause "sinful thoughts to the simple-minded." This is extended to kaddish in the synagogue. She may, however, recite the kaddish at home, in the presence of family members only. "The evil inclination," he concludes, "is present even in a mourner's home."[21] From seventeenth century Amsterdam, where a woman said kaddish at home and not in the synagogue for practical reasons only, we have arrived three

---

[20] R. Uziel, *Mishpetei Uziel*, OC 13.

[21] R. Chaim David haLevi, *Ase Lekha Rav*, vol. 5 (Tel Aviv, 5743/1983) 334–36.

hundred years later at a place where sexual polarity enters the human question of how to structure the grieving process so as to permit equal access and opportunity to all. The *Be'er Heitev, Gesher haChaim, Mishpetei Uziel* and *Ase Lekha Rav* all manifest a restricting of the decision in the Amsterdam case. While they may agree that the outcome in the Amsterdam case was acceptable in the particular circumstances relevant to it, they are dealing with different situations and use the variant details as part of the justification of limiting the original decision. R. Bachrach's fear of change is taken up and projected to a much greater degree than the legal reasoning explaining his judgment.

But such fear of women—or fear of change clothed as such—is absent in a vocal minority of halakhic decisions. Rabbi J.B. Soloveitchik, ruled that a woman, be she even the only woman present, may say kaddish in the synagogue.[22] That a woman may say kaddish with a group of ten or more men, even if she is the only person doing so, is consistent with R. Bachrach's analysis of *kiddush HaShem*. It is interesting that Rabbi Aaron Soloveitchik, in a 1993 publication,[23] argues against the *Chavot Yair* on the grounds of the changing nature of the Jewish community. In positing this argument, Rav Aaron incorporates precisely the thinking of another Chicago rabbi in an earlier era, Rabbi Moshe Leib Blair.[24] Both responsa recognize the alienating quality of some of the *teshuvot* examined above, as well as the possible political repercussions of holding fast to legal abstractions which seem to ignore the fundamental Jewish concept of woman as person created in the image of God. Let us look first at the more recent responsum.

Rav Aaron begins by quoting the *Chavot Yair* and then says:

> It seems now that some Jewish men and women are fighting for the equality of women with men in regard to *aliyot* for women. Since this is the case, if Or-

---

[22] See Joel Wolowelsky's letter-to-the editor in *HaDarom* 57 (5748/1988) 157–58. See also Sara Reuger, "Kaddish from the 'Wrong' Side of the Mehitzah," *On Being a Jewish Feminist*, ed. Susannah Heschel (NY, 1983) 177–81.

[23] R. Aaron Soloveitchik, *Od Yisrael Yosef Beni Chai* (Yeshivat Brisk, 1993) 100, n32.

[24] I am grateful to the late Rabbi Isaac Nadoff of Omaha, Nebraska (formerly of Chicago), for sending me the Blair responsum. Rabbi Blair was born in Dvinsk in 1897 where he received *semikha*. He died in Israel in 1967, having written the responum referred to here around 1950 while living in Chicago (email communication from Aviva Cayam, granddaughter of Rabbi Blair).

thodox rabbis will prevent a woman from reciting kaddish in a place where doing so is a possibility, the influence of Conservative and Reform rabbis will greatly increase. Therefore it is prohibited to prevent a woman [daughter] from saying kaddish.[25]

This responsum acknowledges that the Halakha can—and indeed has—granted to women the right to recite kaddish. It does not deal with the reasons offered in the earlier responsa which rule in the negative, but clearly affirms the positive possibility as being within the realm of Halakha. That halakhic authorities must rule leniently is due to the changing status of women as it has been interpreted in both Conservative and Reform Judaism. The argument seems to be: to prohibit what is permissible—and surely understandable—in the context of mourning rites, hilkhot aveilut, is to invite alienation from the tradition. Gender should not in this case be the grounds for withholding from women the time-honored way in which the state of mourning has been marked in Judaism.[26]

Rabbi Blair's responsum is more detailed than Rav Aaron's. He begins by enumerating three reasons why a woman (he refers specifically to a daughter) should be obligated to say kaddish. First, she is obligated in all the laws of mourning of which kaddish is an integral part. Second, the reasons for saying kaddish—giving solace to the soul of the deceased and redeeming the dead from Gehenna through sanctifying God's name—definitely apply to a woman. Rabbi Blair here uses R. Bachrach's argument of kiddush HaShem to support his stance. And third, kaddish may be considered not only as part of the obligations of mourning, but also within the category of prayer. As such, women are not exempt but are obligated.[27] Then he brings earlier precedents, primary among which is the Amsterdam case. He proceeds to argue against the interpretation of ben as "son" rather than "offspring," and to lament the practice of hiring a man to say kaddish in the absence of male progeny. In both cases he brings strong evidence to make his case.

---

[25] My free translation from R. Aaron Soloveitchik, op. cit.

[26] This notion has also influenced behavior at the graveside. It is no longer uncommon for traditional women to help shovel earth over the coffin once it has been put in place.

[27] Rabbi Blair analyzes the well-known dispute as to whether prayer is of rabbinic or biblical origin and discusses sources in the Mishna and Maimonides' Mishne Torah.

I want to take special note, however, of the next section of Rabbi Blair's responsum. In it he gives an unusual and sharp interpretation of the last part of R. Bachrach's argument in the Amsterdam case. He says: The last words of the *Chavot Yair* require explanation. He is speaking of a case in which the father directed that ten men should learn Torah in his home for twelve months and after the learning [each time] the daughter should say kaddish.

> This is truly erecting one's own pulpit and rescinding the custom of Israel, be-
> cause also in the synagogue only men, and not women, say kaddish after
> learning. But he is not speaking about the kaddish of eleven months that a
> woman says from the women's gallery or even during the time of *shiva* in her
> home when [at least] ten men are praying. On this certainly it is inappropriate
> to say that it "derides rabbinic enactments."[28]

The narrow focus of Rabbi Blair's responsum is to obligate a daughter's recitation of kaddish in the case when there are no sons. He ends a main section of his discussion by quoting Rabbi Yekutiel Greenwald's *Kol Bo Al Avelut*, in which Greenwald inveighs against the practice of hiring a man to say kaddish when there is a surviving son. "Certainly," Rabbi Blair concludes,

> this frivolous action [of hiring a stranger] most decidedly applies to a daughter,
> since she is obligated according to the law, and she is able to come to the syna-
> gogue to say kaddish. Therefore, according to my humble opinion, it is impor-
> tant for all rabbis of our time to explain to a daughter who is mourning a parent
> that since there is no son, it is upon her that the obligation falls to come to
> synagogue to say kaddish and not to hire anyone.[29]

But the broader center of interest is the saying of kaddish by a woman—spouse, daughter, mother or sister—even in cases where she is not the sole mourner. Rabbi Blair summarizes his position in four brief statements. He says:

> It is not my intention to be unduly stringent in regard to the mourning of a
> daughter, but merely to uphold the law that the daughter is obligated to recite

---

[28] My translation from R. Blair's independently printed responsum, "Does a Daughter Have a Duty to Say Kaddish?" Chicago. See n24 above.

[29] *Loc. Cit.* The phrase "twelve months" in the *Chavot Yair* may refer to the practice of saying kaddish for eleven months and one day, i.e., into the twelfth month.

kaddish. On the contrary, in my opinion her obligatory recitation is a leniency, and in the laws of mourning the more lenient view prevails.

Also, if there will not be ten women in the women's section to answer "Amen," this also would not preclude her saying kaddish, since the law (*dine*) is that all those who say kaddish should recite it together in unison; if so, the "Amen" with which the men respond applies as well to her kaddish.

And when it is said that custom (*minhag*) erases law (*halakha*), this is only in the case of a communal enactment (*takanat tzibur*), and we do not find such an enactment regarding the circumstance of a daughter's saying kaddish when there is no son.

I want to emphasize here to the rabbis of our country who oppose this legal decision (*pesak halakha*) that in the time of the Geonim when the custom (*minhag*) to say kaddish began, many sages of Israel, such as Rav Hai Gaon, were opposed. And what do we see now? That the kaddish is included in the general category of mourning, and is as important in mourning as a commandment of biblical origin (*mitzva de'oraita*). The kaddish brings many male Jews to the synagogue and causes them to become more involved in Judaism. This will occur also with female Jews; we would bring them closer to Jewish life and to our holy Torah.[30]

Rabbi Blair is clearly concerned with the possible alienation of women from the tradition.

Women whose attempts to cope with grief and honor their deceased were stymied due to "custom" or halakhic cavil ("if there not be ten women") ought rather to be encouraged to participate in the long-established and accepted Jewish way of mourning, the recitation of kaddish. The identification with the community of Israel at a time of personal loss can only strengthen one's bonds to Judaism.

By citing the case of Rav Hai Gaon, Rabbi Blair indicates that movement, evolution and development are intrinsic to the halakhic process, the nature of which is to apply eternal ideals and principles within specific historical contexts. Rav Hai Gaon's opposition to kaddish did not alter its eventual inclusion as part of mourning. Neither should contemporary opposition to women saying kaddish deter its establishment, if not as halakhic obligation in

---

[30] See n28 above.

the manner Rabbi Blair would prefer, at the very least as strongly encouraged social and religious custom.[31]

Expanding the logic implicit in the Amsterdam case—if a woman can say kaddish at home, it is understood that she most certainly can and should, say kaddish in the synagogue—is supported by another discussion of the issue in an article by Rabbi Yehuda Herzl Henkin. R. Henkin writes:

> Certainly the reciting of kaddish by a woman is not a difficulty from the responsa of the *Shevut Yaacov* and *Knesset Yechezkel*, who wrote that a woman may not recite kaddish at all in the synagogue, *since they wrote only according to their custom*.... [emphasis mine][32]

Rabbi Henkin makes clear reference to social custom as a significant factor in determining the acceptability or discouraging of behavior that is permissible, but may not, in certain historical periods, have been widespread. Rabbi Henkin's discussion is of especial note because it engendered a rather sharp response in an essay written by R. Reuven Fink[33] While the original *pesak* was

---

[31] See Simcha Fishbane, "'In Any Case There Are No Sinful Thoughts'—The Role and Status of Women in Jewish Law as Expressed in the *Arukh Hashulhan*," *Judaism* 42.4 (Fall, 1993): 492–503. Dr. Tamar Ross, writing in the same journal, seems to make a similar claim as to the workings of the halakhic process. But in her essay, "Can the Demand for Change in the Status of Women be Halakhically Legitimized?" (478–92), Ross recognizes the legitimacy of change only in regard to the individual woman; women *qua* women, i.e., as a group, should not pressure for halakhic change. This is, I believe, quite an extraordinary suggestion, especially when coupled with Ross' claim that the unresolved problem of *agunot* "reflects the continuing tension between the Law as it is, and the world as it is, and not any bias or animosity by male *poskim* against Jewish women" (487). The naivete expressed here was also manifested in Ross' plenary address at the opening of the Second International Conference on Orthodoxy and Feminism, Feb. 15, 1998. Compare the analysis in Zvi Zohar, "Traditional Flexibility and the Modern Strictness: Two Halakhic Positions on Women's Suffrage" *Sephardi and Middle Eastern Jewries*, ed. Harvey E. Goldberg (Indiana University Press, 1996) 119–33 and Nissan Rubin, "Coping with the Value of the *pidyon ha'ben* Payment in Rabbinic Literature—An Example of a Social Change Process" *Jewish History* 10.1 (Spring, 1996): 39–62.

[32] Rabbi Yehuda Herzl Henkin, "The Reciting of Kaddish by a Woman" (Hebrew) *HaDarom* 54 (5745/1985) 34–38, subsequently republished in *Responsa Bnei Banim*, vol. 2, responsum 7. Esp. page 43, paragraph two and n1. This passage is from page 43.

[33] R. Reuven Fink, "The Recital of Kaddish by Women," *Journal of Halacha and Contemporary Society* (Spring, 1996): 23–37. See R. Yehuda Henkin's letter in response, in the *Journal of Halacha* (Fall, 1997): 97–102 and R. Fink's rebuttal of R. Henkin's letter,

written around 1948 by Rabbi Yosef Eliyahu Henkin, the article in *HaDarom*[34] written by Rav Henkin's grandson, Rabbi Yehuda Herzl Henkin, is a clear exposition of the original analysis. In an as yet unpublished volume, R. Yehuda Henkin responds to the criticisms of Rabbi Fink.[35] The positions stated and their rebuttals illustrate well the tug of war within halakhic circles in regard to what seems a minor issue—a woman coming to shul to say kaddish. As we shall see, the sensitivity of Rabbis J.B. Soloveitchik, Aaron Soloveitchik, and Moshe Leib Blair, Yosef Henkin, and Yehuda Henkin is quashed by current opinions, which seem to regard the "freedom" to grieve given to women as a grave threat to the tradition.[36] Rabbi Fink, in fact, ends his analysis by stating:

> It would therefore seem that an attempt to 'improve' or alter our sacred traditions... [is] both pernicious and dangerous.... Tampering with the synagogue's customary practices is clearly a step fraught with great danger.[37]

What are Rabbi Fink's objections? First, when women say kaddish in the *ezrat nashim*, they are not saying it with a *minyan*. As various halakhic sources demonstrably illustrate, the *ezrat nashim* must be regarded as an extension of the male sanctuary. To say otherwise is to ban all traditional *women* who come to *daven*, hear the weekly Torah reading, and occasionally say *birkhat*

107–108.

[34] *HaDarom*, ibid.

[35] Originally written as a letter responding to R. Fink's rebuttal letter (see n33 above), the *Journal of Halacha* did not agree to publish it.

[36] In IM, OC 5:12, Rav Moshe Feinstein mentions, as an aside in response to another issue altogether, that "...in every generation it has been customary that sometimes... a woman who is a mourner will come to shul to say kaddish...." Thus, that a woman could—and that women did—recite kaddish is here a given. Why this question, at this time, has come to arouse such intense emotional responses is an important issue. It seems as if Rabbi Fink, Rabbi Lau and others feel acutely the gauntlet of challenges feminism has posed to Halakha. It is always easier to be strict. But, a stringent position lacks both common sense and evidence of social responsibility when the tradition is so clear. The motivation seems to be, "We won't be like *them*"; rather than "Let's continue to accommodate the needs of women as mourners."

[37] Fink, 37.

hagomel[38] to the land of Oz. To say that women come to shul but are not in shul is to forever exclude all females from the prayer community of *klal Yisrael*. There is a patent absurdity in this claim, which through legal abstraction denies the reality of real people, real men and women, and relegates the synagogue to a most exclusive men's club. Fink's claim is halakhic cavil. The second criticism is that Rabbi Yehuda Henkin gives inadequate support for his interpretation of his grandfather's *pesak*. This objection may be dismissed in an outright manner, as Fink does not even refer to R. Yosef Henkin's original discussion in his footnotes.[39] But let us respond nonetheless. What R. Yosef Henkin argues is that the early responsa which prohibited women from saying kaddish, especially in shul, were based on synagogue practice of the time. He describes the custom which predominated in the time both of the *Rishonim* and *Achronim*. Prevailing synagogue practice was for one mourner to recite kaddish on behalf of all mourners present and to stand at the prayer leader's table while doing so. A woman could not be this representative in the *minyan*. Current custom, R. Yosef Henkin continued to argue, is for each person to say kaddish in his place, a place which may surely also be, then, *her* place. R. Fink's language, "If he could demonstrate that when the divisions against a woman saying kaddish were rendered, the local custom was for only one person only [sic] to say the kaddish, he might then have a tenable argument,"[40] is sharp, brusque, and unscholarly. If he wishes to invalidate R. Henkin's claim about the change in custom, he must bring evidence to the contrary. In addition, contrary to R. Fink's interpretation, R. Henkin does not say that the earlier negative decisions were based "solely"[41] on the evolution of an altered custom. Surely other factors were involved, including different social attitudes towards women. But they are not the focus of R. Henkin's discussion. R.

---

[38] See Rochelle L. Millen, "*Birkhat Ha-Gomel*: Cultural Context and Halakhic Practice," *Judaism* 43.3 (Summer, 1994) and "Communications," *Judaism* 44.1 (Winter, 1995). Also Henoch Goldberg, "The Obligation of Women to Recite Birkhat Ha-Gomel," (Hebrew) *Shana beShana* (Jerusalem: Heichal Shlomo, 1990) 231–39. Rabbi Blair also took note of this question.

[39] Fink, 34.

[40] *Loc. Cit.*

[41] Fink, 37.

Fink's claim of exclusive causation is thus both illegitimate and simplistic.[42] In addition were one to go through the complete responsa of the *Shevut Yaakov* and *Knesset Yechezkel* in regard to kaddish quoted earlier in this article, one would immediately notice that not only do they oppose a daughter's reciting kaddish in shul, but they also analyze the hierarchy of precedence as to which one man among the mourners should say kaddish for all the mourners.[43] Clearly this supports R. Henkin's description of earlier synagogue practice.

It is to be noted as well that this very change in custom described by R. Henkin indicates, very simply, that changes in religious observance, custom, ritual—even Halakha—do occur. They occur all the time. R. Fink's notion that recent discussions of women and kaddish camouflage an attempt to "improve" our traditions is simply a distorted reading of the very halakhic processes he claims to wish to protect. Customary practices today will not necessarily be customary practices tomorrow.

R. Fink's third criticism of R. Henkin, that women reciting kaddish in the women's gallery along with male mourners is not accepted among sephardim is irrelevant. When my husband taught sephardi high school girls in Netivot in 1976–77, the girls neither took *lulav* and *etrog* nor sat in the *sukka*. That "all our women are *chashuvot*" is stated by the *Rama*, not R. Yosef Caro.[44] Indeed, the differences between women's involvement in *mitzvot* in sephardi and ashkenazi communities is testimony to the impact of cultural context on the corpus of Halakha, the very aspect of halakhic development against which R. Fink is arguing.

It is of some interest that R. Yosef Henkin makes the same point about kaddish made by Rabbi Blair and implied by Rabbi Aaron Soloveitchik:

> It is known that were it not for kaddish, many would refrain from teaching prayer to their sons and would not come to synagogue. When they come because of kaddish they also come a bit closer to Judaism the rest of the year, and

---

[42] See for instance, Jonathan Sacks, ed., *Orthodoxy Confronts Modernity* (New Jersey: Ktav, 1991), as well as Jacob Katz, *Tradition and Crisis* (NY: Free Press, 1961) and *The Shabbes Goy* (JPS, 1989).

[43] Cf. Rabbi Yehuda Henkin's forth-coming book *Equality Lost* (Jerusalem: Urim Publications, 1998). I thank Urim Publications for sharing this manuscript with me.

[44] See *Shulchan Arukh, Hilkhot Pesach* 472: 4 on which the *Rama* states "all our women are called *chashuvot*."

for this reason itself one should not rebuff the young woman (*na'ara*) either, since it fosters closeness to Judaism.[45]

An overview of the recent halakhic literature finds *poskim* for the most part, adopting the restrictive interpretations of the Amsterdam case. Although a responsum of Rabbi Yitzchak Weiss refers to the practice of female mourners coming to shul to recite kaddish,[46] the legal literature is predominantly negative. This is so despite the increase of this practice in many synagogues. Were kaddish not being recited by women, legal decisors would not have to inveigh against its being said in a female voice. This voice *is* being heard, yet the attempts to silence it are powerful. The chorus of nay-sayers includes R. Meshulam Roth,[47] R. Yitzchak Yaacov Fuchs,[48] R. Yisrael Meir Lau,[49] R. Eliezer Waldenberg,[50] R. Moshe haLevi Sternberg,[51] R. David Auerbach,[52] and R. Reuven Fink[53] (as analyzed above). Those who accept the female voice of kaddish (as discussed in specific responsa) are R. Moshe Leib Blair, R. Aaron Soloveitchik, R. Yehuda Herzl Henkin, and an earlier *posek*, R. Eliezer Zalman Grayefsky.[54] Rabbi J.B. Soloveitchik specifically permitted a woman to recite kaddish even if she is the only person in the congregation to do so.[55]

As I read through the various texts which restrict woman, seeing her as sexual object or by nature so private that kaddish is an inappropriate public

---

[45] *Kitvei haGri"a Henkin*, vol. 2, 6. Quoted in R. Yehuda Herzl Henkin's manuscript.

[46] R. Yitzchak Weiss, *Responsa Minchat Yitzchak* 1:133. See also n35 above.

[47] *Responsa Kol haMevaser* 2:44.

[48] *Halikhot Bat Yisrael* (Jerusalem, 1983) 157.

[49] *Sefer Yachel Yisrael*, vol. 2 (5752/1992) 478–80, n90.

[50] *Responsa Tzitz Eliezer* 14:7.

[51] *Hilkhot Nashim* (Jerusalem, 1987) 133–34.

[52] *Halikhot Beta* (Jerusalem, 1983) 72–73.

[53] See n33 above.

[54] Cited in David Golinkin, "Women and the Mourner's Kaddish" (Hebrew), *Responsa of the Va'ad Halakha of the Rabbinical Assembly of Israel*, vol. 3 (5748/5749) 76–77. Grayefsky, originally from eastern Europe, died in England in 1899. The discussion on kaddish is in his volume *Kaddish le'Olam*, 11–12.

[55] See n22 above.

gesture, the fear of women as autonomous, independent, competent persons is a persistent—and resonating—undercurrent. Women are accountants, lab technicians, genetic researchers, academics, lawyers, teachers, executives, physicians, scientists, mothers and care-givers. Women can do anything, but ought not to say kaddish in shul—even if Halakha says women can do so? This is anomalous and unacceptable. It is using seventeenth-century circumstance to adjudicate for women of our day.

Legal change within religious traditions is by nature a slow, conservative process. Ultimately what seems a ponderous pace is protective of tradition; finding the fit of eternal principles and historical context is an on-going, pull and push series of interactive and interdependence actions.[56] It is clear that in the case of the female voice of kaddish, roadblocks, however inappropriate, are still being erected.

When Sarah Schenirer decided in 1914 to clothe the Jewish girls and women of Cracow in the "spiritual garments" of Torah learning, her efforts were endorsed by the Belzer rebbe and later by the *Chafetz Chaim*.[57] In his famous responsum in answer to critics on the religious right, the *Chafetz Chaim* argued that changing social conditions allowed the community to disregard earlier prohibitions against women learning Torah. The female voice of Torah study was now, he proclaimed, a *mitzva*.[58] Likewise, it is neither *shtut* nor *chukha telula*, derogatory terms meaning "foolishness," "like a joke," "a mockery," descriptions used by an early *posek*[59] to describe a daughter's recitation of kaddish.

What can we see from this survey of the responsa? Until recently, when accretions having to do with sexuality crept into the literature—an obvious interpolation with the aim of precluding female participation when no other grounds existed—it was clear that of course women could, and did, say

---

[56] See Gershom Scholem, "Revelation and Tradition as Religious Categories in Judaism," *The Messianic Idea in Judaism* (NY: Schocken, 1971) 282–304.

[57] Deborah Weissman, "Bais Yaakov: A Historical Model for Jewish Feminists," *The Jewish Woman: New Perspectives*, ed. Elizabeth Koltun (NY: Schocken, 1976) 139–49.

[58] An excerpt of the responsum of the *Chafetz Chaim* appears in *Ha'Isha vehaMitzvot* (Hebrew), ed. Elyakim Ellinson (Jerusalem: Torah Dept., WZO, 1979) 158.

[59] The *posek* is the *Beit Lechem Yehuda*, who brings this quote from the *Knesset Yechezkel*. See R. Yekutiel Greenwald, *Kol Bo al Avelut* (Feldheim, 1973) 375, n33.

kaddish. There is obvious precedent based on the understanding of kaddish as an essential part of the mourning process as well as an effort to elevate the soul of the deceased. That women could and did say kaddish does not diminish the fact that such recitation was always an exception to the social norm. Despite Rabbi Blair's emphasis on "duty," women did not take on the obligation of kaddish as was done in the case of *teki'at shofar.*[60] However, this is changing as the practice becomes increasingly prevalent. The responsa continued and continue to deal with the issue on an *ad hoc* basis.

The underlying struggle in the responsa has always been the tension between woman as mourner and the public arena of prayer. As in all legal cases, both positive and negative decisions create social realities and patterns of thinking which are then difficult to alter. In a general society where women were, in some sense, neither seen nor heard, the Halakha, though possessing the adaptability, was not ready to deal with female experience on a broad scale.[61] Piecemeal changes, spurred by specific questions and situations, occurred. Social and cultural factors became obstacles to a more generous, and legitimate, interpretation of the texts. To state the obvious, woman's place in both general and Jewish society, and man's uncomfortability with woman as a public person, autonomous and in charge of herself, affect the rendering of religious law, especially when—and perhaps because—the decision-making body is all-male.

Standing from within the tradition, and fully cognizant of the lag between social reality and changes in religious law, it becomes crucial to identify areas of opportunity and equality extended to female experience, even while more fundamental shifts within the tradition may be occurring. Upon knowledge of these opportunities depends the continuing development of a new social reality, one in which women as a matter of course are included in kaddish. Some responsa, as noted, respect and even applaud the need for and appropri-

---

[60] See Arlene Pianko, "Women and the Shofar," *Tradition* 14.4 (Fall, 1974): 53–63.

[61] This is, of course, still the case in certain Jewish circles. See, for instance, Tova Reich's description of her mother's funeral in Israel and her treatment as a daughter of the deceased in "My Mother, My Muse," in the "Hers" column, *The New York Times Magazine* (Nov. 6, 1988). Another example is in "The New Look of Liberalism on the Court" by Jeffrey Rosen in *The New York Times Magazine* (Oct. 5, 1997) where Supreme Court Justice Ruth Bader Ginsburg refers to daughters being prohibited from saying kaddish.

ateness of these prospects. In the face of continued narrowness and rigid interpretations of the Amsterdam case, the authors of these responsa are courageous. They acknowledge the role of history in the development of Halakha and the absolute personhood of woman, a personhood not to be compromised by demanding women submit themselves to formulations deemed anachronistic. While change derives from resolute, bold decisors, it also emanates from the individuals and groups who alter their practices. When women will make kaddish a *sine qua non* aspect of observance of mourning, then, much as in the case of shofar, its recitation will become accepted—and expected—practice.

Between Thought and Action:
The Role of Intent in the Performance of *Mitzvot*

Gilla Ratzersdorfer Rosen

What matters more: intentions or actions? Is the essence of a *mitzva* to be found in the act itself, or in the experience of the relationship with the Almighty? One way of approaching these questions is to ask: whether *kavana* (intention, consciousness, devotion)[1] is required in the performance of *mitzvot*. This question has engaged Jewish thinkers in many spheres from Kabbala to Halakha to ethics and has remained tantalizingly unresolved in Halakha for hundreds of years.

Kavana in the Mishna

In the Mishna this issue is explicitly raised with regard to three well-known *mitzvot*: *keri'at Shema*—the daily recitation of the *Shema*; *teki'at shofar*—shofar-blowing on *Rosh haShana*; and *keri'at haMegilla*—the reading of the *Megilla* on Purim.

The Mishna in *Berakhot* (2:2) states:

> If one was reading the Torah [and reached the passage of the *Shema*] and [simultaneously] the time for recital of the *Shema* arrived; if one directed one's heart (*kiven libo*)[2]—one has fulfilled one's obligation [to recite the *Shema*]; and if not, one has not [fulfilled one's obligation].

---

* I wish to thank my entire family for their patience while I was writing this paper and for their thoughtful insights. I am especially grateful to my son Shlomo Dov for bringing to my attention many fascinating sources and for the pleasure of working through ideas together. Thanks also to my brother, Joseph Ratzersdorfer, for reading and commenting upon the manuscript.

[1] The word *kavana* comes from *kivun*, direction, and suggests focusing or attunement. The various meanings of *kavana bemitzvot* will be discussed below.

[2] The word *lev* (heart) in *Tanach* and *Chazal* may signify metaphorically either what we would call today heart or mind (or some combination thereof).

It is paralleled by a Mishna in *Megilla* (2:2):

> If one was writing [copying], expounding, or correcting [a *Megilla*]; if one directed one's heart [i.e., had *kavana*] one has fulfilled one's obligation [to read the *Megilla*] and if not, one has not.

In the same vein, the Mishna in *Rosh haShana* (3:7) reads:

> If a person was passing behind a synagogue or one's house was close to the synagogue and one heard the sound of the shofar or of the *Megilla* [reading]; if one directed one's mind/heart one has fulfilled one's obligation but if not one has not. Although both heard one directed his heart and one did not.

In all three of these *Mishnayot*, *kavana* seems to be an essential and indispensable component in the performance of the *mitzva*. This reading is enhanced by the aggadic passage which follows the Halakha quoted above:

> "And it came to pass, when Moses held up his hand, that Israel prevailed..." (Ex. 17:11). But could the hands of Moses make war or lose a war? It is rather to teach you: As long as Israel was looking upwards and subjecting their hearts to their Father in Heaven—they prevailed, and if not—they fell. Likewise, you may say, "Make for you a fiery serpent, and set it upon a pole; and it shall come to pass, that whosoever is bitten, when he looks at it, he shall live" (Num.21:8). But could the serpent cause to die, or could the serpent cause to live? Rather when Israel looked upwards and subjected their hearts to their Father in Heaven—they were healed, and if not—they perished....

It is worth noting that all of these three halakhic *mishnayot* refer to *post facto* situations—*bedi'avad* (as do many *mishnayot*). The individual either was taken unawares or was engaged in a related activity with another intention in mind (in halakhic terminology: *mit'asek*). Thus, these *mishnayot* do not clarify the manner in which a person should theoretically perform *mitzvot*. Nevertheless, it would seem clear that the underlying assumption is that *mitzvot* should, in the first instance, (*lekhatchila*) be performed with *kavana*. The Torah speaks of serving God (i.e., performing *mitzvot*) "with all one's heart."[3] This reading

---

[3] See Deut. 11:13 and the *Sifre* there. See *Ramban* on *Rambam*'s *Sefer haMitzvot*, Positive Commandment 5. *Ramban* considers it a specific positive commandment to perform *mitzvot* with *kavana*. See also Numbers 15:39. "And you shall remember... and

is bolstered by the Mishna's inclusion of the aggadic section in tractate *Rosh haShana*. It totally negates the importance of Moses' action and the object he used and puts the entire emphasis on the uplifted gaze and more importantly its psychological effect—they subjected their hearts to their Father in Heaven.[4]

The Mishna does speak about the ideal (or at least—an ideal) form of performance of the *mitzva* of *tefilla*. It reads:

> One should only stand up to recite the *tefilla* [the *Shemone Esrei* or standing prayer] from a sense of reverence. The pious men of earlier times would wait an hour and then pray, so as to direct their hearts to Heaven. (*Berakhot* 5:1)

This Mishna introduces quite a number of new facets. Pivotal for our concerns, is the way in which the term *kavana* is used. The phrase is not simply to direct one's heart and mind—or possibly simply one's attention—as in the previous *mishnayot*. It is to direct one's heart "to heaven." Combined with the term *koved rosh* at the beginning of the Mishna, this parallels the aggadic section at the end of tractate *Rosh haShana*.

What are the possible meanings, so far, for the term *kavana* in the *Mishna?* The three halakhic *mishnayot* cited all employ the expression *"kiven libo"*— focused or directed his/her heart (or mind/attention). This seems to imply consciousness, awareness, concentration. But consciousness of what? One might suggest a mechanistic concentration upon the act. The act of hearing the shofar or the *Megilla* would include the effort of listening, attending. The act of reading would include the attempt at comprehension, the attention to content. However, such a reading would be difficult in the case of *keri'at Shema* where the individual was already reading. It also would not be consistent with the aggadic material which follows the Mishna in *Rosh haShana*.

On another level, *kavana* might connote the intention to perform a *mitzva*. Concentration might be upon transformation of the action into a particular *mitzva*. This reading of *kiven libo* would be analogous to the phrase in Mishna *Bekhorot*—"mitkavnim leshem mitzva."

---

do." See *Sdei Chemed* 76, page 316. With regard to interpersonal *mitzvot* see below. Other authorities consider *kavana* a Rabbinic obligation. See *Sdei Chemed* 61, page 297.

[4] This aggada may actually be suggesting a far more radical position. The question would be not whether *kavana* must accompany actions but whether actions must accompany *kavana*. See the *Rambam*'s position below. See also n22 below.

At first, when they would perform the act with the intention (*mitkavnim*) of ful-filling the *mitzva*, the *mitzva* of *yibum* took precedence over the *mitzvah* of *chalitza*. But nowadays, (since) they are not intent on fulfilling the *mitzva*.... (Mishna *Bekhorot* 1:7)

The Mishna regarding *tefilla* clearly goes beyond either of these definitions of *kavana* speaking of directing the heart or mind to Heaven. This would suggest not only concentration upon the act or even the *mitzva* but also devotion. The *mitzva* creates the link to God—the moment in which the individual turns to God. Thus *kavana* may have a whole range of meanings from the intention to perform a *mitzva*, to concentration upon an action or text, to the sustaining of a relationship with God through an act's performance. Although all of these *mishnayot* clearly require *kavana*, nevertheless, a conclusion that the fulfill-ment of all *mitzvot* is contingent upon *kavana* cannot necessarily be drawn. These three *mishnayot* might represent a unique category of *mitzvot* which require *kavana*.

The *mitzvot* of *keri'at Shema, keri'at haMegilla* and *teki'at shofar* share certain distinct qualities. First of all, they are all positive commandments, not prohibitions. Secondly, they are all *mitzvot bein adam lamakom*. Thirdly, all three require minimal physical action for their performance. Speaking, reading and certainly hearing are not necessarily considered actions in all contexts.[5] Thus they may warrant mental *kavana* because of their lack of external activity. Furthermore it is certainly possible that conscious attention (an aspect of *kavana*) is to be considered an integral part of the act of hearing or reading or speaking.

The *mitzva* of *tefilla* exemplifies the same characteristics. It is a positive commandment *bein adam lamakom* with a limited sphere of "action." Furthermore, *tefilla*—which is defined as "service of the heart"[6] may be an even more extreme example of a *mitzva* which is built upon a strong mental or emotional component. Thus, the requirement of *kavana* and especially its specific form described in this Mishna, may not be essential in the perform-ance of all *mitzvot*.

---

[5] Whether or not speech is to be considered an action in Halakha is discussed in a number of contexts in the Talmud. See for example, *Shavuot* 21a.

[6] *Ta'anit* 2a and *Sifre* to Deut. 11:13.

Thus, we have generated two related groups of questions. Firstly, what is meant by the term *kavana* in these *Mishnayot* and might the Mishna be referring to different forms or degrees of *kavana?* And secondly, would the *kavana* requirement apply to all *mitzvot*, or only to *mitzvot* which shared the characteristics delineated above?

Kavana in the Temple

There is another area of Halakha in which the issue of intent in the performance of a *mitzva* is a central concern in the Mishna. That is the sacrificial system. The first four chapters of the tractate of *Zevachim* and the parallel first two chapters of the tractate of *Menachot* deal almost exclusively with the need for the correct intentions and the consequences of incorrect intentions.[7] However, the emphasis is on the effect of intentions and other thoughts on the object—the sacrifice—not the individual bringing it. Thus, some aspects of these *mishnayot* are not directly applicable and relate to other areas of Halakha.[8]

In general, the halakhic discussion of *kavana* did not incorporate the *mishnayot* regarding the sacrificial system except in relation to *tefilla*[9] (possibly because conclusions cannot necessarily be drawn from laws pertaining to the *Beit Hamikdash* to other areas of Halakha.)

---

[7] These *mishnayot* deal in great part with the biblical prohibition against eating *piggul*. (Lev. 7:15–18 and 19:5–8) *Piggul* refers to an offering about which the priest who sacrificed it entertained a disqualifying thought while it was ritually slain or offered up. See *Sefer haChinukh Mitzva* 144. (However, according to the *Tosafot* the thought does not have any consequences unless it is actually spoken. See *Pesachim* 63a. תוספות ד"ה רב' מאיר).

[8] In general, the term *kavana* is used by the Mishna when the emphasis is on the status of the individual (has he or she performed the *mitzva*) and the term *leshem* (for the sake of) is used when the emphasis is on the validity of the finished product—for instance, a Torah scroll must be written *lishema*. See "*lishema*" in J.D. Eisenstein, *Ozar Dinim uMinhagim: A Digest to Jewish Laws and Customs* (Tel Aviv, 1975) 196. A full analysis of the relationship between these two concepts is beyond the scope of this paper. Another use of the term *lishema* will be discussed below.

[9] See *Shulchan Arukh, Orach Chaim (Hilkhot Tefilla)* 98:4 "Prayer is in the place of the sacrifices. And so, one must be attentive that it should be analogous to the sacrifices and no extraneous thought should be mingled with prayer in the same way that thoughts [can] disqualify sacrifices." Isaiah 1:11–15 parallels sacrifice and prayer.

Nevertheless, two *mishnayot* are, I believe, essential for an understanding of the Mishna's discussion of *kavana*. One Mishna reads:

> The sacrifice is slaughtered for the sake of six things: [The person performing the sacrificial service must have in mind that it is] for the sake of the particular sacrifice, for the sake of the one who is offering, for the sake of God's name, for the sake of fire-offerings, for the sake of the savor rising from the alter, and for the sake of pleasing God. (*Zevachim* 4:6)

This Mishna brings together a whole spectrum of thoughts and emotions. It begins with the most mundane and specific—the intention to consecrate the particular offering and moves on to the *kavana* to be part of the general service before God. It includes the desire that the sacrifice actually be accepted as a devotional act before God. It is not difficult to transfer these forms of *kavana* to the observance of *mitzvot* in general[10].

The second Mishna which relates to our discussion, forms the conclusion of the tractate of *Menachot*. This particular Mishna is discussed in both Halakha and ethical literature:

> It is said of the burnt-offerings of cattle (Lev.1:9): "An offering made by fire of a sweet savor"; and of the burnt-offerings of birds: "An offering made by fire of a sweet savor," and of the meal-offering, "An offering made by fire of a sweet savor," to teach that it is the same whether a person offers much or little, if only the person directs his [or her] mind to Heaven. (*Menachot* 13:11)[11]

This theme—that it is *kavana* rather than quantity (or even quality) which is pleasing before God—was extended to *mitzvot* in general and especially to Torah study and prayer.[12] Just as generally a poorer person brought an offering of flour, likewise many people do not have the ability or the opportunity to

---

[10] Although this Mishna refers to the priest performing the sacrificial service and it is debated whether it applies halakhically, its discussion of the human relationship to different aspects of holiness remains relevant.

[11] There are textual variants here. The printed version of the Gemara reads "*libo*"—"his heart," but the printed version of the Mishna reads "*da'ato*"—"his mind."

[12] See *Berakhot* 5b and *Shavuot* 15b. See the *Ramban*, *Ritva*, and *Rashba* on *Shavuot* 15b who argue that the Torah sometimes requires the best quality sacrifices possible, only because of the psychological effect on the person bringing it.

study and pray for long periods. Thus "better a small amount of supplication with *kavana* than much without."[13]

The Unwitting Sinner

Let us return to our initial questions regarding our three *mishnayot*. These *mishnayot* deal with positive commandments. What about prohibitions? Is *kavana* a necessary component when committing a transgression? Interestingly, this issue is explicitly raised in the Torah itself. The Torah establishes a category of *shogeg*, unintentional or unwitting sin. It describes unintentional homicide (with some degree of negligence):[14] The Torah further posits an entire halakhic category of unintentional performance of a transgression. It legislates the bringing of a sacrifice (*korban chatat*) to atone for unintentional transgressions.[15]

However, the parameters defining an unintentional transgression for which an individual is held responsible vary among the *mitzvot*. In the case of homicide, the individual guilty of manslaughter (*rotze'ach beshogeg*) who must flee to a city of refuge is someone who knows that murder is forbidden and kills someone by mistake—the death of another human being is the unforeseen unintended consequence of his actions. In the case of Shabbat, for instance, the Mishna explains that the *shogeg* is one who intentionally performs the entire action, but does not intentionally commit a transgression. He or she forgets some salient fact, for instance, that the action is prohibited or that the day is Shabbat. Despite gray areas, the Halakha recognizes and defines different degrees of intentionality and consequential culpability. These range from the *anus* (one compelled to act) to a *mit'asek* (one who unwittingly

---

[13] *Shulchan Arukh, Orach Chaim* 1:4. But what about a rich person who brought only an offering of flour, with *kavana*? And would not a longer supplication with equivalent *kavana* be preferable to a small amount? Is quantity irrelevant? See *Tosafot Yom Tov* on *Pirkei Avot* 2:16, *Taz* on the *Shulchan Arukh* ibid., *Sefat Emet* on Parshat Vayikra and *Be'ur haChassidut leShas*. Yishai Chasidah, ed. (Jerusalem, 1975) 14.

[14] If he [the killer] thrusts [the victim] down accidentally and without malice, or throws any object at him without planning to kill him. Even if it is a stone that can kill, if he did not see the victim. (Num.35:22–23). See also Exodus 21:12–13.

[15] Lev. ch. 5.

performs one action in the process of doing another) to *shogeg* (unintentional or unwitting transgression) to a *meizid* (one who sins intentionally).[16]

When it comes to performing a *mitzva*, there are, of course, also many possible levels of consciousness and intentionality. However, the Torah does not create a parallel special category for unintentional *mitzvot*. Thus, either an individual is considered as having fulfilled a *mitzva* or not—in which case, he or she may have the opportunity or even the obligation to repeat the action. Of course, over and beyond, fulfilling the minimal requirements a *mitzva* may be performed on many different levels.

In general, direct halakhic parallels have not been drawn between the unintentional or unwitting sinner and the person lacking *kavana* in the positive performance of *mitzvot*.[17] Nevertheless, the different classifications and analyses of levels of consciousness and intent in the performance of transgressions discussed in the Mishna and Gemara are useful in analyzing the psychological processes which accompany the performance of *mitzvot*. It is also deeply thought-provoking to follow when and why comparisons between the commitment of transgressions and the performance of *mitzvot* break down.

The second exclusionary principle which we noted above was that all three *mitzvot* cited in the Mishna depict *mitzvot bein adam lamakom*—ritual *mitzvot*.

Would the conclusions drawn apply to *mitzvot bein adam lechavero*—interpersonal *mitzvot*? This question will be dealt with at the end of this paper, but for the moment, we will assume that we are dealing specifically with *mitzvot* solely between the individual and God.

The third principle noted was that these three *mitzvot* are all particularly dependent upon the mental state of the individual. Would the same *kavana* be required in the performance of other *mitzvot*? This question brings us to the discussion in the Gemara.

---

[16] The issues are complex. For some examples of the various types of unintentional transgressions and the differing circumstances in which an individual is considered culpable, see Mishna *Shabbat* 7:1, *Rambam Hilkhot Shabbat* 1:8–14, *Hilkhot Shegagot* 2:1–8 and.7:1–4, and *Hilkhot Shavuot* 1:9–13 and 3:5–11.

[17] An exception in which a rule in the Gemara about the unintentional performance of a transgression is later used to explain the performance of a *mitzva* without *kavana*—will be discussed below.

The Talmud Defines Broad Principles

The Jerusalem Talmud does not debate the issue. It seems to accept the Mishna's requirement of *kavana* and to apply it to the performance of *mitzvot* in general, reconciling any divergent texts.[18] However, the Babylonian Talmud totally reopens the whole question. First of all, it assumes a particular definition of *kavana*—the intention to fulfill a *mitzva*. Secondly, the Gemara both broadens and sharpens the discussion by introducing the case of another type of *mitzva* in a different situation.

The Gemara in *Rosh haShana* opens the discussion of the Mishna about *teki'at shofar* with a story: "They sent to inform the father of Samuel that if an individual is compelled by force to eat matzah [on Pessach] he or she thereby fulfills the religious obligation" (*Rosh haShana* 28a).

It is to be presumed that the individual in question did not intend (at least at that moment) to perform the *mitzva* of eating matzah. In fact, it would seem that he or she did not even have the intention to eat (i.e., perform the act). He or she may not have known that it was Pessach. It is even possible that the individual had no awareness of the meaning of his or her act as a *mitzva*.

The Gemara asks, "who compelled him to eat?" And Rav Ashi answers that it was Persians. Thus Rav Ashi negates the possibility that the *Beit Din* or a fellow Jew applied the force—creating a situation in which *kavana* to perform the *mitzva* might have developed during the process.[19] On the contrary, it sounds probable that the individual was objecting to eating the matzah. Thus it is also possible that the individual consciously did *not* want to fulfill the *mitzva*.

Nevertheless, despite the lack of any assurance of the most minimal level of positive *kavana*—it was ruled that the individual involved had fulfilled the *mitzva* of eating matzah. This ruling would seem to be in stark contradiction to our three *Mishnayot*. Furthermore, the Gemara proceeds to create a general

---

[18] See *Pesachim Yerushalmi* 10:3 [37a]. The position of the Talmud *Yerushalmi* will be discussed further below.

[19] On whether or not the *kavana* of another Jew or of a *Beit Din* can substitute for the *kavana* of the individual performing the *mitzva*: see *Chullin* 31b with regard to a woman dipping in a *mikva* but note the special nature of the *mitzva* of *tevilla* as a preparatory act. For a discussion of this question see *Sdei Chemed* 62, 302–3, 305.

principle applying even to the *mitzva* of *teki'at shofar* from this ruling about matzah:

> Said Rava:[20] "This would imply that if one blew the shofar simply to make music, one has fulfilled one's religious obligation." Is this not obvious? It is the same thing! You might argue that in the previous case the All Merciful prescribed that matzah should be eaten, and the individual has eaten. [But] in this case, it is written "a memorial of blowing the shofar" and this man is merely amusing [literally: occupying] himself.

The Gemara suggests that we might have differentiated between the *mitzvot* of matzah and shofar because the actual commandment in the Torah to blow the shofar is expressed as a *mitzva* of remembrance (demanding a conscious component). But Rava rejects the differentiation. The Gemara concludes that Rava is of the opinion that "*mitzvot* do not require *kavana*."

Of course the Gemara immediately asks: What about our *mishnayot* which demand *kavanat halev* in the case of *keri'at Shema*, *teki'at shofar*, and *keri'at Megilla*? The Gemara answers that it is possible to harmonize Rava's position with our *mishnayot*: "Did not the Mishna refer to *kavana* to perform the *mitzva*? No, [not necessarily]" It may only refer to *kavana* to actually read or hear. It is possible for a person to proofread or type up a text without any attention to processing the actual meaning of the words. Would we say that a good typist has "read" what he or she has typed? In the case of *keri'at Shema* the individual described in the Mishna may have been a *sofer* correcting a *Sefer Torah* who reaches the passage of the *Shema*. The Mishna legislates that the *sofer* must attend to the act in order to actually "read." This mechanistic reading of the Mishna is bolstered by the Mishna about *Megilla* reading, which actually describes someone who was copying, expounding or correcting the text and not "reading" in the normal sense.[21]

---

[20] Some *Rishonim* had a text which read Rabbah not Rava.

[21] This is only one of a number of possible understandings of this Gemara. Other possibilities include: that the individual did not actually read correctly (or he pronounced the words phonetically since he was checking the written text) or that he read without meaning to (*mit'asek*), his reading being a by-product of his wish to scan the texts. See *Rashi* and *Tosafot* on *Rosh haShana* 28b and 33b and *Rashi*, *Tosafot* and especially Rebbenu Yona (page 13 in the *Rif*) on *Berakhot* 13a.

Likewise, the Gemara suggests that the person surprised by the sound of the shofar might have mistaken it for some other sound. Thus without *kavana* consciousness or awareness—he might have physically heard the sound of the shofar but not mentally processed it. The *mitzva* of hearing the shofar presumes the mental component of identifying the sound. Thus, a person blowing the shofar to make music could still be performing the *mitzva*. The assumption of the Gemara is that these difficulties are particular to the process of hearing and reading and could not apply to other *mitzvot* which entail actions like eating or shaking a *lulav*.

Of course, such a reading distances our original three *Mishnayot* from the more aggadic passages about *kavana* in the Mishna—which require "*kavanat lev*"—not just attention to action, but an experience of one's relationship with God. But it is possible that the Mishna purposely juxtaposes passages describing different types of *kavana*. Thus it legislates a minimal standard of *kavana* and at the same time subverts that minimal standard and points to the ideal of a deeper form of *kavana*.[22]

In contrast to Rava's view, the Gemara in *Rosh haShana* also describes the practice of Rabbi Zera who required *kavana* to perform the *mitzva*—at least in the blowing of the shofar. It also notes the opposing view that *mitzvot* do need *kavana*.

The Gemara understands that although the position that "*mitzvot* do not need *kavana*" is not explicitly mentioned in the Mishna—it is part of an age-old controversy. The Gemara in *Pesachim*[23] brings two *beraitot* (*tannaic*

---

[22] According to Dr. Frankel the Mishna allows the aggadah to present alternative and even contradictory religious emphases through the juxtaposition of halakhic and aggadic texts. See his analysis of our text in Yona Frankel, "*HaYachas ben Halakha leAggada*," *Darkhei haAggada vehaMidrash*, vol. 2 (Givataim, 1991) 484–87.

The Halakha may demand a minimal standard while the aggadah reflects the aspirations of Judaism. If so, a halakhic study of the question of *kavana*, will only yield a partial understanding of Jewish thought on the subject; (a limitation inherent in this paper). Nevertheless, the basic ideals should be expressed by and therefore comprehensible within the halakhic structure. Thus the view that "*mitzvot* do not need *kavana*" must also be understood from a philosophical and psychological perspective. See the *Meiri*'s introduction to the *Beit haBekhira* (his commentary to the Talmud) and an analysis of his views in Elyakum Krombein "*Kavanat haLev beMitzvot—Erekh mul Halakha beTorato shel Rabbenu Menachem Meir*," *Netu'im* 4 (Yeshivat Har Etziyon): 9–32.

[23] *Pesachim* 114b.

extra-Mishna sources) which contradict each other with regard to the eating of *maror* at the *seder*. One view maintains that even if *maror* was eaten without *kavana*, the individual has fulfilled his or her obligation. The other view—that of Rabbi Yossi—requires a person to eat *maror* a second time. The Gemara concludes that there was a *tannaic* controversy over *kavana*. It explains various *machlokot* (controversies) in the Mishna on the basis of the fact that some *tannaim* held that *mitzvot* do need *kavana* while others held that they do not.[24] According to such an analysis, our three *Mishnayot* only represent the tip of the iceberg. Either they are representative of all *mitzvot*, and all *mitzvot* need *kavana*. Or they reflect exceptional circumstances and most *mitzvot* do not need *kavana*.[25]

What seems to emerge from the Gemara is a picture in which all or most of the *mitzvot* are subsumed under one general principle. *Kavana* is understood as the intention to perform a *mitzva*. This entails ideally an awareness of the meaning of the act, a consciousness of being commanded by God and the intention to do His will, and consciousness at that particular moment of what one is doing. Either all *mitzvot* require such *kavana* or none do. (Some *mitzvot* simply require a certain level of mental attention). There are two possible exceptions: *keri'at Shema* and *tefilla*. Other passages in the Gemara describe aspects of *kavana* specific to them, such as "the acceptance of the yolk of heaven" (*kabalat ol malkhut shamayim*) during the recitation of the first line of the *Shema*.[26]

The *Rishonim* Examine *Mitzvot* Individually

The controversy over whether *mitzvot* as a whole need *kavana* in order for their physical performance to be endowed with meaning endured throughout the period of the *Geonim* and the *Rishonim*. For instance, the *Rif* and the *Rosh*

---

[24] See *Pesachim* 114a–b with regard to *maror* and *Eruvin* 95b with regard to *tefilla* and *Chullin* 31a with regard to *shechita*.

[25] It is also possible that a *Tanna* who held that *mitzvot* do not need *kavana* would disagree with the Mishna's opinion in the case of *Megilla, Shema*, and shofar.

[26] *Berakhot* 13b (on *Shema*) and 28b–31a (on *tefilla*). The *Rishonim* were divided as to whether the *kavana* required by the Gemara for *Shema* stemmed from the general form of *kavana* or not. For an analysis see Rabbi Yosef Dov Soloveitchik, *Kuntrus beInyanei Keri'at Shema: Shiurim leZekher Aba Mori z"l* (Jerusalem, 1983) 27–28.

maintain that *mitzvot* do need *kavana*; the *Rashba* and the *Re'a* that they do not.[27] However, some of the *Rishonim* redefined the issue. They split up the *mitzvot* arguing that for some types of *mitzvot*, *kavana* was absolutely necessary while not for others. The *Rambam*, ruled that the *mitzva* of *teki'at shofar* can not be fulfilled without *kavana* to fulfill the *mitzva* (as suggested by the Mishna within its context), but that eating matzah can (as ruled in the Gemara).[28] However, the *Rambam* did not divulge his logic. He did not

---

[27] The *Rif* on tractate *Rosh haShana* mentions only the position of Rabbi Zera who required *kavana*. Most authorities conclude that he always requires *kavana*. The *Rosh* on *Shulchan Arukh*, OC explicitly requires *kavana*. The *Tur* disagrees. See *Tosafot* on *Pesachim* 115a. See the *Ran* on *Rosh haShana* (page 14 in the *Rif*) for a summary and analysis of some of the different positions. See also the *Tur*, OC 589 and the *Beit Yosef* there. For an analysis of the position of the various *Rishonim* see R. Shimon Levi, "*Mitzvot Tzrikhot Kavana*," Shmaatin 120 (1995). This article also discusses many other issues relating to our subject. See also Rabbi Pinchas Yehoshua Kaganoff, "*Be'inyan Mitzvot Tzrikhot Kavana*," *Sefer Moreshet Zvi* (New York) 69–76.

[28] *Rambam, Mishne Torah, Hilkhot Chametz uMatzah* 6:3 "A person who eats matzah without the intention to fulfill the *mitzva*—e.g., gentiles or thieves force him to eat—fulfills his obligation," and *Hilkhot Shofar* 2:4: "A person who occupies himself with blowing the shofar in order to learn does not fulfill his obligation. Similarly, one who hears the shofar from a person who blows it casually does not fulfill his obligation. If the person hearing had the intention of fulfilling his obligation, but the person blowing did not have the intention of facilitating the latter's performance of the *mitzva*, or the person blowing had the intention of facilitating his colleague's performance of the *mitzva*, but the person hearing did not have the [correct] intention, he did not fulfill his obligation. Rather, both the person hearing and the one allowing him to hear must have the [proper] intention."

Similarly, the *Rambam* ruled in *Hilkhot Megilla* 2:5: "A person who was reading the *Megilla* without [the desired] intent does not fulfill his obligation. What is implied? That he was writing [a *Megilla*], explaining it, or checking it: If he had the intent to fulfill his obligation with this reading, his obligation is fulfilled. If he did not have this intent, he did not fulfill his obligation."

However, with regard to *keri'at Shema*, the Ramban gave an interesting ruling. He wrote: "One who recites the first verse of *keri'at Shema* without intention, does not fulfill his obligation." However he added, "One who recites the rest without intention fulfills his obligation. Even a person studying Torah in his usual way or proofreading these portions at the time of *keri'at Shema* fulfills his obligation provided he concentrates his intention for the first verse." For an analysis of the *Rambam*'s position on *keri'at Shema* see: Rabbi Yosef Dov Soloveitchik, 27–33.

In the case of the *mitzva* of shaking the *lulav*, the *Rambam* made two seemingly contradictory rulings. See *Sukka* 41b–42a. *Rambam* rules in this commentary to the Mishna that

explain whether or not *mitzvot* in general need *kavana* or whether one of these two *mitzvot* was an exception. The *Maggid Mishna* found this discrepancy so startling that he suspected a mistake in the text of the *Rambam*![29]

Essentially, two different structural analyses emerged. Rabbenu Yona argued that according to the view that "*mitzvot* do not need *kavana*," a *ma'ase*—a physical action, can take the place of *kavana*. Thus, in practice *mitzvot* like eating matzah or shaking a *lulav* do not need *kavana* but *teki'at shofar* or blessings before food—do. According to him, those who accept the view that "*mitzvot* do not need *kavana*" do not include *mitzvot* dependent on thought and speech.[30] The *Maggid Mishna* suggests that the *Rambam* may hold this view.[31]

Avraham the son of the *Rambam* independently comes to a similar conclusion, having also been troubled by the question. He argues that the problem originates not in the *Mishne Torah* but in the Talmud itself (which accepts contradictory decisions with regard to shofar and matzah). Similar to Rabbenu Yona, he explains that the rule that *mitzvot* do not require *kavana* only applies to *mitzvot* which are performed via a physical action. However, he includes reading and speaking in the category of actions. Thus he differentiates between someone who only hears the *Megilla* and who needs *kavana* to perform the *mitzva* and someone who actually reads it (who does not need special *kavana*).[32]

---

the *mitzva* of *lulav* can be performed without *kavana*. However, he does not include this possibility in *Mishne Torah, Hilkhot Shegagot* 2:10.

The discussion on this *sugya* also relates to the halakhic situation in which a person has *kavana not* to perform a *mitzva*. See *Beit Yosef* on the *Tur*, OC 589 s.v. *vetzarikh* and *Chaye Adam* 68:9.

[29] *Maggid Mishna* on *Mishne Torah, Hilkhot Shofar* 2:4. (Considering the *Rambam* on *Shema* (previous note), the *Maggid Mishna* himself is surprising).

[30] *Talmid Rebbenu Yona on Berakhot*. Printed as *Rebbenu Yona al haRif* page 11 (end of the first chapter). He adds: "...since speech is the expression of one's thoughts [literally: speech is in the heart]. If one does not concentrate on what one is saying and [one] is not performing an action, it is as if one has not done any aspect of the *mitzva*."

The *kavana* which Rabbenu Yona refers to may very well be only paying attention (not intending to perform a *mitzva*).

[31] op cit. However, note that the *Rambam* demands fuller *kavana*.

[32] *Responsa Birkat Avraham* 34.

The *Ravad* and the *Ran*, on the other hand, argued that one could generalize in practice from the cases of *Megilla, Shema* and shofar and that the *Rambam* accepted the view that "*mitzvot* need *kavana*." In fact, almost all *mitzvot* need *kavana*—the *mitzva* to eat matzah is the exception. The *Ran* drew a parallel from the laws regarding prohibitions. The Gemara states that in the case of acts from which one derives physical pleasure (specifically eating and sexual acts), a person who transgresses inadvertently (*mit'asek*) must bring a sacrifice (for unintentional transgressions). Although conscious intention to perform the action was lacking, the pleasure which the individual experienced removed him or her from the category of *mit'asek* to that of someone who had sinned.[33] The *Ran* argues that here, similarly, the individual who ate matzah should be considered to have performed the *mitzva*.[34]

How could pleasure take the place of *kavana* to perform a *mitzva*? This question may relate to the function of *kavana*. Does *kavana* endow the action itself with meaning or even help to create its status as a *mitzva*? Or is *kavana* necessary only in order to cement the link between the individual and the act which he or she performs whether a *mitzva* or transgression? If it is the latter, it is possible to understand how pleasure could take the place of *kavana*.[35] Alternatively, the *Me'iri* argues that *kavana* itself is always required but that through the pleasurable experience one would certainly acquire at least some small degree of awareness and *kavana*.[36]

According to both Rabbenu Yona and the *Ran*, one must assume that the Gemara does not necessarily accept Rava's claim that eating matzah is analogous to blowing the shofar. The *Beit haLevi* (a few hundred years later) agrees and suggests a third interpretation of the *Rambam*. He returns to the

---

[33] *Sanhedrin* 62b.

[34] See the *Ran* on *Rosh haShana* 28b (printed with the *Rif*, page 14).

[35] For a discussion of this issue see Sharon Isaacson "*Shitat haRambam beDin Mitzvot Tzrikhot Kavana*" *Shnaton Torani shel Matan* (Matan Torah Journal, 1992). For an alternative explanation see: Rabbi Yosef Dov Soloveitchik, 30–31.

The analogy is nevertheless difficult. In the case of transgressions pleasure takes the place of the intention to act. But in our case, it must take the place of *kavana* to perform the *mitzva*.

[36] See the *Meiri*'s introduction to his *Beit haBechira* (Jerusalem, 1965) 17–18. For an analysis of the *Meiri*'s position see Krombein.

Gemara's original assumption that the *mitzva* of shofar might be exceptional because it is called *zikhron teru'a*—a remembrance of blowing. According to the *Beit haLevi*, the *Rambam* thought that although *mitzvot* do not need *kavana*, the Torah specifically requires that the *mitzva* of shofar be performed with "memory and the awareness of one's heart and mind."[37]

Returning to Rabbenu Yona's interpretation that action could replace *kavana*, the question in the case of a *mitzva* dependent upon speech might even be reversed. Could *kavana* replace action? Could one fulfill the *mitzva* of *keri'at Shema* or *tefilla* by thinking about the words rather than saying them? Could one say, in this case that "thought is [to be considered] like speech"?[38]

The *Rambam* in his *Guide to the Perplexed* went even further turning the whole discussion on its head. It is not, he argued, that the purpose of *kavana* is to enhance prayer or the performance of *mitzvot*. Rather, it is the moments of prayer and *mitzvot* which give the individual the opportunity to develop *kavana*:

> Know that all the practices of worship, such as reading the Torah, prayer, and the performance of the other commandments, have only the end of training you to occupy yourself with His commandments, may He be exalted, rather than with matters pertaining to this world; you should act as if you were occupied with Him, may He be exalted, and not with that which is other than He...[39]

---

[37] Rav Yosef Dov Ber Soloveitchik, *Beit haLevi*, part 3, 51:2.

[38] The question arises in *Berakhot* 20 with regard to *keri'at Shema*.

The *Rambam* ruled that although in the first instance one should pronounce blessings, one could fulfil the *mitzva* of blessings via thought. (*Rambam, Mishne Torah, Hilkhot B'rakhot* 1:7). The *Or Zaru'a* applied this ruling to *keri'at Shema* as well. (See also *Rabbenu Mano'ach* in the *Kesef Mishna* on *Hilkhot Keri'at Shema* 2:8).

The *Shulchan Arukh* ruled that if unable to speak, one should, even in the case of *keri'at Shema*, meditate upon the words. (*Shulchan Arukh, Orach Chaim* 62:4). However, most commentaries understood that according to the *Shulchan Arukh* one did not actually fulfill the *mitzva* in this manner. See the *Be'ur Halakha* on the *Shulchan Arukh*, ibid for a summary of the issues see also the *Be'er Heitev* ibid who discusses the suggestion that understanding of the text of the prayer is mandatory if fulfilling the *mitzva* via meditation. For a discussion of the positions of *Rambam* and *Tosafot* see Nachum Lem, "*Hirhur keDibur Dami*," *Hilkhot veHalikhot* (Jerusalem, 1990) 83–92.

[39] *Rambam*'s *Guide to the Perplexed* 2:51. This may be an echo of the halakhic-aggadic message of the *mishnayot* in tractate *Rosh haShana* with which we began.

Motivation and *Kavana*

The Gemara also struggles with a related and sometimes overlapping issue—
that of motivation. It seems obvious that it is possible to be genuinely
religiously inspired and yet fail to muster *kavana* while performing a particular
mitzva. Though less obvious, it is also possible to act with the correct *kavana*
to perform *mitzvot* and yet when one examines one's true motives for keeping
mitzvot—to find them wanting.[40]

Whereas the discussion so far assumed that an individual might simply lack
kavana, the issue of motivation must deal with people's inappropriate and
downright offensive reasons for doing *mitzvot*. In such cases there is a far
greater temptation to disqualify the *mitzva*—a sense that the wrong intention
can transform and contaminate the act and even create a *chilul HaShem*
(desecration of God's name). A discussion of this problem takes place on both
a halakhic and an (emotionally charged) aggadic plane. The Talmud relates:

> Rabbah b. Bar Chana said in the name of R. Yochanan: What is meant by the
> Scriptural text: "For the ways of the Lord are right, and the just do walk in
> them; but transgressors do stumble therein"? This may be applied to two men
> both of whom roasted their paschal lambs, and one of them ate his with the in-
> tention of performing the commandment, *(leshem mitzva)* while the other ate
> his out of gluttony. To him who ate with the intention of performing the com-
> mandment [applies], "The just do walk in them," while to him who ate merely
> to enjoy a substantial meal, "But transgressors do stumble therein." Said Resh
> Lakish to him: "Do you call him 'wicked'!" Granted he has not performed the
> commandment to perfection *(mitzva min hamuvchar)* has he not, however,
> eaten of the paschal lamb? *(Horayot* 10b)[41]

---

[40] Pointed out to me by Chananel, my son and *chavruta.*

[41] I am interpreting here the term *lishema (for its sake)* as referring to one's general
motivation and *kavana* as referring to one's intention or consciousness at the time of
performance of the *mitzva*.

Resh Lakish in *Pesachim* 114b comments that the Mishna implies that *mitzvot* do need
kavana. A number of resolutions have been offered such as the *Ran*'s distinction between
mitzvot which involve physical pleasure and those which do not. However, see also
Yerushalmi Pesachim 10:3 [37a].

While this discussion might have related only to *kavana* at that moment, the Gemara goes on to discuss motivation.

> Rabbi Nachman Bar Isaac said, a transgression committed *lishema*—with good intent, is greater than a *mitzva* performed *shelo lishema*—for ulterior motives [or possibly, with no intent].[42]

The Gemara however cannot accept the severity of this view citing Rav Yehuda who said in the name of Rav:[43]

> An individual should always engage in Torah study and the performance of *mitzvot*, even for ulterior motives, because even (Torah and *mitzvot* performed for) ulterior motives will ultimately lead to Torah study and the performance of *mitzvot* for their own sake.

Everyone is encouraged to keep the *mitzvot* whatever his or her level of religious inspiration at the time.[44]

Furthermore, in the Gemara *Pesachim*, Rava argues that even *mitzvot* performed for ulterior motives are still meritorious. He points out that a *tannaic* source affirms that women who do not work all week because they live lives of leisure are nevertheless rewarded for the fact that they don't work on Friday

---

[42] See Urbach's reading of this passage in E. Urbach, *The Sages* (Jerusalem, 1979) 398–99. (See also pages 392–99 for a full discussion of *Chazal* on *kavana*.) Is Rabbi Nachman bar Isaac highlighting the value of the well-intentioned transgression or the inferiority of a *mitzva shelo lishma?*

[43] The Gemara amends the dictum to read: that a transgression committed with good intent is equal to a precept performed for ulterior motives.

[44] This passage is also refuted by a passage in *Berakhot* 17a See Urbach, ibid., 394–95 for a review of the Halakha's resolution of the conflict. See also *Pirkei Avot* 1:3.

See Norman Lamm, *Torah for Torah's Sake in the Works of Rabbi Hayyim of Volozhin and his Contemporaries*, 190–273, which deals with problematic motivation in the study of Torah as well as with differing definitions of *lishema* and their relationships to each other.

Yeshayahu Leibovitz points out that these two forms of service of God (*lishema* and *shelo lishema*) are already explicit in the Torah itself. He demonstrates that the first two paragraphs of the *Shema* are diametrically opposed to each other. The first paragraph describes service of God out of love, while the second outlines material reward and punishment. Yeshayahu Leibovitz, *Sichot al Pirkei Avot ve'al haRambam* (Jerusalem, 1979) *sichot* 19–20, 73–74; Yeshayahu Leibovitz, *He'arot leParshiyot haShavu'a* (Jerusalem, 1988) 116–17.

afternoon.[45] He explains that for those who perform the *mitzvot* for their own sake "God's loving-kindness extends beyond the heavens" (as described in Psalms 106:5); but even for those who perform *mitzvot* for ulterior motives "God's loving-kindness extends 'unto' the heavens" (Psalms 57:11).

Halakha ultimately accepted the validity—despite their deeply problematic nature—of both *mitzvot* and Torah study for ulterior motives and in exceptional circumstances, of transgressions performed with good intentions.[46]

Later Developments

By the time of the *Shulchan Arukh*, the issue of *kavana* had still not been resolved. The *Shulchan Arukh* ruled that we follow the view that *mitzvot* need *kavana*.[47] The *Magen Avraham* understood that it is a case of *safek* (doubt as to how to behave). We should, as usual, take a lenient approach with regard to Rabbinic decrees and a stringent approach with regard to biblical laws.[48] The *Chaye Adam* suggested that if a *mitzva* was performed within the appropriate context, it would be valid even without *kavana*. Even if the person was not concentrating at that moment, it would not disqualify the action.[49] For

---

[45] *Pesachim* 50b. Note that this is consistent with *Rava*'s position in Gemara *Rosh haShana* that *mitzvot* do not need *kavana*. Note also that Rava has extrapolated from a lack of action or transgression (which may not technically require *kavana* at all!) to the performance of a *mitzva*. For a discussion as to whether the issue of *kavana* generally applies to refraining from committing a transgression. See *Sdei Chemed*, page 316.

[46] See *Megilla* 15a–b and subsequent halakhic discussion in which Esther is praised for sinning in order to save the Jewish people. A fuller discussion of this issue is important but beyond the scope of this paper.

[47] *Shulchan Arukh*, OC 60:4.

[48] *Magen Avraham*, ibid., subsection 3.

[49] See *Chaye Adam* 68:9. The *Mishna Berura* accepts this view. See *Mishna Berura* and *Be'ur Halakha* on *Shulchan Arukh*, ibid. This view emerges from passages in the Talmud *Yerushalmi*. In *Pesachim*, Rabbi Yohanan's statement that one fulfils the *mitzva* of eating matzah whether or not one has *kavana* is qualified (and reconciled with the Mishna's requirement of *kavana*) by the understanding that: "יוהכא כיון שהיסב חזקה כיון" "Here [in this case] since he was leaning, it is assumed that he had *kavana*."

Likewise, the Mishna in *Rosh haShana* which reads: "If a person was *passing* behind a synagogue..., and heard the sound of the shofar... if one directed one's heart..." was

instance, a person would not be likely to purchase and then wave around a palm branch, citrus fruit and various leaves, unless he or she invested such an act with meaning. Although, at that particular moment on *Sukkot*, he or she might not be thinking about the *mitzva*, the intention to perform a *mitzva* would be clear.[50] However, it was suggested that it is always necessary, even in the case of eating matzah where conscious *kavana* may not be demanded, to know that the *mitzva* exists in order to perform it.[51]

This group of decisions taken together generally created an important perspective. On the one hand, the average Jew could fulfill *mitzvot* regularly even if unable to invest his or her actions with *kavana* at all times. At the same time, the symbolic significance of the performance of *mitzvot*—with *kavana* was not lost. The Halakha created an opportunity for individual effort in the space between minimal obligation and the ideals of thoughtful intention, devotion, and joy in the performance of *mitzvot*.

An interesting sideline which emerges from the issue of *kavana* relates to the supererogatory performance of *mitzvot*—a serious issue for women today. If the essence of the *mitzva* lies within the act itself, a person voluntarily performing a *mitzva* should need no unusual *kavana*. However, if the essential aspect is the willing performance of God's will, then there might be a difference in this situation. In the case of an obligation, there is an explicit bond between God and the individual which is recognized and strengthened through

---

clarified in the Talmud *Yerushalmi* as an individual who was (casually) passing by. However, if they stood still, it is to be assumed that he or she had *kavana.*

[50] With regard to the *mitzva* of Torah study, (or rather, of involvement with the words of Torah—*la'asok bedivrei Torah*), Rav Soloveitchik describes an emotional engagement with Torah which includes two kinds of consciousness. One is an "acute awareness" when actually intellectually involved in Torah study. In a striking tour de force, Rav Soloveitchik likens this "accute awareness" to a mother's experience when playing with her child. The second is a "latent awareness" of Torah similar to a mother's constant, unbroken awareness of her child's existence (even when she is occupied with other matters). If one extends this concept to other *mitzvot*, one might speak of an emotional involvement with a *mitzva* which would create a latent awareness of that *mitzva*. This latent awareness might function as a minimal form of *kavana*. Rav Joseph B. Soloveitchik "On the Love of Torah: Impromptu Remarks at a Siyyum," *Shi'urei haRav*, ed. Joseph Epstein (NY, 1974) 102–4.

[51] It was argued that the Gemara purposely discussed a case in which the individual was forced to eat matzah rather than one in which he or she was unaware of the *mitzva*. See *Shulchan Arukh*, OC 475:4.

human action. However, a person taking a *mitzva* upon themselves might need to consciously relate to the particular bond which he or she is creating in order to endow it with meaning.[52]

Prayer with *Kavana*

In the case of *mitzvot* like *keri'at Shema, kavana* was understood by definition to have another added dimension—the comprehension of and attention to the meaning of the text. With regard to both *Shema* and the *Amida,* the *Shulchan Arukh* ruled that in order to have fulfilled the *mitzva,* one must have comprehended and concentrated on the first section at the least.[53]

---

[52] For comparison, note the discussion in the Gemara regarding whether the prohibition of *bal tosif* (adding *mitzvot* or creating additions to existing *mitzvot*) would apply if one performed a *mitzva* at an inappropriate time without *kavana* (even according to the view that *mitzvot* do not need *kavana*). *Rosh haShana* 28b. See also *Chokhmat Shlomo, Shulchan Arukh,* OC 589.

Note also the responsum of Rabbi Moshe Feinstein with regard to feminism and women wearing *tzitzit* (OC 4:49) in which he does not apply the principle that observance will lead to correct motivation (*mitokh shelo lishma ba lishma*) to the performance of supererogatory *mitzvot,* but rather demands a purity of intent and motivation. (However, the issue of highly problematic motivation may be the overriding problem in this case.)

However, a number of authorities have ruled that even if one does not have *kavana* during the first blessing, one has fulfilled the *mitzva* of *tefilla* and one has not uttered *berakhot levatala* (invalid blessings). See the halakhic review and analysis in R. Ovadia Yosef, Responsa *Yabi'a Omer, Orach Chaim,* 3:9.

In addition, Yeshayahu Leibovitz has argued that an emotional outpouring, or an intense involvement with the content of *tefilla,* do not constitute the ideal forms of performance of the *mitzva* of *tefilla.* He maintains that the simple intention to serve God by performing the *mitzva* of *tefilla* is not only valid, but superior (to an emotional/intellectual experience of *tefilla*), because the *mitzva* of *tefilla* is thus performed truly *lishema*—not for one's own material or psychological benefits. Yeshayahu Leibovitz, *Sichot, sichot* 9–12, 50–69.

[53] *Shulchan Arukh,* OC 60:5, 63:4, and 101:1. There are various opinions as to whether this is because one only needs *kavana* at the beginning of the performance of a *mitzva* or whether it is because of the special content of those opening sections. (See the discussion above of the *Rambam*'s position on *Shema.*) Rabbi Avraham the son of the *Rambam* argued that it might be because of either one or both reasons. (*Responsa Rabbi Avraham ben haRambam* 80). In a responsum regarding pietistic practices he addressed the issue of the Halakha's practical as well as aspirational aspects: "anything which increases *kavana* of the heart in prayer is praiseworthy... the Rabbis made enactments which people can manage... for if they had ruled that one can not fulfil the *mitzvot* of *keri'at Shema* and

The history of *kavana* with regard to prayer has been surprising—oscillating back and forth. *Tefilla* has been regarded essentially either as an obligation—stemming from the *mitzva* of "service of the heart"[54] or as an opportunity given by God to approach Him for mercy.[55] Rabbi Eliezer held in the Gemara that a person who felt that he or she could not pray with *kavana* should not pray at all—a view which is not expressed with regard to any other *mitzva*.[56] Rambam accepted this view. He also ruled that if one prayed the *Amida* without *kavana* (at least during the first blessing) one had not performed the *mitzva* and would need to repeat the prayer.[57] Rabbi Yosef Caro spoke eloquently and movingly about *kavana* in the *Shulchan Arukh*. Nevertheless, he wrote "One should not pray in a place in which there is something which prevents one from having *kavana* nor at a time when one's mind is disturbed. However, in our time we are not particular about this as we do not have so much *kavana* in prayer."[58] In addition, the *Rama* ruled that: "Nowa-

---

tefilla without *kavana* throughout, only exceptional individuals would [only] occasionally manage to fulfill these *mitzvot*. Therefore they enacted the most minimal standard possible—*kavana* in the first sentence of *keri'at Shema* and the first blessing of *tefilla*." (*Responsa Rabbi Avraham ben haRambam* 62). Rav Soloveitchik points out that the *kabalat ol malkhut shamayim* (*the acceptance of the yolk of heaven*) inherent in the first line of the *Shema* functions as the essential core of the entire *Shema* and makes any other *kavana* (such as the *kavana* to perform the *mitzva* of *Shema*) totally redundant and unnecessary. Rabbi Yosef Soloveitchik, 32.

[54] *Rambam, Sefer haMitzvot*. Positive Commandment 5 and *Mishne Torah, Hilkhot Tefilla* 1.

[55] *Ramban* in his critique on the *Rambam. Sefer haMitzvot*, ibid.: "It is a quality of God's lovingkindness that He listens and answers when all are calling to Him." See also the two possibilities in Rabbenu Yona on *Berakhot* (page 4 in the *Rif*) s.v. *eizehu ben olam haba.*

[56] *Berakhot* 30b. See also *Eruvin* 65a: "Rabbi Eliezer ruled: A man returning from a journey must not pray for three days..." See also *Berakhot* 34b which requires a minimum of *kavana* during the first blessing.

[57] *Rambam, Mishne Torah, Hilkhot Tefilla* 4:1, 4:15–16 and 10:2. *Rambam* writes in chapter 4 that "Any prayer which is not [recited] with *kavana* is not prayer. If one prays without *kavana* one must pray again..." However, in chapter 10 he limits the obligation (post facto) to *kavana* during the first blessing. The source for his ruling is *Berakhot* 30b: "Rabbi Yohanan said: 'I saw Rabbi Yannai pray and then pray again.' Rabbi Yirmiyah said to Rav Zeira: 'Perhaps originally he did not have *kavana.*'"

[58] *Shulchan Arukh*, OC 98:2. The *Shulchan Arukh* nevertheless required that one repeat the *Shemone Esrei* if one had not said the first blessing with *kavana*.

days we don't repeat prayers for lack of *kavana*, for if during the repetition it is likely that one still won't concentrate why should one repeat it?"[59] However, over the last 150 years various authorities have ruled in accordance with Rabbi Eliezer's view in the Talmud. They have made room for the individual to skip *tefilla* when unable to have *kavana*, and to pray (and repeat prayers) when he or she feels able to concentrate.[60]

In the case of *tefilla*, the Mishna also describes a directional form of *kavana*: "So as to direct their hearts to their Father in Heaven." In fact, there are reflected both in Halakha and in aggadah three different senses of the way one should direct one's heart and mind:[61] The first is the Halakha that one should turn toward the Temple mount, an idea first expressed by King

---

[59] *Shulchan Arukh,* OC 101:1. For a philosophical understanding of this development see Nachum Lem, "*Veha'Idna Ein Chozrin Bishvil Chesron Kavana,*" *Hilkhot veHalikhot* (Jerusalem, 1990) 68–74.

This position originates from the Talmud *Yerushalmi.* But the *Yerushalmi* had left it open for the individual to evaluate his or her own capability to pray with *kavana* even the second time around: "Rabbi Yirmiya said in the name of Rabbi Elazar that if one prayed and did not have *kavana,* then if one knows that in repeating one will have *kavana* one should pray [again]." *Yerushalmi Berakhot* 2:4.

[60] The *Arukh haShulchan* thought that if one felt that one would be unable to concentrate at least on the first blessing of the *Amida*—one should not pray (OC 101:1-1). The *Mishna Berura* thought that one should repeat the *Amida* if one could eliminate the source of one's previous distraction (OC 96:2). Rav Ovadia Yossef ruled that a traveller who could not concentrate intentionally skip praying and make up the missed prayer during the next *tefilla* (*Yabi'a Omer* 3:9). It is told that the Chazon Ish did not make blessings when he became sick in his old age because he had always previously said them with *kavana.* For a general history of the sources see "Kavanah for Prayer in Jewish Law" in Seth Kadish, *Kavana* (Aronson, 1997) 1–43 See also R. Asher Meir, *Mishna Berura Shiur* 54 of the Yeshivat Har Etzion Virtual Beit Midrash.

An awareness of these developments gives one a greater understanding of the chassidic-mitnagid divide over the value of correct timing versus *kavana* in prayer. Additionally, the age-old custom of women not to pray the *Amida* consistently may be seen, in part, in light of the circumstances of their lives, which did not enable them to pray with *kavana.* See discussion in R. Dovid Auerbach, *Sefer Halikhot Beita* (Jerusalem, 1983) 39.

[61] For a discussion of these three motifs in *Chazal* see Uri Arlik, "*Makom haShekhina beToda'at haMitpalel,*" *Tarbiz* 65: 315–29.

Solomon, the bodily orientation reflecting the inner *kavana*.[62] The second, is that one should pray towards God in Heaven.[63] The third is that one should feel that one is standing immediately before the *Shekhina* (the Divine Presence).[64] This type of sense of almost tangible physical relationship with the Infinite Divine Presence is unique to *tefilla*. It was understood by Rav Haym Soloveitchik to be not only a detail in how to physically position oneself or even an aspect of *kavana*. Rather, the mental awareness of being present before the *Shekhina* according to Rav Chaim constitutes an indispensable part of the actual act of *tefilla*.[65]

Interpersonal *Mitzvot* and *Kavana*

All of the discussion so far has been with regard to *mitzvot bein adam lamakom*. If we proceed to an analysis of *mitzvot bein adam lechavero—*

---

[62] I Kings 8:27–45. and Mishna *Berakhot* 4:5–6 and *Rambam, Mishne Torah, Hilkhot Tefilla* 5:3.

[63] *Yevamot* 105b. *Rambam*, ibid., 5:4: "his heart should be open upwards as if he is standing in heaven." See also King Solomon's prayer cited above and *Talmid Rabbenu Yona al Berakhot* 22b. In addition, many sources discuss a correspondence between the earthly Temple and its celestial counterpart.

[64] *Berakhot* 31b and *Rambam*, op. cit, 4:16. "What is meant by *kavana*? One should clear one's mind of all thoughts and envision oneself as standing before the *Shekhina*." In *Berakhot* 31b R Joshua ben Levi says: "It is forbidden to sit within four cubits of one praying." Rav Hai Gaon explained that this is "because it is a place of the presence of the *Shekhina*. A proof of this is that, when a person finishes his prayer he must take three steps backward and afterward offer a parting farewell." cited in B. Lewin, ed., *Otzar haGeonim* (Jerusalem, 1984) 1:74 and in E. Wolfson, "Iconic Visualization and the Imaginal Body of God: The Role of Intention in the Rabbinic Conception of Prayer," *Modern Theology* 12.2 (1996): 137–62.

Elliot Wolfson argues that "The term *kavana*... refers to an internal state of consciousness by means of which the worshipper creates a mental icon of God, the function of which is to locate the divine presence in space. In this state of consciousness the phenomenal boundaries of inside and outside dissolve for only by means of the internal image does the worshipper experience the divine as external" (139–40).

[65] *Chidushei Rabbenu Chaim haLevi: Chidushim veBe'urim al haRambam, Hilkhot Tefilla* 4:31, page 6. See also n57 above. According to Rav Chayim, this is the indispensable form of *kavana* referred to in ch. 4. (Ch. 10 refers to concentration on the meaning of the text of the *tefilla*, which is of course desirable throughout but obligatory only in the first blessing.)

mitzvot which guide interpersonal behavior—our entire conception so far of *kavana* becomes, I believe, inadequate. A new framework needs to be incorporated and an added dimension of *kavana* is revealed.

Do *mitzvot bein adam lechavero* require *kavana*? This question has been of interest especially with regard to *tzedaka*, charity. It has surfaced more often in contemporary responsa than in the past and has elicited various responses. One approach builds upon the distinctions defined by Rabbenu Yona. As explained above, Rabbenu Yona differentiated between *mitzvot* solely dependent upon mental activity and those *mitzvot* which incorporate an action (*ma'ase*) which would therefore not require *kavana*. If one accepts this dichotomy, interpersonal *mitzvot* would not require *kavana*. Interpersonal *mitzvot* generally exemplify a greater degree of *ma'ase* than most classic *mitzvot bein adam lamakom* because they leave behind a tangible impact (*roshem*). For example, if we compare the *mitzva* of shaking the *lulav* to the *mitzva* of giving *tzedaka*—both involve an action by an individual. However, in the case of *tzedaka* a change in the situation has been affected. Moreover, it is this particular outcome not the actual action which is the desideratum. No one is interested in changing a *lulav* by shaking it or for that matter, destroying matzah by eating it. Conversely if a sick person needs care, the act of *bikur cholim* is performed by satisfying his or her needs. When a guard-rail must be built on a roof to prevent people falling off it is precisely the presence of the guard rail which is the clear objective of the *mitzva*.

Most interpersonal *mitzvot* are not continuous obligations but rather issue from the needs of others and the general circumstances.[66] (This actually creates

---

[66] Some forms of *tzedaka* such as *pe'a* (leaving the corner of one's field for the poor) are always incumbent upon the individual but even their observance is linked to satisfying the needs of the poor. See Mishna *Pe'a* 1:2 and 4:5.

The *Maharal* holds a totally divergent view, maintaining that even interpersonal *mitzvot* are only for the benefit of those who perform them. See *Gur Arye, Bamidbar* 19:1. And *Tiferet Yisrael* 86 (202).

The *Rishonim* debated a related issue—whether or not one should say a blessing when performing *mizvot bein adam lechaveiro*, such as giving charity (*tzedaka*). One of the main issues was the fact that the goal of a *mitzva* such as charity can only be achieved via the acceptance of help by the recipient. Thus the giver is dependent upon the recipient to fulfill his or her *mitzva*.

the converse problem—the best intentions coupled with what would seem to be an appropriate action may still fall short. For instance, to what extent is one obliged to investigate in order to insure that one's *tzedaka* actually helps the intended individuals?) A person who gives *tzedaka* effectively for an ulterior motive has nevertheless transferred the money and benefited the recipient. While this act may not encompass the full potential for holiness in the *mitzva*, since the goal has been achieved are we to assume that a *mitzva* has been performed?[67]

Whether or not interpersonal *mitzvot* require *kavana* (even according to those who are of the opinion that generally *mitzvot* do need *kavana*) remains a subject of halakhic controversy. There are those who maintain that despite the fact that it is usually the outcome rather than the action which is of paramount importance, nevertheless, *kavana* is required.[68] Others maintain that since *kavana* is irrelevant to the recipient of help, *kavana* is not mandatory. According to some authorities, it may not even be required *lekhatchila* (*a priori*).[69] The subject may not be important for the individual's self-evaluation. If the essential aspect of *tzedeka* is that the needs of the poor are cared for— the individual's focus should be on that and not on his or her own *mitzva*

The *Rambam* ruled that one only makes a blessing on positive commandments which are *bein adam lemakom* (*Mishne Torah, Hilkhot Berakhot* 11:2) and this is the majority opinion. However, Rabbenu Eliyahu used to make a blessing upon rising for an elderly person and other similar *mitzvot*. It is interesting to ponder whether religious practice would look different today if blessings were recited on interpersonal *mitzvot* and they were consequently granted more weight. *Asaf: Sifran shel Rishonim Teshuvot uPoskim uMinhagim*, 199–206; *Perush Rabbenu Eliyahu miLondrish* (Mossad haRav Kook) 32; *Avudraham haShalem* (Jerusalem) 17–21.

Rav Yechiel Weinberg suggests a totally different reason for the lack of a blessing on interpersonal *mitzvot*. See below.

[67] The argument is that if the action is only a means toward the *mitzva* which is essentially a particular outcome, then there is no need for *kavana* in the performance of the action. For a discussion of this principle and of other *mitzvot* which might fall into this category see Elimelech Vinter, "*Mitzvot Tzrikhot Kavana*," *Shmaatin* 88–89 (1987).

[68] Rav Shlomo Zalman Auerbach maintained that it would seem that even the construction of a parapet requires *kavana*. See *Minchat Shlomo, siman* 1, "*be'Inyan Mitzvot Tzrikhot Kavana*" and *Responsa Or leTzion*, vol. 2, 45:4.

[69] For a review of the authorities holding this position with regard to charity, see R. Ovadia Yosef, *Chazon Ovadia*, "*BeDin Mitzvot Tzrikhot Kavana*," ch. 29, 541–43.

count.[70] However, the question may be very important in terms of the religious individual's attitudes towards others such as the secular Jew. If a fellow Jew who does not view *tzedeka* as part of his or her covenant with God nonetheless lives a life of giving—to what extent can the religious Jew feel linked to the secular Jew in the halakhic—covenantal sense?[71]

The evaluation of *kavana* in interpersonal *mitzvot* must relate to another question besides the issue of the practical effects of these *mitzvot*. The ideal content of the individual's *kavana* as defined above—as the intention to perform a *mitzva*—may be too narrow and limiting. Let us take an example from another sphere—Shabbat. It is possible to rest on Shabbat "because it's a *mitzva*" without an awareness of the symbolism of Shabbat. But it is far preferable to be aware that Shabbat is a testimony to God's creation of the world.

In the case of *tzedeka* or visiting the sick or any number of interpersonal *mitzvot*, the relationship with the recipient of help is of paramount importance. *Kavana* to perform a *mitzva* without an empathetic emotional relationship towards the recipient would be hollow indeed and could adversely affect the recipient. Is it preferable if one is motivated by a love or pity for the other or by the command of the Almighty? What would be the *kavana retzuya*—the ideal form *of kavana*?

It is, I believe, important to argue that the ideal form of *kavana* would not be the wish to perform a *mitzva* on this particular occasion. Rather it is the urge to do *chessed*, the sense that one must act on the basis of love for the other. This view was indeed put forth by Rav Yechiel Weinberg (author of the *Sridei Eish*) in a discussion as to why one does not make a blessing on

---

[70] Rav Henkin in his responsa actually asks a questioner what practical difference it makes since "if one clothed the poor without *kavana* to perform a *mitzva*, the poor person is still clothed." And as for fulfilling the personal *mitzva* of *tzedaka* he adds—the minimal amount required *mide'orayta* (biblically) is very small. For a succinct analysis of the issues see R. Yehuda Herzl Henkin, *Responsa Bnei Banim*, vol. 3 "*Kavana beMitzvot ben Adam leChavero*," 38.

[71] *Rambam* related to this question when he wrote about the "gentile who keeps *mitzvot*." See *Mishne Torah, Hilkhot Melakhim* 8:11. The two different versions of this text extant (based upon a difference of one letter in the Hebrew) are diametrically opposed to each other.

mishlo'ach manot on Purim. He argues that since the goal of *mishlo'ach manot* is "to increase peace, love, and friendship," it is preferable if one gives from one's free-will, not just because of the commandment. "And," he continues, "such is also the case of *tzedeka*—one who gives out of compassion or out of love of the Jewish people is preferable to one who gives because of a command or compulsion."[72]

This leads us to a description of a deeper and more encompassing form of *kavana*. True *kavana* in *mitzvot ben adam lechavero* extends beyond the particular *mitzva* one is fulfilling. It entails the realization that it is God's will that one acts with *chessed*. It acknowledges that one's urge to do *chessed* or to work towards justice are aspects of one's *tzelem elokim*—one's divine image. This *kavana* is an expression of the commandment that "Thou shall walk in his ways";[73] "as he is merciful, so you shall be merciful. As he is compassionate, so you shall be compassionate."[74]

This approach suggests that an individual need not experience conflict between his or her autonomous ethical sense and the obligation to observe *mitzvot*. On the contrary, *kavana* in the case of interpersonal *mitzvot*, suggests the cultivation within the self of *ratzon Eloki*—the divine will. The innate ethical sense becomes developed through religious inspiration and behavior.[75]

---

[72] *Sridei Eish*, OC 46. Rabbi Weinberg relates his view to *Rambam*'s contention that people who refrain from evil because that is their natural tendency are greater than people who do so solely because they are obliged to. See *Rambam*'s *Shmone Perakim* (Introduction to *Pirkei Avot*) ch. 6.

[73] Deut. 28:9. See also Deut. 11:22.

[74] *Sifre* to Deut. 11:22 and *Shabbat* 133b. See also Lev. 19:2 and Deut. 10:17–19.

[75] See Rabbi Avraham Yitzchak haCohen Kook, *Orot haKodesh*, Introduction 3:26.

In conclusion, a *mitzva* ideally forms a bond between the Almighty and the finite individual. Nevertheless, a tension is often experienced between the principle that *rachmana liba ba'i*—God desires the heart, and the halakhic importance of the performance of *mitzvot* in their exact form. *Kavana* is the attempt to come to terms with this tension by bringing together heart, mind, and action in the performance of *mitzvot*. The pursuit of *kavana* is the daily challenge of every religious Jew.

III. THE COMMUNITY

Historically, rabbinic discourse has been dedicated to two levels of concern, the personal and the communal. Thus it is fitting that a section of this work be devoted to communal questions.

In this section, the concerns of women and society are explored. From the young woman formally joining Jewish society as an adult at her Bat Mitzvah to the woman who may master certain halakhic knowledge and tradition to the point of being regarded as a halakhic adjudicator, the relevance of these issues today are evident. These discussions can set the stage for coming generations of Torah scholars, as they seek both halakhic and meaningful applications of the Law.

The Bat Mitzvah in Jewish Law and Contemporary Practice

Erica S. Brown

The ceremony that marks the Bar Mitzvah is a relatively late addition to the corpus of Jewish law and practice. For the girl, the Bat Mitzvah celebration is an even later development and arguably, still in formation. Significantly, the Talmud makes no mention of festivities comparable to contemporaneous practice. In *Pirkei Avot* (*Ethics of our Fathers*) we read about the age of thirteen as the acceptance of the commandments, but the age is only one of many in the expanse of Jewish life. "At five for Scripture, at ten for Mishna, at thirteen for *mitzvot*, at fifteen for Gemara, at eighteen for marriage..."[1] The age of thirteen is one of several stages in a young man's spiritual and educational development. The current practice of celebration is rooted in a Midrash on Genesis 25:27, "The boys grew," referring to Esav and Yaacov:

> Rabbi Elazar said: A man must see to the needs of his son until he is thirteen, from there onwards he must say: "Blessed is He who released me from the responsibility of this one."[2]

The blessing did not evolve into an actual ceremony until much later. In the sixteenth century, R. Shlomo Luria, discusses whether or not a meal on the day of the Bar Mitzvah is considered a *se'udat mitzva*, a festive meal to commemorate a commandment. He determines that it would qualify as long as the boy gave a halakhic discourse during the meal.[3] Thus, the celebration was still in formation four hundred years ago which, in the span of rabbinic literature, makes this a rather late legal development.

Why the development of a male ritual rather than one for both genders evolved at this time is unclear when the purpose for the celebration is pre-

---

[1] *Pirkei Avot* 5:25.

[2] *Bereishit Rabba* 63:10.

[3] R. Shlomo Luria, *Yam shel Shlomo, Bava Kamma* 7:37.

sumably the same regardless of gender. Rabbi Alfred S. Cohen in his article on the topic in the *Journal of Halacha and Contemporary Society* asks this important question:

> ...the rationale for making a celebration for a boy who reaches the age of thirteen arises from the fact that a person has to give thanks for achieving a higher level of religious responsibility. Since a girl of twelve undergoes the very same elevation in status, progressing to a level where she has to observe all the *mitzvot* incumbent upon a Jewish woman, does it not follow that there should be the identical obligation to make a party for her?[4]

Jewish educational institutions and parents who express the same concern have, in the last decades, tried to create more religious depth to mark the occasion for girls. Realizing that this entrance into Jewish adulthood, if not significant, can be a farewell to Judaism—especially if compared to the opportunities offered the male at the same life interval—parents and educators have explored new and old ritual observance for the young woman. The ones currently employed by parents anxious to ensure that their daughters feel this important religious transition are usually more a matter of personal predilection than uniformly prescribed, or expected, tradition. More often than not, because no standard ceremony has been adopted in ritually observant communities, the attempt at making religion more egalitarian has led to boys and girls having the same costly party, sometimes devoid of spiritual content. Lisa Aiken in her book, *To Be a Jewish Woman*, mentions that in the absence of uniform ritual for the Bat Mitzvah that, "The possibilities are endless."[5] One wonders what she means by this. Even if this were the case, perhaps the range of alternatives should not be endless. While some use the ambiguity of Jewish law on the matter as an opportunity to craft unusual and poignant ceremonies, the fact that there is no consistent practice, endorsed by the rabbinic community, leaves the girl—perhaps not fully realized until much later in life—a

---

[4] Rabbi Alfred S. Cohen, "Celebration of the Bat Mitzvah," *Journal of Halacha and Contemporary Society* 12 (1986): 8. In this article I will move from primary sources to secondary sources, the latter consisting mostly of articles reviewing various legal aspects of the Bat Mitzvah celebration. Several of these articles brought new halakhic sources to my attention.

[5] Lisa Aiken, *To Be a Jewish Woman* (N.J.: Aronson, 1992) 241.

sense that her passage is more a matter of invention than of tradition.

This article is a plea for the Orthodox rabbinic establishment to create a *uniform* ceremony that acknowledges the significance of a young woman's entering the adult world of *mitzva* observance. The halakhic analysis that follows will try to demonstrate where, within the framework of Jewish law, there may be more room to include young women in ritual performance. Yet these represent only a few suggestions to stimulate more thought about the issue of a girl's religious development in general. When a discussion of Bat Mitzvah becomes tied to a host of other potentially explosive issues—as it has—we lose sight of the most significant question: what do we have to do as rabbis, parents, and educators to ensure that the next generation of Jewish women will be spiritually demanding, ritually observant, and fully educated?

In order to properly explore Jewish legal writings on the possibilities open for the Bat Mitzvah celebration, we will look at three of several customs that are central to the day of celebration: the blessing traditionally recited by the father over the son, the speech or *derasha,* and the commemorative meal or *se'udat mitzva.*[6] Then we have to put the legal discussion within a broader picture of halakhic development to see the limitations on new ritual for this event, why they exist and what direction might be fruitful for a preservation of the spirit of Halakha while at the same time acknowledging the changing demands placed on Jewish women today. This will be framed by a brief discussion of maturity in Jewish law, an area where boys and girls share more similarities in Jewish law than differences. Although the discussion is rather technical (and physical) regarding what constitutes maturity in Jewish law, it is

---

[6] Rabbi Michael Broyde has brought to my attention the need for rituals which demonstrate that the girl entering Jewish adulthood can now fill the religious obligations of others. Presumably, under the general rubric of the *mitzva* of *chinukh*, she has been observing most commandments up until this point. The Bat Mitzvah shows a change of status by filling another's responsibility for commandment performance. This can be accomplished by any number of commandments. More than any of the other observances of the day, Rabbi Broyde feels that this is central to the meaning of the Bat Mitzvah. Although I agree in principle with his conclusion, I think that there are certain accepted "norms" for the Bar Mitzvah celebration which can be meaningful and of educational value for the Bat Mitzvah as well, providing that they are halakhically permissible, of course. To merely point to one area to mark the occasion, such as allowing the young woman to make a blessing over bread for her guests, would be to strip the day of other aspects which have also become integral to Jewish rites of passage.

not inconsequential to the discussion of Bat Mitzvah generally. Can we see from the halakhic discourse any broad guiding principles of rabbinic thought on adolescence and responsibility?

Maturity in Jewish Law

Maturity is defined in Jewish law as the age at which an individual becomes responsible for commandment performance. This is technically defined as twelve years and one day for a girl and thirteen years and one day for a boy. A Mishna in *Nidda* confirms this new stage of "halakhic maturity":

> At eleven and one day, a girl's vows are inspected; at twelve and one day, they are valid. At twelve and one day, a boy's vows are inspected; at thirteen and one day, they are valid. Before this age, even if they were to say, "We know to whom we are vowing, to whom we are donating," their vows are not vows and their donations are not donations. After that age, even were they to say, "We do not know to whom we are vowing, to whom we are sanctifying," their vows are vows and their donations are donations.[7]

Before the prescribed ages, even were they mature enough to realize the implications of the oaths they had just taken, the children's vows would not be valid. Once they each respectively reach a certain age, even were they not mature enough, they are legally bound by their own words. Thus, the Mishna acknowledges that at a very definite date, children become ready to enter the legal world of adults and to assume responsibility for the way they speak and act regarding the performance of Jewish law. However, maturity is not only defined by some mental transition that translates into action at twelve and thirteen, but also by the physical transformation that is assumed will take place during early adolescence. The Mishna in *Sanhedrin* records that the onset of puberty is also significant for the observance of Jewish law.

> "A stubborn and rebellious son": when does he become liable to the penalty of a stubborn and rebellious son? From the time that he produces two hairs until he grows a beard around [by which is meant the hair of the genitals, not that of the face, but the sages spoke in polite terms]....[8]

---

[7] Mishna *Nidda* 5:6.

[8] Mishha *Sanhedrin* 8:1.

The *Shulchan Arukh* describes those who can participate in a quorum as, "males, free men, adults who have [at least] two pubic hairs."[9] Hence, for males, there is a correlation between the onset of puberty and liability or responsibility. Maimonides makes a distinction, in the physical realm, between males and females.

> A girl, after twelve years of age, even were she not to have signs [two pubic hairs], not beneath and not above, is considered an adult. Boys are as their signs... A boy until thirteen is termed a *katan* and *tinok* even if he has a few hairs before this time; this is not as a sign but [considered like] a mole... when he is thirteen years old and one day and older he is termed a *gadol* and an *ish*.[10]

Yet, elsewhere, Maimonides makes no distinction between boys and girls and the significance of physical maturity coinciding with their respective ages:

> A girl of twelve and a day and a boy of thirteen and a day who have brought forth two hairs are considered as adults with regard to all of the commandments and are obligated to complete [the fast on Yom Kippur]. But if they have not brought forth two hairs, they are still minors and their completion of the fast is of a rabbinic status.[11]

The *Shulchan Arukh* follows Maimonides' position on this matter in *Hilkhot Yom haKippurim* and mimics his language:

> A girl of twelve and one day and a boy of thirteen and one day who has brought forth two hairs are considered adults with regard to the all of the commandments and must complete [the fast] from the Torah but if they have not brought forth two hairs then they are regarded as minors and complete the fast as a rabbinic obligation only.[12]

At the time when a child shows physical signs of adulthood, he or she must begin to accept more adult responsibilities. Despite the fact that a distinction might be made for girls and boys as to the significance of puberty for *mitzva*

---

[9] *Shulchan Arukh*, OC, 55:1.

[10] Maimonides, *Mishne Torah, Ishut* 2:9–10.

[11] Maimonides, *Mishne Torah, Shvitut Esor* 2:11.

[12] *Shulchan Arukh*, OC 616:2.

observance, it is clear that maturity of mind and of body coincide regardless of gender and that full adult status is only accorded by the Torah to one who begins to show physical signs of puberty. Boys and girls both move into adulthood physically but spiritually the divergence begins. As this relatively silent and private passage expanded into a more elaborate, public, event, the differences between the male and female public performance became high-lighted.

The responsibilities that are assumed at this stage of development are rela-tively clear for males, from the wearing of *tefillin* to participation in daily synagogue prayer. For the female, according to Jewish law, the major rite of passage mentioned in the Talmud is fasting on *Yom Kippur*: "At the age of twelve, they must fast to the end of the day by biblical law, referring to girls."[13] The age of puberty does not mark for the female an added sense of outward communal responsibility or the acceptance of ritual other than the commandment just mentioned which is also incumbent upon the boy. "As far as religious responsibility is concerned, although a girl becomes so obligated at puberty, she never has the wide range of personal obligation that a male assumes. In addition, there are no central symbols, representing new roles, similar to the male's *tallit* and *tefillin*."[14] Although the body of Jewish law becomes incumbent upon the girl at this age, there are no public signs or an understood communal activity that represent rites of passage into adulthood. One cannot overstate the difference between the nature of *mitzvot* like the acceptance of personal prayer and fasting, and *mitzvot* like *tefillin* and communal prayer where the child is expected to perform in the company of a community with outward symbols of maturity. There are also outward displays of acceptance into the community on the actual day of the Bar Mitzvah that are not permitted or demanded of the girl on her Bat Mitzvah. It is to these that we turn to now.

The Blessing of the Parent

The blessing that the father invokes upon his son's Bar Mitzvah has become a

---

[13] *Yoma* 82a.

[14] Cherie Koller-Fox "Women and Jewish Education: A New Look at Bat Mitzvah," *The Jewish Woman: New Perspectives*, ed. Elizabeth Koltun (NY: Schoken, 1976) 35.

central symbol of this rite of passage—the hightening of the child's independence and the relaxing of adult supervision. If so, it would seem appropriate that
the same blessing be recited for a girl. In order to understand the current
practice and explore future possibilities, we must first understand what the
blessing signifies.

Even though the recitation of the *Barukh Sheptarani* blessing is the shortest
part of the ceremony, it represents the beginning of the ritual of Bar Mitzvah,
according to the Midrash cited earlier. According to the *Magen Avraham*, the
Polish seventeenth century scholar, R. Avraham Gombiner, the blessing frees
the father from punishment for the son's transgressions as the child assumes
responsibility for his own actions.[15] Until that age the father is responsible for
the religious education of his son, and the child's misconduct is attributable to
poor training on the part of the father.[16] Consequently, the blessing is central
because its meaning is seminal to what the Bar Mitzvah signifies, the assumption of adult responsibilities and the parting of parental responsibility. The
blessing recited is a dramatization, on a certain level, of an encounter between
generations and a symbolic separation. R. Yehuda Henkin in his work of
responsa, *Benei Banim*, evokes Yitzchak to explain the nature of the blessing.
Yitzchak raised two sons, Yaacov and Esav, who took two very different life
paths. This demonstrates that despite all that a parent can invest in a child,
children have other influences and make life choices that go outside of the
parental domain. It is for this that the parent makes the blessing, releasing
himself of the culpability for choices which do not accord with his own will.[17]

The sixteenth century commentator, the *Levush*, R. Mordechai Yaffe, posits
a novel interpretation for the blessing's meaning; he says that the child
actually recites it to free himself of the father's sins, concurring with the

---

[15] *Magen Avraham*, OC 225:5. See also, *Chokhmat Shlomo*, ad loc.

[16] See also the *Pri Megadim* for the blessing as a release of the father from the educational responsibilities for his son. This has consequences for whether or not the blessing is
recited over daughters since if the father has no responsibility to educate his daughter then
the blessing would have no substantive meaning and would not, therefore, be recited.

[17] R. Yehuda Herzl Henkin, *Bnei Banim* 18. For a lovely explanation of the blessing's
meaning as the child transforming sin into merit and the father acknowledging this through
recitation of the blessing, see R. Eliyahu Shlessinger, *She'alot uTeshuvot Sho'alin
veDorshin*, vol. 1 (Jerusalem, 1997) 70–74.

biblical notion that the sins of the fathers are visited upon the children.[18] This is in contrast to one rabbinic authority who writes that the punishment of the son is in itself a punishment for the father and that the blessing need not be read according to the *Levush's* interpretation.[19] The *Divrei Chamudot*, R. Yom Tov Lipman Heller, criticizes this interpretation as forced and brings the more traditional understanding of the verse.[20] The *Chokhmat Shlomo*, a later nineteenth century commentary on the *Orach Chaim* of the *Shulchan Arukh*, R. Shlomo Kluger, adds that the concept of the child being punished for his father's sins, a complex idea that has conditions, is operative during adulthood as well and would, therefore, serve no purpose at this juncture.[21] The language of the blessing also does not suggest that it is the son reciting this blessing over the father.[22]

The blessing, traditionally recited by the father, signals not only the parental cessation of responsibility for commandment performance, but enhances the child's sense of independence. Therefore, it would seem that this blessing should likewise be recited for the Bat Mitzvah, who is also under the guidance and training of her parents until she assumes responsibility for her actions. To this, halakhic decisors have generally followed one of two courses. The first assumes that the father is not essentially responsible for the education of his daughter and the second, in contradistinction, holds that the father is responsible for his daughter until marriage, and since the blessing is one of relinquishing responsibility, its recitation would be inappropriate.

The *Magen Avraham, Pri Megadim* and *Kaf haChayim* concur that no blessing is involved for the daughter because they rule that the education of the daughter is in the mother's domain. Both the *Pri Megadim*, R. Yosef Te'omim in the eighteenth century, and the *Kaf haChayim*, R. Yaacov Hayim Sofer of the twentieth century, claim that as the father might give the girl in marriage while still a minor, he would not recite the blessing because she comes of age in her husband's home. The *Kaf haChayim* adds that she is under her father's

---

[18] *Levush*, OC 225:5.

[19] R. Henkin, 18.

[20] *Divrei Chamudot, Perush le-Piskei ha-Rosh, Berakhot* 9:30.

[21] *Chokhmat Shlomo*, OC 225:5.

[22] R. Henkin, 18.

domain until she marries, minor or not, and he cannot relinquish responsibility for her.[23] He challenges the *Levush*'s novel interpretation that the child says this blessing and not the father. If the girl gets married as a minor, she affects, according to his opinion, the fate of her husband and her father and should not be liable for the sins of both. Consequently, the father does not recite the blessing for her. His answer reflects what might have been a modern day reality, that women were married or betrothed while still minors and that a shift in the father's responsibilities should occur for the girl when she marries and not at the age of twelve. Should the modern reader find this alarming, the *Shulchan Arukh* states that even for boys, the optimal performance of the command to marry should take place when the boy assumes the performance of all *mitzvot*, at thirteen.[24]

The *Pri Megadim* adds that, "...even if we require a father to educate his young daughter, not many commandments apply to her anyway."[25] He implies that as she has few commandments to perform, the father's responsibility to educate her is minimal and he need not obsolve himself from a responsibility so insignificant. Modern halakhic decisors and writers have queried the traditional approach to the recitation of this blessing. R. Hanoch Grosberg challenges this interpretation, saying that women must observe all *mitzvot lo ta'ase, mitzvot ase* not bound by time, *and* many that are. He concludes with a question, "Why not recite a blessing for a daughter?"[26] R. Moshe haLevi Sternberg, citing R. Ovadia Yosef,[27] permits the recitation without "*shem umalkhut*" in his compilation, *Hilkhot Nashim*.[28] R. Yitzchak Nissim, former Sephardic chief rabbi of Israel, took this one step further and changed the text of the blessing to reflect a change of gender: "*Barukh Shepatrani Me'onsha shel Zot.*" His justification is that the daughter also requires an education and

---

[23] See OC 225:15 for the three commentaries mentioned on this issue.

[24] *Shulchan Arukh, Even haEzer* 1:3.

[25] OC 225:5. See *Eshel Avraham*, ad loc.

[26] R. Hanokh Grosberg, *HaMa'ayan* 13.2, 41.

[27] R. Ovadia Yosef, *Yabia Omer* 6:29.

[28] R. Moshe haLevi Sternberg, *Hilkhot Nashim* (Jerusalem: 1986) 22. He mentions that there are *achronim* who do not permit the recitation since it requires a quorum and women do not constitute one.

that while the traditional reading of the Midrash from which the blessing was culled uses the word, "*ben*," it can connote children and not only sons. Therefore, he concludes that a blessing may be recited over a daughter but without "*shem umalkhut*," mention of God's name and kingdom.[29] Lest the recitation of the blessing without "*shem umalkhut*" is looked upon less seriously since it withholds God's name, there are several *poskim* who suggested the same apply for the boy since there is no mention of this blessing in the Talmud itself.[30]

Rabbi Getzel Ellinson, author of several contemporary works on women and Jewish law, in his appendix to *Ben haIsha leYotzra*, posits that if the *Pri Megadim* did not obligate the father in the blessing because the mother educates her daughters,[31] then why not have the mother recite the blessing? The same would apply to the thinking of the *Magen Avraham* and the *Kaf haChayim*. This innovative ruling would depend on two factors: (1) the establishment of a responsibility for the mother to educate her daughters, and (2) according to the *Levush's* reading, an affirmative answer to the question: are the sins of the mother transferable to her children such that the recital of the blessing is necessary? Although the *Magen Avraham* rules that "perhaps all commandments are like *Yom Kippur* (with regard to a girl's obligation) and daughters must be trained in their performance, nevertheless the responsibility for this training does not devolve upon the mother.[32] R. Ellinson brings two points to challenge this view: (1) the mother is at home with the daughter and therefore, more likely to train her in the performance of commandments, and (2) a mother is closer to her daughter and can more readily influence her.[33] Here, too, generalizations which may not always hold true are made that lead

---

[29] R. Yitzchak Nissim, *Noam* 7.4.

[30] See, for example, R. Shlessinger 3.

[31] See *Nazir* 29a in the name of Reish Lakish: "A man is obligated to train his son but not his daughter."

[32] *Magen Avraham*, OC 343:1.

[33] R. Getzel Ellinson, *Bein Ha'Isha Leyotzra* (Jerusalem: World Zionist Organization, 1987) 182. He supports this with the position mentioned by R. Hisda in *Ketubbot* 102b, that when parents are divorced the daughter remains with the mother even though the father pays for support, showing that the mother, in this instance, must educate the daughter.

their writer to certain halakhic conclusions. Is it true that a mother is home more with her daughter and that this ensures that the mother is educating her? Equally perplexing is the assumption that the daughter is closer to the mother and that this closeness will result in a stronger Jewish influence. Rather than showing that the mother is directly commanded to teach her daughters, R. Ellinson insists that because of certain factors—the mother's being at home and closer to her daughter than the father—Jewish education or transmission of values will occur naturally. This is not compelling enough proof to overturn the rulings of well-known halakhists, as sympathetic as one may be with R. Ellinson's conclusion.

Regarding the issue of a mother being implicated in the suffering of her children for her own sins, R. Ellinson mentions several possibilities in the affirmative and concludes that should the child recite this blessing, she is freed from her mother's sin. He even entertains the possibility of the mother reciting the blessing for the son as well.

As one can see with a range of legal commentaries both classic and modern, the conclusions arrived at in regard to saying the blessing for a girl are based on assumptions about the girl's lifestyle and education. Classic commentators generally followed one of four positions:

1) The girl does not have to be thoroughly educated since her obligations are minimal and therefore there is not much for the father to be free of in terms of educational responsibility.

2) The father is not under a technical command to educate his daughter, and therefore, it would not be appropriate to make a blessing freeing himself from a responsibility he never had to undertake.

3) The father is not yet free of responsibility to his daughter. This responsibility continues until she gets married.

4) According to the *Levush*'s reading, since the girl herself would be making the blessing—and she may be married at the time, we are not sure who is responsible for her behavior, such that she can absolve him through the blessing. Therefore, no blessing is made.

Modern halakhic commentators have questioned many of the above assumptions; some have done so by making assumptions of their own. On the whole, today, girls are assumed to require more educational background for active Jewish lives, especially when the prospect of betrothal and marriage is farther off in the future than at age twelve.

The *Derasha*

As mentioned earlier, the recitation of a speech by the Bar Mitzvah was the subject of discussion by the *Maharshal*. Applying it to women touches upon the broader question of a woman's participation in the public arena and in synagogue rites specifically. R. Moshe Feinstein forbids any synagogue involvement on the part of the Bat Mitzvah.[34] Some Orthodox synagogues trying to be both sensitive to tradition and to the changing needs of Jewish women have tried to incorporate a girl's remarks after the service, making her speech part of the synagogue service and yet not "officially" in the midst of the service. To circumvent this problem altogether, some rabbis address the Bat Mitzvah in the synagogue or the girl speaks off synagogue premises. The rabbi's comments to the Bar Mitzvah are an important acknowledgment of a future life in the public sphere and validates his entry into the community of worshipers. Regardless of whether or not the girl herself speaks, the rabbi's comments would serve the same function for her as for the Bar Mitzvah. Rabbi J. David Bleich writes that the rabbinic notable, R. Jacob Ettlinger, "sanctioned the institution of such observances in Germany in order to combat the inroads of the early Reform movement, and himself delivered addresses on such occasions."[35]

Today, many twelve year-old girls' birthdays pass without mention in the synagogue sanctuary, without comments that are direct and focused at the Bat Mitzvah herself. The rabbinic address can convey expectations for her in study, synagogue life and commitment to Jewish values and the community. Without public acknowledgment that these expectations are in place, she may not set them for herself or she may get the message implicitly that there are no such expectations. Saying nothing is not the same as doing nothing. The absence of addressing each child, boy or *girl*, as potential members of the Jewish community, conveys a message in its silence.

Today, an increasingly common practice is to make a *siyum* marking the completion of a primary Jewish text in preparation for the occasion. While study is always a worthwhile endeavor and should be encouraged, the study, in

---

[34] R. Moshe Feinstein, *Iggerot Moshe*, OC 1:104.

[35] R. J. David Bleich, *Contemporary Halakhic Problems*, vol. 1 (NY: Ktav, 1977) 77.

itself, is not qualitatively different from any other the Bat Mitzvah may undertake before or after her twelfth birthday. Thus, once again the question arises as to whether or not there exist rites related to this life passage. Again, uniformity also becomes an issue, since not every young woman (nor every young man) will have the background or intellectual composition to embark on this kind of task. Some ambitious young women may complete major works while others will use the same term, "*siyum*" to signify much more limited achievement. Nevertheless, the *siyum* has become a more popular custom recently because it is both a substantive educational accomplishment for the Bat Mitzvah and because, in explaining her choice and the meaning of the work she has studied, she has the opportunity for public discourse and recognition.

The *Se'udat Mitzva*

The *Magen Avraham* contends that parents should make a festive meal for the Bar Mitzvah of their son as they would on the day of his wedding.[36] The *Maharshal* illustrates the need to make a festive meal by referring to the story of Rabbi Yosef, a blind scholar quoted in the Talmud. Since he was blind, he was exempt from the performance of several commandments. He said that he would have rejoiced and made a feast had he heard that he was obligated to perform all the commandments, despite his disability.[37] The *Maharshal* writes that if Rabbi Yosef would have made a party on that occasion then one should certainly make a festive meal for a child's assumption of *mitzvot*.

R. Yitzchak Nissim who earlier questioned why a blessing was not made for the Bat Mitzvah, also thought it significant to have a celebration in the form of a festive meal for a girl.

> ...it seems to me that a feast made on the day a girl becomes subject to the *mitzvot*, on her twelfth birthday, is a *se'udat mitzva*, just as that of a Bar Mitz-vah, for what is the difference? It is a worthy custom... if invited to such an occasion one is obligated to attend.[38]

---

[36] *Magen Avraham*, OC 225:2.

[37] *Kiddushin* 31a.

[38] R. Nissim, page 4. Regarding the obligation to attend a festive meal, see *Pesachim*

R. Ovadia Yosef, former Sephardic chief rabbi of Israel concurs with R. Nissim's opinion and cites the *Ben Ish Chai*'s (R. Yosef Chayim haBavli) position in the nineteenth century that such an occasion is significant:

> The day a girl assumes the obligation to observe the commandments, even in the absence of a festive meal, should be a festive day for her. She should wear her Shabbat clothing, and if possible put on a new dress and recite over it, "*Shehechiyanu*," bearing in mind when reciting the blessing that she is assuming the yoke of the commandments and it is a good sign... We do so in our family.[39]

Modesty

R. Grosberg states that although it is important to hold a festive meal, it should be done in the home rather than in public. R. Moshe haLevi Sternberg writes that, "just as one organizes a commemorative meal for the Bar Mitzvah, so too are most accustomed to make a meal for the Bat Mitzvah since it marks her entrance into *mitzva* observance and she is obligated in keeping all the commandments for women."[40]

R. Bleich assumes that R. Grosberg's insistence that the affair be celebrated at home is for, "reasons of modesty."[41] R. Cohen also explains the distinction in the festivities for boys and girls as rooted in modesty.

> It has never been our way to put women in the forefront of public attention; this accounts for many instances wherein we treat boys and girls or men and women in different ways. Having a girl be the center of attention in a synagogue celebration of her attaining maturity would be antithetical to our concept of *tzni'ut*, but one can readily appreciate that a celebration for her at home, with her family and friends, is more appropriate within the context of *tzni'ut*.[42]

113b and the *Rashbam* there.

[39] R. Ovadiah Yosef, *Yechave Da'at* 2:29 and *Ben Ish Chai, Re'e* 17.

[40] R. Sternberg, 22.

[41] R. Bleich, 78.

[42] R. Cohen, 11. See R. Baruch Rakovsky *haKatan veHilkhotav* (Jerusalem, 1996) 169, where he writes emphatically of the need for modesty and relates it to not making the celebration in a synagogue. He does, however, permit a celebration to take place, but does

R. Moshe Sternbuch in *Teshuvot veHanhagot* uses the same rationale to forbid a father from reciting the blessing, since it implies that the girl would be standing before him at the time and "it is not in the way of modesty to come with his daughter before the public and bless."[43] The call for modesty is reflected in many responsum dealing with women and an enhanced role in Judaism. But modesty is not only a quality for women but espoused by the whole Jewish community and modesty is not always in conflict with the promotion of genuine religious feeling. Ideally, the two operate in confluence. Dr. Joel Wolowelsky comments on this phenomenon: "...honesty also requires avoiding simplistic answers to complex questions. For example, *tzni'ut* (modesty) is a core value in the halakhic community. But one cannot simply dismiss a suggestion by invoking the cry of modesty when our community regularly accepts analogous activities as modest and acceptable."[44] While we cannot readily dismiss the issue of modesty since it is a "core value" nor should we be quick to dismiss the views of those great scholars who see these practices as a breach of modesty; we can nevertheless question the use of the term. We generally use the term as a statement of humility or in contradistinction to physical exposure. Thus a person behaves immodestly if he or she speaks arrogantly or dresses in a revealing way. Naturally, the latter involves some degree of subjectivity. Curiously, we also associate this term more with female behavior than with male. Even the *Oxford English Dictionary* has as one of its definitions of "modesty" the association with women: "Womanly propriety of behavior; scrupulous chastity of thought, speech and conduct." Yet, the way it is often used in current rabbinic literature is that even when the act is a religious one, the fact that it may involve a public appearance or

---

not call it a *se'udat mitzva*. See also Rabbi Sha'ul Yisraeli, *Responsa beMare haBazak*, vol. 2 (Jerusalem: Rubin Mass, 1995) 18–19 where he ruled that the celebration of a Bat Mitzvah, though preferably not the celebratory meal, may take place within the synagogue—if the purpose is "for the increase of the fear of Heaven and the acceptance into *mitzvot* (*ol mitzvot*) for the girls and the families, and this—through a Torah *derasha* (as it should be in all instances)." R. Yisraeli then adds in a footnote: "Consequently, this [the Bat Mitzvah celebration with words of Torah in the Synagogue] is truly a *mitzva*, and like a Torah study class (*sheharei ze devar mitzva mamash kmo shi'ur torani*)."

[43] R. Moshe Sternbuch, *Teshuvot veHanhagot*, vol. 1 (Jerusalem: 1992) 156.

[44] Joel B. Wolowelsky, *Women, Jewish Law and Modernity: New Opportunities in a Post-Feminist Age* (NY: Ktav, 1997) 5.

performance deems it inappropriate. Is it immodest to give a *dvar Torah* (Torah speech or discourse) in public? Is it immodest for a father to recite a blessing over his daughter when she turns Bat Mitzvah, even if it means that she will appear in public? To use one example, the *Chatam Sofer*, in trying to explain why women were not lighting Chanukkah candles, writes that since the custom in Israel was to light outside the home and since this would lead to women being outside close to nightfall, women behaved modestly and refrained from lighting outside. In the Diaspora, although the custom was no longer to light outside, the behavior of women, nevertheless, did not change.[45] Yet, what this also means is that women were denied, according to this view, the privilege of participating in what Maimonides calls a "most beloved commandment."[46] The sacrifice required to behave modestly, according to the definition of modesty offered by some *poskim* can, in some cases, contravene spiritual growth and active participation. Under the blanket clause of modesty, we can squelch many complicated issues without giving them the multifaceted consideration they deserve. And were we to pit the values of modesty against public performance and acknowledgment, would modesty always win out if our concern is developing an inspired future generation of Jewish women?

Imitation of Reform and/or Gentile Practice

The other limitation on the festive meal, put forward most vigorously by R. Moshe Feinstein, is that the Bat Mitzvah is an imitation of practices performed by non-religious Jews, notably imitating the confirmation service.

> Concerning those who wish to conduct a formal celebration for a Bat Mitzvah, under no circumstances is it to be held in a synagogue, which is no place for an optional function. A Bat Mitzvah celebration is surely optional and even trivial and cannot be permitted in a synagogue, especially since it was instituted by Reform and Conservative Jews. However, if a father wishes to make some festivity in his home, he may do so, but there is no reason to consider it a *se'udat mitzva*.[47]

---

[45] R. Moshe Sofer, *Chiddushim*, *Shabbat* 21b.

[46] *Mishne Torah, Hilkhot Chanuka* 4:12.

[47] R. Feinstein, ibid. See Rabbi Shlomo Aviner, *Am keLavi*, vol. 1 (Jerusalem, 1983) 322–

R. Moshe echoes the opinion of R. Aaron Walkin, a Lithuanian born rabbi born in 1865, who saw that the ceremony smacked of reform.

> It is forbidden to arrange gatherings of men and women, young and old, to celebrate a daughter's reaching maturity, not only because of the promiscuity involved, but also because anyone who arranges such gatherings is imitating Gentiles and irreligious Jews and the Torah has warned us against following Gentile practices. Who will remove the dust from the eyes of such reformers... It is not right for men and women to mingle even when the Torah is read and everyone stands in awe; how much more so must this be avoided on more light hearted occasions when no *mitzva* is involved. We must not deviate from our fathers' customs even when no shadow of transgression is involved, and certainly when grave prohibitions are involved.[48]

R. Walkin's cites a number of serious reservations about the Bat Mitzvah ceremony: (1) there will be a mingling of genders and the possibility of promiscuous behavior, (2) the imitation of Gentile practices, (3) the imitation of irreligious Jews, (4) the deviation from the customs of our fathers. Both R. Walkin and R. Moshe do not regard the Bat Mitzvah as a *mitzva*, and, therefore do not obligate any acknowledgment of the occasion.

More recently, R. Moshe Sternbuch has also followed this mode of thinking.

> It is well known that the Reformers celebrate a daughter's coming to *mitzvot* with a large festive meal as for a son and such a party is completely forbidden (*issur gamur*), and a change from the ways of our fathers and any party which is motivated by the purpose of making women and men equal—as do the nations of the world—is completely forbidden. And in making a large celebration for the Bat Mitzvah, their intent is only to prove that women are like men.

24, where he points out that in his own estimation, the Halakha is "not in accordance with what [R. Moshe Feinstein] said" on this issue of Bat Mitzvah. This he shows by bringing some of the sources noted in this paper and concluding that "A Bat Mitzvah celebration is grounded in the holy foundations of the words of our Sages (*yesoda beharerei kodesh shel divrei Chazal*), and that the decided majority of the great Torah personalities of our time ruled that this is a *se'udat mitzva*." Rabbi Aviner also cites Rabbi Amram Aburbi'ah who noted that having a Bat Mitzvah celebration was an ancient custom in Jerusalem (*minhag kadmon birushalayim*).

[48] R. Aaron Walkin, *Zekan Aharon*, OC 1:6.

Even though among us we are not accustomed to have a Bat Mitzvah at all, nevertheless in a place where it is the custom to call several of her friends and family together for a small meal—that has no similarity to a festive meal for the Bar Mitzvah of a man—since it is not a large meal and it is only for women, I do not see in it an *issur*, and since people are accustomed to this there is no need to eliminate it since it is not a public matter and it is not like the Bar Mitzvah.[49]

In R. Sternbuch's responsum, one can detect that the underlying concern is against the in-roads of feminism and its adoption by more liberal segments of the Jewish community in imitation of the "nations of the world." Unlike R. Walkin who mentions the imitation of non-Jewish practice, R. Sternbuch concentrates on the women's movement as the main motivating factor to have a Bat Mitzvah and the aspect which should be of most consternation to the traditional Jew. Evident from R. Sternbuch's language is that his community does not have any form of celebration even though he permits a small celebration within limitations.

It is difficult to understand R. Walkin's worry over imitating non-Jewish behavior. The Christian confirmation is not celebrated until age sixteen and does not involve any practice which is similar to the Bat Mitzvah. More to the point is his contention that the Bat Mitzvah as practiced in traditional communities was an imitation of the Reform confirmation for a girl, which, depending on the community, can take place at different ages, even for middle-aged and elderly women.

One can contrast the opinion of these authorities with the famous responsum of the *Sridei Eish*, R. Yechiel Weinberg (d. 1966), who had a very different response to the changes he witnessed:

A practice [of Gentiles] which is not a norm of idolatry is prohibited only if done in order to imitate them. Some authorities oppose the Bat Mitzvah celebration on the grounds of "You shall not follow their ways" (Leviticus 18:3). However, the initiators of this practice claim that they intend thereby to inculcate in the girl's heart a feeling of love for the commandments and pride in her Jewishness. It does not matter that Gentiles also have celebrations on the maturing of their sons and daughters; they follow their traditions and we follow

---

[49] *Teshuvot veHanhagot* 115, 156.

ours. They pray and kneel in their churches and we kneel and bow down and render thanks to the King of Kings, the Holy One, blessed be He. Some oppose the Bat Mitzvah celebration because earlier generations did not practice this custom. Indeed this is no argument. In previous generations it was not necessary to give daughters a formal education since every Jew was full of Torah and piety; the very atmosphere of every Jewish settlement was thus infused with the spirit of Judaism. Girls who grew up in a Jewish home imbibed the Jewish spirit naturally, as if from their mother's breasts. Now, however, times have changed radically; the influence of the street destroys in our children any semblance of Judaism.

Sound pedagogic principles require that we celebrate a girl's reaching the age of obligation to fulfill commandments. Discrimination against girls in celebrating the attainment of maturity has an adverse effect upon the self-respect of the maturing girl who in other respects enjoys the privileges of the so-called women's liberation.[50]

R. Weinberg, in the continuation of this responsum, concurs with R. Moshe's conclusion that the ceremony should not be held in a synagogue despite the fact that he writes persuasively of the ceremony's value. Here, what is different is not the conclusion of the responsum but its language. While some may see little difference in the two positions if the conclusion is the same, R. Weinberg does sound more encouraging. As text-people, observant Jews should always be and usually are sensitive to the use of language. For example, in the flaming controversy over women's prayer groups, R. J. David Bleich and the five rabbinic signatories of a responsum published in the *Beit Yitzchak* journal in 1985, both R. Bleich and the group were not permissive, and the language of the responsum was harsh. There was suspicion of the women's motives, questioning of the value of the endeavor, and a blanket statement that "*ein anu achra'im lahen*," "we are not responsible for them."[51] The behavior of these women did not warrant rabbinic guidance and the rabbis saw themselves absolved of responsibility to them. In analyzing the responsum, Rabbi Jonathan Sacks, chief rabbi of the British Commonwealth wrote of the main signatory:

---

[50] R. Yechiel Weinberg, *Sridei Eish* 3:93.

[51] R. H. Schacter, *Tzei Lakh be'Ikvei haTzon*, *Beit Yitzchak* 17 (1985).

He accused women of wanting innovation for its own sake, of seeking publicity and of rebellion against Jewish tradition. What is more, such prayer groups never existed in the past; and when in doubt, we should follow only the existing customs. Besides which, if today we allow a significant change in Jewish custom, others will draw the conclusion that further changes are permitted, with tragic consequences for Jewish law... The women's motives should also be examined. Undoubtedly, he argued, the move to create separate women's prayer groups was influenced by the general mood created by the women's liberation movement, which might therefore be forbidden as *chukat hagoy*.[52]

The very same elements that were used in questioning the origin and practice of the Bat Mitzvah arise in the treatment of women's prayer groups. Contrast the skepticism with R. J. David Bleich's language on the same issue in *Contemporary Halakhic Problems*:

For many women, the feminist movement has spawned reflection rather than rejection. Religious introspection and self-analysis with a view to seeking higher levels of spiritual awareness and enhanced observance are to be applauded. Thus, the newly awakened assertiveness of women in our society may well become a positive tool leading to their increased involvement in the religious life of the community. It is imperative that this singular opportunity be seized and be utilized to maximum advantage in fostering the spiritual enrichment of all members of the community.[53]

Even though both are skeptical of the value of women's prayer groups and neither permit them, R. Bleich did not cast aspersions on the spiritual animus of the women involved, and in direct opposition to the position, *"ein anu achra'im lahen,"* encouraged finding ways to use women's new roles as "tools" for enriching the community.

R. Weinberg also presents a challenge to R. Moshe, R. Walkin and R. Sternbuch in his position on the changes of the female role in Judaism.[54] Where R. Walkin in particular saw this advance as a challenge to the "customs

---

[52] R. Jonathan Sacks, "Three Approaches to Halakha" a paper given for the Fifth Immanuel Jacobovits Lecture, Jews College (London) (March 10, 1987) 5.

[53] R. J. David Bleich, *Contemporary Halakhic Problems* (NY: Ktav, 1989) 120–21.

[54] See also R. Weinberg's lengthy responsum on *"kol isha," Sridei Eish* 2:8.

of our fathers," R. Weinberg saw this as an opportunity to heighten self-respect and involvement in Judaism for the girl. He also acknowledges that the mimetic method of passing down tradition has been broken in our times and that this necessitates a more deliberate response to modernity.

R. Weinberg's language in his responsum highlights a critical distinction between intent to perform an action because it is a Gentile practice and the desire to perform a religious act because it is inherently worthwhile. He notes that when Gentiles pray and Jews pray, their acts may resemble one another's but are not for the sake of imitation. The Bat Mitzvah would not be imitative of Gentile behavior, regardless of its possible non-Jewish origin because it serves a legitimate need in Judaism, to inculcate a girl with a love of Judaism and observance of Jewish law. R. Weinberg, elsewhere in this responsum, writes that if the concern were only with its non-Jewish origins, then no distinction should be made between the Bat or Bar Mitzvah, and neither should be celebrated.

The Bat Mitzvah and Rabbinic Responses to Modernity

One can see in this small but significant area of Jewish law, two opposing approaches to normative changes in society. One would be remiss in studying rabbinic literature on the issue of Bat Mitzvah without putting it into the larger framework of concerns. The question of Bat Mitzvah involves the inter-relation of four separate questions, all of which have been noted, to a certain extent, by rabbinic authorities:

1) Has this celebration risen in popularity because of feminism and what should the Jewish response be to that phenomenon?
2) Is there any halakhic precedent for such an occasion and is one needed?
3) Will Orthodoxy be perceived as imitating Reform or Conservative practices by allowing or encouraging the Bat Mitzvah in particular and innovation in general?
4) To what extent must one we be concerned with imitating non-Jewish behavior when discussing Jewish ritual practices?

It is in no way the intent of this author to attempt to answer any of these questions but merely to demonstrate that the issue became explosive because of these four sensitive questions. While some may be alarmed at the extreme positions recorded earlier, it is a rabbinic responsibility when answering every question, to put an answer forward which speaks to the perceived future welfare of the Jewish community.[55] Rabbis who sense that feminism, innovation, and imitation of Gentile practices are the results of a modern culture, estranged from the values of Torah Judaism, will usually take a stringent view. Others who view them as opportunities to invigorate Judaism and to incorporate more public female participation in Jewish life, tend to be more permissive. The creation of new customs has always aroused both excitement and cautious skepticism. A tradition thousands of years old cannot afford quick leaps to match societal norms at the expense of preserving its spirit. Time has always been the measure of whether or not halakhic "experiments" will work within a system of tradition.

In the camp that is skeptical of the Bat Mitzvah's origins, the concern for imitation of liberal Jewish, or Gentile, behavior, especially in the synagogue, was the most significant factor in their stringent position. Perhaps that explains why, generally, the sephardic *poskim* cited here were more supportive of some form of Bat Mitzvah. Whether in predominantly Muslim countries or in the State of Israel, they did not have to contend with the larger societal issue of imitating Christian rites of passage. Currently, the influence of liberal Jewish behavior is more of a factor in the United States than elsewhere. Not living under these clouds, the sephardic *poskim* had more liberty to be permissive. Zvi Zohar, while not dealing with the issue of Bat Mitzvah per se, demonstrates this observation in his article, "Halakhic Responses of Syrian and

---

[55] There are meta-questions which may be raised here regarding the nature of rabbinic authority in general. One specific question that is central to this discussion is in regard to the rabbinic community's serving as barometers and commentators on social change. For example, rabbis who deal in questions of medical ethics are usually informed by physicians regarding the technicalities of procedure and practice, areas in which we can assume there are limitations on the rabbi's expertise. Yet, in other areas, such as the social or psychological impact of a trend or phenomenon which possibly impact on Jewish law, the rabbinic attitude has been more fluid. Often, it seems, that the rabbis who make psychological assumptions that are included in a statement of their position on an issue are the very same who denigrate the role of any outside force, such as psychology or philosophy on Halakha. For more on related issues, see Moshe Sokol, ed., *Rabbinic Authority and Personal Autonomy* (NJ, 1992). In particular, see articles by Lawrence Kaplan, "Daas Torah: A Modern Conception of Rabbinic Authority," and Moshe Sokol, "Personal Autonomy and Religious Authority." His distinctions between different "grades" of autonomy are useful for addressing the issue at hand. I am grateful to Rabbi Elie Holzer for his insights on these meta-questions and for his comments on this article.

Egyptian Rabbinical Authorities to Social and Technological Change."

> ...the rabbis had no need to define themselves as members of one camp or another and, paradoxically, their options in formulating halakhic responses to new situations evolving in the life of their congregations were, therefore, more open and diverse.[56]

In Ashkenaz, external factors usually succeeded in limiting the scope of this celebration. And that is part of the problem.[57] The one question that is not in our list is, in my view, the most important and the least discussed—with the exception of a few comments by R. Weinberg—in all of the rabbinic debate: What happens to the girl?

The Bat Mitzvah Girl

What happens to the girl in the absence of a meaningful, demanding, spiritually uplifting entry into the world of *mitzvot*? Do we only have to consider the more "political" concerns? Are we more worried about the statement that the ceremony makes to the non-Jewish world, liberal Jews, and our co-religionists than we are to what it says to the twelve year old girl? For all of the broad concerns about what the Bat Mitzvah represents as a statement about feminism, innovation, and modernity—and these are significant factors—we lose sight of what the Bat Mitzvah means to a young girl who may have no clue about "*chukat hagoy*," feminism, or the *Sridei Eish*. It is not infrequent that a middle aged woman will recount the passing of her Bat Mitzvah to me as a non-event in her family. She may have received a new dress and there was a *kiddush* in her synagogue where her father said a few words. Some did not even get that. And whatever happened, it was a fraction of the attention that

---

[56] Zvi Zohar, "Halakhic Responses of Syrian and Egyptian Rabbinical Authorities to Social and Technological Change," *Studies in Contemporary Jewry*, vol. 2, ed. Peter Y. Medding (Bloomington: Indiana University Press, 1986) 19.

[57] A different approach is presented by Solomon Freehof in his article, "Ceremonial Creativity among the Ashkenazim," *Beauty in Holiness*, ed. Joseph Gutman, (NY: Ktav, 1970), where he writes that the Bar Mitzvah is an example of ashkenazi creativity: "...the ceremony itself as an entity and as a widespread regular observance was an original creation... We see, therefore, that the ashkenazim had developed a unique ability in ceremonial creativity. It was the power of visualizing. It can be called an artistic ability, to mold religious laws and doctrines into outward and enduring physical form."

their brothers received on the very same occasion. Many will say that that is when they turned their interests elsewhere. If Judaism was not interested in them, they weren't interested in it. Intelligent women, who, on the cusp of adulthood, experienced indifference to their religious future, may still be observant of Jewish law, but received a clear message of silence about active participation that still influences them in their adult lives. That silence spoke loudly to them. While I cannot demonstrate the correlation between Bat Mitzvah and a meaningful Jewish future empirically, I can say through intuition and through countless conversations with adult women that the Bat Mitzvah is a seminal experience in developing intellectual and spiritual curiosity about Judaism and the performance of its commandments.[58]

---

[58] On a broader note, there has been more attention paid lately to the psychological development of adolescents and specifically teen-age girls struggling with issues of self-esteem. In *Making Connections: The Relational Worlds of Adolescent Girls at Emma Willard School*, a group of educators and psychologists took a careful look at what girls of this age were thinking and doing in the context of one school. Carol Gilligan, one of the book's editors and a noted Harvard scholar who has written extensively on women and girl's educational development, had this to say:

> Adolescence poses problems of connection for girls coming of age in Western culture, and girls are tempted or encouraged to solve these problems by excluding themselves or excluding others—that is by being a good woman, or by being selfish. Many current books advocate one or the other of these solutions. Yet the problem girls face in adolescence is also a problem in the world at this time: the need to find ways of making connection in the face of difference. Adolescence seems a watershed in female development, a time when girls are in danger of drowning or disappearing.

(Carol Gilligan, "Teaching Shakespeare's Sister: Notes from the Underground of Female Adolescence," *Making Connections: The Relational Worlds of Adolescent Girls at Emma Willard School*, eds. Carol Gilligan, Nona P. Lyons, and Trudy Hammer (Cambridge, Ma: Harvard University Press, 1990) 9–10. I am also grateful for my extensive conversations with Nona Lyons, a co-editor of the book, in making me aware of the urgency of the matter and drawing my attention to recent literature on adolescent girls.)

Although Gilligan's work reflects a case study in one school of girls mostly well into their adolescent years, her observations, nevertheless, should make us contemplate our own situation "back home," so to speak. At this time of watershed, with introspection and sensitivity, we can make sure that Judaism for the twelve year old girl does not "drown or disappear" but helps the young woman enter a time of increased study, *chesed* activity, and communal awareness. Where the middle class white adolescent female may be foundering in her search for identity and increased connection to the outside world, the Jewish equivalent must be anchored and nurtured and welcomed into a world that is both spiritually meaningful and demanding. We have to pay careful attention to what educators

Where do these intuitive thoughts lead in terms of an actual celebration? They emphatically do not lead to where we currently are. The attempt to make a Bat Mitzvah more like a Bar Mitzvah in terms of the party, in my opinion, is worse than the message of silence. R. Moshe, while not being a supporter of Bat Mitzvah innovation, did not show great support for modern Bar Mitzvah celebrations either, claiming that such occasions were responsible for a great deal of Shabbat desecration and that, "...it is well-known that they have brought no one, not even the Bar Mitzvah, any closer to Torah and *mitzvot*."[59] Many think that by having the same lavish affair, number of guests, and excess of gifts, we are helping the Bat Mitzvah achieve equality with the Bar Mitzvah. The girl will hopefully produce a piece of Torah but, again, as so often happens, the speech is written by the parents and comprehensible only to them and their adult company. The celebration loses its focus on the child's spiritual composition and becomes an occasion to impress others with words, food, and entertainment that hold little, or no, Jewish meaning for the child. And yet, because there has been no uniform celebration for the Bat Mitzvah put forward by the rabbinic establishment, people are left to their own devices.[60] To put it simply:

---

and psychologists are alerting our attention to and see how, within the framework of Halakha, we can address some of the pitfalls of female adolescence.

Again, the question of whether *poskim* acknowledge that such research can impact on halakhic decision making is not clear. Generally, halakhic discourse follows a very structured and well-established pattern. Whether or not that pattern will ever include other "disciplines" is an issue which is beyond the scope of this paper.

[59] R. Moshe Feinstein, OC 1:104.

[60] "Left to their own devices" presents the real danger for the Bat Mitzvah ceremony. Look, for example, at two suggestions for active rites of passage. Nina Freedman, "When a Jewish Woman Comes of Age" (*Sh'ma*, 6.3, April 2, 1976), suggests that a girl should mark her coming of age with immersion in a *mikva* following the onset of menstruation. This, she claims, would help her come to terms with her "physical womanhood" and would be a personal celebration of "self-awareness." This may have the opposite effect and signal to the girl that this new stage in her life is marked by something physical not spiritual, and something sexual, which is not in any way marked for the Bar Mitzvah. One can only imagine the problems potentially caused by this potential sanction of premarital inter-course. Koller-Fox in her article cited earlier got together with her class of girls and "agreed upon the idea of designing a blue satin headband, with a meaningful verse from the Bible of prayer book embroidered on it" (40). In the absence of a uniform practice, Koller-Fox asked her twelve year olds what they wanted to do. They came up with a

...ignoring current developments in this way reflects a non-halakhic attitude. Instead of examining the basis of certain *takkanot* to see whether they still have meaning and purpose, the rabbinical establishment is afraid of any change and anything new. In certain areas, of course, life itself has taken over.[61]

Life has taken over and has left the laity to decide. In the absence of rabbinic guidance, the female equivalent to the male ceremony is sadly becoming the norm. In other periods of time where the position of women in society altered, rabbinic leaders and educators understood that Torah education for women had to be magnified in its intensity in order to match the needs of secularly well-educated women. Whether we turn to R. Samson Raphael Hirsch, Sara Schenirer, the *Chafetz Chayim*, or the *Sridei Eish*, we see models of piety who also understood that Jewish women faced difficult transitions that required flexibility. Ignoring these developments or disparaging them only alienated leaders from the very women who needed guidance, and possibly turned the women themselves away from Torah observance. Today we see, in areas of women's education, the fruits of their flexibility in all segments of the Orthodox community. In recent years, we have turned from the controversy over women's education to women's roles in the public sphere and in ritual performance. Here, too, a strict adherence to Jewish law coupled with flexibility and sensitivity to language need to be the rubric under which we think about these issues. R. Baruch Rakovsky, one rabbi who did not permit the Bat Mitzvah to take place in a synagogue on the grounds of modesty, nevertheless acknowledges in a footnote the significance of the Bat Mitzvah in today's climate:

> Since now there has been a change in the generations and girls are educated in non-Jewish or secular schools which are not concerned with imparting in the hearts of their students a love of Torah, fear of Heaven, or admirable character traits, therefore, on the day that the girl arrives at the acceptance of *mitzvot*, it is fitting to do this [have a celebration] with happiness and at that time to educate her in her obligations in Torah and *mitzvot*...[62]

"religious" headband.

[61] R. Eliezer Berkovits, 80–81.

[62] R. Rakovsky, ibid., see n42 above.

In summation, R. Moshe's words are a clarion call for spiritual authenticity. Perhaps that is why we read nothing of such a ceremony in talmudic times. Thirteen marked an age, only one of many, where religious expectation became a reality. But the same was true for the five year old learning to read the weekly *sedra* and the ten year old picking up his first copy of the Mishna *Berakhot*. Only by ensuring that the early pieces and milestones are in place, i.e., a background of study and commitment, will the future dates have any meaning. And even with all of the background pieces in place, the Bat—and Bar—Mitzvah ceremony must focus on the child and the implicit messages she or he receives from the adult world of Judaism. Rabbinic leaders cannot cower in the face of modernity's challenges at the expense of a future generation of halakhically observant, knowledgeable young women and future Jewish mothers. A responsible rabbinate will work toward a more uniform practice that can effectively deliver the Jewish community's expectations to the young girl with active rites of passage. The components of that ceremony are, as of yet, unclear, but are currently under exploration. In the absence of responsible rabbinic guidance, life will take its own course and the laity will decide, much to the spiritual detriment of our Jewish future. More than any issue of feminism, innovation, and materialism, the planners of the modern day Bat Mitzvah—the parents, the rabbi, the educator—must put themselves in the mind of the twelve year old girl and think what will most enhance her chances of growing into an observant, spiritual, and humanitarian Jewish adult.

Red Strings:
A Modern Case of Amulets and Charms

Rachel Furst

At the entrance to the women's section of the *Kotel*, an old lady hovers, rain or shine, waiting with outstretched palm for a generous passer-by to offer her a coin. Often, she will press the giver to accept a length of red string in return, mumbling blessings for health, happiness, successful marriage, and raising of righteous children.

What is the significance of the red "bendela" this old lady offers? In Israel, one notices a growing number of men and women, and teenage girls in particular, with red threads knotted around their wrists. Does this red string (חוט אדום) have any basis in halakhic literature or practice? Is it an entirely unfounded, recently-developed folk custom with no backing from traditional sources? And above all, does the wearing of such a "charm" infringe upon any halakhic prohibitions regarding amulets and folk-medicine?

The primary talmudic source which discusses the halakhic status of charms is the Mishna and its corresponding Gemara on *Shabbat* 67a.

> One may go out with [and carry on Shabbat] the egg of a grasshopper, the tooth of a fox, and a nail from the cross for medicinal purposes, these are the words of Rabbi Meir. The Rabbis [however,] prohibit [carrying these items] even on weekdays due to [the prohibition regarding] the ways of the Amorites.

The Mishna enumerates various charms which were believed to have medicinal value, and therefore, according to Rabbi Meir, are permissible to carry on the Shabbat because they fall under the heading of medicinal purpose (משום רפואה). The rabbis, however, prohibited these same charms, deeming them Amorite practices (דרכי האמורי), the Amorites being one of the seven nations that the Jewish people were instructed to destroy upon entering the Land of Israel, who regularly engaged in such activities.

The category of Amorite practices is related to the prohibition in *Vayikra* 18:3 of "ובחוקותיהם לא תלכו," not following the customs of the non-Jews. This prohibition is also cited in *Shmot* 23:24 and in *Vayikra* 20:23. The ban on the laws of idol-worshippers (חוקות העכו״ם) is a clear-cut, Torah-based prohibition, which the *Sefer haChinukh* rules is in effect in all places, at all times, for both men and women.[1]

Rashi on *Shabbat* (67a) understands Amorite practices to be a type of divination (נחוש), which would be included under the prohibition of "ובחוקותיהם לא תלכו."

The *Beit Yosef* in the name of the *Smag* explains that Amorite practices would fall under both the prohibition against divination as well as that against laws of the non-Jews (חוקות הגוים).

> Their laws are the puzzling [practices] and Amorite practices are the divining [practices]. And if with regard to all of [these practices it is] taught "This is of the Amorite practices," the *Smag* explained that there are two [types of] Amorite practices: one which falls under [the prohibition of] *nichush* and one which falls under [the prohibition of] laws of the idol-worshippers.[2]

The *Encyclopedia Talmudit* paraphrases the commentary of the *Ba'alei haTosafot* to define Amorite practices as practices stemming from the laws of idol worshipers (חוקות העכו״ם)[3] which are not directly associated with the idol worship itself but with other foolish and futile practices of these nations.[4]

Although the Torah does not explicitly list a prohibition against charms, the *Jewish Encyclopedia* mentions an interesting Biblical source for a specific prohibition regarding the possession of charms.[5] In chapter 35 in *Bereishit*, immediately after the incident of Dina's rape in the city of Shechem, Yaacov prepares to approach Beit-El where he will offer sacrifices of thanksgiving. He commands his household accordingly in verse 2: "Remove the foreign gods that are in your midst." Verse 4 records the actual carrying-out of this command, stating, "And they gave to Yaacov all of the foreign gods that were in their possession and the earrings that were in their ears." The removal of

---

[1] ספר החנוך מצוה רסב, ״שלא ללכת בחוקות הגוים.״

[2] ב״י, יו״ד קעח, ד״ה ״אסור ללכת.״

[3] סנהדרין נב ע״ב, ד״ה ״אלא כיון דכתיב בשריפה,״ עבודה זרה יא ע״א, ד״ה ״ואי חוקה היא.״

[4] אנציקלופדיה תלמודית, בעריכת הרב שלמה יוסף זוין, כרך שביעי, ״דרכי האמורי,״ עמי תשי״ו.

[5] "Amulet," *Jewish Encyclopedia*, ed. Isidore Singer (NY: Funk and Wagnalls, 1901) 1:546–50.

jewelry is obviously an addition to the original command. The addition implies a connection between the foreign gods they possessed and the trinkets they wore, seemingly as a type of charm connected to idol-worship.

In the opinion that was accepted as Halakha, Rabbi Meir (or according to the Jerusalem Talmud's version, Rabbi Yossi) permitted the use of the charms listed in the Mishna on *Shabbat* (67a) because of their medicinal purpose. What are the parameters of this category? Can additional charms, such as red strings, be considered medicinal forms as well? Since the claim that certain folk-practices have value because of their medicinal purpose was the basis of the Gemara's leniency regarding specific charms, precisely defining the boundaries of this classification by addressing issues of incantations vs. tangible charms, preventative vs. reactionary medicine, and the nature of string itself as a form of medication will aid us in determining whether the red string practice we are concerned with qualifies for this permissive ruling.

The Gemara on *Shabbat* (67a) qualifies the term "medicinal purpose" (משום רפואה) by stating:

> Abaye and Rava who both said, anything which has in it medicinal purpose does not have in it [the prohibition regarding] the ways of the Amorites, thus [that which] does not have in it medicinal purpose has in it the ways of the Amorites.

A discussion among the medieval commentators which is of supreme relevance to our topic surrounds the precise definition of the term "medicinal purpose" (משום רפואה),. *Rashi* defines:

> That its cure is apparent, such as the drinking of a cup [of medicine] and the bandaging of a wound. And we challenge, "thus [that which] does not have in it, etc."—such as an incantation which is not recognized as being medicinal— "has in it the ways of the Amorites"![6]

The *Rosh* counters *Rashi*'s claim, arguing on the basis of the Gemara itself, which lists specific incantations and deems them permissible, that the requirement regarding medicinal purposes relates only to an action whose medicinal

---

[6] רש״י, שבת סז ע״א, ד״ה ״שיש בו משום רפואה.״

value is questionable and not to an incantation.[7] However, aside from their debate on this particular point, both commentators agree that according to the Gemara, the use of a tangible charm which does not have a proven, recognized, medicinal purpose is prohibited. Maimonides follows this line of argument, maintaining in *Hilkhot Shabbat* of his *Mishne Torah*: "A person may go out with [and carry on Shabbat]... any object which is for medicinal purpose, that is, that which the doctors deem to be [medicinally] useful."[8]

The *Rashba*, however, maintains that if there is doubt as to medicinal value, "מן הספק מותרין" (out of uncertainty, they are permitted); in other words, the outright prohibition of the Gemara affects only those charms for which clear proof against medicinal value exists.[9] This opens the door for the *Ritva* to argue:

> That the Torah did not prohibit [practices] except for things of invalidity that are done without any point. And therefore, even something which is not a compress and not a bandage, if it has in it medicinal value, such as a charm or the like, it is permitted.[10]

It is interesting to note that the *Ritva* does not include charms in the category of valueless practices. Thus, according to some medieval commentators (such as the *Ran*, in addition to the *Ritva*), a charm that is kept for its possible health benefits could be permitted.[11]

We have suggested that the permissibility of charms depends on the belief in their medicinal value. As sources which are to be examined in the following sections testify, many of those who wear red strings today believe that they are a charm for good luck related to marriage, children, prosperity, etc. Could

---

[7] ראייש, מסכת שבת ו׳:ט.

[8] משנה תורה, הלכות שבת יט׳:יג.

The actual words of the *Rambam* are: "ובכל דבר שתולין אותו משום רפואה" whose exact intent is somewhat ambiguous. "שתולין" generally means "that are suspended," but it is unclear whether the *Rambam* was referring to pendants or to other charms that might be hung on the wall, etc.

[9] חדושי הרשב״א, שבת סז ע״א, ד״ה "כל דבר שיש בו רפואה אין בו משום דרכי האמורי."

[10] חדושי הריטב״א, שבת סז ע״א, ד״ה "כל דבר שיש בו רפואה אין בו משום דרכי האמורי."

[11] ר״ן, פסחים ל ע״ב בדפי הרי״ף, ד״ה "כל דבר שיש בו משום רפואה."

these benefits be loosely defined as health benefits, thus permitting the use of such an amulet?

In his recently published book *Kuntrus Tamim Tehiye haShalem*, Rabbi Yaacov Moshe Hillel claims that charms of this nature do not fall within the boundaries of medicine and are therefore questionable.

> ...But those charms which are for other matters, such as for love and for favor, for livelihood and for success, to release a prisoner from prison, etc., we still have not found a permissive ruling for them in the words of the rabbinic authorities, who base their rulings on that which was said by our rabbis, may they rest in peace, "Anything which is for medicinal purpose, etc." [12]

Others believe, however, that the red strings are a charm which offers protection against all negative effects of the evil eye. This type of protection could conceivably be construed as medicinal as it would constitute protection against future illness.

Thus, a point which requires clarification is whether for medicinal purpose (משום רפואה) applies only to charms that are used after a malady has been diagnosed or whether the category extends to charms used as preventative medicine. The red string practice, as we have defined it, would fall into the latter group.

A *beraita* that is quoted in an earlier discussion on *Shabbat* (66b) leads one to believe that preventative charms are fundamentally permissible.

> The Rabbis tell, One may go out with a preserving stone [carried by women during pregnancy] on Shabbat, and attributed to Rabbi Meir they said, even with the weight of a preserving stone. And not [because] she has miscarried [previously], but lest she miscarry, and not [only if] she became pregnant, but lest she become pregnant and miscarry.

In his comments on the Gemara on *Shabbat* (67a), the *Shiltei Giborim* similarly claims that such charms are permissible.

> And my teacher, my Rav, explained in his rulings that it was not permitted for medicinal purspuses (משום רפואה) except for one who is sick and needs curing; but what they do to protect from sickness, so that it won't come, this

---

is of the Amorite practices. [However,] I already explained in *Kuntrus haRa'ayot* that even to protect him from the sickness is permitted...[13]

The *Shiltei Giborim* goes on to prove his claim that preventative charms are permissible on the basis of another Gemara in tractate *Shabbat*. So although there are dissenting opinions among the medieval commentators, one could justifiably claim that on this basis alone there is not sufficient evidence to black-list red strings.

However, clear sources do exist to support the claim that strings, by nature, cannot be classified as legitimate medical remedies. With regard to the prohibition of carrying on Shabbat, the *Tur* states: "It is prohibited to bind a string or drawstring on the wound to go out with it [on Shabbat], because since they do not cure they are a burden [which it is prohibited to carry on Shabbat]."[14]

The *Bach* explains the *Tur*'s ruling: "In explanation, a mere string or mere drawstring without a cotton rag or sponge or all these which are considered such, here it is prohibited to bind on the wound, because since they do not cure they are a burden."[15]

Most rabbinic authorities emphasize that string in itself cannot be considered to have medicinal value and therefore, by its very nature, a red string would not fall under the category of permissible charms. It is necessary to note that there is, however, an apparently dissenting opinion found in the Jerusalem Talmud in a parallel Mishna to ours in the tractate *Shabbat*.

> The sons may go out with [and carry on Shabbat] knots and the sons of kings with bells—and every man [is included in this statement], except that the Rabbis spoke in the accepted form. One may go out with [and carry on Shabbat] the egg of a grasshopper, and the tooth of a fox, and a nail from the cross for medicinal purposes, these are the words of Rabbi Yossi. Rabbi Meir prohibits [carrying these items] even on weekdays due to [the prohibition regarding] the ways of the Amorites.[16]

---

13 שלטי גבורים, שבת ל ע״ב בדפי הרי״ף, אות ג, ״לשון ריא״ז.״

14 טור או״ח שא.

15 ב״ח, או״ח שא, ד״ה ״יוצאין במוך וכו׳.״

16 ירושלמי, שבת ו :ט [ח].

The *Yerushalmi* records the same three charms as our Mishna on *Shabbat* (67a), but precedes them with an additional permissive ruling regarding knots or bands—קשרים, hence the connection to string—and bells. In explanation of the permission accorded to these additional items, the *Korban haEida* on the *Yerushalmi* maintains that the reason here is also for medicinal purposes (משום רפואה) as knots and bands clearly have medicinal value.

> "One may tie knots and hang [them] around [one's] neck for medicinal purpose, and I did not know for which malady," [these are the words of] *Rashi* [on the corresponding Mishna in the Talmud]. And to me it appears that it is appropriate for all the illnesses...[17]

Thus, according to the opinion expressed by the *Korban haEida*, the string aspect of red "bendelas" would not be sufficient reason to prohibit the practice.

The idea that string, or knots, can be considered a medicinal cure leads us directly to the question of whether one is required, or even permitted, to rely on clearly outdated medical opinions. A point emphasized by many of the medieval commentators is that in order to qualify as medicinal (רפואה), medical practices have to be "מצד הסברא," to have some logical basis, and so the argument surrounding the issue of medical advice given by *Chazal* has direct relevance to our discussion of charms today.

Maimonides addresses this issue in his *Guide to the Perplexed*, where he claims that the only folk-medicine which is permissible are those practices which stand up to practical inquiry, "שמחייב אותו עיון הטבעי."

> And do not allow to trouble you those which they permitted such as the nail of the cross and the tooth of the fox, because these, in those times, were thought (חשבו בהן) to have been proven by trial and therefore were followed for medicinal purposes (משום רפואה)...[18]

Rabbi Yosef Kapach, who translated the *Guide* from its original Arabic, added in his notes that the word *chashvu* in the above quote is a translation of the

---

[17] קרבן העדה, שבת ו:ט, ד"ה "בקשרי פואה."

[18] מורה הנבוכים להרמב"ם, חלק ג, לז.

Arabic word *th'an* "טّיّן," which connotes "an incorrect thought which comes to mind, seemingly on the basis of a mistake or a digression."[19]

Such a meaning lends additional emphasis to Maimonides' claim that one is allowed to rely on the medical opinions of *Chazal* even if it is clear that they were rendered based on misinformation. This opinion is so uncharacteristic of Maimonides that the *Rashba* comments on the passage quoted above:

> We did not know which to put into practice from the words of the Rav... And perhaps the Rav would say that even what is attributed in their books to a charm, we should not believe, since the essence of their agenda is chaos and futility in the affairs of sorcerers. But what the Rabbis said, we will believe and rely on to carry out acts from what they permitted and approved as a charm. And the Rav has placed us in great confusion.[20]

The *Rashba* concedes that his own opinion on dealing with the medical advice of *Chazal* is to rely on what the Talmud deemed permissible.

> And if so, it is permissible to rely on the experience of the ancients, and we do not prohibit them until that experience is tested verifiably before our eyes [and proven false], for behold, [with regard to] the nail of the cross and the tooth of the fox, we are permitted to rely on the experience of the ancients, and just like we rely on the scholars of medicine regarding those medicines which natural logic does not derive.[21]

However, he also extends this permissive ruling beyond *Chazal* and claims that it is acceptable to rely on the charms and amulets of any soothsayer who has experience in the field.

> And not on the scholars of the Torah and the scholars of medicine alone, but on all people who say they are experienced in this area they [the Rabbis] permitted us to rely on, such as the preparers of amulets, for behold, they [the Rabbis] permitted the amulets, be they [made] of roots [or] be they written...[22]

[19] מורה הנבוכים, תרגום לעברית ע"י יוסף קאפח. ירושלים: מוסד הרב קוק, 1977. עמ' שנט, הערה 40.

[20] שו"ת הרשב"א השלם, חלק א, קסז.

[21] Ibid.

[22] Ibid.

The *Rashba* does note, though, that it is unclear whether Maimonides himself intended to go so far as to permit amulets prescribed by those other than *Chazal*.

In a more recent ruling, the *Chavot Yair* suggests that today it may no longer be permissible to follow the medical advice of *Chazal* since the exact meaning of the ingredients and measurements prescribed has been lost over the years. Additionally, the physical constitution of people today is different from that of previous generations, and it is likely that ancient medicine will no longer be effective. He concludes, though, that the weakening of the human constitution has been proportional to the weakening of the effectiveness of the ingredients used in such folk-medicine.[23]

Red strings around the wrist are certainly not recognized by modern medicine and logical support for their effectiveness as a charm is limited. Even relying on broad interpretations of medicinal purpose (משום רפואה), to claim that they have medicinal value today seems far-fetched "מצד הסברא."

Despite the lack of clear halakhic support for red string amulets, sources suggest that such a practice existed in various Jewish communities throughout the ages. It is unclear though, whether early customs involving red strings are in any way related to the practice that is gaining popularity today.

At the grave site of Rabbi Meir Baal HaNess in Tiberias, an elderly man who sells red strings that have been wrapped around the tomb and other religious paraphernalia, quotes the book of *Yehoshua* as the original source for the red string practice. In *Yehoshua* (2:18–19), the two spies who are sent into Jericho by Joshua to gather strategic information, warn the prostitute Rachav, a Jericho-native who saved their lives by hiding them from city authorities, as follows:

> Behold, when we come into the land, you shall bind this cord of scarlet string (תקות חוט השני) in the window through which you lowered us down, and your father, and your mother, and your brothers, and all of your father's household you shall gather into your house... and anyone who is with you in the house, his blood shall be on our heads if a hand is laid upon him.

---

[23] שו"ת חות יאיר רלד.

The *Targum* translates "תקות חוט השני" as "תורא דחוט זהוריתא," a band of crimson string. After serving Rachav as a mark of immunity during the destruction of Jericho, the red string became a universal symbol of protection from destructive forces. Similarly, another possible source for red as a color of protection is the blood of the paschal lamb smeared on the doorposts of Jewish homes in Egypt on the eve of the Plague of the Firstborn.

The *Tosefta Shabbat* that relates to the Mishna on *Shabbat* (67a), which has been under discussion, is perhaps the clearest reference to the existence of a red string practice in an earlier period. It explicitly includes red string (חוט אדום) in a list of superstitious customs which are considered Amorite practices.

> These things are from the ways of the Amorites: he who cuts his hair in the fashion of the Gentiles, and he who makes a plait [in his hair], and one who is unable to control his sexual appetite, and one who drags her son between the dead, and one who ties a pad to his thigh and a red string on his finger... behold, this is from the ways of the Amorites.[24]

In his multi-volume work *Tosefta Kifeshuto*, Saul Lieberman notes that such a practice was common and tolerated in his own community, as well as in towns across Poland during the advent of epidemics.

> This charm was very common in the Old World... and mainly, the crimson string was used as an amulet for children. And my memory is that in this manner, they hung a red string on the necks of children in my town Mottela at the time of the measles epidemic and there was no protest on their hands, and thus was the custom even in the countries of Poland.[25]

In terms of the specific form of the practice we are concerned with, which involves tying a red string around the wrist, it is interesting to note that Lieberman later quotes an alternate version of the *Tosefta* which he attributes to a 15th-century book, the *Menorat haMa'or*: "And in *Menorat haMa'or*, section 4, page 444: 'Rabbi Zadok says, One who ties on his hand a red sting, behold, this is of the Amorite practices.'"[26]

---

[24] תוספתא, שבת ז:א.

[25] שאול ליברמן, תוספתא כפשוטה, (נויארק: הוצאת בית המדרש לרבנים שבאמריקה, תשכ"ב) 82, ד"ה "חוט אדום על אצבעו."

[26] תוספתא כפשוטה, 96, ד"ה "ר' לעזר בי ר' צדוק או' הרי זה מדרכי וכו."

With regard to contemporary forms of such a practice, the July 23, 1887 edition of *HaMelitz*, a Hebrew daily published in St. Petersburg, reports an incident similar to that which Lieberman recalls as having occurred in his hometown.

> For about a month, the word has been out in the district city of Sovalk [sic] that the rabbi of the city has instructed parents whose sons and daughters have not yet reached thirteen years to tie on the hands of these children, and on a part of their necks, a string of crimson, saying that this is a wondrous charm for safeguarding against the epidemic; he means to say, [the one] that will be coming within our midst.[27]

The reporter maintained that the roots of such a foolish, baseless practice were based on the manipulation of a shrewd businessman rather than on any intrinsic association:

> Many cast doubt as to whether this matter really came forth from the rabbi in the big city—indeed, his greatness in Torah is known to everyone, he is also wise and intellectual, and what would come over him to [cause him to] instruct making such a charm? There are those who say that this pronouncement came forth from one of the shopkeepers, because in his shop this merchandise (red strings) was stocked in great quantity, with virtually no turnover. He tried to be clever and remove it from his shop without total loss; lo and behold, his cleverness managed to procure him great profit.[28]

The *Jewish Encyclopedia* records that in Germany, until present times, red cords with corals were worn as a protection against the evil eye and that in Hamburg, spools of red silk were regularly wound around a newborn's wrist to protect the mother and child.[29]

After studying the *Tosefta*, which states explicitly that tying a red string around one's finger is considered Amorite practice, one might question how red string (חוט אדום) could possibly escape the related prohibition. In response,

---

[27] *HaMelitz* 163, July 23, 1887, cols. 1730-31.

[28] Ibid.

[29] "Superstition," "Childbirth," *Jewish Encyclopedia*.

medieval and post-medieval commentators, as well as contemporary scholars, have come up with a number of solutions.

Firstly, it is possible to claim, as Lieberman does in the paragraph quoted earlier from *Tosefta Kifeshuto*, that the prohibition of the *Tosefta* is not relevant to our case.[30] "And apparently, we have only what the rabbis prohibited, and they mentioned nothing but his finger. But on the remaining parts of the body, it is permissible."[31] The *Tosefta* prohibits a red string specifically around the finger. Since many of the practices *Chazal* deemed Amorite practices (דרכי האמורי) fall into the Amorite category only because they were common among idol worshipers, the prohibition would not necessarily apply to red string tied around any other part of the body—in our case, the wrist— which was not common practice among the Amorites.

Assuming then, that our red string practice is not addressed by the *Tosefta*, the question becomes: can one extend the boundaries of the prohibition to include specifics not mentioned by either the *Tosefta* or the Gemara?

Rabbi Eliezer of Metz, one of the twelfth century *Ba'alei haTosafot*, states unequivocally in his *Sefer Yeraim* that the practices listed in the Talmud may not be treated as logically-arranged categories nor viewed as random examples; rather, they are to be treated as specifics derived not by way of logic but by tradition, and therefore, are not open to additions.

> And the Rabbis explained what [were] the practices and laws that they regularly carried out for the sake of their statutes in [the tractate] *Shabbat* in the chapter *BeMa Isha Yotza*, and in the *Tosefta* of *Shabbat*, all that was passed on to the Rabbis [regarding practices] that were included [under the Torah prohibition of following], their laws is recounted. And one may not add to them, and they are not logically derived, but passed down [traditionally].[32]

This ruling is quoted by the *Hagahot Maimoniyot* on the Maimonides *Hilkhot Avoda Zara*.[33]

---

[30] תוספתא כפשוטה, 82, ד"ה "חוט אדום על אצבעו".

[31] Ibid.

[32] ספר יראים שיג.

[33] הגהות מיימניות, הלכות עבודת כוכבים א:א, אות א.

In a particularly sharp statement, the *Rashba* sounds even more extreme than the *Year'im* in his claim that the Talmud's list of prohibited charms is based entirely on tradition rather than on any type of logic or natural order.

> It seems that everything which was not prohibited in the Gemara [together] with those that were counted among the practices of the Amorites, it is not for us to prohibit them, because the charms are not known to us and we may not pass judgment on them [based on] the well-known natural order.[34]

Yet the *Bach*,[35] while agreeing that there is no prohibition involved with any practice not explicitly mentioned in either the Mishna or *Tosefta*, tempers these opinions by creating a new category for practices that seemingly fit the description of Amorite practice (דרכי האמורי)despite being excluded from the Talmud's list—one must be separated, or distanced, from them. "צריך להיות נבדל מהם" While it may not constitute an exact prohibition, the imperative "to be separated" "צריך להיות נבדל מהם" is not to be brushed aside either.

But even those who believe that the current red string practice is actually included among the prohibited charms of the *Tosefta* can maintain that we do not accept the *Tosefta* as Halakha and thus, continue to permit the practice. This seems to be the opinion of the *Beit Yosef* in trying to explain the continuing prevalence of the practices that were black-listed by the *Tosefta*.

> And indeed, many things are taught in that *Tosefta* which have in them Amorite practices and many people fail [in this regard] and no one pays attention. And perhaps it implies that it is not [necessary to] be concerned that [things are] משום דרכי האמורי except for the things which were mentioned in the Gemara alone, and all other things that are taught in the *Tosefta* are not [accepted as] Halakha, for were that not the case, the Talmud wouldn't remain silent with regard to them.[36]

The *Maharik*, however, maintains that there is no difference between the practices listed in the *Tosefta* and those listed in the Gemara itself. Thus, it

---

could be inferred that he supports including the examples of the *Tosefta* in the ban that applies to the practices listed in the Mishna and Gemara.

> And there I studied from the *Tosefta* of *Shabbat*, and you will not find there [in the *Tosefta*] even one [practice] that was not divination or an astonishing thing whose cause is not known such as those which the Talmud brings at the end of [*Shabbat* Chapter 4]...[37]

On the basis of this *Maharik*, it is difficult to justify ignoring the red string (חוט אדום) prohibition of the *Tosefta*.

An alternate solution is that of the *Shirei Korban* on the corresponding Talmud *Yerushalmi*, who brings up the following possibility with regard to Amorite practices: "And it is shocking that the world is not vigilant [with regard to] this matter, and I do not know the reasoning. And it is possible, seeing that traces of the Amorites have been lost, that they were not concerned with this matter."[38] This somewhat radical statement implies that although certain practices—for example, those listed in the *Tosefta*—were included in the original Torah prohibition of Amorite practices, due to the fact that the Amorites themselves are no longer around to exert their negative influence, the prohibition no longer applies.[39]

On the other side of the fence, the *Bach* maintains that the mere fact that red string (חוט אדום), which is mentioned explicitly in the *Tosefta* as Amorite practice, was at one point connected with idolatrous customs, is reason enough to prohibit its use today.

> And in any case, it appears that those things which are explicit in the words of the rabbis in [*Shabbat* Chapter 6], and in the *Tosefta* of *Shabbat*, and in additional sources, even though the idolaters in certain places do not practice them nowadays, it is forbidden for [a member of] Israel to practice them, because seeing as this custom was already established with reference to their statutes, it

---

[37] שו״ת מהרי״ק, שרש פח, ובי״י יו״ד קעח, ד״ה ״אסור ללכת.״

[38] שירי קרבן, שבת ו:א.

[39] The *Shirei Korban* notes that a similar reasoning is used by the *Rama*, YD 12:2 regarding a particular Halakha of *shechita*: יש בכך כוכבים עובדי דרך דאין הזה ובזמן ״הגה להתיר בדיעבד.״

would appear as though he were conceding to them and to their statutes if he were to follow similar customs that had previously been [their] law.[40]

Another questionable aspect of the red string (חוט אדום) practice is not related to its function as a charm, per se, but rather to its color. *Chazal* apparently had reservations about the color red based on its conspicuous nature and consequently, its intrinsic connection to other nations who do not conform to the Jewish values of modesty and humility. In certain cases, the rabbis even went so far as to prohibit the wearing of red garments and accessories.

For example, in his glosses on *Hilkhot Avodat Kokhavim* of the *Shulchan Arukh*, the *Rama* comments with regard to the prohibition of dressing in the fashion of pagans (עכו"ם), "And all this is not prohibited except for that matter which the idolaters practiced for the sake of licentiousness, for example, that they customarily wore red clothing and it is the clothing of princes..."[41]

Here the *Shakh* notes with reference to the *Maharik*, "That it is not the way of the modest to have red in their dress, and the color black is the way of modesty and humility... And additionally, it is our tradition to be strict regarding the wearing of red by the people of our nation, [thus writes] the *Maharik*."[42]

The *Maharik*'s ruling is actually based on a Halakha of the *Rif* in *Sanhedrin* (פרק בן סורר ומורה), which prohibits Jews from wearing red shoelaces or sandal straps, because that was the color worn by Idolators, while Jews traditionally wore black.[43] The *Rif* goes so far as to maintain that if an Idolator publicly demands of a Jew to change his shoelaces to red, the Jew must choose to be killed rather than consent.

The *Maharik* emphasizes that the *Rif*'s prohibition regarding sandal straps is specifically connected to the color red, and not merely to any color deemed fashionable by idolaters:

But if the Gentiles would make their straps black, the Jews would not [be required to] make themselves different. For if we do not contend accordingly

---

[40] ב"ח, יו"ד קעח, ד"ה "אסור ללכת בחוקות עובדי כוכבים ואצ"ל וכו."

[41] רמ"א, יו"ד קעח:א.

[42] ש"ך, יו"ד קעח:א, ד"ה "מלבושים אדומים כו."

[43] רי"ף, סנהדרין יז ע"ב, בדפי הרי"ף.

[i.e., that this is the Halakha], then Rav Alfasi [the *Rif*] should not have said "Because the nations customarily use red, etc." but rather, he should have said, "Even the shoe-strap is prohibited, for instance, when the nations make the straps of their sandals in one color and the Jews in another color." Instead, it is certain, from the fact that he felt it necessary to specify the colors, that we can deduce that he [the *Rif*] mentioned red and black specifically.[44]

Once again, however, it is unclear whether this prohibition can be applied to garments or accessories other than the sandal straps under discussion. It seems unlikely that such an extrapolation would be accepted. But although the negative connotations ascribed to the color red and the related prohibitions discussed by *Chazal* do not carry enough weight to outlaw our red strings on their own, they do add to the charges brought against the red string practice.[45]

Yet another aspect of today's red string practice which involves possible prohibitions is its association with tombs.

Charity-collectors at the *Kotel* generally claim that the red strings they distribute have been wound around the tombs of *Rachel Imenu*, Rabbi Meir Baal HaNess, the Baba Sali, or others, lending the charms additional holiness. When confronted, several of these string-distributors reported that their source for such a practice was the Baba Sali, the contemporary, kabbalistic leader of the Moroccan community in Israel who unfortunately never committed any of his teachings to writing.

The only related, written source that research for this article produced was that which was quoted by Professor Daniel Sperber in the fifth volume of his *Minhagei Yisrael* regarding the binding of a string seven times around the stomach of a woman in childbirth.[46] In the book by BenZion Yehoshuah Raz about the history of the Jews of Afghanistan, the author reports an actual

---

[44] שו״ת מהרי״ק, שרש פח.

[45] One exception to the generally negative association *Chazal* attach to the color red is that which is brought down in the continuation of the Gemara previously referred to on Shabbat (67a). The Talmud suggests painting the trunk of an ailing fruit tree red, so as to attract the attention of passers-by who will be moved by the plight of the tree and offer prayers on its behalf.

[46] דניאל שפרבר, מנהגי ישראל: מקורות ותולדות (ירושלים: מוסד הרב קוק, 1995) ד:שיז.

incident that took place, which quite intriguingly connects not only the binding of string and the tombs of the righteous, קברי צדיקים, but also *Rachel Imenu*:

> Avrahamoff tells us of a woman in childbirth who had complications with her delivery, and the old women went out to the tombs of the righteous and wrapped string around them and afterwards wrapped the string around the stomach of the birthing woman seven times. [By one account] the infant was saved, but the woman died at the time of the birth. The midwife then announced that the woman had become [similar to one] whose fate is that of Rachel *Imenu*, who died in childbirth (זאווגי).[47]

It is not noted here whether the string was specifically red.

The relevance of this aspect of the red string (חוט אדום) practice is the possibility that after being wound around a tomb, a string becomes set aside specifically for the use of the deceased (מוקצה למת). Thus, one who then uses it for his own purposes would be violating an איסור הנאה, a prohibition regarding illegal benefiting from the dead.

The basis of this argument is a *beraita* quoted in *Megilla* (29a) which states "The rabbis teach: In the cemetery, one does not exhibit frivolity, nor shepherd animals, nor channel water sewers, nor pick grasses. And if he did pick, [he must] burn them in their place out of respect for the dead."

The *Ran* comments with regard to the prohibition of picking the grass, "'And if he did pick, [he must] burn them in their place' because they are prohibited regarding benefit [from the dead]."[48]

The medieval commentators argue as to whether the prohibition applies to the surrounding land of the entire cemetery or only to the plot of land above the actual grave. There is much debate as to the exact intention of Maimonides in his blanket statement: "cemeteries are prohibited regarding benefit,"[49] and, his addition of several prohibitions not mentioned in the *beraita* including eating, drinking, doing work, and learning in the cemetery.

After discussing the varying opinions, the *Shiltei Giborim* on *Sanhedrin* concludes that according to Maimonides, all of the laws of holiness (קדושה),

---

[47] בן-ציון יהושע-רז, מנדחי ישראל באפגאניסתאן לאנוסי משהד באיראן (ירושלים: מוסד ביאליק, 1992).

[48] ר"ן, מגילה ט ע"ב, בדפי הרי"ף, ד"ה "ת"ר בית הקברות אין נוהגין בהן קלות ראש וכו'."

[49] משנה תורה, הלכות אבלות יד:יג.

which apply to a synagogue apply to a cemetery as well, namely that the holiness of the place is transferred to its implements (כלים),[50] which are then prohibited from any other use.[51] This prohibition might apply to our case if we can assume that once it is wound around the tomb the string takes on the characteristics of an implement, such as the cover on the coffin of the deceased.

The *Yerushalmi* in *Megilla* states more explicitly: "Throwing an implement before the coffin of the deceased, within his four cubits [which constitute halakhically-recognized personal space] [makes the object] prohibited regarding benefit."[52] In our case, the string wrapped around the tomb would be classified as the implement which comes within four cubits of the deceased.

The difficulty in comparing the cases mentioned (and other similar situations addressed in halakhic literature) with red string is that all of the examples given involve objects which were placed or thrown onto the grave for the purpose of the deceased or the tomb itself. The red string, which is wrapped seven times around the tomb, however, is placed there for the express purpose of removing it and cutting it up for distribution, which might alter its halakhic status. Thus, while prohibitions involving benefit derived from tombs is certainly an additional facet of the red string חוט אדום practice whose permissibility is questionable, much research remains to be done in this area, along with the issues of *segula* and *minhag*.

The premise which is at the root of all prohibitions regarding charms, witchcraft, and other shady practices of idolaters is the belief that the positive precept "Simple-hearted should you be with *HaShem*, your God"— "תמים תהיה עם ה' אלקיך" is a cornerstone of man's relationship with the Master of the Universe.[53]

In the words of R. Yaacov Moshe Hillel in his *Kuntrus Tamim Tehiye*: "In the matter of success in all of his endeavors, surely man must conduct himself with simplicity and with belief in his creator. And his strength is in naught but

---

[50] See Jerusalem Talmud *Megilla* 3:1 and corresponding Gemara.

[51] שלטי גבורים, סנהדרין טו ע"א, בדפי הרי"ף, אות פ.

[52] *Yerushalmi Megilla* 23b.

[53] *Devarim* 18:13.

his very mouth, through prayer and in supplication that his path will be successful."[54]

The majority of sources cited in this article raise questions as to the halakhic legitimacy of such a practice as wearing a red string. If convincing proof of an outright prohibition is lacking in the deliberations on individual facets of the practice, the sum total of the arguments presented certainly points in the direction of something forbidden (איסור). Furthermore, were it possible to distance red string from every one of the halakhic questions raised, it would still be difficult to maintain that the practice conforms to the spirit of being simple-hearted before God, "תמים תהיה".

---

[54] 75.

Women and the Issuing of Halakhic Rulings

Chanah Henkin

Any discussion of women's religious roles needs to go back to Devorah *HaNevi'a* (the Prophetess).

ודבורה אשה נביאה אשת לפידות היא שפטה את ישראל בעת ההיא. והיא יושבת תחת תמר דבורה בין הרמה ובין בית אל בהר אפרים ויעלו אליה בני ישראל למשפט.

And Devorah was a prophetess, a woman of Lapidot, she judged Israel at that time, sitting beneath the date-palm of Devorah, between Rama and Beit El in the Mount of Efraim, and Israel went up to her for judgment. (Judges 4:4–5)

"She judged Israel"—this is the biblical precedent brought in the halakhic discussion of two issues: (a) Can a woman serve in a public position of authority ("*mesima*")? (b) Can a woman judge? An examination of how the *Rishonim* treat this issue will establish for us the parameters within which we need to evaluate *pesika*, the issuing of halakhic rulings, by women.

The talmudic sages, perhaps not entirely at ease merely with the spiritually charismatic personalities of the biblical period, ascribe to them the more familiar identities of profound Torah scholars. This is true for both men and women. "Abraham observed the entire Torah" (*Yoma* 28b). "The daughters of Zlafchad, they are learned, they expound the law, they are righteous (*chachmaniyot hen, darshaniyot hen, tzidkaniyot hen*)" (*Bava Batra* 8). "Amram was head of the Sanhedrin" (*Shmot Rabba* 1:13). "The house of study of Shem" (*Targum Yerushalmi, Toldot* 25:22). This is also the basis for their understanding of Devorah. "…She judged Israel (*hi shofta et Yisrael*)"—what was her activity?

In *Devarim* 17:15, we read:

שום תשים עליך מלך אשר יבחר ה׳ אלקיך בו מקרב אחיך תשים עליך מלך לא תוכל לתת עליך איש נכרי אשר לא אחיך הוא.

You shall place upon you a king whom *HaShem* your God will choose, from amongst your breathren you shall place upon you a king, you shall not place upon you a gentile who is not your brother.

The Midrash Halakha *Sifre* (Ibid.) comments: "*Melekh velo malka*," a king and not a queen. What the *Sifre* is saying is that the verse could have been constructed more economically, without the repetition of "*tasim alekha melekh*." The verse could have read: *Som tasim alekha melekh mikerev achekha asher yivchar HaShem Elokekha bo*, etc.—you shall appoint a king from amongst your brethren whom *HaShem* your God has chosen etc. Since Hebrew is gender specific but the male voice is commonly inclusive of both genders in the Torah, the repetition of *melekh*, male king, in the first two clauses therefore teaches that we may appoint only a male.

Rambam in *Mishne Torah, Hilkhot Melakhim* (1:5) expands this to all public roles of authority (*kol mesimot*):[1]

אין מעמידין אשה במלכות שנאמר עליך מלך ולא מלכה וכן כל משימות שבישראל אין ממנים בהם אלא איש.

We do not set up a woman in kingship, as it is written, "'upon you a king,' and not a queen." And likewise, to all positions in Israel, we appoint only a man.

Rambam's ruling becomes relevant to the topic of *psikat* Halakha by women via the *Radbaz* (R. David b. Zimra, 16th c., Egypt) who, in his commentary on *Mishne Torah*, asks (ibid.): How can *Rambam* assert that a woman cannot be appointed to a *mesima?* Devorah was a prophetess who judged Israel, and that is certainly a *mesima*! He answers:

לא קשיא שהיתה מלמדת להם המשפטים, א"נ ע"פ הדבור היה.

This is not a challenge, for she taught them the laws. Alternatively, it was according to the Almighty's command.

She was not actually a judge, but rather "she taught them the laws." Alternatively, she was indeed a judge, but she bypassed the restriction that applies to other women because God appointed her. In his first answer, "*shehayta melamedet lahem hamishpatim* (she taught them the laws)" *Radbaz* does not mean she was a grade school *dinim* teacher. She judged *Israel*, and if judging is interpreted as teaching the law, then she decided Halakha. She issued halakhic rulings for the nation. And *Radbaz* is telling us that this interpretation

---

[1] The process by which *Rambam* expands the scope of the prohibition is discussed by *Rav* Moshe Feinstein in Responsa *Iggerot Moshe, Yore De'a* 2:44.

that Devorah *paska halakha*, issued halakhic rulings, is not inconsistent with *Rambam*'s objection to *kol mesimot,* nor with anything else *Rambam* wrote.

The *Tosafot* (12th–13th century) reach the same conclusion, but through a different process. Their problem is not "*melekh velo malka*" or "*kol mesimot,*" but rather the prohibition against women judges. From the Gemara in *Shavuot* (30a) and *Nidda* (49b) it can be determined that a woman is ineligible to judge, and this is stated explicitly in the Jerusalem Talmud.[2] *Tosafot* (*Shavuot* 29b) challenge this with the precedent of Devorah. They answer:

איכא למימר שהיתה מלמדת להם הדינים, א״נ לפי שהיתה נביאה היו מקבלים אותה עליהם

We must say that she taught them the laws, or alternatively, that because she was a prophetess, they accepted her upon themselves.

According to *Tosafot*, the Gemara can be upheld so long as we make either of two assumptions: (a) Devorah was a *poseket*—"*hayta melamedet lahem hadinim*"—and not a courtroom judge, or (b) she was indeed a judge, but the objection of Halakha is not to the act of judging by a woman but rather to the coercive aspect of her appointment. If all litigants *voluntarily* accept her judicial authority, she can judge. Because Devorah was a prophetess, Israel willingly accepted her authority.

Ramban (Nachmanides), representing 13th century sephardic tradition, also offers two alternative explanations of Devorah's judging (*Chiddushei haRamban, Shavuot* 30a):

וכן אמרו בירושלמי שאין האשה מעידה ואין האשה דנה ומאי דכתיב והיא שפטה את ישראל פירושו מנהגת שעל פיה ובעצתה היו נוהגין זה עם זה כדין מלכה ואע״ג דאמרינן בספרי שום תשים עליך מלך ולא מלכה נוהגין היו בה כדין מלכה אי נמי מקבלין היו דבריה ברצונם.

And likewise, in the Jerusalem Talmud, they said, a woman does not testify and does not judge. And what of: "she judged Israel"? It means that she was a leader, like a queen, and that according to her decision and counsel they conducted their affairs with each other. And even though we say in the *Sifre*, "'You shall place upon you a king,' a king and not a queen," they conducted

---

[2] *Sanhedrin* 3:6.

themselves as if she was a queen. Alternatively, they accepted her words voluntarily.

The term *shofet* (judge) during the pre-monarchial period in Israel was used synonymously with political leader; and when we speak of Yehoshua or Gidon as *shoftim*, we do not mean they were courtroom judges, but rather heads of state. Ramban explains that in like fashion Devorah, who was a *shofetet*, was leader of the nation. This raises the question: is not the leader of the nation for all intents and purposes a king, whether we use the term or not? Yet, continues *Ramban*, we can maintain that Devorah was the leader of the nation without any conflict with the principle of '*melekh velo malka*,' because she was not officially appointed king, but rather the people acted as if she were king; we thus arrive at the same point implicit in *Tosafot*, that it is the procedure of *appointment*, and not the act of serving in the position, that is halakhically objectionable. According to *Tosafot*, Devorah could have functioned as the supreme judge so long as she was not formally appointed. According to *Ramban*, she was *de facto* political leader, because everyone voluntarily accepted her leadership.

The second explanation *Ramban* gives is that Devorah indeed judged Israel, but here again, they accepted her judicial decisions of their own volition. *Ramban* differs from *Tosafot* on this last point in that *Tosafot* explain that Israel accepted Devorah as a courtroom judge because of her status as a prophetess. *Ramban*, on the other hand, mentions only the general legal mechanism through which anyone can be accepted—"*mekablin hayu devareha birtzonam* (they voluntarily accepted her words)." The implication of *Tosafot* is that such acceptance might be appropriate only for a Divinely ordained prophetess, while no such limitation is implied by *Ramban*.

The applicability of voluntarily acceptance to any woman becomes absolutely clear in the writings of *Ramban*'s disciple, *Rashba* (*Chidushei haRashba*, Shavuot 30a):

ואי״ת הא כתיב והיא שפטה את ישראל י״ל דלא שפטה ממש אלא מנהגת כשופטים
ששפטו את ישראל ואע״ג דאמרינן בספרי שום תשים עליך מלך ולא מלכה התם לא מנו
אותה אלא היו נוהגים בה כדין מלכה והיו נוהגים על פיה ואי נמי שופטת ודנה שהיו
מקבלים אותה כדרך שאדם מקבל אחד מן הקרובים.

And if you say: Indeed, it is written, "And she judged Israel," one must say that she did not actually judge, but was a leader, like the judges who led Israel. And despite our saying in the *Sifre*, "'You shall place upon you a king,' a king and not a queen," she was not appointed, but they conducted themselves as if she were a queen. Alternatively, she was a coutroom judge, and they voluntarily accepted her as one accepts a relative.

He brings the same two options as does *Ramban*, Devorah as head of state or courtroom judge, but concludes regarding courtroom judge, "*kederech she'adam mekabel echad min hakrovim*," as one accepts a relative. *Rashba* informs us that Devorah, if we posit that she was a courtroom judge, was accepted through a mechanism open to anyone. Just as one party may accept a blood-relative of the other party to judge him, even though the halakha normally forbids a blood-relative from judging, in like fashion Israel voluntarily accepted her authority.

This same position is articulated by *Ran*, R. Nissim of Gerona, (14th century; *Shavuot*, chapter 4, ד״ה שבועת העדות):

והא דכתיב גבי דבורה והיא שפטה את ישראל לאו שופטת קאמר אלא מנהגת, ואע״ג דאמרינן בספרי שום תשים עליך מלך ולא מלכה התם לא מנו אותה אלא נוהגין היו על פיה, וא״נ שופטה ודנה היתה שהיו מקבלין אותה כדרך שאדם מקבל אחד מן הקרובים.

And that which is written regarding Devorah, "she judged Israel"—a judge is not implied, but [rather] a leader. And although we saw in *Sifre*: "'You shall place upon you a king,' a king and not a queen," there they did not appoint her, but acted according to her words; alternatively, she was a judge, for they accepted her as one accepts a relative.

To summarize thus far:

1) Among the *Rishonim*, *Rambam* alone speaks of a general stricture against appointing a woman to a position of public authority.
2) *Radbaz* explains that positing that Devorah was a *poseket* is not problematic for *Rambam*, despite the above strictures.
3) *Ramban*, *Rashba*, and *Ran* are prepared to posit that Devorah was a political leader.
4) *Tosafot*, like *Radbaz*, posits that Devorah taught them the laws, i.e., was a *poseket*.

Finally, none of the *Rishonim* has any problem with Devorah's having engaged in the act of judging, so long as she was not appointed.[3]

There is yet a third halakhic issue in the context of which the subject of *pesika*, halakhic ruling, by a woman, arises. Another *Rishon*, *Sefer haChinukh*, writes in *Mitzva* 152 that, while inebriated, one is prohibited from either entering the Temple or issuing a halakhic ruling, *hora'a*:

שלא להכנס שתוי במקדש, וכן שלא להורות, כלומר שלא נדון בדבר מדיני התורה בעוד
שיהא האדם שיכור.

Not to enter the Temple inebriated, and likewise, not to issue a halakhic ruling.
In other words, not to interpret a Torah law while drunk.

Sefer haChinukh continues that the prohibition against issuing a halakhic ruling while drunk applies equally to men and to a *"learned woman who is worthy of issuing a ruling."*

ונוהג איסור ביאת מקדש בשכרות בזמן הבית בזכרים ונקבות, ומניעת ההוריה בכל מקום
ובכל זמן בזכרים, וכן באשה חכמה הראויה להורות.

This prohibition of entering the Temple while drunk applies during the time of
the Temple to males and females, and the prohibition against ruling [while
drunk], [applies] in all places and at all times, to males and likewise to a
learned woman who is worthy of ruling.

Earlier, in *Mitzva* 78, *Sefer haChinukh* rules that the *mitzva* of following the majority opinion in deciding Halakha applies equally to men and women. The *Minchat Chinukh* comments that in a law requiring a formal *beit din* such as in monetary or capital cases, a woman is ineligible to rule. But in *issur veheter*,

---

[3] *Iggerot Moshe*, ibid., no. 45:

והקושיא ואע"ג דאמרינן בספרי דלא קאי על מה שהיתה דנה דלישב בדין לא הוי כלל
באיסור דמינוי אלא כשנתמנה להיות משופטי העיר, אך הוא מדין אחר שאשה פסולה לדון
כשם שפסולה להעיד, וע"ז תירץ הרמב"ן דלא דנה דנה כלל ושפטה את ישראל פירושו שהנהיגה
את ישראל שעל פיה ובעצתה היו נוהגין זע"ז כדין מלכה, והקשה ע"ז קושיא אחרת דא"כ
פסולה מהא דספרי מלך ולא מלכה ותירץ שלא מינוה למלכה אלא ששמעו לדבריה כמו
למלכה. ואח"כ תירץ על הקושיא דפסולה לדון, א"נ מקבלין היו דבריה ברצונם היינו שלא
בכפיה והפסול לדון אינו עצם הפס"יד אלא הכפיה.

See also R. Ben Zion Meir Chai Uziel, *Piskei Uzziel, Choshen Mishpat* 44.

matters religiously proscribed or permitted, we accept the opinion regardless of who constitutes the majority, whether they be learned women or men.[4]

R. Chaim Yosef David Azulai, the eminent 18th century Jerusalem-born sephardi sage, rules in his *Birkei Yosef* that although a woman cannot judge, she can *pasken*, issue a halakhic ruling,[5] and this is the meaning of "*hayta melamedet lahem hadinim*" in *Tosafot*. He writes that the fact that a woman can issue a halakhic ruling is proven by *Sefer haChinukh* who, in *Mitzva* 83, agrees that a woman cannot judge, and on the other hand, in *Mitzva* 152, writes that a woman may not issue a halakhic ruling while drunk. This opinion of the *Birkei Yosef* is cited by the *Pitchei Teshuva*.[6]

This position, I want to stress, is *non-controversial*. Nowhere within the *Rishonim* or the *Achronim* is there an opinion that the Halakha prohibits in principle the issuing of a halakhic ruling by a woman.[7]

---

[4] R. Yosef Babad (Lvov, Poland, 1869):

ונר' שאם חכמי הדור חלוקין באיזה דין באו"ה חוץ דינים שצריך ב"ד בשעת מעשה כמו דיני
נפשות או דיני ממונות והולכין אחר הרוב אין חילוק דאפילו חכמים קטנים מצטרפים לרוב
אם הם חכמים ואל תסתכל בקנקן וכו'. וכן נשים חכמניות כמו דבורה ששופטת את ישראל.
כן באיזה דין הבא שצריך ב"ד צריכים ב"ד כשר אבל לענין מחלוקת באיזה דבר אין שום
חילוק רק מי שהוא חכם חשבינן דעתו יהיה מי שיהיה כנ"פ.

[5] *Choshen Mishpat* 7:12:

אף דאשה פסולה לדון מ"מ אשה חכמה יכולה להורות הוראה וכן מתבאר מהתוספות לחד
שינויא דדבורה היתה מלמדת להם דינים. וכן תראה בסי' החנוך דבסי' פ"ג הסכים דאשה
פסולה לדון ובסי' קנ"ב בענין שתוי כתב וז"ל ומניית ההוריה וכו' וכן באשה חכמה הראויה
להורות וכו' עיי"ש.

[6] *Choshen Mishpat* 7:5.

[7] *Iggerot Moshe,* ibid., 60, in discussing the controversy between R. Yochanan and Resh Lakish in the Jerusalem Talmud *Terumot* 8:4 concerning handing over criminals to the authorities, inquires why the "wise woman" in II Samuel 20 is so-called, as her ruling is ostensibly in conflict with *ab initio* Halakha. R. Feinstein takes for granted *the fact* that a woman can issue a ruling. He challenges only the *nature* of her ruling, which he later defends.

There is, however, one midrashic source which seems to deny women the right of ruling. In *Bamidbar Rabba* 10:5 Manoach, father of Shimshon, in explaining why he asked the angel to confirm his wife's report (in *Shoftim* 20), is quoted as saying "women are not *bnot hora'a*, and one can not rely on them." However, (a) the context implies that testimony, not halakhic ruling, is being referred to, (b) Manoach is a non-authoritative figure in midrashic lore, and (c) no such statement is found elsewhere in rabbinic literature.

On the other hand, issuing halakhic rulings requires wide knowledge of Halakha, in addition to which there are many and detailed *klalei pesika*, rules for issuing a halakhic decision. For instance, in *Nidda* (7b), we learn that we do not issue halakhic rulings based upon the aggadah, nor do we rule from the Mishna. In *Bava Kama* (30b) and *Shabbat* (12b), we learn the principle "*halakha ve'en morin ken*," that under certain circumstances one is not even permitted to publicize the actual Halakha, lest the community permit themselves to be negligent in related areas. This is found also in *Beitza* (28b), *Chulin* (15a and 15b), and *Menachot* (36b).

Because *hora'a*, issuing a halakhic ruling, is laden with such responsibility, R. Yehuda Hanasi (in *Sanhedrin* 5b) established the *takana*, ordinance, that a disciple may not rule without the *reshut*, the authorization, of his teacher.

Finally, the Gemara in *Sota* (22a) and again in *Avoda Zara* (19b) warns against those who issue halakhic rulings although unqualified to do so. "*Rabim chalalim hipila—ze talmid chakham shelo higi'a lehora'a umore.*" But, "*va'atzumim kol harugeha—ze talmid chakham shehigi'a lehora'a ve'eino more.*" "'[*Hora'a*] has felled many'—that is a scholar who has not reached the stature of ruling and yet rules; 'and great are her fallen'—that is a scholar who has indeed reached the stature of ruling yet does *not* rule."

So what of women? Will they remain in the category of *rabim chalalim hipila*, unqualified candidates for *hora'a* who might fell many, or will women reach the level of *va'atzumim kol harugeha*, those scholars who *should* issue rulings lest "great are her fallen"?

First of all, I want to say—as the head of a learning institution which is qualifying women to address questions of *hilkhot nidda* in practice—we should stop using the term *poskot*. I turn to the rabbis and to the women who are using the term and I beg them to stop. It is not accurate, not constructive and it will not result in *poskot*. *Ein habrakha metzuya ela bedavar hasamuy min ha'ayin*, constructive changes will not be made in the glare of spotlights.[8]

---

[8] This applies with even greater force to talk of the *semikha* (ordination) of women as "rabbis," with its unwanted implications of competition with men for pulpits and other community positions. *Semikha* has long lost its original meaning of "laying on of hands" by rabbi to student in an unbroken chain stretching back to Moshe, a chain which was broken in talmudic times. Rather, *semikha* today is a *heter hora'a*, permission given by a rabbi/teacher to a student permitting the student to issue halakhic rulings in the locale of, or during the lifetime of, the teacher. Technically, in the absence, or with the death of, the

We are embarked on a tantalizing journey toward *va'atzumim*, learned women with the profound Torah scholarship, force of religious personality, and penetrating insight which will lead the community to seek them out as halakhic authorities, perhaps initially specializing in areas of Halakha which relate to women or which demand mastery of highly technical, scientific material. As we proceed along this journey, we should not casually and prematurely use a terminology that presumes a greater level of Torah accomplishment than we have yet achieved. A process is underway, and it can only be harmed by sensationalism.

Second, our major concern must be the Halakha. Not for the purpose of empowering women, but enabling women to observe *mitzvot* meticulously, to blossom with the full richness of the fabric of the religious experience.

In order to meticulously observe the Halakha, women need women! For reasons of modesty, women do not wish to, and often will not, discuss a *hilkhot nidda* question with a man. The consequences of a *shayla* (question pertaining to Jewish law) not asked can range from improper observance of the Halakha to marital anguish and even to infertility. As little as ten years ago, we had no solution to this problem. Today, we are witnessing, before our eyes, with profound emotion and gratitude to *HaKadosh Barukh Hu*, the emergence of a first generation of talmudically-literate women who will be able to advise other women in this field. They are committed to the Halakha and devoted to

---

teacher, *semikha* is no longer required; nor is it required in order to give a halakhic decision in the abstract, as opposed to a ruling in a specific case, nor to merely citing an explicit ruling in the *Shulchan Arukh* or other accepted text. See *Shulchan Arukh, Yore De'a* 242:7, 9, 13.

Nevertheless, in particularly sensitive and difficult areas such as arranging writs of divorce, *semikha* has become mandatory, as well as in order to assume an appointed position as rabbi or halakhic authority of a community (*Arukh haShulchan* 29). It has also become customary to grant a partial *semikha* to permit the awardee to rule in certain halakhic areas even though not in others, such as *yore yore* without *yadin yadin*. One can envisage the equivalent of a *heter hora'a* being given to qualified women in areas such as *hilkhot nidda*, or even in parts of *hilkhot nidda*, without using the term *semikha* and without the title of "rabbi."

My husband, Rabbi Yehuda Henkin, noted a further consideration, based on *Yore De'a* 242:11. When necessary "*le'afrushei me'isura*," to keep someone from sin, a student can rule even without *semikha*. Particularly in the area of *hilkhot nidda* where many women will not and do not consult a male rabbi because of the intimate nature of the topic, it may be *le'afrushei me'isura* to train and encourage women to answer other women's questions.

their fellow women. We must utilize this precious new resource of learned women to inspire piety and devotion to Torah in other women.

Third, we are living in challenging times, when gender roles are changing and family structures are weakening. We must weigh carefully the results of the changes we are making upon our families. As we assume new roles uplifting to our spirits and enabling us to apply our new scholarship for the benefit of *Am Yisrael*, we must make certain that we are not falling short of the proper nurture of our children or abandoning the joys of a large family.

There is a tension within Judaism between formalized and spontaneous religiosity, and even within God between *din* (the Divine quality of judgment) and *rachamim* (mercy). *Rachamim* wants to create the world in order to give man the opportunity to excel; *din* wants to prevent man's failure. This struggle asserts itself regularly in the Midrash. In Gemara *Berakhot* (7a), God prays that His mercy will successfully conquer His *midat hadin*. To a certain extent, historically this tension was resolved by the balance between the traditional male and female roles. *Chesed*, deferral to others' needs, requires time, a requirement which the domestic role has, through the ages, nobly accommodated. The Gemara brings several incidents contrasting the halakhically meticulous *tzedaka* of the *talmid chakham* husband with the preferable *chesed* of his presumably less-learned wife. The dangers to the delicate balance between *din* and *rachamim*, between formalized and spontaneous behavior, comes not from higher Torah learning for women but from the roles men and women are already playing in an increasingly impersonal and technological society. When we create new role models for women's religious leadership, we must ensure that they represent not only great learning but also personal piety, commitment to family and to *chesed*, and excellence in *middot* as well.

Secular Studies at the Volozhin Yeshiva

Maidi Katz z"l

The question of the permissibility of philosophic inquiry and of secular learning has long been a source of disagreement in Jewish thought and has often caused conflict within the Jewish community. In the early days of Rabbinic Judaism various injunctions[1] were invoked against study of certain materials such as *chokhmat yevanit*[2] and *higayon;*[3] these terms are not clearly defined in the Talmud and later interpretations have run the gamut from the prohibition of a today unknown sign language[4] to the prohibitions of logic[5] and philosophy.[6] Similarly, the reasons for these injunctions are ambiguous in the Talmud and both heresy and *bitul Torah* arguments have been offered as explanations.[7] Thus, depending on the historical context, these terms have been interpreted and reinterpreted by Jewish scholars each of whom was striving to maintain and defend his own particular world view.[8] Varying

---

[*] This paper was written in 1985 while studying at the Bernard Revel Graduate School of Advanced Jewish Studies of Yeshiva University in New York.

[1] It is not always clear in the Talmud whether they are meant as actual prohibitions or merely as good advice.

[2] *Menachot* 64b, 99b; *Sota* 49b; *Bava Kamma* 82b.

[3] *Berakhot* 28b.

[4] *Rashi* on *Menachot* 64b.

[5] R. Hai Gaon interprets *higayon* as logic: "כמו חכמת האמנטיקו"." See *Otzar HaGeonim LeMasekhet Sanhedrin* 491.

[6] Nachmanides, *Kitvei Ramban*, vol. 1, ed. Chevelle (Jerusalem: haRav Kook, 1963).

[7] Jewish males are obligated to learn Torah day and night; when time is spent not learning Torah (unless it is spent in a sanctioned activity) it is considered *"bitul Torah."*

[8] For example, the interpretations of the pro-philosophic schools: Joseph ibn Caspi (Muslim Spain) says in his ethical will (*Hebrew Ethical Wills*, Israel Abrahams, ed.) that *higayon* cannot be interpreted as logic, because clearly *Chazal* would not have prohibited such a beneficial activity. Similarly, R. Jacob Anatoli (13th century) in his introduction to *Melamed haTalmidim* says that מנעו בניכם מן ההגיון applies only to young people who are

attitudes to philosophic inquiry and to secular studies caused the focus of the conflict to shift back and forth along a spectrum ranging from the permissibility and value of secular culture and learning in general,[9] involving possible problems of *bitul Torah*, to heated debate about the possible consequences of philosophic study, such as heresy.[10]

In the Eastern European Jewish communities (Lithuania, Poland, and Russia) of the 16th and 17th centuries, neither the issue of secular learning in general nor the issue of philosophy in particular was the source of much controversy. The Jewish communities during that period experienced an inward turning and focused their attention primarily on talmudic studies and on pious living. Judaism became a closed system of thought.[11] Even according to those historians who maintain that Jewish scholars of this period continued to incorporate rationalist Maimonidean philosophy into their own beliefs,[12] it hardly appears that these intellectual activities made major inroads on the narrow focus of Jewish life or disrupted the Jewish communities to any discernible extent. Attempts were made to define the parameters of *chokhmat yevanit*[13] and *higayon*, in as much as they were part of Talmud study, but these prohibitions were not subject to prolonged or acrimonious debate.

However, at the end of the 19th century a curious event occurred: the Eitz Chaim Yeshiva in Volozhin was closed by the Russian government on the grounds that it did not meet the secular studies requirements previously imposed upon it.[14] In order to fully understand why this happened at that

---

not mature enough to study the sciences. On the other hand, those who opposed philosophic study interpreted the statement differently. For example, we find in *Minchat Kena'ot* (15th century) that the prohibition of *higayon* is equated with that of philosophic study. Similarly, R. Joseph Haviva (15th century) writes in his commentary to *Megilla* 25b:

"חכמת ההגיון מושכת לב האדם... ולא יהיה חפץ בתורה וישכח מה שלמד."

[9] For example, during the *Haskalah* period (19th century).

[10] For example, during the Maimonidean controversy.

[11] Jacob Katz, *Exclusiveness and Tolerance* (London: Oxford Univ. Press, 1961) ch. 12.

[12] See for example: Ephraim Kupfer, "*Ledemuta haTarbutit sheYahadut Ashkenaz VeChakhameha beMe'ot ha-14 ve-15.*" *Tarbiz* 42: 113–45. See also: J. Ben Sasson, *Mishnato Ha'Iyunit shel ha'Ramoh* (Jerusalem, 1948).

[13] For example, Maharal, *Sefer Netivot Olam* ch. 14.

[14] Samuel Ettinger, "Volozhin," *Encyclopaedia Judaica* 16:218.

particular time (1892) and in that particular place (Russia), we must first investigate what in the 18th and 19th centuries caused the renewed stir concerning secular studies, what were the prevalent attitudes among the Jews towards these studies, and how the Russian government came to be involved in an issue which seemingly should have been the concern of the Jewish community alone.

Without a doubt, the advent of the *Haskalah* movement (late 18th century) usually associated with Moses Mendelssohn (Germany, 1729–1786), was intimately connected to the resurgence of the debate over secular studies. Among other objectives, the proponents of the *Haskalah* ideology wanted secular studies recognized as a legitimate part of the curriculum in the education of every Jew, both because of their unwavering faith in rationalist-intellectual inquiry and because of their wish for closer relationships with the non-Jewish community.[15] The *Haskalah* movement started and was most widespread in western and central Europe, but by the early 19th century its influences were felt in eastern Europe as well.[16] As in Germany, the groups of *Maskilim* pressed for imposition of reforms on the masses such as change of the traditional dress to the European clothes of the period and for the establishment of modern Jewish schools in which the students would be taught both secular studies and Jewish studies.[17] An anti-talmudic mood was prevalent among groups of *Maskilim*; in 1848 a teacher in the Rabbinical Seminary in Warsaw, Abraham Buchner, wrote a book entitled *Der Talmud in Seiner Nichtigkeit* (*The Talmud in its Emptiness*), and Joshua Heschel Schorr in Galicia claimed that the legal decisions of the Talmud were outdated socially and spiritually, though the Talmud is an important source of historical information.[18] Slowly but surely, the less radical of the new *Haskalah* ideas

---

[15] Zevi Scharfstein, *History of Jewish Education in Modern Times*, vol. 1 (NY: Ogen, 1945) 65–66.

[16] Ibid., 241–45. Scharfstein notes that there had been "*Maskilim*" for quite some time, but not as part of a larger movement. Scharfstein states that the Russian *Haskalah* developed as a result of internal, as well as external influences.

[17] Yehuda Slutsky, "Haskala," *Encyclopaedia Judaica* 7:1447–49.

[18] Ibid., 1436.

began to have an impact even upon the more traditional Jewish circles, creating tension within the Jewish communities.[19]

The *Maskilim* were not alone in their desire to reform the Jewish community. The Russian government, for its own reasons, also wished to change the very nature of the Jewish communities under its rule;

> The question of the enlightenment of the Jews began to interest the Russian government, especially at the beginning of the 19th century, after the partition of Poland, when Russia received dominion over a large Jewish population. To the Russian government, the lives of the Polish Jews, with their autonomous communities, their own religious and educational institutions and their own courts, appeared to be a government within a government. The autocracy in Russia, considering this autonomy an infringement on its own power, sought to destroy this way of life, to subjugate the Polish Jews and to imprint upon them the Russian way of life.[20]

Early in the 19th century (1802), a government commission established to study the "Jewish problem," recommended that certain regulations be enacted which would force the Jews to mend their ways. Among these was the decree that Jewish children study in Russian schools. The government's efforts however, were largely ineffective, and in 1840 renewed attempts were made to rectify the situation. The new commission, after consulting with Max Lilienthal,[21] decided to establish government-run Jewish schools. Lilienthal was sent

---

[19] The development of the haskalah movement and analysis of its goals and motives is clearly too broad a topic to be dealt with here, considering the scope of this paper. For a general overview of the movement see Slutsky, "Haskalah" in *Encyclopaedia Judaica*. For a collection of primary haskalah sources concerning these issues see Yehuda Slutsky, *Tnu'at haHaskalah beYahadut Russia* (Jerusalem: *HaChevra haHistorit haYisra'elit*, 1977).

[20] Scharfstein, 244. This area to requires a more detailed analysis which is not within the scope of this paper. The Hebrew original reads:

שאלת השכלת היהודים החלה לעניין את ממשלת רוסיה ביחוד בראשית המאה הי״ט, לאחר חלוקת פולין, כשקבלה רוסיה אוכלוסיה יהודית רבת נפשות אל תחת חסותה. חיי היהודים הפולנים עם האבטונומיה שלהם, מוסדות דתם וחינוכם ובתי דיניהם נראה לרוסיה כממשלה בתוך ממשלה. השלטון האבטוקראטי ראה בזה הסגת גבולו ובקש להרוס את ארחות החיים האלה ולהכניע את היהודים הפולניים לעצמו. כמו כן רצו לטבוע עליו את חותם החיים הרוסיים.

[21] Max Lilienthal, originally from Munich, was a well known, influential *Maskil*.

to the major Jewish communities to help overcome resistance there and to convince the Jews of the good intentions of the government. By the end of the 1840s these schools (elementary schools of two grades) as well as two state-run rabbinical seminaries were in fact established. In addition, new laws were passed concerning the *chederim* in an attempt to integrate secular studies there as well. By 1859, however, it became apparent that these requirements would not and could not be met and the regulations concerning the teachers and the curriculum were abolished on the condition that the students receive minimal secular education outside of the *chederim*. Also at this time, the government ceased operating the elementary schools of the second level in order to give Jews an incentive to attend the non-Jewish public schools.[22]

It was against the backdrop of this turmoil in Jewish education created by the *Maskilim* and the Russian government that Yeshivat Eitz Chaim (the "Volozhin Yeshiva") was founded, flourished, and eventually became the prototype for all Lithuanian *yeshivot*. R. Hayim b. Isaac Volozhiner (1749–1821), a student of the Vilna Gaon, established the yeshiva in 1803 for a variety of often disputed reasons:[23] to counteract the perceived decline of Torah study, to provide much needed teachers and leaders for the Jewish community, to institute a logical approach to analysis of the Talmud,[24] and to counteract Hasidism. "Secular studies" was not a real issue in R. Hayim's time since neither the *Haskalah* movement nor the Russian government had as yet picked up momentum in pursuing their goals or in finalizing their choice of means. In any event, R. Hayim's ideology concerning secular studies was probably akin to that of the Vilna Gaon: subjects which increase and deepen one's comprehension of Torah should be studied, in order that one may reach the broadest and fullest understanding of Torah within one's capabilities.[25]

A number of factors distinguished this new yeshiva from previous *yeshivot*: it was an independent institution supported not by the local community but by

---

[22] For a more detailed description of these events see Scharfstein, 10.

[23] Saul Stampfer, *Three Lithuanian Yeshivot* (unpublished dissertation, Hebrew University, 1981) 17.

[24] Logical analysis of the Talmud might have been used to counteract the arguments of the *Maskilim* about the irrationality of the Talmud.

[25] Stampfer, 26.

the whole Lithuanian Jewry; it had a teaching staff; the students did not have to board; each student was largely responsible for himself and his own learning; the methodology in learning was analytic and synthetic—analyzing "various details of many scattered and complex *halakhot* to join them together and establish general rules."[26] It is told that there were students studying around the clock in the *beis medrash* (study hall) so that the voice of Torah learning should never stop; though this story may be exaggerated it does reflect R. Chaim's philosophy that the world's existence is dependent on Torah study.[27]

In 1821, R. Isaac, R. Chaim's son, became the head of the yeshiva and served in that capacity until his death in 1849. The government closed the yeshiva in 1824 but it continued to operate openly, with close to 200 students.[28] In 1842, during his travels through Russia, Lilienthal met with R. Isaac to ask for his support in the establishment of Jewish schools under government auspices (see page 5), he was greatly impressed with R. Isaac's breadth of knowledge and intellectual curiosity:

> He [R. Isaac] spoke the German, Russian, and Polish languages very fluently and though being unacquainted with the literature of any of these languages he understood it well, that the reforms of the scholars could be delayed no longer, and though feeling somewhat uneasy about the fate befalling his Yeshiva, when these reforms would be carried out, he did never hesitate to recommend an alteration of the educational system.[29]

The *Haskalah* periodical *Ha'asif* describes R. Isaac in a similar vein: "[R. Isaac] also attached himself to the enlightened people of his generation, maybe from this will arise benefit to the people...[R. Isaac] gave his sanction to the commentary and translation of the Pentateuch...."[30] His personal views,[31]

---

[26] Gedalyahu Alon, "The Lithuanian Yeshivas," *The Jewish Expression*, ed. Judah Goldin, trans. Sid Leiman, (NH: Yale University Press, 1976) 458–59.

[27] Stampfer, 21.

[28] The reason for the closure is unclear, but was probably related to the government's policy of reform of Jewish education.

[29] As quoted in Stampfer, 248, from Max Lilienthal, "My Travels in Russia," *American Israelite*, vol. 2 (1856) 52.

[30] *Ha'Asif* 3 (1887) 240. The original Hebrew reads:

however, did not find expression in the running of the yeshiva; we have no evidence whatever of a broadening of the curriculum.[32]

In 1843, R. Isaac was chosen to participate in a Jewish conference convened by the government in Petroburg, to discuss the future of Jewish education.[33] Though forced to accept the government's plans,[34] he took advantage of the meeting to reaffirm the official government recognition of the yeshiva which his father had obtained in 1813.

In 1849, upon R. Isaac's death, R. Eliezer Isaac Fried (R. Isaac's son-in-law) became head of the yeshiva and R. Naphtali Zvi Yehuda Berlin (*Netziv*), the second son-in-law of R. Isaac, was appointed his deputy. When R. Fried died in 1854, the *Netziv* took his place. Because of a severe disagreement about the administration of the yeshiva between the *Netziv* and R. Joshua Heschel, a group of rabbis was called in to settle the controversy. Finally, in 1853, R. Berlin was appointed head and R. Joseph B. Soloveitchik (R. Chaim Volozhiner's grandson) his deputy. R. Soloveitchik left Volozhin in 1865 and R. Raphael Shapira (the son-in-law of the *Netziv*) was appointed in his stead. Upon R. Shapira's departure in 1881, R. Chaim Soloveitchik took his place. Clearly then, the stability in Volozhin was provided by R. Berlin, as he was the continuous thread running throughout the period 1849–1892, the time in which the *Maskilim* and the government gradually increased the pressure for change in Jewish educational institutions and the effects of the *Haskalah* slowly began to take hold in the yeshiva.[35] And in fact, R. Berlin's attitudes and opinions did seem to be crucial in shaping the yeshiva, as he was involved more than anyone else in its administration.[36]

הוא התחבר גם למשכילי דורו אולי יצמח מזה תועלת להאומה... [הוא] נתן הסכמתו על הביאור
ותרגומו על התורה.

[31] These descriptions of his views, coming from *Maskilim*, may have been exaggerated in order to lend further credence to their own views.

[32] Stampfer, 34.

[33] S.K. Mirsky, ed., *Mosdot Torah be'Eiropa beVinyan ubeChurbanam* (NY: Ogen, 1956) 33.

[34] Scharfstein, 275.

[35] Stampfer, 38.

[36] Mirsky, 50.

The attitude of the *Netziv* to secular studies per se was not a negative one; in fact he seems to have agreed with the Vilna Gaon's position, as he states in his commentary *Harchev Davar* on Genesis 45:16:

> And from this we understand that 'external wisdom' [external to the Torah, i.e., secular studies] is called 'daughter' and in the plural 'daughters,' in that they are not the main principles of [the structure of] the world but join together to expand upon the Torah...and the Torah assists those people [who diligently study Torah with great love] to reach a deeper understanding of the 'external wisdoms' in order that they may fully understand the words of the Torah in the areas that require knowledge of the 'external wisdoms.'[37]

Again in his commentary *Ha'emek Davar* to Exodus 37:19 and Numbers 8:2: "...And behold the six stems of the candelabrum together with the middle stem are the seven areas of 'external wisdom' which are secondary to the Torah. And that the Torah requires [knowledge of] them for all the details of measure and similar subjects...."[38] In his commentary *Harchev Davar* to Deuteronomy 32:3, the *Netziv* stipulates that the person studying secular subjects be well-versed in Torah studies first: "...in growth, the main element is the rain [the Torah]... and afterwards it is good to sweeten one's strength with the 'external wisdoms' which are the sun. This is not true, however, before one has studied Torah sufficiently; in that case the 'external wisdoms' are not beneficial...."[39]

In his responsa, R. Berlin reaffirms this position. There is no prohibition against learning the language of the country or against secular studies in

---

[37] The original Hebrew reads:

ומזה אנו מבינים דחכמת חיצונית מכונה בשם בת וברבים בשם בנות באשר אינם עיקר בנין עולם אלא מצטרפות להרחיב בנין התורה...דקאי על שוקדי התורה באהבה ואלו שהגיעו לכך התורה מסייעת להם להבין ולהשכיל בחכמות אחרות כדי לעמוד על ד״ת בעניינים הנדרשים לה.

[38] The original Hebrew reads:

והנה ששה קני מנורה עם הנר האמצעי הן המה שבע חכמות חיצוניות הטפלים לתורה. ושהתורה צריכה להם להתפרש בכל פרטי שיעורין וכדומה...

See also his commentary to Numbers 8:4.

[39] The original Hebrew reads:

אבל סדר הגידול העיקר הוא הגשם...ואח״כ טוב להמתיק עוד כמו ע״י חכמת חיצוניות שהוא השמש. מה שא״כ בעוד לא גדל בלימוד אין חכמת חיצוניות מועיל...

general, or even, in certain instances, in taking foreign names and changing one's style of clothes. In fact he recommends that:

> The Rabbi and the community leaders should see to it that the students be learned in Torah and, if the students are required by the government to study secular subjects, this too should be done under the supervision of the Rabbi and the leaders of Israel, so that the teacher [of the secular subjects] be a God-fearing person. This would be impossible were each person to see to his son's education himself, as he would be unable to choose a religiously upright teacher. Consequently, he would prevent his son from studying secular subjects against his [the son's] will and thus would cause the son to rebel against his parents and follow a crooked path in order to attain knowledge of secular subjects.[40]

Why then was the *Netziv* so opposed (as we will see he was) to any introduction of secular studies into his yeshiva, especially at a time when he was under tremendous pressure to do so? Though a *Maskil*'s harsh description of the mistreatment of students who read newspapers and books may be exaggerated,[41] it does seem that study of such material was frowned upon by the administration,[42] even though the *Netziv* did read newspapers himself![43] This problem too is addressed in his responsa:

> ...This is the way of the Torah, that its perfection and completeness is only attained by one who devotes himself exclusively to its study... it is impossible to be a great Torah scholar at a time when one is involved in other matters. And all great Torah scholars who are also learned in secular subjects, did not study the secular subjects until they had devoted themselves exclusively to Torah [for

---

[40] Naftali Zevi Yehuda Berlin, *Mayshiv Davar* (Responsa) 1:44. See also 4:71. The original Hebrew reads:

יתעסקו בזה הרב וראשי הקהילה שהיו התלמידים גדולי תורה וגם אם יצטרכו ע״פ המלכות ללמוד
לימודי חול ג״כ יהא בהשגחה מהרב וראשי ישראל שיהא המורה ירא אלקים, וזה אי אפשר אם
יהיה כל אחד דואג לבניו ואין בידו לברור איזה מורה הגון ומחזיק הדת, על כן הוא מבריח את בנו
מלמודי חול בעל כרחו וזה גורם שהבן בועט בהוריו והולך בדרך עקלקלות כדי להשיג למודי חול.

[41] *HaShachar* 8 (1877) 112–19.

[42] Stampfer, 78.

[43] M. Berlin, *Raban shel Yisrael* (NY: Mizrachi, 1943) 112.

a period] or until after they had already achieved greatness in Torah study; but together [Torah and secular studies] it is impossible to attain perfection in study.[44] Thus, R. Berlin did not feel that secular studies per se necessarily involved the prohibition of *bitul Torah*, though he was opposed to introduction of secular studies into the curriculum of Yeshivat Eitz Chaim; time devoted to things other than Torah would detract from the purpose and mission of the yeshiva; maintenance of great Talmudic scholars and rabbis as the very form of Jewish existence.

Nevertheless, private study of *Haskalah* journals and papers as well as some writing of Hebrew poetry was widespread in the yeshiva in its later years,[45] though only as a peripheral activity. And in fact, it seems that generally the study of *Haskalah* material was not so much borne of rebellious spirits or of burning desires to reform Jewish society, as of wishes to become well-respected, dignified members of the Jewish community.[46] The official line of the administration was one of disapproval, but often the matter was simply ignored.[47] Even when punishment was forthcoming, it was of more lenient form than the punishments given for deeds which were considered sinful per se, such as contact with women.[48]

Towards the end of the 19th century, as the *Haskalah* movement was increasingly accepted by many Jews,[49] groups of students renewed their efforts to involve the yeshiva in *Haskalah* activities in an organized fashion:[50] there

---

[44] *Mayshiv Davar* 1:44. The original Hebrew reads:

זה דרכה של תורה, שאין עמלה ותכליתה מתקיים אלא במי שמפנה כל ראשו בה... ואי אפשר
להיות גדול בתורה בשעה שעוסק בדברים אחרים. וכל גדולי תורה שהמה גם חכמים בלימודי חול,
אינם אלא שנתעסקו בלימודי חול קודם ששקעו ראשם בתורה או אחר שכבר נתגדלו בתורה, אבל
ביחד אי אפשר להגיע לתכלית הלימוד.

[45] Stampfer, 77–80.

[46] Stampfer, 76: In the later years of the 19th century, it was already accepted by many that one must be well-read in order to achieve good standing in the community.

[47] As quoted in Stampfer, 78, from "Yeshivat Volozhin," *Shevivim* 1:61.

[48] Stampfer, 79.

[49] Ibid., 115–16.

[50] Ibid., 100–1: in these years (1880s) a general tendency towards student organization was evident in the yeshiva.

was one unsuccessful attempt to establish a "*Haskalah* club" at the yeshiva and later, certain students began publishing a *Haskalah*-type newsletter.[51] Clearly these efforts mark the change in the attitude of the yeshiva students and may have partially caused the final closing of the yeshiva in 1892.[52] A contemporary describes the *Netziv*'s attitude to these changes:

> The *Netziv* saw that the generation was progressively deteriorating, and if he would be strict about the dress and the side-locks of the students their numbers would decrease from year to year and the Torah would, God forbid, be forgotten in Israel; so he started to be more lenient in these matters, and students with cut side-locks and 'partial' *Maskilim* began to appear in Volozhin... Every young man who learned in Volozhin, with a few exceptions, knew more or less, about world events and especially about politics...[53]

Thus it seems that the increasing tolerance of *Haskalah* materials in the yeshiva was a result of the very same belief which prevented the *Netziv* from incorporating secular studies into the curriculum: the belief that the students of the Volozhin yeshiva were vitally important to the continuation of traditional Judaism. Once the *Netziv* realized that he would no longer attract top quality students if he berated them for their side interests, he became more lenient in order to perpetuate Torah study. Nevertheless, his fundamental and official position, remained unchanged, that any serious student should not engage in secular studies simultaneous with his Torah studies at the yeshiva.

The internal problems and developments within the yeshiva were the least of the *Netziv*'s worries; the more pressing problems were the attacks from the outside, from the *Maskilim* and from the Russian government. The *Maskilim* wanted to normalize the Russian Jewish community by changing its system of education and its "outdated" customs. The purpose of the government as stated in a secret communication was to bring the Jews nearer to the Christian population by destroying the study of the Talmud and the prejudices fostered

---

[51] Ibid., 104–5.

[52] Ibid., 127: It seems that some of the students may have complained to the government about the yeshiva's failure to add secular studies to the curriculum.

[53] Ibid., 79.

by it.[54] Thus, though the final goals of the two groups were not identical, their strategies concurred, and they often worked closely in their implementation.

In 1856, the government wanted to close the yeshiva, ostensibly because it had not filed the required reports with the government. The administrator of the Vilna region suggested that they require institution of secular studies in the yeshiva instead, so as not to cause an uproar among the Jews.[55] The government, however, eventually returned to its original plan, for as long as *yeshivot* existed, the graduates of state rabbinical seminaries (see above) would not be accepted by the communities to rabbinical offices. Many *Maskilim* favored this move as they considered the traditional *yeshivot* a drain on the community's finances and thought that traditional Talmud study yielded no practical results.[56] On April 6, 1858, the order was issued to close the yeshiva; many influential Jews beseeched the government to revoke the decree, but to no avail. Nevertheless, the order to close the yeshiva had no practical effect. Subsequently, in May 1859, a law was passed (and reaffirmed in 1879, after a third attempt to close the yeshiva), requiring that secular studies be taught, but this law too, had no practical consequences.[57] The yeshiva continued to flourish, attracting the best students from Russia, England, Germany, Austria, and even America. By the end of the 1880s there were over 400 students, the budget was expanded, and a new building was built.[58] The government, however, had other plans: its demands for institution of secular studies (especially Russian language and literature) became more extensive and this time, more rigidly enforced. Government representatives were sent to inspect the yeshiva. Among these inspectors was Joshua Steinberg, the head of the state rabbinical seminary in Vilna, who, wanting to see the Volozhin yeshiva closed, had no reservation about accurately reporting that the yeshiva had no substantial secular studies program.[59]

---

[54] Eliezer Leoni, ed., *Volozhin: Sifra shel ha'Ir veshel Yeshivat "Eitz Chaim"* (Tel Aviv, 1970) 108.

[55] Stampfer, 118.

[56] *HaShachar* 8 (1877) 161–69.

[57] Stampfer, 120.

[58] Ettinger, *Encyclopaedia Judaica* 218.

[59] See M. Berlin, 141, and Stampfer, 120.

In 1887, S. Poliakov assembled a group of rabbis and Jewish leaders (including the *Netziv* and R. Joseph B. Soloveitchik) in Petroburg to discuss
broad changes in the Jewish educational system. The rabbis reluctantly agreed
to having Russian language taught on premises near the *yeshivot* for those
students who were not familiar with the language,[60] but stipulated that *only* the
Russian language be taught: "...the teacher will not be permitted to have
books of 'free opinions or of romance literature which are foreign to us;
according to the holy Torah they are an abomination and are not desirable for
those who come to the holy yeshiva...."[61] this time the *Netziv*, realizing the
severity of the situation, did make an effort to meet the requirements. A small
group of pious students, considered "volunteers" to help save the yeshiva, was
chosen and received instruction from 7:30 to 9:30 P.M. in a building outside
the actual yeshiva (a fact which infuriated the *Maskilim*) by a non-Jewish
teacher.[62] Apparently, the *Netziv* thought that though secular studies per se
were permissible and would not cause spiritual harm, a *Maskil* teacher might
try to influence the students with heretical views.

The yeshiva continued to function in this manner until the fatal day of Dec.
22, 1891, when the government (possibly prodded by students from the
yeshiva who were *Haskalah* sympathizers as well as by the *Maskilim* themselves) issued "Regulations concerning Volozhin yeshiva." This document
stated that all yeshiva pupils were required to study general subjects to
elementary school standards. Among other things, it also listed necessary
qualifications for teachers in the yeshiva, drastically reduced the numbers of
hours to be devoted to Talmud study to four per twenty-four hour period, and
further reduced the number of students allowed to attend the yeshiva.[63] Of
course, such requirements could not be met without destroying the essential
nature of the yeshiva, a fact the government well realized. The *Netziv* ignored
the regulations and the Volozhin yeshiva was closed on Jan. 22, 1892. Though

---

[60] Stampfer, 120. This agreement was largely because of their fear of Poliakov.

[61] As quoted in Mirsky, 70. The original Hebrew reads:

לא יהיה רשות להמורה הנ"ל להחזיק שם ספרי חפש הדעות וספרי ראמאנעו אשר הם זרה לנו עפ"י
תוה"ק, פגול הם לא ירצו לבא בבית הישיבה הקדושה...

[62] Stampfer, 121. There were either 10 or 50 students; the sources disagree.

[63] *HaMelitz* 32 (1892) 50.

the yeshiva was reopened in 1895, two years after the *Netziv*'s death, and continued to operate until World War I, it never regained its former prestige and prominence.

What then were the crucial factors which interacted to lead the Volozhin yeshiva to its unfortunate demise? Clearly the heated debate was not concerned with the legitimacy of secular studies per se: even the *Netziv* did not believe that the particular subjects which the government and the *Maskilim* wanted taught would lead to heresy. The bone of contention was not even the question of *bitul Torah* as most generally applied: even the *Netziv* felt that certain secular subjects should in fact be studied to deepen one's understanding of and appreciation for the Torah. Ultimately, the question was that of the role and the purpose of the Volozhin yeshiva within the Jewish community. It was only in this context that the *Netziv* felt strongly about the inappropriateness of secular studies in his institution.

In the *Netziv*'s eyes, the maintenance of the Volozhin yeshiva was of vital importance to the continuation of traditional Judaism; his view required that the students be totally immersed in Torah studies to the exclusion of all else, in order that they become the great scholars needed by the Jewish community to counteract the decline in Torah study and observance. Secular studies could play no role here. Of course, his goals for the yeshiva were constantly being eroded by the changing character of the student body in the late 19th century, and it is not at all clear that the yeshiva could have indefinitely maintained the status quo, even barring outside pressures forcing its closure.

For the *Maskilim*, the goal was modernization of the Jewish people. Thus, secular studies were a necessary factor in the development and education of every Jew. Though many *Maskilim* were adamantly opposed to Talmud study and pressed for closing the yeshiva already in the 1860s, it seems that most would have tolerated the Talmud studies were the *Netziv* willing to meet their secular studies requirements. In fact, after the yeshiva's closing in 1892, the *Haskalah* journal *HaMelitz* praised the *Netziv*'s concern for the preservation of the Jewish people and his efforts on their behalf[64] and proceeded to explain what had to be done in order that the yeshiva be reopened by the government: "...even the most zealous people of our generation have come to terms with [the need for]... this small amount of secular studies, because this type of

---

[64] Ibid.

knowledge is necessary and beneficial for every person and contains no poison which impinges upon Torah study or fear of God."[65] Indeed, the *Maskilim* felt that this type of study was necessary *especially* for a community leader: "...[the government] only requested proper order [in the yeshiva] and some secular studies which are necessary for every person and especially for a person who wants to lead a community..."[66] Thus, the *Maskilim* essentially agreed with the *Netziv* in that training leaders was a necessary function of the yeshiva, but they disagreed over the correct training procedures. Had the *Netziv* agreed to the government demands, perhaps the *Maskilim* would have been satisfied. Though purely conjecture, perhaps they even thought that eventually the yeshiva would become another state-run rabbinical seminary.

The Russian government, with goals fundamentally different from those of the *Netziv* and the *Maskilim*, wanted to terminate the existence of all particularistic Jewish institutions and to blur all distinctions between Jews and non-Jews. After coming to the realization that it would be impossible to do this in one fell swoop, the government tried to create what was to be, in effect, a transition period in which Jews would gradually become accustomed to the ways of the non-Jews. The government was essentially attempting to gradually transform Jewish educational institutions out of existence! The *Netziv*'s intransigence made even this impossible and the government opted for its initial goal: by imposing requirements that could not be met, the government provided itself with a pretext for immediate closure of the yeshiva.

Thus, throughout the 19th century the history of the Volozhin yeshiva reflected and was a microcosm of the developments in the Jewish community at large. A community subject to many different influences, which on the one hand did not want to break ties with its past, but on the other, did not want to trail behind the rest of the world remaining "unenlightened." This inner tension was further complicated by external pressure (the government) pushing the Jewish community towards an eventual loss of identity and self worth.

---

[65] Ibid. The original Hebrew reads:

לימודי חול מעטים כאלה... בדורנו כבר השלמו להם אפילו הקנאים והאדוקים, כי ידיעות כאלה נחוצות ומועילות לכל אדם וכי אין בהם ארס מזיק ללמודי תורה וליראת שמים.

[66]*HaMelitz* 32 (1892) 47. The original Hebrew reads:

רק דרשה סדר ומשטר נכון ואיזה לימודי חול, הנחוצים לכל בן מדינה ובפרט להחפץ לעמוד בראש קהל ועדה.

Hence, in its later years, the yeshiva was caught in the midst of a tug-of-war between the *Netziv* (representing the traditional Jewish community opposed to a fundamental change in its structure) on the one hand and the government and the *Maskilim* on the other—two sides, but three groups, with three very different sets of goals. Each group was so determined to meet its goals that the snap of the rope was almost inevitable.

CONTRIBUTORS

Aliza Berger, Ph.D. (Measurement and Statistics), is a researcher and editor for the National Institute for Testing and Evaluation in Jerusalem. She also holds a master's degree in Bible from Yeshiva University. Aliza is married to Dov Cooper.

Erica S. Brown, A.M., M.A. (Judaic Studies); M.A. (Education), serves as the scholar in residence of the Boston Jewish Federation. Concurrently pursuing her doctorate, she is also on the faculty of Ma'ayan and Me-ah—adult education programs in Boston. Previously, Erica was on the faculty of Jews College (London), Midreshet Lindenbaum, and Nishmat, and has published numerous articles relating to Jewish issues. She is married with three children.

Aviva Cayam, D.S.W.; M.S.W.; B.H.L., is a practicing family therapist and social worker. She is a lecturer for AMIT, Hadassah, and other venues for adult Jewish education, and has written a number of articles on Halakha and family. Aviva recently made aliyah with her husband, Dr. Bob Cayam, and their five children.

Rachel Furst is a student at Barnard College in New York and learns part time at Drisha. She has studied at Midreshet Lindenbaum.

Micah D. Halpern, M.A. (History & Jewish Education), is an educator, writer, and Orthodox Rabbi who received his rabbinical ordination from the Harry Fischel Institute in Jerusalem. Micah writes and lectures extensively in the areas of Rabbinics, Holocaust studies, and intellectual history both in America and in Israel, and is the founder and Director of the Jerusalem Center for European Study. He also serves as Israeli essayist and commentator for America On Line.

Susan Handelman, Ph.D. (English Literature), is Professor of English and Jewish Studies of the University of Maryland, a faculty member of the Wexner Foundation for adult Jewish education, and currently, a Jerusalem Fellow for advanced educators. Her areas of specialty include literature and religion, literary theory, Jewish studies, and postmodern Jewish thought. Susan has authored many academic articles, while her books include *The Slayers of Moses: The Emergence of Rabbinic Interpretation in Modern Literary Theory*.

Chanah Henkin, M.A. (Jewish History), is founder and Dean of Nishmat, the Jerusalem Center for Advanced Jewish Studies for Women. Previously, she was the assistant principal of the *mamlachti dati* (state-religious) high school in Bet She'an. She has received the Agrest Prize of the Israel Ministry of Education and the Rabbi Belkin Award of Yeshiva University. Chanah resides in Jerusalem with her husband Rabbi Yehuda Henkin and their six children.

Norma Baumel Joseph, Ph.D. (Religion), is Associate Professor of Religion at Concordia University in Montreal and has lectured and published extensively on women and Judaism, Jewish law, ethics, and religion. She is an activist for women's *tefilla* groups and agunot and appeared in, and was the consultant to, the films "Half the Kingdom" and "Untying the Bonds...Jewish Divorce." Norma is married to Rabbi Howard Joseph and has four children.

Maidi S. Katz z"l, M.S. (Jewish History); J.D., was an attorney as well as an instructor in Talmud, Jewish law, and Bible, which she taught at Drisha, Pardes, Pelech High School for Girls, and the Ramaz Upper School. Her writings include "The Books we Live by," a series which appeared in *American Women's Mizrachi Magazine* from 1984–1987, and "The Married Woman's Ownership and Use of Marital Property in Jewish Law" published in the *Jewish Law Annual*. Maidi was born on September 15, 1962 and passed away on November 11, 1996. May her memory be for a blessing.

Tirzah Meacham (leBeit Yoreh), Ph.D. (Talmud), is Associate Professor of Near and Middle Eastern Civilizations at the University of Toronto. She has prepared a critical edition of Mishna *Nidda* with particular emphasis on halakhic and medical realia, and has recently published a critical edition of *Sefer haBagrut veSefer haShanim*. Tirza has contributed to and co-edited, together with her spouse Professor Harry Fox, *Introducing Tosefta: Textual, Intra-Textual and Inter-Textual Studies*. They have three children.

Rochelle L. Millen, Ph.D. (Religious Studies), is Associate Professor of Religion at Wittenberg University, Ohio, and has also taught at Pardes and Stern College. She has published extensively in the area of Judaic studies and is the editor of *New Perspectives on the Holocaust: A Guide for Teachers and Scholars*. Rochelle is currently working on a volume of halakhic sources regarding women and life-cycle events.

Malka Puterkovski, M.A. (Talmud), has been the head instructor and program coordinator of Talmud and Halakha at Pelech High School for Girls in Jerusalem for the past ten years. Her great interest is introducing women with no previous learning experience to the world of Talmud. Malka is married with four children.

Gilla Ratzersdorfer Rosen, M.A. (Comparative Literature), teaches Talmud and Midrash at Yakar Educational Center in Jerusalem. She has lectured at Pardes, Matan, Nishmat, Jews College (London), and Hebrew University, and is currently pursuing her doctorate, as well as advanced *hilkhot nidda* studies at Nishmat. Gilla is married to Rabbi Michael Rosen and has six children.

Dvora Ross, Ph.D. (Mathematics), is a computer engineer and mathematician. She has studied for many years *chavruta* and in the *batei midrash* of Matan, Yakar, and Hartman. Dvora's areas of specialty include mathematics, computer science, Talmud, and Halakha.

Chana Safrai, Ph.D. (Talmud and Jewish History), is at the Department of Jewish Thought at the Hebrew University in Jerusalem and the Shalom Hartman Institute, and was formerly the Director of the Judith Lieberman Institute of Jewish Studies. She has written as well as edited numerous books and articles in the areas of Rabbinic literature and women's studies.

Deena R. Zimmerman, MD; MPH; IBCLC, is a practicing pediatrician and certified laction consultant. Prior to making aliya, she was Assistant Professor of Clinical Pediatrics at UMDNJ-RWJ Medical School. She is on break from studying *daf yomi* (after completing two cycles) to pursue advanced *hilkhot nidda* studies at Nishmat. Deena is married with four children.

Gili Zivan, M.A. (Philosophy), teaches Bible, Talmud, history, and Jewish philosophy in high school and at the Yakov Herzog Center for Jewish Studies of the Religious Kibbutz Movement. She is a member of Kibbutz Sa'ad and is actively involved with the education and culture of the Kibbutz. Gili is also a Ph.D. candidate at Bar Ilan University and is married with five children.

Devorah Zlochower, M.A. (Political Science), is a graduate of Drisha's Scholars' Circle and is a teacher of Talmud. She has lectured at Drisha and Melton Adult School, as well as on the high school level. Devorah's areas of interest include women and Jewish law and the Talmud. She is married to Rabbi Dov Linzer and has a son Kasriel.

HEBREW SECTION

לאישה פנויה, לכל הפחות כאשר התורם הוא גוי. גם אם "טובים השניים מן האחד,"
אין להעניש את האחת על שלא הגיעה לידי שניים, ולמנוע ממנה להקים משפחה
חד-הורית. אמנם, נשים פטורות ממצוות פרו ורבו, ולכן גם מנישואין, וגם מצוות
חינוך הבנים היא ממצוות הבן על האב, ולא על האם. למרות זאת, כפי שראינו, לחלק
מן הדעות היא חייבת במצוות "לשבת יצרה." במשך השנים קיבלו עליהן רוב הנשים
מצוות אלו, (של פרו ורבו וחינוך), ובאופן פרדוקסלי רבים אף רואים במצוות אלו את
"תפקיד האישה ביהדות," גם אם אינה מחויבת בהן מבחינה פורמלית. לכן, לא נראה
שיש מן ההיגיון או ההגינות במניעת קיום מצוות פרו ורבו וחינוך מנשים שמסיבות
שונות לא נישאו.

כמובן שאפשרות זו אינה מומלצת לכל הנשים. אם אשה מעריכה שסיכוייה
להינשא וללדת ילדים במסגרת משפחה רגילה גדולים דיים, או גם אם אין לה סיכוי
כזה אך אין לה הכוחות המתאימים לעמוד בנטל של משפחה חד-הורית, עדיף שלא
תעשה זאת. אך לאשה המסוגלת לכך, ואינה רואה לעצמה הגיון בהישארותה ערירית,
אין סיבה שלא תעשה זאת.

כפי שראינו, תרומת זרע מתורם יהודי אנונימי מביאה לבעיות הלכתיות רבות.
כמו-כן, אף תרומה מתורם גוי אנונימי יכולה ליצור בעיות: פגיעה בזכותו של הילד
לדעת על מוצאו הביולוגי, וקשיים פסיכולוגיים ביצירת זהותו. לכן, מן הראוי
שהרבנות הראשית משרד הבריאות יסדירו את עניין בנקי הזרע בארץ, כך שכמו
בשבדיה ובאוסטרליה, יותר לילד לגלות את מוצאו בהגיעו לגיל מתאים. לכל הפחות,
כדאי שכמו בארצות-הברית, אפשרות זו תינתן למעוניינים בכך.

שנות הארבעים לחייהן,[קיד] שסיכוייהן למציאת בן-זוג בטרם יעברו שנות הפוריות שלהן קטנים ביותר, וההזרעה היא הסיכוי הטוב ביותר שלהן להקמת משפחה, גם אם לא בצורה המקובלת.

בכל מקרה, כפיית נשים החפצות בילדים להינשא כדי למלא רצון זה, גם אם אין יכולות למצוא שותף מתאים, אינה נראית מוסרית, ובודאי שלא תתרום למוסד המשפחה, או לאושרם ובריאותם של הילדים והוריהם.

הריסת המיסטיקה:
הרב יעקובוביץ' (שם) חושש,

> הולדת ילדים תהפוך באמצעותה עניין שרירותי ומיכני, משולל אותן סגולות מיסטיות ויחסי קירבה אנושיים, העושים את האדם שותף להקב"ה במעשה הבריאה.

יש להזכיר כי ההזרעה אינה באה להחליף את השיטה הרגילה ליצירת ילדים, אלא לעזור במקרים שהשיטה הרגילה אינה ישימה, ללא ניאוף (במקרה של נשים הנשואות לגברים עקרים), או יחסי מין שמחוץ לנשואים (במקרה של נשים פנויות). יחסי הקירבה האנושיים של האמהות וילדיהם, שלא היו יכולים להיוולד בדרך אחרת, והכרת תודתם לקב"ה, יוכלו רק להתחזק בעקבות זאת.

סלידה:
ד"ר אברהם שטיינברג אומר לגבי הזרעה לנשים פנויות:[קטו]

> ברור שמבחינה מוסרית יש במצב זה סלידה רבה יותר מאשר באשה נשואה שלא הצליחה להתעבר מבעלה.

כפי שראינו לעיל, ברור שמבחינה ההלכתית מצבן של נשים פנויות דוקא קל יותר. ד"ר שטיינברג אינו מפרט את הסיבות לסלידתו, אך נראה שהיא נובעת בעיקר מדעות קדומות, או, ממה שהרב פיינשטיין מכנה, "השקפות שבאים מידיעת דעות חיצוניות," (ראו את הציטוט מדבריו בפרק ד לעיל). בקשר לכך אצטט ממאמרה של Gina Kolata בנושא השכפול הגנטי, שפורסם ב- New York Times, ב- 2 בדצמבר 1997:

> ...new reproductive arrangements pass through several predictable stages, from "horrified negation" to "negation without horror" to "slow and gradual curiosity, study, evaluation, and finally a very slow but steady acceptance."

יב. סיכום

כפי שראינו בכל מה שנאמר לעיל, לרוב הדעות אין איסור ממשי על תרומת זרע

קיד כך, למשל, מראות הסטטיסטיקות המצוטטות ב- Jane Mattes.

קטו הרב ד"ר אברהם שטיינברג, "הזרעה מלאכותית לאור ההלכה," ספר אסיא כרך א, תשל"ו, עמ' 128–141.

סובלים מבעיות פסיכולוגיות קלות או חמורות.[קיא]

על כך יש להעיר כי יש הבדל גדול בין משפחות חד-הוריות שונות. במשפחות שעברו גירושין או מוות של אחד ההורים, ודאי שהילד חווה טראומה של אובדן וחוסר-יציבות. כמו-כן, כאשר נערה או אשה צעירה, בגיל העשרה או בתחילת שנות העשרים, נכנסת להריון לא-מתוכנן, כאשר היא עדיין אינה בשלה מבחינה נפשית, וגם אינה מבוססת דיה מבחינת מהלך חייה ומבחינה כלכלית, הילד יסבול מכך. אולם, במשפחות חד-הוריות שבהן האם בוגרת יותר, יציבה ומבוססת, והילד נולד מתוך החלטה וציפייה שלה לכך, המצב שונה.

בכל מקרה, השאלה מתי, ואם בכלל, נימוק של "טובת הילד" יכול לגרום להחלטה שלא ללדת אותו היא מורכבת ביותר. כמובן, מבחינה אידיאלית, עדיף שילד יגדל במשפחה יציבה, שבה יהיו לו או לה שני הורים בוגרים, בשלים, אוהבים, החיים בשלום זה עם זה, ומבוססים דיים כדי להעניק לו את כל צרכיו. למרבה הצער, במקרים רבים, אידיאל זה אינו מושג. אך קיום הורה אחד יציב ובשל, ודאי עדיף על שני הורים שאינם יציבים או בוגרים, או המסוכסכים זה עם זה.[קיב]

מוסד המשפחה:

הרבנים יעקובוביץ',[קיג] וגולינקין (שם) מביעים את חששם להמשך קיום מוסד המשפחה. הרב יעקובוביץ' אומר:

> ההזרעה המלאכותית,... אם תוכנס לשימוש גם בבני אדם, עשויה לנתק הקשר בין הולדת ילדים ונישואים, שהוא הכרחי לקיום המשפחה,... זו תיתן אפשרות לנשים להשביע רעבונן לילדים מבלי להזדקק לבעל ולבית.

והרב גולינקין קובע:

> אם נאמץ את שיטת ההזרעה המלאכותית מתורם לנשים רווקות, נסתום את הגולל על המשפחה היהודית.

למרבה המזל, נראה שהקב"ה ברא את עולמו כך שרצונם ההדדי של נשים וגברים אלו באלו יהיה מבוסס בדרך-כלל גם על "אהבה, אחווה, שלום ורעות," ולא רק על צורך חצוני כלשהו—במעמד חברתי, כספי או בילדים. מאז הוכנסה ההזרעה המלאכותית לשימוש נרחב, לא נראה כי היא גורמת להריסת מוסד המשפחה. נשים רווקות המשתמשות בשיטה זו, הן בדרך-כלל נשים בסוף שנות השלושים או בתחילת

[קיא] כמובן, נשאלת שאלת השאלה: בהשוואה למי? האם יש מישהו שאינו סובל מאיזשהן בעיות פסיכולוגיות?

[קיב] מחקרים בענין זה מצוטטים למשל ב-

Jane Mattes, *Single Mothers by Choice* (Time Books/Random House, 1994) 16.

[קיג] הרב ד"ר עמנואל יעקובוביץ', הרפואה והיהדות, ירושלים, מוסד הרב קוק, תשכ"ו, טו.

לאיבוד הבקרה על מיניות הנשים. כך למשל, אומר הרב יעקובוביץ'.[קז]

> שיטת ההזרעה...תסלול הדרך לפריעת מוסר הרת אסון, שכן באמצעותה תוכל אשה הנאשמת בניאוף לטעון, כי ההריון שלא נגרם, או לא יכול היה להיגרם באמצעות בעלה, הושג על ידי הזרעה מלאכותית...

והרב הענקין:[קח]

> הכלל הוא שאשה-בעלה משמרה,... אבל ע"י אמתלא של הזרעה מלאכותית בטלה השמירה...

בעידן אמצעי המניעה וההפלות המלאכותיות, נראה שאין לטענות כאלה בסיס. נשים הרוצות לנאוף יכולות לטשטש את עקבותיהן בקלות רבה יותר ע"י אמצעים אחרים.

עידוד לזנות:

טענה אחרת היא שהתרת ההזרעה המלאכותית תביא את הנשים לזנות ממש. כך למשל הרב הענקין (שם):

> והרופאים החפשים בדעות ובמוסר או הפרוצים עצמם, יתנו עצה לנאוף ויאמרו, מה לה לזנות באורח עקלקלות, ודא ודא אחת הוא,...

ואילו הרב אמסעל אומר דברים חריפים יותר:[קט]

> והודיעני ידידי... שלמעשה מעשרים נשים המוזרקות, אפשר שאחת תקלוט, וגם זו רק אחרי יסורים,... ורובן אחרי שהן להוטות להתעבר ורואות שבאופן מלאכותי קשה ואינו מועיל, מתמסרות מעצמן לכל דבר פשע...

לטענה כזו, נראה שאפשר לענות רק במאמר חז"ל: כל הפוסל-במומו פוסל.[קי] לגופו של ענין, לפחות בימינו אלו אחוזי ההצלחה מהזרעה מלאכותית גבוהים בהרבה. למעשה, אין הבדל באחוזי ההצלחה מהזרעה או מיחסי מין רגילים (והזרקה לתוך הרחם–IUI–יעילה אף יותר מיחסי מין), אם-כי יש הבדל בין הזרקת זרע מופשר (בו משתמשים היום בד"כ, מחשש להדבקה ב- AIDS), לבין שימוש בזרע טרי.

טובת הילד:

הרב גולינקין (שם) קובע בשם מאמר ב- *Newsweek* כי ילדים במשפחות חד-הוריות

[קז] הרב ד"ר עמנואל יעקובוביץ', הרפואה והיהדות, ירושלים, מוסד הרב קוק, תשכ"ו, פרק טו.

[קח] הרב יוסף אליהו הענקין, "הזרעה מלאכותית," המאור תשרי-חשון ה'תשכ"ה, שנה טז קונטרס א, קמז.

[קט] הרב מ' אמסעל, "עוד פרטים נחוצים באיסור ההזרעה המלאכותית," המאור, תשרי-חשון תשכ"ה, שנה טז קונטרס א, קמז.

[קי] שלחן ערוך, אבן העזר ב:ב.

אינה עניין של פיקוח נפש, או של מצווה כלל, (מכיוון שהאשה אינה חייבת במצוות פרו ורבו), הרי התפשטות האשה בפני הרופא לצורך זה נכלל בגדר "אביזריהו דעריות."

לעומתו, הרבי מסאטמאר,[קג] וכן הרב ולדנברג,[קד] קובעים כי אין עניין של צניעות בפני רופא. רופא טרוד במלאכתו, ואין לחשוש לצניעות בפניו. בכל מקרה, לנשים החוששות לכך, ניתן בדרך כלל לפתור את הבעיה בקלות יחסית: אפשר ללכת אל רופאה-אשה, או לנקוט בדרך של הזרקה עצמית של הזרע לצוואר הרחם.

חשד זנות:

הרב אברהם-סופר אברהם מספר על אשה רווקה בת למעלה מ- 30 שפנתה אליו בבקשת עזרה.[קה] היא ביקשה ללדת באמצעות תרומת זרע, ומכיוון שרצתה להשתמש בזרעו של תורם יהודי, ולא רצתה להסתבך בבעיות הלכתיות, ביקשה שהילד ייולד מזרעו של אדם התורם לבנק הזרע ממילא, וששמו של התורם יישמר במשרד הדתות או הבריאות.

הרב אברהם מעיד שחשב ש"הדבר מכוער," אם כי לא פירט מדוע. סיבה אפשרית אחת שניתנת להבנה מדבריו היא החלוקה בין מקרה של זוג, שבו מדובר באושר של זוג, שלום בית וקיום מצווה—וכאן "רק תאוה של אשה להיות אם" (לטענה זו, ראו פרק ח לעיל). מכל מקום הוא פנה בשאלה לרב אויערבאך. הרב אויערבאך הסכים אתו שלא כדאי לעזור לה, כי בזה היא מביאה על עצמה חשד זנות.

אכן, אפשר לתאר שבמצבים מסוימים, או חברות מסוימות, דבר כזה יביא חשד על האשה. אולם, לא נראה שיש בכך כדי לאסור את המעשה. מעניין לציין כי הרב אברהם, שכתב את ספרו כהארות על השלחן ערוך, הביא סיפור זה כהארה על אבן העזר, (א:יג). בסעיף זה אומר השו"ע כי אשה אינה מצווה על פריה ורביה, והרמ"א מעיר עליו שם כי בכל זאת, אין לאשה לעמוד בלא איש משום חשדא. כלומר, נראה שאם אשה פנויה לא מצאה לעצמה בן-זוג, הרי אין לה דרך להימלט מן החשד בכל מקרה![קו]

איבוד השליטה על מיניות האשה:

מספר רבנים מביעים את דעתם כי התרת עניין זה תקל על נשים לזנות, ותגרום

[קג] הרב יואל טייטעלבוים, האדמו"ר מסאטמאר, המאור, מנחם אב תשכ"ד, שנה ט"ז קונטרס ט, קמה.

[קד] הרב אליעזר ולדנברג, שו"ת ציץ אליעזר, חלק ט,סימן נא, שער ד, הפרייה מלאכותית.

[קה] הרב אברהם-סופר אברהם, נשמת אברהם, הלכות חולים רופאים ורפואה, חלק ד, אבן העזר, סימן א, ירושלים תשנ"ג.

[קו] טענות נוספות שהרב אברהם מביא בשם הרב אויערבאך שם הם חשש ש"הילד יצטער על כך," וכן "יש לחשוש שזרע פגום שנולד בעבירה של מוציא שכבת זרע לבטלה, יתכן שיש לזה השפעה גם על הנוצר מזה."

שלהם אל רחם ישראלית...[צח]

רק הולד שיש לו אב כשר בישראל הוא קדוש ומיוחס, ורק בן כזה יורש את כל כוחות
וסגולות האב הישראלי... ובאם זרע האב הוא של עכו"ם הרי מוחו של הבן וכל מהלך
מחשבותיו ונטיותיו הם של עכו"ם... ולכך התקינו לומר שלא עשני גוי.[צט]

כי איך זה יהיה דמות פרצופו של עם ישראל, אם חס ושלום יכניסו בקרבו לאלפים ולדות
מזוהמות מזרע עכו"ם רחמנא ליצלן.[ק]

כלומר, פוסקים אלו רואים בכך דבר מתועב ואבסורדי. הם אינם מבחינים בין
התבוללות רוחנית, שיכולה להיגרם על-ידי נישואים לגוי וחיים עמו, לבין
"התבוללות" או עירוב אתני שיכול להיווצר על-ידי שימוש בזרעו (והמתרחש אף
ממילא ע"י נישואים עם גרים). לדעת חלק מהפוסקים הנ"ל, זרע גוי הוא מזוהם,
ונטיותיו הטבעיות הרעות של הגוי יעברו דרך זרעו לילד הנוצר מתרומת הזרע.

אכן, הדברים קשים. על-פי מאמרו של דניאל לסקר (שם), ניכרת כאן השפעתם של
דברי הזוהר והקבלה. אך אין בכך כדי לנחם. רק כ- 20 שנה עברו מאז ההתפרצות
הגזענית הנוראה שהביאה עלינו את השואה, מתוך מגמה ל"טיהור אתני" של אירופה
והעולם כולו, לבין כתיבת חלק מן הדברים הנ"ל. נראה שחלקים מעם ישראל ורבניו
לא הפנימו את הלקח המוסרי מאסון זה, ולנו לא נותר אלא להתבייש.[קא]

אולם, אפשר אולי לראות בעייתיות אחרת לגבי השימוש בתרומת זרע מגוי.
אמנם, שלא כבנישואין, התורם אינו יכול להשפיע על חינוכו ודתיותו של הילד, אך
בהנחה שהילד מקבל את מלוא המידע על מוצאו, האם תיווצר אצלו בעיה בתחושת
הזהות העצמית שלו? האם תחושת הזהות היהודית של הילד תפגע? ככל הנראה, דבר
זה תלוי בחינוכו של הילד, וכן בסביבה שבה יגדל, ובמידת קבלתה אותו כיהודי שלם.

יא. שיקולים נוספים

מלבד הטענות שהזכרנו לעיל, מעלים המתנגדים להזרעה מלאכותית שיקולים
נוספים, הלכתיים ומטא-הלכתיים. אנסה להתייחס לטענות אלו, כפי שליקטתי מן
הספרות הדנה בנושא זה:

צניעות:

הרב וייס חושש לצניעותה של האשה בפני הרופא.[קב] לטענתו, מכיוון שהזרקת זרע

[צח] הרב אליעזר ולדנברג, שו"ת ציץ אליעזר, חלק ט,סימן נא, שער ד, הפרייה מלאכותית.

[צט] הרב שלמה האלבערשטאם (האדמו"ר מבאבוב), קונטרס להצלת קדושת ויחוס ישראל,
המאור, תשרי-חשון תשכ"ה, שנה טז, קונטרס א, קמז.

[ק] הרב מ' אמסעל, "עוד פרטים נחוצים באיסור ההזרעה המלאכותית," המאור, תשרי-חשון
תשכ"ה, שנה טז קונטרס א, קמז.

[קא] ראו בענין זה גם את דבריו של הרב דורף במאמרו.

[קב] הרב יצחק וייס, שו"ת מנחת יצחק, חלק ד, סימן ה.

כלומר, הגמרא אומרת : אלמנה אסורה רק לכהן גדול, ואם בכל זאת תינשא לו, הבן הנולד יהיה פגום, (כלומר אסור לכהונה), קל וחומר לאשה השוכבת עם גוי, שאיסורה כולל יותר, שגם ילדה יהיה פגום (כאשר במקרה זה הכונה בעצם לבת, שתהיה אסורה לכהנים). הגמרא מנסה לטעון לגבי כך : והלא מקרה האלמנה בכל זאת חמור יותר, מכיון שגם היא עצמה מתחללת (כלומר נעשית אסורה) לכהונה ע"י שכיבתה עם הכהן הגדול? והתשובה : זה אינו יותר חמור, מכיון שגם האשה השוכבת עם גוי נפסלת בכך לכהונה.

מכך נראה שהבת תהיה אסורה לכהונה רק אם גם אמה אסורה לכהונה, כי במקרה אחר שהבת-וחומר לא יהיה תקף. אך מכיון שבמקרה ההזרעה המלאכותית האם לא קיימה יחסים אסורים,[צג] גם הבת תהיה מותרת לכהונה. מעניין לציין כי לדעת הרב אויערבאך,[צד] מכיון שבמקרה זה הולד כשר, ומכיון שאין ילד כזה אב מבחינה הלכתית (שכן ילד הנולד לאשה יהודיה מגוי מתיחס רק אחרי אמו), הילד יתיחס אחרי אמו גם לענין כהונה ולויה. כלומר, אם האם היא כהנת או לויה, הילד יהיה כמותה.

אולם, למרות הנ"ל, רבים מהפוסקים, מעט מבין המתירים ורוב האוסרים את השימוש בזרעו של גוי, מסתייגים מטעמים אחרים :

> עתה נבאר דין הזרעה מלאכותית מנכרי לתוך גופה של ישראלית, ואף שאך למותר הוא להרבות דברים על הכיעור והזוהמא שבדבר זה... ואין ספק כי טבע האב צפון בבן... אך היות ובשביל רוב הנשים הבאות לשאול על כך... הרי זו ממש שאלת חיים...[צה]

> קשה לחשוב על אבסורד יותר גדול מזה! האם חזרנו ארצה כדי ללדת ילדים שאביהם אינו יהודי?![צו]

> המשוקץ שבדבר לקחת זרע של גוי... שהרי אפילו במינקת נכרית דנו משום שמקבל היונק מתכונות של גוי, קל וחומר כשעיקר זרעו ותכונותיו של גוי בו.[צז]

> ומה נאמר כבר מבחינה זאת כשהמדובר בלקחת שכבת זרע של עכו"ם... הרי כל הדיבורים מיותרים לתאר הכיעור והזוהמא שבדבר וכן החורבן... שיביאו **יצורים** כאלה בקרב בית ישראל... ומה נורא הרעיון... להתיר התבוללות עם גויי הארצות דרך חדירת שכבת זרע

[צג] הרב שלמה זלמן אויערבאך, "הזרעה מלאכותית," נועם, שם, הרב רב בן-ציון מאיר חי עוזיאל, פסקי עוזיאל בשאלות הזמן, ירושלים, מוסד הרב קוק, תשל"ז, סימן נג, והרב משה פיינשטיין, שו"ת אגרות משה, חלק ב, אבן העזר יא.

[צד] הרב שלמה זלמן אויערבאך, "הזרעה מלאכותית," נועם, שם.

[צה] שם.

[צו] הרב דוד גולינקין, "תשובה בעניין הזרעה מלאכותית," תשובות ועד ההלכה של כנסת הרבנים בישראל, כרך ג, תשמ"ח-תשמ"ט.

[צז] מכתב מאחד מגדולי התורה בירושלים, "הזרעה מלאכותית יחוס הילוד," נועם, ספר ראשון, תשי"ח, עמ' קכד.

אלהים אחרים.

מכאן למדו חז"ל שאין להתחתן עם עובדי עבודה זרה, או אף עם גויים בכלל. טעם המצוה מפורש בפסוק: נשואים עם גויים ימשכו את בני הזוג היהודיים לעבוד עבודה זרה, ואולי אף את ילדיהם.

במסכת עבודה זרה (לו ע"ב) מובאות שתי דעות: לדעה אחת התורה אסרה על נישואין עם שבעת העממים, וחז"ל גזרו אף על שאר הגויים, ולפי הדעה השניה יש איסור חיתון על כל הגויים מן התורה, וחז"ל אסרו על יחסי מין עמם אף שלא בדרך נישואין. לדעת התוספות ביבמות טז ע"ב (ד"ה "קסבר"), יחסי אישות עם גויים בדרך זנות מותרים מן התורה, ונאסרו ע"י בית דינו של שם.

בכל מקרה, הילד הנולד מיחסי אישות בין אשה יהודיה לגוי יהיה כשר (יבמות מה ע"ב), אם כי במקרה של בת, היא תהיה אסורה להינשא לכהן[פט]. אשה המקיימת יחסי אישות עם גוי אסורה לכהן אף היא, בתור "זונה," כלומר אשה הנבעלת לאדם שאינו יכול להינשא לה[צ].

המצב לגבי קבלת תרומת זרע מגוי, יהיה כמובן תלוי בגישה הכללית לתרומת זרע. אלה הרואים בתרומת זרע איסור המקביל ליחסי אישות (פרק ד לעיל), יראו גם בקבלת תרומת זרע מגוי זנות, ויאסרו את הבת הנולדת מתרומה זו לכהן[צא].

לעומת זאת, אם יחסי אישות, כפי שטענו בפרק ד, אינם כוללים שום איסור על הזרע עצמו, הרי שקבלת תרומת זרע מגוי עדיפה. היא פותרת, כפי שראינו, את הבעיות ההלכתיות כאשר יש תורם יהודי שאינו ידוע (חשש נשואי אחאים או הולדת ילד שתוקי, חשש צורך בייבום וחליצה, ממזרות לגבי אשה נשואה, וחוסר השרית השכינה כאשר האב אינו ידוע), ואף כשהתורם ידוע, פותרת את החשש להוצאת זרע לבטלה[צב]. ואכן, כל המתירים קבלת תרומת זרע ממליצים על שימוש בזרע גוי.

לגבי שאלת מעמד האשה והבת הנולדת מהזרקת זרע גוי לגבי נישואים לכהן, מסכימים רוב הפוסקים כי אין כל בעיה בכך. לגבי האשה עצמה, אי אפשר לראותה כ"זונה," מאחר שלא היו כאן כל יחסים אסורים עם הגוי, וכך גם אפשר להסיק מן הגמרא בחגיגה (לעיל בפרק ה), בענין העיבור באמבטיה. לגבי הבת, הרי איסור הבת לכהונה נלמד מקל וחומר לגבי אלמנה לכהן גדול. וכך אומרת הגמרא ביבמות (מה ע"א):

מה אלמנה לכהן גדול, שאין איסורה שוה בכל, בנה פגום, זו שאיסורה שוה בכל אינו דין שבנה פגום? מה לאלמנה לכהן גדול שכן היא עצמה מתחללת? הכא נמי: כיון שנבעלה פסלה.

[פט] שו"ע, אבן העזר ד :יט, ז :יז.

[צ] שו"ע, אבן העזר ו :ח.

[צא] הרב אליעזר ולדנברג, שו"ת ציץ אליעזר, חלק ט,סימן נא, שער ד, הפרייה מלאכותית.

[צב] לכל הדעות אין על גוי איסור הוצאת זרע לבטלה.

אומר שזאת "פריצות גדולה שאין כדאי לעשות כן," אלא אם כן הרופא אומר שאי
אפשר אלא בצורה זו. הוא מציע גם אפשרות שיחסי המין יהיו בבית הזוג, ואח"כ
תבוא האשה אל הרופא כדי שיוציא את הזרע מגופה. בכל מקרה, ע"פ הנ"ל נראה
שהתורם צריך להיות נשוי.

הרב ד"ר ברוך נס טוען כי הגמרא בנדה היא אגדתא,[צג] ואין למדין הלכה מן
האגדות, ואין חטא זה של "שחת ארצה"[צד] בכלל מצוות לא תעשה. לכן הוא מתיר
להוציא זרע ע"י אוננות דרך קונדום, כי בדרך זו ההוצאה נקראת "שלא כדרך
הנאתן." וביחס לגמרא ביבמות, הוא אומר שמכיון שמדובר שם באדם שיש שאלה
לגבי יכולתו להוציא זרע, ובית הדין צריכים לראות בדיוק איך ומהיכן הזרע יוצא,
הפתרונות שהוצעו היו של גרוי חצוני.

כל הפוסקים הנ"ל דנים בעצם בשאלת תרומת זרע מאיש לאשתו, אולם לא ברור
אם צריך להיות הבדל בעצם הדין בנוגע לאשה אחרת. לדעת רבים מן הראשונים
קיום מצות פרו ורבו אינו תלוי בנישואין,[צה] כך שלפחות לדעה זו לא נראה שצריך
להיות הבדל בכך לדעת התולים את היתר הוצאת הזרע בקיום המצווה. ובוודאי שכך
גם לדעות (שצוטטו לעיל) שהדבר תלוי ביצירת ילד, גם ללא קיום מצות פרו ורבו.
היחיד הדן ומתיר בפירוש תרומת זרע ל"אשה זרה" (שאינה אשתו של התורם), הוא
הרב דורף.[צו]

הרב אהרן וואלקין מתיר לאדם לתרום מזרעו (אף ע"י אוננות) עבור אשתו, אך לא
עבור אשה אחרת, מכיון ש"הרבה מכשולים יוכל לצאת מזה בערבוב המשפחה."[צז] גם
האנציקלופדיה התלמודית סוברת כך,[צח] כנראה ע"פ דברי הרב וואלקין. לא ברור מה
תהיה דעתו במקרה של תורם ידוע ואשה פנויה, שבו אין בעיה של "ערבוב המשפחה."

סך-הכל, נראה שיש סימוכין להתיר תרומת זרע של יהודי לצורך זה, אם-כי
כאמור, לא לדעת הכל.

י. תורם גוי

בפרשת ואתחנן (דברים ז:ג-ד) נאמר על שבעת העממים:

ולא תתחתן בם: בתך לא תתן לבנו ובתו לא תקח לבנך. כי יסיר את בנך מאחרי ועבדו

[צג] הרב ד"ר ישראל ברוך נס, "בדבר היתר לזרוק ולהכניס זרע האיש לתוך חדרי רחמה של אשה
עקרה כדי שתתעבר," הפרדס, חשון תשי"ח.

[צד] בראשית לח:ט.

[צה] ראו למשל את דברי הרא"ש על כתובות ז ע"ב (אות יב). מן התוספות על יבמות (סב ע"א, ד"ה
"ר' יוחנן") עולה שקיום מצות פרו ורבו תלוי ביחוס הצאצאים אחרי האב, וזה מתקיים גם ללא
נישואין. לעומת זאת הרמב"ם, בהלכות אישות טו:ב, מקשר בין מצות פרו ורבו לבין נישואין.

[צו] דורף, שם.

[צז] הרב אהרן וואלקין, זקן אהרן, מהדורא תנינא, פינסק, תרצ"ב, סימן צז.

[צח] אנציקלופדיה תלמודית, ערך "השחתת זרע," כרך יא, קלב.

איש או באשתו כשהיא נדה, עדיף שיוציא זרע לבטלה.

הרב הדאיא,[עה] שהנו מקובל בעצמו, מושפע מדברי ספר הזוהר, ולכן אוסר על יהודי לתרום מזרעו כלל, ואפילו אם מדובר בהזרקת זרע לאשתו. לעומתו, טוענים אחרים, שהוצאת זרע עבור יצירת ילד אינה לבטלה, ולכן מותר בהחלט להוציא זרע למטרה זו.[עו]

לעומתם, הרב עוזיאל טוען שמכיוון שלדעתו התורם אינו מקיים בכך מצות פרו ורבו, הוצאת זרע זו תהיה לבטלה.[עז] הוא אף מוסיף שגם לדעת הפוסקים שהתורם מקיים בכך את המצוה, הרי שתמיד תהיינה כמה טפות שיאבדו בתהליך זה, והן תהיינה לבטלה, והוצאת זרע "הותרה רק בדרך מנהגו של עולם."

הרב עובדיה יוסף משיב לכך שגם ביחסי מין רגילים חלק מטפות הזרע יאבדו (אם-כי דיוק בדבריו של הרב עוזיאל מעלה שהוא סובר שאיבוד זה מותר ביחסי מין רגילים, "מנהגו של עולם").[עח] בכל אופן הוא אומר שמכיוון שמתקיימת בתרומת זרע מצות פרו ורבו, התרומה מותרת.

הרב ויינברג מוסיף שאפילו לדעת הסוברים שהתורם אינו מקיים בכך מצות פרו ורבו, בכל זאת מכיוון שתרומה זו היא לשם יצירת ילד, היא מותרת.[עט] כך פוסק גם הרב אריאל:[9] לדעתו, אף שהתורם אינו מקיים בכך את המצוה, הולדת ילדים מזרעו פוטרת אותו ממצוה זו, והוא מקיים בכך את מצות "לשבת יצרה."

לדעת הרב משה פיינשטיין יש בעניין זה שני איסורים נפרדים:[פא] הוצאת זרע לבטלה, שאינה רלוונטית בתרומת זרע, ואיסור אוננות ביבמות ובנדה (על פי דעת ר' יוחנן במסכת נדה לעיל, הוא פוסק שאיסור זה הוא מדאורייתא). לכן הוא פוסק שמותר להוציא זרע לצורך, אבל לא על ידי אוננות אלא רק על ידי גרוי חיצוני, כמו שמצויעה הגמרא ביבמות, או על-ידי יחסי מין: אם בשימוש בקונדום, או בשיטות "דש מבפנים וזורה בחוץ." לגבי עצת הרבי מסאטמאר של איסוף הזרע ע"י קיום יחסי מין במרפאה, כך שהרופא יוכל לאסוף שם את הזרע מגוף האשה,[פב] הוא

[עה] הרב עובדיה הדאיא, "הזרעה מלאכותית," נועם, ספר ראשון, תשי"ח, עמי קל–קלז.

[עו] הרב ישראל זאב מינצברג, "הזרעה מלאכותית," נועם, ספר ראשון, תשי"ח, עמי קכ; הרב ד"ר ישראל ברוך נס, "בדבר היתר לזרוק ולהכניס זרע האיש לתוך חדרי רחמה של אשה עקרה כדי שתתעבר," הפרדס, חשון תשי"ח, הרב משה פיינשטיין, שו"ת אגרות משה, חלק א, אבן העזר עא, והרב דוב מ. קרויזר, "הזרעה מלאכותית," נועם, ספר ראשון, תשי"ח, עמי קיא-קכג.

[עז] הרב בן-ציון מאיר חי עוזיאל, פסקי עוזיאל בשאלות הזמן, ירושלים, מוסד הרב קוק, תשל"ז, סימן נג.

[עח] הרב עובדיה יוסף, יביע אומר, ירושלים, תשמ"ו, כרך ב, אבן העזר א.

[עט] הרב יחיאל יעקב ויינברג, שו"ת שרידי אש, שם.

[פ] הרב יעקב אריאל, שו"ת באהלה של תורה, מכון התורה והארץ, תשנ"ח, אבן העזר סט.

[פא] הרב משה פיינשטיין, שו"ת אגרות משה, חלק א, אבן העזר ע.

[פב] הרב יואל טייטעלבוים, האדמו"ר מסאטמאר, המאור, מנחם אב תשכ"ד, שנה ט"ז קונטרס ט, קמה.

הגמרא שם מעידה שבית הלל השתכנעו מנימוק זה, וחזרו להורות כבית שמאי. סוגיה זו מופיעה גם בבבא בתרא (יג ע"א). לדעת התוספות שם (ד"ה "שנאמר לא תהו בראה"), הפסוק "לשבת יצרה" שייך גם באשה. כך פוסק גם המגן אברהם, שאשה חייבת במצות "לשבת יצרה."[עא]

במסכת מגילה (כז ע"א) אומרת הגמרא שמותר למכור ספר תורה כדי לשאת אשה, ומנמקת זאת בפסוק הנ"ל. התוספות במסכת חגיגה (ב ע"ב, ד"ה "לא תהו בראה") מסבירים שהגמרא משתמשת בפסוק זה, ולא במצות פרו ורבו מפני שהוא "אלים טפי" (חזק יותר).

ט. הוצאת זרע לבטלה

כאשר תורם הזרע הוא יהודי, יש לדון אף בשאלה נוספת: האם מותר ליהודי לתרום זרע? האם אין בהוצאת זרע שלא בדרך של יחסי מין רגילים עבירה על איסור הוצאת זרע לבטלה? מכיון ששאלה זו אינה נוגעת במישרין לנושא מאמר זה, אגע בה אך במעט. נזקקים לברור שני נושאים עיקריים: האם בכלל מותר להוציא זרע שלא בדרך של יחסי מין רגילים, והאם הזרקת זרע לאשה פנויה יכולה להחשב סיבה לכך? שאלת הוצאת זרע נידונה בגמרא בשתי סוגיות נפרדות: במסכת נדה (יג ע"א) על המשנה: "כל היד המרבה לבדוק בנשים משובחת, ובאנשים תקצץ." אומר ר' יוחנן:

> כל המוציא שכבת זרע לבטלה חייב מיתה, שנאמר "וירע בעיני ה' אשר עשה וימת גם אותו."[עב]

ובהמשך הגמרא (ע"ב) נאמר:

> ואמר ר' אלעזר: מאי דכתיב "ידיכם דמים מלאו"?[עג] אלו המנאפים ביד. תנא דבי רבי ישמעאל: "לא תנאף" לא תהא בך ניאוף, בין ביד בין ברגל.

ביבמות (עו ע"א) דנה הגמרא באדם שלא ברור אם הוא מסוגל להוציא שכבת זרע, איך ניתן לבדקו אותו. הגמרא נותנת שם עצות כיצד לגרותו אם ע"י חימום איברו או ע"י גרויו בבגדי נשים צבעוניים.

איסור זה של הוצאת זרע התעצם מאד ע"י הזוהר, שהפכו לאחד האיסורים החמורים ביותר.[עד] על פי הקבלה, פוסק השו"ע באבן העזר (כג:א): "אסור להוציא שכבת זרע לבטלה ועון זה חמור מכל עבירות שבתורה." החלקת מחוקק שם מסייג את דברי השו"ע, ופוסק בעקבות ספר חסידים שאם האדם מתירא שיכשל באשת

[עא] שלחן ערוך, אורח חיים קנג:ט.

[עב] בראשית לח:י.

[עג] ישעיהו א:טו.

[עד] Daniel J. Lasker, "Kabbalah, Halakhah, and Modern Medicine: The case of Artificial Insemination," *Modern Judaism* 8.1 (Feb. 1988).

מצות פרו ורבו, ולכן אין הם מתאמצים למצוא היתרים. עקב כך, ברצוני להוסיף כאן כמה מלים בעניין זה.[סו]

בתנ"ך, רצונה של אשה בילדים נחשב מובן מאליו. שרה, רבקה, רחל, וחנה היו כולן עקרות, ונפקדו רק לאחר תפילות ותחנונים. אצל כולן (מלבד רבקה), רצון זה היה חזק למרות שלבני-זוגן כבר היו ילדים משלהם, וכבר קיימו את מצות פרו ורבו. גם שלום-הבית שלהן לא היה תלוי בעניין זה: רחל היתה האשה האהובה על יעקב, ואלקנה ניסה לנחם את חנה באמרו "הלוא אנכי טוב לך מעשרה בנים." תפילתה של חנה להפקד בזרע נחשבת בגמרא (ברכות לא עמ' א-ב) כאב-טיפוס של תפילה בכלל, וממנה נלמדים כללים של תפילת העמידה.

תמר, אמם של זרח ופרץ, ומקימת שושלת בית-דוד, יכולה להיחשב אף האם החד-הורית הראשונה. גם אם ניתן שלא להסכים עם הדרך בה מילאה את מבוקשה (אם כי בנסיבות הדור ההוא, יתכן שלא היתה לה ברירה), הרי רצונה לא נחשב כ"לא לגיטימי," ואף יהודה אמר עליה "צדקה ממני."[סז]

המשנה (יבמות ו:ו) מביאה שתי דעות: תנא קמא סובר שרק האיש מצווה על פרו ורבו, ואילו רבי יוחנן בן ברוקה סובר "על שניהם הוא אומר 'ויברך אותם אלקים ויאמר להם פרו ורבו.'" ההלכה נפסקה כדעתו של תנא קמא: רק האיש חייב במצות פרו ורבו.[סח]

הגמרא, בדונה בהלכה זו (יבמות סה ע"ב), מביאה את סיפורה של אשה שבאה לפני ר' אמי, ותבעה להתגרש ולקבל את כתובתה לאחר שבן-זוגה היה עקר. ר' אמי ענה לה: את אינך מצווה על כך, ולכן אינך זכאית לכתובתך. אך היא ענתה: מה יהיה עלי בזקנתי? ר' אמי השתכנע ופסק לה את כתובתה. מעשה דומה מובא גם לגבי רב נחמן, ושם טענת האשה היתה: "לא בעיא הך אתתא חוטרא לידה ומרה לקבורה?" (האם אותה אשה אינה זקוקה למשענת לעת זקנתה, ולמי שיקברנה לאחר מותה?) גם כאן השתכנע רב נחמן מטענתה. ואכן, כך גם נפסק להלכה, שעקרות הגבר הינה סיבה מספקת לתביעת גט מצד האשה.[סט]

במסכת חגיגה (ב ע"ב), דנה הגמרא באדם שהיינו במעמד של "חציו עבד חציו בן חורין." בית הלל נותנים תחילה פתרון לצורת עבודתו, אך בית שמאי מעירים כי פתרון זה אינו נותן לו אפשרות לשאת אשה. וכך הם אומרים:

> והלא לא נברא אלא העולם אלא לפריה ורביה, שנאמר "לא תהו בראה, לשבת יצרה."[ע] אלא
> מפני תיקון העולם כופין את רבו ועושה אותו בן חורין.

[סו] בהקשר זה ראו הרב משה פיינשטיין, שו"ת אגרות משה, חלק א, אבן העזר י, והרב דורף, שם.

[סז] בראשית לח:כו.

[סח] משנה תורה, הלכות אישות טו:ב, שלחן ערוך, אבן העזר א:יג.

[סט] שלחן ערוך, אבן העזר קנד:ו.

[ע] ישעיהו מה:יח.

סביר שאנשים יטעו לחשוב שבנה שנולד לפני הנישואין הוא בנו של אותו האדם לו נישאה. אולם, לדעת האומרים שילד הנולד מתרומת זרע נחשב בנו של התורם לכל דבר, או לפחות לחומרא, הרי החשש הרביעי, שיפטור את יבמתו לשוק, (כלומר שאם יש לו אח מאביו שמת ללא זרע, אנשים לא ידעו שיש כאן אח שצריך לחלוץ לאלמנתו לפני שתתוכל להינשא בשנית), אכן קיים כאן. מסיבה זאת שוב, לדעה זו, יש להקפיד על תורם יהודי ידוע, או תורם גוי, שבו לא שייך חשש זה.

ענין נוסף שמעלים הפוסקים הוא הסיבה הראשונה שמביאה הגמרא הנ"ל ביבמות לדרישה לחכות לשלשה חודשים בין גירושין או אלמנות לנישואין שניים:

אמר רב נחמן אמר שמואל: משום דאמר קרא: להיות לך לא-להים ולזרעך אחריך[סג] להבחין בין זרעו של ראשון לזרעו של שני.

ורש"י שם אומר:

שאין השכינה שורה אלא על הוודאים, שזרעו מיוחס אחריו.

ושוב תיווצר כאן בעיה בתורם יהודי אנונימי. לעניין תורם גוי אומר הרב פיינשטיין שמכיון שלולד כזה אין אב כלל, אין בו חסרון זה, כי הוא נחשב "ודאי" ולא "ספק."[סד] הרב אויערבאך מעיר לגבי שאלה זו שאמנם אין כאן איסור הבחנה,[סה] מכיון שאין לילד אב, אך בכל זאת, לגבי מה שנאמר בקדושין ע ע"ב, שהקב"ה משרה את שכינתו רק על המשפחות המיוחסות בישראל, הרי ילד זה אינו נקרא מיוחס (אף שהוא אינו רואה כל איסור בהולדת ילד כזה).

ח. הלגיטימיות של רצונה של אשה בילד

כמיהתה של אשה לילדים נחשבת בדרך-כלל אחת מתכונותיה הבסיסיות, ואף המעורכות, כמו הקשר בין האם לילדיה. אולם, בהקשרים אלו, של אשה לא-נשואה, או אשה נשואה היולדת ילד שאינו צאצאו הגנטי של בן-זוגה, יש המפקפקים בלגיטימיות של רצון זה, ורואים בו שאיפה אגואיסטית של האשה גרידא. חלק מהפוסקים האוסרים הזרקת זרע מנמקים את פסיקתם בכך שלא מתקיימת כאן

באיסור ההזרעה המלאכותית," המאור, תשרי-חשון תשכ"ה, שנה טז קונטרס א, קמז, והרב אליעזר ולדנברג, שו"ת ציץ אליעזר, חלק ט,סימן נא, שער ד, הפרייה מלאכותית) טוענים כי אין כל ספק כי במקרה של פטירת בני-זוגן, נשים אלו לא ירצו לספר לבתי הדין שילדיהן אינם צאצאיהם הביולוגים של הנפטרים, ולכן הן עדיין זקוקות לחליצה. לעומת זאת, המתירים (הרב שלמה זלמן אויערבאך, "הזרעה מלאכותית," נועם, שם, והרב משה פיינשטיין, שו"ת אגרות משה, חלק ב, אבן העזר יא) מניחים כמובן מאליו שנשים הפונות בשאלה הלכתית בדבר הזרקת זרע מעוניינות בעצמן לנהוג על-פי ההלכה, ולכן אין כל חשש בדבר.

[סג] בראשית יז:ז.

[סד] הרב משה פיינשטיין, שו"ת אגרות משה, חלק ב, אבן העזר יא.

[סה] הרב שלמה זלמן אויערבאך, "הזרעה מלאכותית," נועם, שם.

הפסול של אביו! כפי שראינו בענין הסדינים בפרק הקודם, רבינו פרץ לא חשש שם למעמד של פסול. לדעת הרב משה פיינשטיין,[נה] מעמד ממזרות נוצר רק ע"י יחסי מין ממש, ולכן ילד שנולד מהזרעה לא יהיה ספק ממזר בכל מקרה: אפילו אם התורם הוא ודאי ממזר, הולד לא יהיה ממזר. ואכן, הוא פוסק כי בדיעבד אם אשה התעברה מתרומת זרע אנונימית של יהודי מותר לולד להינשא לכל.[נו]

הרב סאוויצקי טוען כנגד הרב פיינשטיין שלבן כזה (מתרומת זרע של יהודי אנונימי) אסור להתחתן עם אשה יהודיה (שאינה גיורת),[נז] על-סמך הסעיף ברמב"ם שציטטנו לעיל (הל' אסורי ביאה טו:כז), שאשתו תהיה רק ספק-מקודשת. לעניות דעתי, הבנתו את הרמב"ם מוטעית: אמנם הרמב"ם אומר שיש כאן רק ספק קידושין, אולם בסעיף כ"ט שם הוא אומר בפירוש שבמקרה שאין חוששים לספק ממזרות, מותר לבן להינשא גם אם הקידושין יהיו מסופקים.[נח]

בכל מקרה, גם הרב פיינשטיין מסכים שלכתחילה יש לקחת תרומת זרע מגוי,[נט] ורק בדיעבד אין בתרומת זרע מיהודי אנונימי משום איסור (של ניאוף או ייחוס פסול לילד).[ס] כמובן, ניתן להוסיף לכך גם תורם יהודי ידוע: או תורם שזהותו ידועה בזמן ההזרקה עצמה, או כזה שזהותו תוכל להתברר ע"י הילד בהגיעו לגיל 18.

למרות שרבינו פרץ בציטוט שהבאנו לעיל הזכיר רק את החשש מפני נשואי אחאים, מזכירים אחרים,[סא] כי הגמרא ביבמות (מב ע"א) המעלה את בעית ההבחנה (לגבי נשואי גרושות ואלמנות תוך שלשה חודשים לגירושין או ההתאלמנות), מביאה בשם רבא 4 חששות:

(1) שמא ישא את אחותו מאביו, (2) וייבם אשת אחיו מאמו, (3) ויוציא את אמו לשוק, (4) ויפטור את יבמתו לשוק.

חששות מספר (2) ו-(3) אינם נוגעים לאשה פנויה.[סב] גם אם בעתיד היא תינשא, לא

[נה] הרב משה פיינשטיין, שו"ת אגרות משה, חלק ג, אבן העזר יא.

[נו] הרב משה פיינשטיין, שו"ת אגרות משה, חלק א, אבן העזר י.

[נז] הרב מרדכי סאוויצקי, "בדבר הזרעה מלאכותית בזרע איש אחר," המאור, כסלו ה'תשכ"ח, שנה טז, קונטרס ב, קמח.

[נח] אותה טעות דומני שיש לו גם בהבנת דברי החלקת-מחוקק על השו"ע, אבן העזר ד:לז.

[נט] הרב משה פיינשטיין, שו"ת אגרות משה, חלק א, אבן העזר י ו- עא.

[ס] הרב פיינשטיין אף מתיר לקחת בחו"ל תרומת זרע סתם, כי אפשר לסמוך על-כך שרוב התורמים שם גויים. הרבה פוסקים התקיפוהו על-כך, מטעמים שונים. בכל מקרה, כפי שכתבנו בפרק א, היום אין צורך להשתמש בהיתר זה: בבנקים המוסדרים בארץ ובחו"ל אפשר לדעת בודאות אם התורם יהודי או לא.

[סא] הרב אליעזר ולדנברג, שו"ת ציץ אליעזר, חלק ט, סימן נא, שער ד, הפרייה מלאכותית והרב יואל טייטעלבוים, האדמו"ר מסאטמאר, המאור, מנחם אב תשכ"ד, שנה ט"ז קונטרס ט, קמה.

[סב] מעניין לציין בהקשר זה את ההבדל הבולט בין האוסרים והמתירים את ההזרעה לנשים נשואות בשאלת האימון שהם מוכנים לתת בנשים. האוסרים (הרב מ' אמסעל, "עוד פרטים נחוצים

כפי שראינו בפרק הקודם, לרוב הפוסקים הזרקת זרע מתורם יהודי אנונימי היא בעייתית. בגלל ענין ה"הבחנה" דלעיל ייווצר מצב שבו הילד עלול להינשא לקרובי התורם. אמנם, מבחינה סטטיסטית הסיכוי קטן (ובנקי הזרע המוסדרים, בארץ ובחו"ל, תמיד יגבילו את מספר הילדים הנולדים מזרעו של תורם אחד, כך שאם משתמשים בבנק זרע מוסדר הסיכוי לכך הוא בעצם אפסי), אך יצירת מצב כזה של ספק לכתחילה הוא ודאי לא רצוי, ואולי אף אסור.

מבחינה הלכתית, ילד כזה, שאינו מכיר את אביו, נקרא "שתוקי." לגבי ילד כזה, יתכנו גם בעיות הלכתיות נוספות. המשנה בקדושין (ד:א) אומרת:

שתוקי כל שהוא מכיר את אמו ואינו מכיר את אביו... אבא שאול היה קורא לשתוקי "בדוקי."

והגמרא (קדושין עג ע"א) מפרשת:

בדוקי שבודקין את אמו ואומרת לכשר נבעלתי... אמר רבא : הלכה כאבא שאול.

לפי גמרא זו, אין חוששין במקרה של ילד שתוקי לנישואים אסורים עם קרובי משפחה, אבל יש לבדוק שאביו לא היה בעצמו פסול (ממזר וכדומה), ולכן יש לבדוק את אמו ולפי דבריה לקבוע אם הילד כשר. אולם, במקרה של הזרעה מתורם אנונימי, גם לאם אין כל מושג מי האב. הגמרא בקדושין (עג ע"א) דנה בתחילת המשנה, במקרה של שתוקי ללא בדיקה, ואומרת :

אמר רבא : דבר תורה שתוקי כשר. מאי טעמא? רוב כשרים אצלה ומיעוט פסולים אצלה.

בהמשך הגמרא מפרשת שאם אבי הילד בא אליה, נשתמש בכלל ההלכתי "כל דפריש מרובא פריש" (כל הפורש מניחים שפרש מהרוב), ולכן נניח שהוא כשר, ואילו אם היא הלכה אליו, לא נוכל להשתמש בכלל זה, והילד יהיה ספק ממזר, ולגביו גזרו חכמים "מעלה עשו ביוחסין," והילד יהיה פסול. לגבי מקרה כללי של אשה פנויה, נחשוש שהיא הלכה אליו, ולכן נשתמש בגזירה זו תמיד. כך אמנם פוסק הרמב"ם[נב] (ובעקבותיו גם השו"ע[נג]): אם האם נבדקה וטענה שאבי הילד הוא כשר, הילד או הילדה יחשבו כשרים ויוכלו להינשא ללא חשש, אם-כי נישואיהם יחשבו רק לספק נישואים, מכיון שספק העריות תמיד ישאר. אולם אם האם לא נבדקה, הילד נחשב ספק ממזר, ויוכל להינשא רק לגרים.

במקרה של הזרעה, נראה שניתן לטעון שהאב, או ליתר דיוק זרעו, הוא שפרש ממקומו ובא למקומה של האשה, ולא היא זו שהלכה למקומו של בעל הזרע[נד]. כמו-כן, יש כאן גם שיקול נוסף : האם ילד שלא נולד מיחסי אישות יירש את מעמדו

נב הלכות איסורי ביאה טו : יא–יב, כג, כז–כח.

נג אבן העזר ד : כו, לו–לז.

נד ע"פ הנאמר בטור אבן העזר סוף סימן ו, וכן הרב יחיאל מיכל עפשטיין, ערוך השולחן ד : לד.

מסתפק אם הילד מתיחס אחרי התורם רק לחומרא (למשל לעניין איסור נישואים עם קרובי התורם), אך לא לקולא (כגון לעניין פטירת אשת התורם מחליצה), אך בכל זאת סובר שהתורם מקיים בכך מצות פרו ורבו. הוא מוכיח זאת מן ההלכה לגבי גוי שהתגייר, שילדיו שנולדו לו טרם גיורו פוטרים אותו ממצות פרו ורבו. הלכה זו מראה שניתן לקיים את מצות פרו ורבו גם ללא מעשה מצוה. אחרים המיחסים את הילד אחרי התורם רק לחומרא ולא לקולא, טוענים גם שהתורם לא קיים בזאת מצות פרו ורבו.[מז]

לעומתם, יש גם המבטלים לגמרי את הקשר בין התורם לבין הילד. כך למשל אומר החיד"א,[מח] הטוען שבמקרה של עיבור ללא ביאה אין לילד יחוס אב כלל (ולכן גם לא איסור נישואין עם קרוביו של התורם). לדבריו, רבינו פרץ הזכיר את בעית הנישואין בין אח לאחות רק מתוך שגרת לשונו, כשרצה לצטט את הגמרא ביבמות בעניין הקפדה על ההבחנה, שבמקרה זה של שכיבת האשה על הסדין כולם יניחו שבן-זוגה של האשה הוא אביו של הילד.

דעה אחרת מבטלת לגמרי את דברי רבינו פרץ הנ"ל. הרב אויערבאך טוען שאגדת בן-סירא עצמה מפוקפקת, ואת דברי רבינו פרץ הוא תולה בדעת מיעוט בתוספות.[מט] לדעתו, ישנם שני איסורים נפרדים: איסורי עריות, ואיסורי ממזרות, שאינם תלויים זה בזה. כפי שראינו בפרק ד, הוא אינו רואה כל איסור בהזרעה מלאכותית עצמה. אולם, כפי שלדעתך האוסרים רכיבה על פרד (מדין כלאים), דין זה אינו תלוי בצורת יצירת הפרד ביאה או הזרעה, כך גם בבני אדם. איסור ממזרות דומה לאיסורי כלאים, ולכן למרות שאשה נשואה המקבלת תרומה מגבר יהודי זר לא תיאסר בכך, הרי הולד יהיה ממזר.

דעה נוספת היא הדעה המובאת בשו"ת מערכי לב:[נ] אי אפשר להשוות את המקרה הנ"ל להזרקה, כי אין כאן כל מעשה אקטיבי מצד המעורבים: האשה קולטת את הזרע מאליה מעל הסדין. לעומתו טוען הרב פריעדמאן שזה אינו אפשרי, וודאי היה כאן איזשהו מעשה של האשה (גם אם בשוגג).[נא]

לעניננו, ניתן למצוא כאן חיזוק נוסף לטענה שאין בהזרעה עצמה כל פעולת איסור, ואין להשוותה ליחסי מין. עניין הממזרות הוא כמובן לא רלוונטי לפנויה, אך שאלת החשש מפני נשואי אח ואחות קיימת גם כאן, ובכך נעסוק להלן.

ז. עניין הבחנה

[מז] למשל, הרב מרדכי יעקב בריש, חלקת יעקב, ירושלים, תשי"א, סימנים כד ו-כה והרב עובדיה הדאיא, "הזרעה מלאכותית," נועם, ספר ראשון, תשי"ח, עמ' קל–קלז.

[מח] הרב חיים יוסף דוד אזולאי, ברכי יוסף, אבן העזר, סימן א.

[מט] הרב שלמה זלמן אויערבאך, "הזרעה מלאכותית," נועם, שם.

[נ] הרב יהודה ליב צירלסאהן, שו"ת מערכי לב, קעשנוב, תרצ"ב, עג.

[נא] הרב צבי הירש פריעדמאן, צבי חמד, ברוקלין, תשכ"ה, משפט הנולדים ע"י הזרעה מלאכותית, קונטרסים מא-מג.

וילדה את בן סירא שהיה חכם גדול.

אגדה זו מובאת כבר ע״י הראשונים. הב״ח, בפירושו על הטור (יורה דעה קצה) מצטט
את רבינו פרץ:[מא]

> מצאתי בהגהת סמ״ק ישן מהר״ר פרץ שכתב אשה נדה יכולה לשכב אסדיני בעלה, ונזהרות
> מסדינים ששכב עליהם איש אחר פן תתעבר משכבת זרע של אחר, ואמאי אינה חוששת פן
> תתעבר בנדותה משכבת זרע של בעלה ויהא הולד בן הנדה, והשיב כיון דאין כאן ביאת
> איסור הולד כשר כשר לגמרי אפילו תתעבר משכבת-זרע של אחר כי הלא בן סירא כשר היה,
> אלא דמשכבת זרע של איש אחר קפדינן אהבחנה גזירה שמא ישא אחותו מאביו כדאיתא
> ביבמות.

הרב עובדיה יוסף לומד מדברים אלו של רבינו פרץ שאם אשה נשואה מתעברת
על-ידי הזרקת זרע מגבר זר הולד אינו ממזר,[מב] שכן אין כאן ביאת איסור (למרות
שהוא אוסר על אשה נשואה לעשות זאת לכתחילה, על פי שו״ת מערכי לב שצוטט
בפרק ד), וכן שהילד מתייחס על תורם הזרע (ולכן תהיה בעיה אם הוא לא ידוע,
מחשש שמא הדבר יגרום לנשואי אחאים). כמו-כן התורם מקיים בכך את מצות פרו
ורבו. הוא אף מעיד שביושבו בבית הדין בירושלים יחד עם הרבנים אלישיב וז׳ולטי,
דנו בעניין זה, והיה פשוט לשלשתם שאין הולד ממזר.[מג] דברים דומים אומרים גם
הרבנים אמסעל,[מד] ניימרק,[מה] ואחרים.

החלקת מחוקק, על השלחן ערוך, אבן העזר (א, ס״ק ח) אומר:

> יש להסתפק אשה שנתעברה באמבטי אם קיים האב פרו ורבו ואם מקרי בנו לכל דבר,
> ובלקוטי מהרי״ל נמצא שבן סירא היה בנו של ירמיה שרחץ באמבטי כי סירא בגימטריא
> ירמיהו.

ואכן, חלק מהפוסקים הולכים בעקבותיו, ומסתפקים אם אכן קיים התורם בהזרעה
מלאכותית מצות פרו ורבו, ואם אכן הילד מתייחס אחריו. הרב וויינברג,[מו] למשל,

---

[מא] ע״פ הרב ד״ר אברהם שטיינברג, "הזרעה מלאכותית לאור ההלכה," ספר אסיא כרך א, תשל״ו,
עמ׳ 128–141 ו- Elliot N. Dorff, "Artificial Insemination, Egg Donation and Adoption,"
Conservative Judaism 1996.

הכוונה כנראה לרבינו פרץ בן אליהו מקורבייל, מבעלי התוספות מן המאה השלוש עשרה.

[מב] הרב עובדיה יוסף, יביע אומר, ירושלים, תשמ״י, כרך ב, אבן העזר א.

[מג] הרב עובדיה יוסף, יביע אומר, ירושלים תשמ״י, כרך ח, אבן העזר כא, תינוק מבחנה.

[מד] הרב מ׳ אמסעל, "בדבר איסור הזרעה מלאכותית," המאור, תמוז תשכ״ב, שנה יג קונטרס ח,
קקד.

[מה] הרב אברהם י. ניימרק, "הזרעה מלאכותית-כשרות הילוד," נועם, ספר ראשון, תשי״ח, עמ׳
קמג-קמד.

[מו] הרב יחיאל יעקב וויינברג, שו״ת שרידי אש, ירושלים, מוסד הרב קוק, תשכ״ו, חלק שלישי,
סימן ה (נדפס גם ב"הפרדס", תשרי, תשי״א).

שיכול להנשא רק עם אשה שקרום הבתולין שלה לא נקרע.[לז] כפי שלגבי אשת-איש לא נוכל לומר שהיא מותרת לבעלה אם קיימה עם גבר זר יחסי אישות כאלו שלא היו משירים את קרום הבתולין, כך לא נוכל ללמוד מכך לגבי מצבה לאחר הזרעה מלאכותית.

הב"ח[לז] על הדף שם אינו רוצה לקבל פירוש זה של התוספות, ולכן הוא מתקן את דבריהם, כך שתחילת דברי התוספות שם הם: "ואי **לא** שכיחא דשמואל מהימנא." כלומר אם מקרה שמואל לא שכיח, ובכל-זאת לאחר בדיקת האשה היא נמצאה בתולה, אז נתירה לכהן גדול. בהמשך הוא מסביר את דברי התוספות כאומרים ששאלת הגמרא כאן היא האם היא נטרח לבדוק אם האישה בתולה. אם מקרה שמואל שכיח, אין טעם לבדוק, כיון שמצב קרום הבתולין אינו מעלה ואינו מוריד, ונניח שהיא עולה. כלומר, סה"כ, אם אכן היא קיימה יחסי אישות ובכל זאת נשארה בתולה, הרי היא אסורה לכהן. יוצא מכך שנישואים לכהן גדול תלויים ביחסי אישות ולא במצב קרום הבתולין כמו בדעה הראשונה שהבאנו. הב"ח אינו מפרט את דעתו לגבי המקרה השני, של עיבור באמבטיה.

הרב פירר טוען שלא ניתן להבין את התוספות ללא תיקון הב"ח, משום שלא יתכן שהאשה תהיה מותרת לכהן גדול אם נבעלה ללא קריעת קרום הבתולין.[לז] אם האשה קיימה יחסי אישות עם אדם לא ידוע, נצטרך לחשוש לכך שהוא היה אדם הפוסל אותה לכהונה (כפי שחושש ר' יהושע בן לוי בכתובות יג ע"ב לגבי כהן רגיל), ואז גם אם היא בתולה היא תהיה פסולה לכהונה, ולכן גם לכהן גדול. לכן, יש להוסיף את התיקון, שהיא נאמנת רק אם מקרה שמואל אינו שכיח. הב"ח לא מסביר איך בכל-זאת התעברה אשה נאמנה זו, ולכן,[לט] סביר להניח שהב"ח מתכוון שנתעברה באמבטי, ובמקרה זה היא נאמנת ומותרת לכהן גדול כלומר אשה שנתעברה בצורה כזו, באמבטיה, ללא יחסי אישות, אינה נקראת לא בעולה ולא זונה. וכך, מוסיף הרב פירר, גם לגבי אשה שהתעברה מהזרקת זרע.

ו. אגדת בן-סירא ויחוס הילד

הרב עובדיה יוסף מצטט את אגדת בן-סירא מן הספר פחד יצחק:[מ]

> ...וזהו בן סירא שהיה בן בתו של ירמיהו, והיה בנו, כי ירמיהו היה מוכיח את ישראל על שהיו רוחצים באמבטי ומוציאים זרע לבטלה, ותפסו את ירמיהו והכריחוהו להכנס לאמבטי ולהוציא זרע, ואח"כ נכנסה שם בתו לרחוץ עצמה, ונבלע בה הזרע, ונתעברה ממנו

[לז] הרב אליעזר ולדנברג, שו"ת ציץ אליעזר, חלק ט, סימן נא, שער ד, הפרייה מלאכותית.

[לז] בית חדש, הרב יואל סירקיס (המאה השבע-עשרה).

[לח] הרב בנציון פירר, "בענין פריון מלאכותי," נועם, ספר ששי, תשכ"ד, עמ' רצה–רצט.

[לט] אלא-אם-כן נניח שנתעברה מרוח הקודש...

[מ] הרב עובדיה יוסף, יביע אומר, ירושלים תשמ"ו, כרך ח, אבן העזר כא, תינוק מבחנה.

ההריון.

התוספות בכתובות (ו ע״ב, ד״ה ״רוב בקיאין הן״), וכן התוספות בנדה (סד ע״ב, ד״ה ״שאני שמואל דרב גובריה״), מפרשים אף הם כך את הגמרא.

אם כך, נראה שניתן לדון כך גם לעניינו: כאשר אשה נכנסת להריון משכבת זרע של גבר זר ללא יחסי אישות ביניהם, הרי שאינה נחשבת ״בעולה.״ כלומר דין ההריון כזה אינו כדין איסורי עריות או זנות, ולכן אין איסור בדבר. בנוסף לכך, היא מותרת אפילו לכהן גדול (כהן גדול יכול להינשא רק לאשה בתולה). כלומר, נוכל להסיק מכך שאשה הנכנסת להריון משכבת זרע של גוי תהיה עדיין מותרת לכהן,[לא] ואשה נשואה תהיה מותרת לבן-זוגה אף אם קבלה תרומת זרע מגבר זר. כך אמנם פוסקים, למשל, הראשון לציון הרב בן-ציון מאיר חי עוזיאל,[לב] הרב משה פיינשטיין,[לג] והרב בנציון פירר.[לד]

לעומת הפירוש הנ״ל לגמרא, התוספות במסכת חגיגה (ד״ה: ״בתולה שעיברה״), מבינים את רש״י אחרת (כנראה ללא פירושו המשלים במסכת שבת), ואומרים:

> ופירש רש״י שהיא אומרת בתולה אני. ואי שכיחא דשמואל מהימנא... ולהר״י נראה דטרחינן לבודקה... ואי דשמואל לא שכיח לא טרחינן ומוקמה בחזקת בעולה.

כלומר, בעלי התוספות מבינים את שאלתה הראשונה של הגמרא כך: אם מקרה שמואל שכיח, כלומר אם המצב שאשה שנותרת בתולה לאחר קיום יחסי אישות הוא שכיח, אז (לטענתם, ע״פ רש״י) האשה נאמנה—נאמין לה שהיא בתולה, למרות הריונה, ונתיר לה להינשא לכהן גדול (רש״י שם סובר שיתכן גם שמדובר במצב שהשניים כבר נישאו, אך התוספות מניחים שמדובר בשאלה לפני הנישואין). רק אם מקרה שמואל אינו שכיח, נניח שהעובדה שהיא מעוברת מוכיחה שאינה בתולה (ואפילו לא נטרח לבדקה), ולכן היא אסורה לכהן גדול. כלומר, ההיתר לכהן גדול תלוי במצב קרום הבתולין, ללא קשר לקיום יחסי אישות. אם-כן, במקרה השני, של עיבור באמבטיה, תהיה האשה גם-כן מותרת לכהן גדול.

גם המשנה למלך[לה] על הרמב״ם (הלכות איסורי ביאה יז:יג), מפרש שדברי בן-זומא בגמרא (שם), הם, שההיתר לכהן הגדול תלוי במצב קרום הבתולין, אך אומר שדברים אלו של בן-זומא אינם להלכה.

הציץ אליעזר מעיר שאם כך, אין ללמוד מגמרא זו דבר לגבי מצב אישה שהתעברה בהזרעה מלאכותית, מכיוון שכאן מדובר בדין מיוחד של הכהן הגדול,

---

[לא] למרות האיסור על נישואי כהן לאשה ששכבה עם גוי (הנקראת בלשון הכתוב בויקרא כא:ז ״זונה״). ראו שו״ע, אבן העזר ו:ח.

[לב] הרב בן-ציון מאיר חי עוזיאל, פסקי עוזיאל בשאלות הזמן, ירושלים, מוסד הרב קוק, תשל״ז, סימן נג.

[לג] הרב משה פיינשטיין, שו״ת אגרות משה, חלק א, אבן העזר י.

[לד] הרב בנציון פירר, ״בענין פריון מלאכותי,״ נועם, ספר ששי, תשכ״ד, עמ׳ רצה–רצט.

[לה] רבי יהודה רוזאניס (המאה השמונה-עשרה).

דבריו):[כח]

והערער של כתר"ה על זה בא מהשקפות שבאים מידיעת דעות חיצוניות שמבלי משים משפיעים אף על גדולים בחכמה להבין מצות השם יתברך בתורה הקדושה לפי אותן הדעות הנכזבות, אשר מזה מתהפכים ח"ו האסור למותר והמותר לאסור, וכמגלה פנים בתורה שלא כהלכה הוא, שיש בזה קפידא גדולה אף בדברים שהוא להחמיר, כידוע מהדברים שהצדוקים מחמירים... ואני ברוך השם שאיני לא מהם ולא מהמונם... הנה עצם הדין הוא דבר ברור ופשוט שאיסורי עריות הם במעשה הביאה ואינו משום הזרע שיולד מזה.

והרב שלמה זלמן אויערבאך אומר בפשטות,[כט] (עמ' קמז):

הרי בהזרעה מלאכותית ליכא כלל עבירה.

ה. עיבור באמבטי

עצם אפשרות העיבור של אשה ללא מגע מיני, והתוצאות ההלכתיות לכך, מופיעות לראשונה בגמרא חגיגה (יד ע"ב–טו ע"א):

שאלו את בן זומא: בתולה שעיברה, מהו לכהן גדול? מי חיישינן לדשמואל, דאמר שמואל יכול אני לבעול כמה בעילות בלא דם, או דלמא דשמואל לא שכיחא? אמר להו: דשמואל לא שכיח, וחיישינן שמא באמבטי עיברה.

מפשט הגמרא לא ברור מה יהיה הדין בכל המקרה. האם במקרה שמקרה שמואל שכיח (כלומר שכיח שגבר יקיים יחסי אישות עם בתולה בלא לקרוע את קרום הבתולין), ונוכל לתלות שכך הבתולה התעברה, היא עדיין מותרת לכהן גדול, וכך גם במקרה שנטען שהתעברות באמבטיה שכיחה. נראה סביר לומר שבמקרה הראשון האשה אסורה, ובמקרה השנייה היא מותרת, אך בכל זאת בשני המקרים מופיעה המילה "חיישינן."

רש"י, בפירושו על מסכת שבת,[ל] מסביר שהמילה חיישינן ("אנו חוששים") מופיעה לפעמים גם לקולא, ומביא לדוגמא את הגמרא כאן: לגבי התעברות באמבטיה כתוב "חיישינן," למרות שהכוונה היא שהאשה עדיין מותרת לכהן גדול. מכך שהוא מביא רק מקרה זה ולא את המקרה הראשון (שמואל), נראה שהוא סובר שבמקרה הראשון המילה מופיעה במובנה הרגיל, לחומרא. כלומר, אם מקרה שמואל שכיח, ואנו חוששים שאשה בתולה בהריון קיימה יחסי אישות עם אדם כמו שמואל, שלא קרע את קרום הבתולין שלה, הרי היא אסורה לכהן. אך אם מקרה שמואל אינו שכיח, אנו נניח שהיא נכנסה להריון באמבטיה, ללא יחסי אישות, והיא מותרת. סך הכל יוצא שההיתר לכהן גדול תלוי בעצם קיום יחסי אישות ללא תלות במצב קרום הבתולין או

[כח] הרב משה פיינשטיין, שו"ת אגרות משה, חלק ב, אבן העזר יא.

[כט] הרב שלמה זלמן אויערבאך, "הזרעה מלאכותית," נועם, ספר ראשון, תשי"ח, עמ' קמה–קסו.

[ל] שבת קנא ע"א, ד"ה "ושמואל אמר."

של פנויה איסור דאורייתא, איסור דרבנן, או שיש איסור רק במקרה של אשה
מופקרת, ולא כאשר מדובר ביחסי אישות קבועים של אשה פנויה עם גבר ספציפי,
המוגדרים יחסי פילגשות ומותרים.

הרמב"ם (הלכות אישות א:ד) סובר שיש על אשה פנויה איסור דאורייתא.[כה] הוא
לומד זאת מן הפסוק בדברים כג:יח: "לא תהיה קדשה מבנות ישראל." בהלכות נערה
בתולה (ב:יז) הוא מביא איסור נוסף, על האב, שלא יפקיר את בתו לזנות, (וכן שלא
יהיה סרסור שלה כזונה). לאיסור זה הוא מביא נימוק הדומה לנימוק שמביא
הרמב"ן בעניין אשת איש:

> אבל אם הניח בתו הבתולה מוכנת לכל מי שיבוא עליה גורם שתמלא הארץ זמה... שאם
> תתעבר ותלד לא יודע בן מי הוא

אולם, כאמור, בכל מקרה זהו איסור על האב, ומדברי הרמב"ם שהבאנו לעיל, שאין
קשר בין איסורי עריות לבין שכבת הזרע, נראה שגם כאן, עצם האיסור יחול על יחסי
המין עצמם, ולא על כניסת הזרע לגוף האשה.

הראב"ד חולק על הרמב"ם בשני המקורות הנ"ל, ואומר שאין איסור כאשר אשה
פנויה מייחדת עצמה לאיש אחד. כך אומר גם הרמב"ן. הוא מפרש את הפסוק
בדברים כמוסב על בית-הדין, שלא יניחו לבנות ישראל להיות זונות העומדות בפרשת
דרכים או בקובה של זונות. כך הוא מסביר בפירושו לתורה, וכך גם בהשגותיו על ספר
המצוות של הרמב"ם (שרש חמישי).

החלקת מחוקק[כו] (על שו"ע, אבן העזר כו:א) אומר שיש על פנויה איסור דרבנן,
וטוען שזו גם דעת הראב"ד (למרות שפשט דברי הראב"ד אינו נראה כך).

מכל מקום, לא נראה שיש איזו סיבה לאסור על אשה פנויה את עצם
המעשה של קבלת תרומת זרע, לכל הפחות לא משום איסורי עריות. אם-כי, על-פי כל
החששות הנ"ל, מובן שעדיף שהתורם יהיה ידוע, כדי שלא נגיע למצב שבו אכן "לא
יודע בן מי הוא." אפשרות נוספת, כפי שנראה להלן, תהיה להשתמש בזרעו של תורם
גוי, משום שאז לא יהיה לילד אב במובן ההלכתי, ושוב יתבטלו החששות האלה.

למרות שע"פ הנאמר לעיל, לא נראה שניתן למצוא איסור מפורש לגבי עצם מעשה
ההזרקה עצמה, חלק מן הפוסקים רואים במעשה זה דבר אסור. כך למשל הרב
מרדכי יעקב בריש אומר:[כז]

> כמובן שמצד דתנו האיסור ברור ומבורר שלא לעשות דברים כעורים ומעוכרים כאלו
> הדומים למעשי ארץ כנען ותועבותיהם.

על-כך עונה הרב משה פיינשטיין דברים חריפים (בתשובה לערעור של רב מסוים על

[כה] כך סוברים גם הרא"ש והטור.

[כו] רבי משה לימא מבריסק.

[כז] הרב מרדכי יעקב בריש, חלקת יעקב, ירושלים, תשי"א, סימנים כד ו-כה.

וביחס לכתוב בויקרא לגבי ניאוף (יח:כ), אומר הרמב"ם בספר המצוות, מצוות לא תעשה שמ"ז:

> הזהיר מגלות ערות אשת איש, והוא אמרו יתברך "ואל אשת עמיתך לא תתן שכבתך לזרע"... ולשון מכילתא: "לא תנאף" למה נאמר? לפי שהוא אומר "מות יומת הנואף והנואפת" ענש שמענו. אזהרה מנין? תלמוד לומר "לא תנאף." אחד האיש ואחד האשה. ולא כמו "ואל אשת עמיתך," כי היא האזהרה שאינה כוללת נואף ונואפת, אבל היא האזהרה לנואף בלבד.

כלומר, בכל מקרה, פסוק זה מתיחס אל הגבר בלבד. הרמב"ן, בהשגותיו לספר המצוות, אינו מעיר דבר על דברים אלה של הרמב"ם. כלומר, מעיר הרב מאיר פרידמאן,[כב] גם אם הרמב"ן סובר כי הטעם הנוסף שהוא מביא בויקרא, של ערבוב הזרע, הוא להלכה, הרי טעם זה מתיחס אל הגבר בלבד. לדבריו, יש להבין את דברי הרמב"ן שם, שאי-הידיעה הודאית של מקור הזרע יביא "תועבות גדולות ונוראות לשניהם," כמוסבים על הבעל והבועל, ולא על האשה.

הרב יהודה ליב צירלסאהן, בעל שו"ת מערכי לב,[כג] מעלה טענה אחרת:

> הנה אשת איש... שכבת הזרע שבתוך מעיה מהאיש האחר, הישראלי, אסורה מצד עצמה, לענין שהנוצר ממנה הוא ממזר, בין שבאה במזיד ובין בשוגג.

כלומר, לדעתו, העובדה שילד שנולד מזנות של אשה נשואה הוא ממזר, גם כאשר הזנות נעשתה בשוגג, מוכיחה שיש על שכבת הזרע איסור בפני עצמה, גם אם לא נכנסה לגוף האשה בדרך הרגילה, אלא, כפי שהוא מגדיר, "שלא כדרך הנאתה." לכן לדבריו יש איסור דאורייתא על הזרקת זרע של תורם זר לאשה נשואה.

כפי שראינו לעיל, דבריו אלה עומדים בניגוד לדברי הרמב"ם, שאין שום איסור על שכבת הזרע עצמה. כמו-כן, כפי שנראה להלן (פרק ו), לדעת רוב הפוסקים במקרה של הזרקת זרע לאשה נשואה הילד אינו ממזר, כי ממזרות נגרמת רק ע"י יחסי מין, ולדעת אחרים מדובר בשני איסורים שונים: איסורי עריות (של קירבה גופנית), ואיסורי כלאים של יצירת ממזר. בכל מקרה, דבריו אינם נוגעים לאשה פנויה (וכן לתרומת זרע מגוי לאשה נשואה, שכן ילד הנולד לאשה יהודיה נשואה מגוי אינו ממזר בכל מקרה).[כד]

לגבי אשה פנויה, המצב כמובן יהיה יותר פשוט. לכל הדעות, אין על יחסי מין של אשה פנויה דין מות או כרת. הראשונים חלוקים לגבי השאלה האם יש על יחסי מין

[כב] הרב צבי הירש פריעדמאן, שם.

[כג] הרב יהודה ליב צירלסאהן, שו"ת מערכי לב, קעשנוב, תרצ"ב, עג.

[כד] מעניין להזכיר כאן את דעתו של הרב נעם זוהר ("עד כמה 'קנויה' אשה לבעלה?" שדמות (1989) 110) הטוען כי הרעיון התיאורטי מאחרי הכללת שכבת הזרע באיסור ניאוף הוא שקנין הנשואין של אשה אינו כולל רק את מיניותה הפיזית, אלא גם את יכולת הפריון שלה. כלומר כאשר אשה נישאת לאיש היא מצווה להקנות לו את הבלעדיות גם לגבי יחסי מין, וגם לגבי אבהות לילדיה.

וכך אומר הרב יואל טייטעלבוים: [יט]

שאדרבא עיקר האיסור הוא הכנסת הזרע, לא הביאה.

ולגבי העובדה שהמקורות מדברים על "ביאת איסור," הוא אומר:

כי אותה ההזרעה המלאכותית... היא המצאה חדשה.. לכן אמר הלשון שלא היה ביאת
איסור... ודרך החכמים בלשונם כן... שדבר בהווה באופן שהיה אז מציאות להביא זרע
לתוך האשה במעשה.

הרב משה פיינשטיין טוען כנגדם: [כ]

הנה עצם הדין הוא דבר ברור ופשוט שאיסורי עריות הם במעשה הביאה ואינו משום הזרע
שיולדו מזה, דלכן אין שום חילוק בהאיסורים בין ראויה להוליד ובין אינה ראויה להוליד
כגון קרחה ואילונית... ולכן ברור שאף מה שכתב הרמב"ן בפירושו... ח"ו שיעלה על דעתו
שזהו טעם האמת וליתן יד לפושעים הרשעים שהזכיר האבן עזרא... אלא שהזכיר שיש עוד
חומר בערוה דאשת איש אף שזה לא מעלה ולא מוריד לענין האיסור והעונש... ולולא
דמסתפינא הייתי אומר שמ"ואפשר" עד "ויהנכון" אינו מדברי הרמב"ן אלא איזה תלמיד
טועה כתב זה, אבל בכל אופן אין זה להלכה.

הרב צבי הירש פריעדמאן מעיר כי בקריאה זהירה של כל דבריו של הרמב"ן, ברור כי
הטעם לשימוש במלים שכבת זרע הוא, לדעתו של הרמב"ן, מה שמובא לאחר הדברים
"ויהנכון בעיני": [כא] להדגיש כי איסור הכרת הוא ביאה ממש (המשגל), ולא קריבה של
ערווה (כגון חיבוק ונישוק). ענין האבחנה הוא הווא אמינא (הנחת ביניים) אפשרית,
אך לא המסקנה הסופית. הוא מביא בספרו גם את מכתבו של הרבי מלובביץ' (שם,
עמ' 38) המסכים עמו בדיוקו בדברי הרמב"ן.

לעומת הרמב"ן, אומר הרמב"ם דברים מפורשים יותר. בפירושו למשניות, על
המשנה במסכת סנהדרין (ז:ד), הוא אומר:

והנה הגיע לי מקום שאזכיר בו עיקרים גדולים מאד מעניני העריות: ...ואין להוצאת
שכבת זרע בענין חיוב העונשין סרך בשום פנים...

ובמסכת הוריות (ב:ד) לגבי דינו של גבר שבזמן יחסי אישות עם אשה התגלה לו שהיא
נדה:

ועשה שבנדה הוא כשנתטמא בעוד שהוא בא עליה שנצוה אותו שיתפרש ממנה... אבל ראוי
לו שיעמוד על עניו ויבטל מתנועות... ואם הוציא שכבת זרע אין בכך כלום שהוצאת שכבת
זרע בעריות לענין העונשין אין מוסיף איסורא ולא גורע.

[יט] הרב יואל טייטעלבוים, שם.

[כ] הרב משה פיינשטיין, שו"ת אגרות משה, חלק ב, אבן העזר יא.

[כא] הרב צבי הירש פריעדמאן, צבי חמד, ברוקלין, תשכ"ה, משפט הנולדים ע"י הזרעה מלאכותית,
קונטרסים מא-מג.

הפוסקים הדנים בשאלה זו דנים בעיקר במקרה הזרקת הזרע לאשה נשואה מזרעו של גבר זר. עיקר דיונם נסב סביב הפסוקים בויקרא (יח:ו, כ):

אִישׁ אִישׁ אֶל כָּל שְׁאֵר בְּשָׂרוֹ לֹא תִקְרְבוּ לְגַלּוֹת עֶרְוָה, אֲנִי ה'... וְאֶל אֵשֶׁת עֲמִיתְךָ לֹא תִתֵּן שְׁכָבְתְּךָ לְזָרַע לְטָמְאָה בָהּ.

כותרת הקטע באיסורי הערוה מפרשת כי האיסור הוא איסור קרבה גופנית, וכן בפרוטם של רוב איסורי הערוה בפרק לשון האיסור היא "גילוי עֶרְוָה," שמשמעה קרבה גופנית. אולם לגבי איסור ניאוף, האיסור מתואר כ"נתינת שכבת זרע." האם ניתן ללמוד מכך משהו לגבי איסורי הערוה בכלל וטעמם, או לגבי איסור אשת איש בפרט?

הרמב"ן בפירושו על הפסוק שם אומר:

אמר ר' אברהם [אבן עזרא] כי המשגל לשלשה חלקים נחלק: האחד לפריה ורביה, והשני להקל מלחות הגוף, והשלישי לתאוה הנמשלת לתאות הבהמות. ואמר הכתוב "לְזָרַע," וטעמו **אפילו** לזרע, והיא אסורה לגמרי.

ואפשר כי אמר "לְזָרַע," להזכיר טעם באיסור כי לא יודע הזרע למי הוא, ויבואו מזה תועבות גדולות ורעות לשניהם. ולא הזכיר זה בעונש, כי אפילו הערה בה ולא הוציא זרע יתחייב, ולכך אמר "וְיִשְׁכַּב אִישׁ אוֹתָהּ שִׁכְבַת זֶרַע," כי בעבור הזרע תהיה קנאתו. וכן בשפחה חרופה הזכיר שכבת זרע, כי האסור בעבור שיוליד זרע מן השפחה.

והנכון בעיני, כי בעבור היות אשת עמיתו אסורה לו לגמרי, לא ינקה כל הנוגע בה, הוצרך לומר "לְזָרַע." שאם אמר "לֹא תִתֵּן שְׁכָבְתְּךָ" בלבד, היה נראה שיזהיר אפילו השוכב עמה לחבק ולנשק. וכאן בחייבי כריתות יזהיר, על כן הוצרך להזכיר שכיבה לזרע, לפרש כי **במשגל** יזהיר. והוא הטעם בשפחה חרופה, שהיא כאשת איש...

ורבותינו דרשו באשת איש למעט איש משמש באבר מת, ואמרו בשפחה חרופה שאינו חייב אלא בגמר ביאתו כמו שמפרש ביבמות."

כמה מן הפוסקים, כרב ולדנברג,[יז] או הרב יואל טייטעלבוים, הרבי מסאטמאר,[יח] רוצים ללמוד מדברי הרמב"ן כי טעם איסור ניאוף הוא שהוא מביא לאי-ודאות בזיהוי אביו של הילד הנוצר מיחסים אלו ("כי לא יודע הזרע למי הוא"). טעות כזו אינה תלויה בקרבה הגופנית עצמה, אלא בכניסת זרע הגבר אל רחם האשה. הם מביאים גם את דברי הרב אהרן הלוי בספר החינוך, על האיסור "לֹא תִנְאָף" (פרשת יתרו, מצוה ל"ה), המביא טעם זה כאחד הטעמים לאיסור ניאוף:

משרשי מצוה זו, כדי שיתישב העולם כאשר חפץ השם... וכן רצה שיהיה זרע האנשים ידוע של מי הוא ולא יתערבו זה עם זה...

[יז] הרב אליעזר ולדנברג, שו"ת ציץ אליעזר, חלק ט, סימן נא, שער ד, הפרייה מלאכותית.

[יח] הרב יואל טייטעלבוים, האדמו"ר מסאטמאר, המאור, מנחם אב תשכ"ד, שנה ט"ו קונטרס ט, קמה.

במכתב זה הוא אומר:

בדבר זריקת הזרע שכתבו בשמי שהתרתי מצאתי לנכון להודיע שאני לא התרתי אלא
בשעת הדחק גדול... וחלילה לשום רב להורות היתר בנידון זה מתוך ספרי... אכן מכיון
שיש לחוש עדיין שיקילו בזה להורות אלה שאינם ראויים לדון בענין חמור כזה... צריך
לגדור גדר שלא יתירו זה בשום אופן אף רב היותר מובהק.

אך למרות זאת, ספרו משה אגרות המשיך להתפרסם עם התשובות להיתר, ובכרך
יותר מאוחר של ספרו,[יד] בשנת תשכ"ו הוא כותב:

ולהלכה הוא ברור כמו שכתבתי בספרי, וכל המאמרים שנכתבו בירחונים הם דברים
הבדוין מסברת עצמם נגד דברי רבותינו הראשונים והאחרונים ואף נגד מקומות שהזכירו
בעצמן.

בכל זאת, הוא מוסיף שם שלמעשה עדיף שלא להתיר מטעם שלום בית
(ההיתרים שפרסם עסקו כולם בזוגות נשואים).
בתשובה אחרת הוא כותב:[טו]

הנה ממה שכתבתי בתשובותי... כולם אמת וברור לדינא, לא שייך להתחרט מהם וליכא
שום חששות בזריקת זרע של נכרים, אבל למעשה לא הוריתי לעשות כן מטעם שלענין קיום
מצות פרו ורבו לבעלה אין זה כלום,... ושייך שיצא מזה קנאה גדולה לבעלה ולכן אין זה
עצה טובה.[טז]

ד. האם איסורי הערוה בתורה כוללים גם את מעשה ההזרעה המלאכותית?

רבים מהדיונים ההלכתיים סביב מעמדה ההלכתי של הזרקת זרע סובבים סביב
הפרטים האחרים הקשורים במעשה זה: האם לגבר מותר להוציא שכבת זרע שלא
בדרך של יחסי אישות, מעמד הילד הנולד, ועוד. אך השאלה הראשונה שיש לשאול,
בבואנו לחקור שאלה זו, היא האם יש איזה שהוא איסור במעשה ההזרקה עצמו.
האם האיסורים המיניים בתורה עצמם כוללים איסור גם לגבי העברת זרע ללא
קרבה גופנית בין הגבר לאשה.

[יג] הרב צבי הירש פריעדמאן, צבי חמד, ברוקלין, תשכ"ה, משפט הנולדים ע"י הזרעה מלאכותית,
קונטרסים מא-מג.

[יד] הרב משה פיינשטיין, שו"ת אגרות משה, חלק ג, אבן העזר יד.

[טו] הרב משה פיינשטיין, שו"ת אגרות משה, חלק ד, אבן העזר ה.

[טז] כלומר, הוא מסתייג מהוראת היתר הלכה למעשה מטעמי שלום בית. טעם זה כמובן אינו נוגע
לאשה פנויה. למעשה, ישנם גם זוגות נשואים רבים המשתמשים בהיתריו (ובהיתרי הפוסקים
האחרים המתירים את הדבר). לעתים רבות ההסכמה בין בני הזוג, והרצון המשותף לגדל ילדים,
הם כאלו שלא ייווצר בעיה כזו, ולעתים דווקא קבלת תרומת הזרע והולדת הילד, אף שהיא
מתורם זר, תביא אצלם לשלום בית.

המאה ה- 20. אומנם, תשובות מעטות בענין זה נכתבו אף בסוף המאה הקודמת, אך הבעיה התעוררה בכל חריפותה כאשר שיטה זו הפכה ליותר נפוצה, וכאשר הרופאים התחילו להשתמש בה אף להזרקת זרע מתורם זר, ולא רק מאיש לאשתו.

הויכוח הפך לסוער ביותר עם פרסום פסקיו של הרב משה פיינשטיין,[א] שהתיר שימוש בתרומת זרע לאשה נשואה מתורם גוי, בשנים תשי"ט ותשכ"א. אומנם, עוד לפני כן, בשנת תשי"ח, פרסם הירחון התורני "נועם" סדרה שלמה של מאמרים העוסקים בשאלה זו, וביניהם אף מאמרים מקילים (ביניהם בולט מאמרו של הרב שלמה זלמן אויערבאך,[ח] אך פסקיו של הרב פיינשטיין שנכתבו הלכה למעשה, גרמו לסערה.

כתב-העת החרדי המאור, שיצא לאור בארה"ב, התגייס למערכה, בראשות עורכו הרב מאיר אמסעל. בשנים תשכ"א–תשכ"ה התפרסמו בו מאמרים רבים וחריפים, כולם בגנות המעשה. האדמו"ר מבאבוב אף קרא להחרמתה של כל אשה שתשתמש בהזרעה מלאכותית.[ט] מאמרים בנושא המשיכו להתפרסם גם בכתבי-עת ושו"תים אחרים, לאיסור ולהיתר, אך הם לא הגיעו בחריפותם למאמרים שהתפרסמו במאור.

כדי לסבר את האוזן, אביא כאן כמה מן הדברים הקשים שנכתבו כנגדו של הרב פיינשטיין. בשנת תשכ"ד אומר הרב עזרין (בלא להזכיר את הרב פיינשטיין בשמו):

וברור אצלי דכל מי שמתיר זה, אומר אני עליו, שאין שם לא חכמה ולא גאונות, אלא חסרון דעת תורה בעלמא, והוא הגורם שעל ידי זה יהיה הדור פרוץ בזנות, כבימי דור המבול ר"ל.

ואילו הרב אמסעל, עורך המאור, אומר:[יא]

והנה לא אמנע טוב מבעליו, מכבוד ידיד הגאון מהר"מ שליט"א, לאמר בכל גלוי לב, שעל הוראותיו לאיסורא בודאי יש לסמוך עליהן, כי מכיון שאסר הרי ברור שאין עוד מקום בזה להתיר, אבל לתשובותיו להיתרא, יש להתייחס אליהן בכל הזהירות, כי כחא דהיתר של הגאון הזה שליט"א, עולה פי כמה על כל המקילים שהיו בישראל.

בשלב מסוים הופעל לחץ רב מאד על הרב פיינשטיין, ובשנת תשכ"ה הוא נאלץ לפרסם "מכתב התקפלות,"[יב] (המכתב מופיע בספרו של הרב פריעדמאן,[יב] בעמוד 34.

[א] הרב משה פיינשטיין, שו"ת אגרות משה, חלק א, אבן העזר י ו-עא.

[ח] הרב שלמה זלמן אויערבאך, "הזרעה מלאכותית," נועם, ספר ראשון, תשי"ח, עמ' קמה–קסו.

[ט] הרב שלמה האלבערשטאם (האדמו"ר מבאבוב), קונטרס להצלת קדושת ויחוס ישראל, המאור, תשרי-חשון תשכ"ה, שנה טז, קונטרס א, קמז.

[י] הרב יודא ארי עזרין, המאור, אייר-סיון תשכ"ד, שנה טו, קונטרס ז, קמג.

[יא] הרב מ' אמסעל, "עוד פרטים נחוצים באיסור ההזרעה המלאכותית," המאור, תשרי-חשון תשכ"ה, שנה טז קונטרס א, קמז.

[יב] מינוחו של הרב נעם זוהר, "עד כמה 'קנויה' אשה לבעלה?" שדמות (1989) 110.

תאי-זרע בזרעו של האיש, ניתן להשתמש בשיטה זו כדי להגביר את סכויי הכניסה להריון של אשתו מזרעו. אולם במקרים רבים, זרע הגבר פגום מדי, ויש להשתמש בזרעו של תורם זר.

בעוד הזרקת הזרע לרחם האשה מצריכה תמיד התערבות רופא (או לכל הפחות אדם מיומן אחר), הזרקה לצואר הרחם, הנחשבת בעלת סכויי הצלחה קטנים יותר, יכולה להתבצע על-ידי האשה עצמה. מספר בנקי-זרע בארה״ב אף מעבירים סדנאות הדרכה לנשים המעוניינות בכך. בארץ, אולי מכיוון שהזרקת זרע על-ידי רופא ממומנת טיפול הממומן על-ידי קופת החולים, אין הדבר מקובל במסגרת זרע המועבר באמצעות בנקי הזרע. אך כמובן שהדבר מתבצע באופן פרטי, למשל במקרים של זוגות הנמצאים בעיצומם של טיפולי פוריות ואינם מעוניינים שהצורך בקיום יחסי-מין במועדים קבועים יפגע בחיי האישות שלהם, או כאשר זוג מחליט על הורות משותפת אך אינו מעוניין בבניית קשר אינטימי-זוגי בין בני הזוג, אם בשל חוסר התאמה ביניהם, ואם בשל סיבות אחרות.[1]

קופות החולים בארץ מחויבות לממן טיפולי פוריות בהזרעה מלאכותית לנשים המעוניינות בכך, עד להולדת שני ילדים. כאשר האשה נשואה יתבקש בן-זוגה לחתום על הסכמתו לדבר. ישנם בארץ מספר בנקי זרע, השייכים לבתי-החולים השונים, והתורמים אליהם הם בעיקר סטודנטים. התרומה היא אנונימית, האשה (או הזוג) אינה מקבלת כל מידע על התורם, ואף התורם אינו יודע אם אכן הופרו נשים מזרעו. חלק מבתי-החולים שומרים עבור נשים דתיות מספר מנות של ״זרע גוי״—תרומת זרע של תורם שאינו יהודי (בהמשך נראה את ההשלכות ההלכתיות לכך), אם מסטודנטים זרים הלומדים בארץ, ואם ממנות זרע שיובאו מארה״ב במיוחד לשם כך.

בארצות-הברית, בנקי הזרע הם פרטיים, והאשה (או הזוג) יכולה לקבל פרטים נוספים רבים על התורם: היסטוריה רפואית של המשפחה, גילו, מוצאו, דתו, הרכב משפחתו, השכלתו, ותחביביו. לעתים מצורף לתרומה גם מכתב או מסר של התורם אל המשתמשים בזרעו, קלטת המוקלטת בקולו, או תמונה שלו. במספר בנקים ישנה אף אפשרות לילד הנולד מתורם מסוים לקבל את פרטיו של התורם ואף להיפגש עמו כאשר יגיע לגיל 18, כפי שהדבר נעשה במקרי אימוץ (בבנקים אחרים יקבל הילד סרט וידיאו של התורם בהגיעו לגיל זה). בארצות אחרות, כשבדיה ואוסטרליה, מתן אפשרות זו של ״פתיחת התיק״ בגיל 18 היא חובה. בבנקי הזרע בארץ הדבר נחשב אסור על-פי החוק, ובמקרים רבים כל המסמכים היכולים להצביע על זהות התורם יושמדו לפני שהילד יגיע לגיל זה.

ג. הויכוח ההלכתי

שאלת ההזרעה המלאכותית עוררה מחלוקת חריפה ביותר בין הפוסקים בתחילת

---

[1] בתל-אביב קיים ה״מרכז להורות אחרת״ המקשר בין נשים רווקות (בד״כ בגילאי ה- 30—40), לבין גברים, רובם-ככולם הומוסקסואלים, המסכימים על הורות משותפת על לילדים הנוצרים בדרך זו.

הזרעה מלאכותית לאשה פנויה

דבורה רוס

א. הקדמה

שאלת ההזרעה המלאכותית לנשים פנויות, הולכת ונעשית מעשית יותר ויותר בשנים האחרונות. נשים רבות, בארץ ובחו"ל, המוצאות עצמן לא נשואות בגילאי ה- +35, מחליטות שלא לוותר על אמהות, ובוחרות בדרך זו.

בספרות הרבנית נידונה שאלת ההזרעה המלאכותית בעיקר לגבי נשים נשואות. בחיפושי אחר מקורות למאמר זה, נתקלתי רק בשני מאמרים שהתמקדו בשאלה לגבי נשים פנויות. מצד אחד, הרב בנציון פירר, רבה של ניר-גלים, שהכריע להיתר,[א] ומצד שני הרב גולינקין, מן התנועה המסורתית, שפסק לאיסור.[ב] אחרים, שדנו בכתביהם בעיקר בעניין הנשים הנשואות, הוסיפו הערה צדדית לגבי פנויות, אם להיתר (כגון הרב יחיאל וויינברג[ג]) ואם לאיסור (כגון הרב אליעזר ולדנברג[ד] והד"ר אברהם שטיינברג[ה]).

במאמר זה ברצוני לסכם ולנתח את הבעיות ההלכתיות הכרוכות בכך, כמיטב הבנתי, ולהראות כי יש בסיס מוצק דיו (גם אם לא מקובל על כל הפוסקים), להתיר הזרעה מלאכותית באשה פנויה.

ב. רקע כללי

שיטת ההזרעה המלאכותית, של החדרת זרע לגוף האשה שלא על-ידי יחסי מין, (לצוואר הרחם–ICI, או לרחם עצמו–IUI), נכנסה לשימוש ע"י הרפואה המודרנית במחצית השנייה של המאה ה- 19. תחילה שמשה לפתרון בעיותם של זוגות נשואים, כאשר נתגלו בעיות בפוריותו של הגבר. כאשר הבעיה היא הפרעה אנטומית או מיעוט

---

* ברצוני להודות לד"ר ש"י וולד על עזרתו בלימוד הנושא, לאסתר ישראל על שיחותנו המרובות בעניין, ולרב נעם זוהר על הערותיו המועילות.

[א] הרב בנציון פירר, "בעניין פריון מלאכותי," נועם, ספר ששי, תשכ"ד, עמ' רצה–רצט.

[ב] הרב דוד גולינקין, "תשובה בעניין הזרעה מלאכותית," תשובות ועד ההלכה של כנסת הרבנים בישראל, כרך ג, תשמ"ח–תשמ"ט.

[ג] הרב יחיאל יעקב וויינברג, שו"ת שרידי אש, ירושלים, מוסד הרב קוק, תשכ"ו, חלק שלישי, סימן ה (נדפס גם ב"הפרדס", תשרי, תשי"א).

[ד] הרב אליעזר ולדנברג, שו"ת ציץ אליעזר, חלק ט,סימן נא, שער ד, הפרייה מלאכותית.

[ה] הרב ד"ר אברהם שטיינברג, "הזרעה מלאכותית לאור ההלכה," ספר אסיא כרך א, תשל"ו, עמ' 128—141.

של: "נשתטו ביותר"! וזהו הנימוק לכך שמותר לו לעזוב אותם. משום כך מסיר הרמב"ם מהבן את החובה לטפל בהוריו באופן אישי-ישיר, ומורה לו לקיים את מצוות "כיבוד הורים," במצב המסוים הזה ע"י שליח מטעמו שידאג לכל מחסורו של ההורה שנשתבשה דעתו.

בנוסף לרגישות ולהתחשבות במצבו הקשה של הבן שיקול חשוב בפני עצמו, שכדאי היה שיהיה חלק בלתי נפרד ממערך השיקולים בעניין זה, קיים צד נוסף בדבר והוא החשש שאם הבן יחויב להישאר עם ההורה שנטרפה דעתו, הוא יגיע חלילה, לכך, שללא רצון וללא שליטה הוא יעבור על מצוות "כיבוד ומורא הורים," שהרי מתוך כעס, רגשות תסכול וחוסר אונים, שנובעים מהמצב הקשה שבו הוא נמצא, לא רק שהוא לא יטפל באביו או באמו, שכה זקוקים לדאגתו, אלא אולי אף גרוע מכך!

יהי רצון שיקויים בנו מה שאנו מבקשים כל בוקר בתפילתנו :
"ואל תביאנו... לא לידי ניסיון ולא לידי ביזיון"

פסק ההלכה של הרמב"ם אם הוא פסק לפי מה שכתוב מפורשות בתלמוד. המשותף לתשובותיהם הוא הבנה שונה ממה שהבינו קודמיהם את הפרטים שמרכיבים את "עובדא דרב אסי."

הגדיל לעשות הרש"ש ר' שמואל שטראסון שהסביר את משפט הסיום של הסיפור כמשפט שמשמעו חרטה עמוקה של רב אסי על נטישתו את אמו וממילא ברור שאין לפסוק הלכה בהתאם להתנהגותו אלא ההפך ממנה! יש לציין שהפוסקים שקיבלו את השגתו של הראב"ד שייכים לזרם הפסיקה האשכנזית.

לסיום המאמר ברצוני להעיר:

נמצאו בדברי פוסקי ההלכה לדורותיהם ותפוצותיהם, שיקולים שונים ומגוונים כדי להטיל את אחריות הטיפול בהורה שנטרפה דעתו על בנו, אם ע"י חיובו לטפל בהורה בעצמו או לדאוג שמישהו אחר יעשה זאת. השאלה הבסיסית שעמדה בבסיס הכרעתו ההלכתית של כל אחד מהפוסקים היתה: מהי הדרך הטובה ביותר לטיפול בהורה שנטרפה דעתו, כך שיסופקו כל צרכיו (הפיזיים והנפשיים) מצד אחד, ושבנו לא יעבור על איסורים שונים מהצד השני.

אך לאחר עיון מעמיק בדבריהם של הפוסקים השונים, נראה לי שמשפט משמעותי אחד בפסק ההלכה של הרמב"ם, לא זכה להתייחסות ישירה ולהסבר מספק בדברי הפוסקים, ולא נכנס כשיקול במערכת השיקולים שהובילו לפסיקת ההלכה.

כוונתי היא לתנאי שמתנה הרמב"ם:

> מי שנטרפה דעתו של אביו או של אמו משתדל לנהוג עמהם...
> **ואם אי אפשר לו לעמוד מפני שנשתטו ביותר**, יניחם וילך לו...

מה משמעותו האמיתית של תנאי זה? מהו אותו הדבר שבגללו מסיר הרמב"ם את החובה מהבן לטפל במו ידיו בהוריו, ומורה לו להעביר את הטיפול לאדם אחר? האם הבן מגיע למצב ש: "אי"א לו לעמוד" משום שמצבם דורש דרך טיפול מסוימת שאינו יכול לעשותה, שיקול שנמצא בדברי הפוסקים, או ש: "אי"א לו לעמוד" **נפשית** בכך שהוא רואה את הוריו במצב הנורא של איבוד השפיות? הקושי הנפשי שכרוך בטיפול באדם שנטרפה דעתו יכול להיות גדול הרבה יותר מקושי הפיזי שכרוך בטיפול באדם שהוא נכה בכל גופו ותלוי באופן טוטאלי בזולתו לסיפוק צרכיו, וזאת כשמדובר בזר שמטפל, קל וחומר כשמדובר בבן שצריך לראות את הוריו במצב שפל ויירוד כזה של אבוד כושר האבחנה בין טוב לרע ואבוד הקשר עם המציאות הסובבת.

נראה לי שדיוק בלשונו של הרמב"ם נותן בסיס לדרישה שגם השיקול הזה של הקושי **הנפשי** של הבן יהיה חלק ממערך השיקולים של כל פוסק בבואו להכריע הלכה בעניין רגיש כל-כך.

הרמב"ם מנמק את התנאי: "ואם אי אפשר לו לעמוד" בנימוק: "מפני שנשתטו ביותר!" אולי התכוון הרמב"ם לכך שמעבר לקושי הפיזי שכרוך בטיפול בהורים שנטרפה דעתם, **בנם לא מסוגל יותר נפשית, לעמוד בכך שהוא רואה את הוריו במצב**

בהבנתו המיוחדת את המשפט: "אי ידעי לא נפקי" דוחה הרש"ש את דברי
הפוסקים שהגנו בעוצמה רבה על פסק ההלכה של הרמב"ם מפני השגת הראב"ד
בטענה, שהרמב"ם היה מחויב לפסוק כפי שפסק בגלל התקדים בתלמוד, ואין דרך
לפסוק באופן שונה. הרש"ש מסביר שכל פוסק שהבין כמוהו את משפט הסיום של
הסיפור היה חייב לתמוה ולהשיג על דברי הרמב"ם ולפסוק אחרת או אפילו ההפך
ממנו.

סיכום:

בסיכום סקירת הדעות השונות מצטיירת ה"תמונה ההלכתית" הבאה:

הרמב"ם במאה ה-12, הניח את התשתית לעיון בסוגיא זו, בקובעו להלכה
שבשלב ראשון החובה והאחריות מוטלת על הבן, או הבת, לטפל באביו או אמו
שנטרפה דעתם ככל שיש לאל ידו, אך מרגע שאין באפשרותו להוסיף ולדאוג להם
"יניחם... ויצווה לאחרים להנהיגם כראוי להם."

הראב"ד בהשגתו לא מקבל את דבריו של הרמב"ם וקובע: "אין זו הוראה נכונה"
ביקורתו של הראב"ד הניבה דרכים שונות ל"הגנה" על פסק ההלכה של הרמב"ם, ע"י
נושאי כליו ופוסקים אחרים ואלו עיקרי דבריהם:

הרמב"ם היה מחויב להכריע הלכתית כפי שהכריע וזאת על סמך תיאור התלמוד
את שקרה לרב אסי, לכן אין מקום כלל להשגת הראב"ד. אף שלא מוזכר בתלמוד ולו
ברמז שרב אסי מינה אדם אחר שיטפל באמו אין ספק שכך עשה וכך ראוי לעשות
במצב דומה וזאת משום שקיים הגיון בבסיס ההיתר/דרישה שבן שהוריו לקו בנפשם
יעזבם ויצווה לאחרים לנהגם כראוי **להם:** מצד הבן, הלכה זו נועדה למנוע כישלון
במצוות "כיבוד הורים," אם בגלל דרישות שלהם שהוא לא יוכל/ירצה למלא או
מחשש שהטיפול המיוחד שהם זקוקים לו במצבם, הוא מסוג כזה שאסור לו לעשותו
כמו קשירה, הכאה, וכדומה. מצד ההורה, אם אדם זר יטפל בו משנטרפה דעתו הוא
יתבייש ממנו ולא יתנהג בצורה חסרת רסן לחלוטין, כפי שאולי היה מתנהג, לו בנו
היה אתו, משום שבפני הבן אין לו בושה כל-כך.

עד המאה ה-16 רובם המכריע של הפוסקים נוקטים בגישתו של הרמב"ם, ודוחים
את השגת הראב"ד. ניתן להזכיר כמאפייני גישה זו את: בעל מגדל עוז, הר"ן, ר' יוסף
קארו והרדב"ז. יש להעיר שכולם פוסקי הלכה מזרם הפסיקה הספרדית.

החל מהמאה ה-16 חל פיצול בשרשרת פסיקת ההלכה בשאלה הנדונה:

הזרם האחד: פוסקים הממשיכים את דרך קודמיהם וקובעים את ההלכה כשיטתו
של הרמב"ם ואף מציעים הסברים ונימוקים לשיטה זו. בהם: ר' יחיאל מיכל הלוי
אפשטיין בעל ערוך השולחן ור' אליעזר וולדנברג.

הזרם השני: יסודו בדברי המהרש"ל ר' שלמה לוריא, שקיבל את השגת הראב"ד
וקובע להלכה **שאסור** לבן לעזוב את הוריו שלקו בנפשם והוא אחראי לשלומם
ולסיפוק כל צורכיהם. פוסקים המאוחרים למהרש"ל כמו: ר' יהושע פאלק, ר' דוד
הלוי, ר' יואל סירקיס ועוד, מצדדים בגישתו ההלכתית ופוסקים כמותו. כל הפוסקים
שנמנים על זרם פסיקה זה שילבו בדבריהם תשובה לשאלה: כיצד יתכן להשיג על

הב"ח מחדד בדבריו את האבחנה בין אמו של רב אסי שביקשה בקשות לא
סבירות ומחשש ל"מעידה" במצוות "כיבוד הורים" עזב אותה רב אסי, דבר שמותר
הלכתית, לבין מצב של הורה שאיבד את שפיותו כך שאין לו יכולת אבחנה בין טוב
לרע, והקשר שלו עם המציאות הסובבת אותו רופף (אם בכלל קיים) ובמצב זה על
הבן מוטלת החובה לדאוג לו ולמלא את צרכיו הפיזיים על הצד הטוב ביותר,[מו] ובשום
פנים אין להעלות על הדעת שמותר לבן לעוזבו.

החכם האחרון שיובאו דבריו הוא הרש"ש, ר' שמואל שטראסון שחי בוילנא
במאה ה-19, וכתב הגהות וחידושים למסכת קידושין. הרש"ש מסביר פרט אחד
מ-"עובדא דרב אסי" באופן שונה מכל המפרשים והפוסקים שקדמו לו. הסברו, מאיר
באור שונה **מהותית** את שאירע לרב אסי ואת ההשלכות ההלכתיות שאמורות לנבוע
מכך:

אמר אי ידע לא נפקי. ולי נראה דרצה לומר: אי ידעי דתיזל אבתרי ותמות בדרך לא נפקי
מבבל! דחשש פן טורח הדרך או עזיבתו אותה גרמו מיתתה! וניראה לי דכן פירש גם כן
הראב"ד בפי"ו מהלכות ממרים, ה"י, דרב אסי חזר בו ממה שהלך מאצלה ומוצל בזה
מגמגום הרי"ן ו"הכסף משנה" עליו ומעובדא דא דרב אסי![מז]

הרש"ש מבין את המשפט שאומר רב אסי בסוף הסיפור: "אי ידעי לא נפקי!" **כמשפט**
של חרטה עמוקה על עזיבתו את אמו בבבל. כשהוא שומע שאירעה של אמו בא לא"י,
עולה חשש בלבו שבעצם העזיבה שלו אותה הוא גרם באופן עקיף או ישיר למותה
ולכן זו היתה טעות גדולה לעוזבה ולעלות לא"י. הרש"ש מוסיף ואומר שלסברתו, כך
הבין גם הראב"ד את המשפט: "אי ידעי לא נפקי." צריך לזכור שהראב"ד לא
מתייחס בדבריו כלל לסיפור התלמודי שעליו, לפי טענות הפוסקים, התבסס הרמב"ם
בקובעו שהבן יכול לעזוב את הוריו.

מדברים אלו ניתן להסיק שאם אכן הבנתו של הרש"ש את המשפט "אי ידעי לא
נפקי" היא נכונה ואם באמת כך הבין גם הראב"ד את משפט הסיום של הסיפור -
שרב אסי מתחרט חרטה עמוקה על שבחשבון לה שאין על עזיבתו את אמו משום שאולי גרם
בעקיפין למותה , ברור שלא רק שאין ללמוד מ"תקדים רב אסי" שמותר לעזוב הורה
שנשתבשה דעתו, כפי שפוסק הרמב"ם, אלא שההפך הוא הנכון:

יש ללמוד מכך איסור מוחלט. אין לעזוב הורה, במיוחד לא כשהוא במצב של
טירוף הדעת וחוסר יכולת לטפל בעצמו, משום שעזיבתו של הבן, יכולה במקרים
קיצוניים, לגרום למותה של ההורה, אם בגלל שאין מי שיספק את צרכיו הבסיסיים
ביותר כמו אוכל ושתיה ואם בגלל שנטישתו תגרום להידרדרות נוספת במצבו הנפשי
של ההורה מתוך צער וכאב, בעקבות נטישת הבן.

[מו] גישתו ההלכתית של הב"ח מבוטאת גם בדבריו של ר' צבי הירש אשכנזי "החכם צבי" שחי
במזרח אירופה במאה ה -17. בשו"ת חכם צבי (תוספות חדשים) סימן כ. ירושלים , תשנ"ה.

[מז] הגהות וחידושי הרש"ש למסכת קידושין לי"א ע"יב, ד"יה : "אי ידעי לא נפקי" בסוף המסכת
בדפוס וילנא.

על כך שבגמרא לא מתואר שרב אסי דאג שמישהו אחר יטפל באמו, וזאת לפי הסברו, משום שאולי אמו של רב אסי היתה כבר במצב כזה שאף אחד אחר לא היה יכול לטפל בה ולכן מותר היה לבנה לעזוב אותה ולעלות לארץ ישראל.

השאלה שנוצרת עם הבנת שתי הנקודות האחרונות בדבריו של ר' יהושע פאלק היא: האם באמת כאשר ההורה הוא במצב כל כך קשה שאפילו אחרים אינם יכולים לטפל בו, יש לבנו רשות מפוסקי ההלכה לנטשו? האם במצב קיצוני כזה של תלות אדם בזולתו יש להניח להורה שלא שולט במעשיו ובוודאי שלא מסוגל לדאוג לעצמו לצרכיו הבסיסיים ביותר למות ברעב או להיכנס למצב של סכנה שהוא לא מודע לה, שתגרום למותו?

ניתן למצוא התייחסות לשאלה זו בדברי ר' דוד הלוי מחבר טורי זהב לשולחן ערוך שחי בפולין במאה ה-17:

> ונראה שעיקר תמיהתו (של הרא"בד) על שיצוה לשומרים דזהו ליתיה בגמרא, ועל זה תמה הרא"בד: מה חשב הרמב"ם שהוסיף ציווי לאחרים לשומרים כיוון דעל כך לא מהני לה שמירה, דאי מהנה למה ילך, ויניחנה, הלא אפשר לה בשמירה, ואם אי אפשר לשמור מה מהני ציווי לאחרים בשמירה וכן ראיתי בדרישה וכן עיקר!^[מד]

ר' דוד הלוי מחדד בדבריו את הנקודה של יכולת השמירה ואחריותו של הבן: ממה נפשך, אם ההורה הוא במצב השמירה עדיין מועילה לו ודאי שהבן צריך לשמור עליו ואם הוא הגיע למצב מדורדר כל כך שלא ניתן עוד לשמור עליו מדוע להורות לבן "שיצוה לאחרים לשומרים" כפי שהורה הרמב"ם, הרי זה ממילא לא יעזור!

מדבריו של ר' דוד הלוי מתברר שעל הבן מוטלת האחריות לדאוג להורה שהגיע למצב של טירוף הדעת בכל מקרה, משום שלא יעלה על הדעת שבמצב קשה כל-כך כאשר אפילו שמירה לא תועיל לו, בנו ינטוש אותו לבדו, בידיעה ברורה שנטישה זו יכולה לגרום במישרין או בעקיפין אפילו למותו של ההורה, שהרי הוא במצב שאיננו יכול לדאוג אף לא לצרכיו הבסיסיים, כפי שהוסבר.

ר' יואל סירקיס שחי בפולין במאה ה-17 בחיבורו: בית חדש על הטור, מבטא בדבריו מעין סיכום של הגישה ההלכתית הרואה בבן אחראי לשלום הוריו **במיוחד** כשמצבם הנפשי מחמיר:

> ואני אומר: דעת הרא"בד היא דהההיא אמא לא נטרפה דעתה אלא זקנה היתה, ולפי שלא היה יכול להשתדל לה בעל כרצונה הלך ממנה כדי שלא יעבור יותר על מה שתצווה אותו עוד ולא יוכל לקיים. **אבל משנטרפה דעתו שצריך שמירה "יתירה" אין הדעת נותנת שניחם וילך לו ... ואם כן אינו מחוייב כי אם להאכילם ולהשקותם ולשומרם והיאך ילך לו** וכן יראה מדברי רבי' שהסכים לדעת הרא"בד והכי נקטינן ודלא כמו שפסק בשו"ע להקל כהרמב"ם.^[מה]

מד טורי זהב לשולחן ערוך, יורה דעה רמ, סעיף קטן יד.

מה בית חדש על הטור, שם.

זאת?מב

באשר ל"תקדים רב אסי," המהרש"ל רואה **אי התאמה ברורה** בין ה"תקדים"
למצב המתואר ברמב"ם. לדעתו, אמו של רב אסי **לא היתה מטורפת כזו שצריכה
שמירה עקב שגעונה** אלא שהיא ביקשה בקשות לא סבירות ורב אסי התקשה לעמוד
בהן (לא ברור מהתיאור בתלמוד באיזה קושי מדובר, אולי גם קושי נפשי) ולכן הוא
עזב אותה. יש לשים לב שהמהרש"ל לא עוסק בביקורת התנהגותו של רב אסי, אך
חשוב לו לקבוע שאין בסיפור תלמודי זה, משום תקדים שעל פי יש לפסוק הלכה בדבר
חובותיו של בן כלפי הוריו שלקו בנפשם בצורה קשה כל כך שהם זקוקים לשמירה
כדי שלא יעשו להם כל רע, משום שזהו אינו המקרה שמאפיין מצב זה.

ר' יהושע פאלק תלמידם של המהרש"ל והרמ"א–חי בפולין בסוף המאה ה-16,
מתייחס בחיבורו דרישה לטור, להשגת הראב"ד. לאחר שהוא מביא את דברי
הפוסקים שקדמו לו הוא כותב:

> ולי נראה דשפיר השיגו ורצונו כיון שכתב הרמב"ם יצווה לאחרים וכי' שמע מינה דאפשר
> לאחרים שינהגו בו ואפילו הכי אינו חייב הוא לנהוג בעצמו! **ואין הוראה נכונה:** דאם
> אחרים יכולים לנהוג בו כראוי, כל שכן הוא שיודע לעשות רצון אביו. אם כן חייב הוא
> בעצמו לנהוג, דבשלמא בעובדא דגמרא, לא נזכר שיצווה לאחרים, ואפשר דמיירי שהיתה
> כבר נשטתה עד שאי אפשר לשום אדם לנהוג בה, אבל אם אפשר לאחרים, כל שכן דאפשר
> לו וחייב! והכי דייק לשון ההשגה שכתב כש הוא יניחם למי יצוה לשומרם, דמשמע שכל
> שהוא אינו יכול לנהוג בו כל שכן אחרים..."מג

ר' יהושע פאלק הולך בדרכו ההלכתית של רבו המהרש"ל ומפתח אותה. קיימות
בדבריו שלוש נקודות שחשוב להבין:

א. מתוך שהרמב"ם כתב: "ויצוה לאחרים להנהיגם כראוי להם" מכאן שמדובר
על מצב שבו "אחרים" יכולים לטפל בהורים ולכן, לדעתו, אם אחרים יכולים לעשות
זאת, קל וחומר שעל הבן מוטלת החובה ההלכתית-מוסרית לדאוג להוריו לפני
האחרים, במיוחד שהוא-בגלל קרבתו להוריו, ידע לטפל בהם באופן הטוב ביותר
משום שהוא מכירם יותר מכל אחד אחר. כך מובנת שאלת הראב"ד "למי יצווה
לשומרם?" אכן, אין בעיה טכנית למצוא אדם זר שיטפל בהם, ואולי, יש לכך אפילו
כמה יתרונות אלא שר' יהושע פאלק רואה את זה, בכל מקרה, כאפשרות הפחות
טובה מכך שבנם יטפל בהם.

ב. רק במצב שגם אחרים לא יכולים לטפל בהורים שנטרפה דעתם, גם הבן פטור
מלעשות זאת.

ג. בניגוד למהרש"ל בעל הדרישה רואה ב"עובדא דרב אסי" תקדים שיש ליישבו
עם פסק ההלכה של הרמב"ם והוא עושה זאת תוך שהוא חוזר על דברי קודמיו ועומד

מב יש לשים לב שאין בדברי המהרש"ל התייחסות לדברי קודמיו שמצאו יתרונות או אפילו **הכרח**
שזר יטפל בהורים.

מג ר' יהושע פאלק, דרישה לטור, יורה דעה , רמ:ב.

מתוארים בתלמוד מתאימים למצב המתואר ע"י הרמב"ם?

כבר נכתב שאין רמז או סימן גלוי בתלמוד לכך שרב אסי דאג למישהו אחר שיטפל באמו והרמב"ם קובע שכך צריך הבן לנהוג. אך בנוסף לכך קיימת נקודה נוספת של אי התאמה לכאורה בין התיאור בתלמוד למצב שמתואר בדברי הפוסקים: האומנם היתה אמו של רב אסי במצב כזה כמו שמתואר במקורות ההלכתיים שהובאו? האם בגלל שביקשה מבנה גבר נאה כמוהו ניתן לקבוע שהיא היתה במצב כזה של טירוף בלתי נשלט שהטיפול בה חייב לעבור לאדם זר?

זאת ועוד, גם אם נניח שבאמת הגיעה אמו של רב אסי לדרגת טירוף כזו, ואף אם נניח שרב אסי דאג שמישהו אחר יטפל בה כראוי, האם לא היה צריך רב אסי להישאר במרחק סביר ממנה, כדי לוודא שהיא אכן מקבלת את הטיפול הראוי לה מאותו אדם זר? האם הגיוני לומר שלשמירת מצבה, רב אסי עזב אותה ועלה לא"י מרחק רב באותם הימים והתנתק ממנה עד כדי כך שהוא לא ידע שהיא נפטרה?

תמיהות אלו מעוררות בהכרח את השאלה האם יש ללמוד הלכה בשאלת חובתו של בן כלפי הוריו שלקו בנפשם, מתיאור ההתנהגות של רב אסי בתלמוד, או שזהו מקרה פרטי המתאר מצב מסויים ולכן אין ללמוד ממנו הלכה גורפת לענייננו?

"מי שנטרפה דעתו של אביו": שינוי מגמה בשרשרת הפסיקה מהמאה ה-16

דברי הפוסקים שהובאו בפרק הקודם מייצגים נאמנה את המגמה השלטת בהשתלשלות ההלכה עד המאה ה-16. רוב מוחלט של הפוסקים מכריע כדעת הרמב"ם: החובה הראשונית מוטלת על הבן לטפל בהורה שלו שנשתבשה דעתו ורק כשהוא לא יכול יותר לעשות זאת עליו להעביר את הטיפול לאדם אחר. כל פוסק מצא דרך המיוחדת לו להסביר את פסק הרמב"ם, אם ע"י עיגונו בסיפור התלמודי ו/או ע"י נתינת הסבר להגיון הפנימי שעומד בבסיסה של הלכה זו. עד לאמצע המאה ה-16 לא נמצא פוסק שיצדיק את השגת הראב"ד, יסביר את ההגיון שעומד מאחריה ואף יתמודד עם הקביעה שמ"עובדא דרב אסי" ניתן לפסוק אך ורק בדרכו של הרמב"ם.

הראשון שעושה זאת הוא המהרש"ל ר' שלמה לוריא שחי בפולין במאה ה-16 והיה אחד הפוסקים המרכזיים, המשמעותיים והמשפיעים ביותר על הפוסקים האשכנזיים שבאו בעקבותיו. המהרש"ל בחיבורו על מסכתות התלמוד, ים של שלמה, לאחר שהוא מצטט את דברי הפוסקים שקדמו לו ואת השגת הראב"ד, הוא כותב:

> **ואני אומר שיפה השיגו** אם יניחם וילך לו מי יצוה לשומרם כמו שכתב **ואינו דומה לעובדא דאמא דרב אסי**, דשם לא היתה מטורפת בעניין שצריכה לשמירה אלא שאלה כהוגן מרוע הלב, ע"כ חלף הלך לו למקום שלא תראה אותו![מא]

המהרש"ל מקבל את גישת הראב"ד, שבאופן **מהותי** אין לפסוק שהבן יעזוב את הוריו משנטרפה דעתם שהרי אם הוא לא יטפל בהם ממי אפשר לצפות שיעשה

מא ר' שלמה לוריא המהרש"ל, ים של שלמה למסכת קידושין א:סב, פולין תרכ"ב.

הראב"ד, כתב ר' יחיאל מיכל הלוי אפשטיין, שחי ברוסיה הלבנה במאה ה-19, בחיבורו ההלכתי, ערוך השולחן:

> ואין זו השגה. דנ"ל דהרמב"ם הכי קאמר דידוע שהמשתגעים ביותר, בהכרח לאוסרם בזיקים ובחבלים והבן אין ביכולתו לעשות בעצמו כן ולכן מצווה לאחרים והוא יילך לו.[לט]

כסיכום לגישה הלכתית זו, ראוי להביא את דבריו של ר' אליעזר וולדנברג, בעל שו"ת ציץ אליעזר, שחי בא"י במאה הנוכחית (יבל"א). אל הרב וולדנברג מופנית שאלה שעניינה: "מי שאמו נטרפה דעתה עליה אם הבן מותר לקושרה בחבל אל כסא כדי שלא תשתולל?"[מ] כדי לענות תשובה לשאלה זו סוקר הרב וולדנברג את דברי הפוסקים שהופיעו במאמר זה ובסיכום סקירתו הוא מצדד בגישה ההלכתית של הרדב"ז ובעל ערוך השולחן. לדעתו, ניתן למצוא סימוכין לגישה זו ע"י דיוק בלשונו של הרמב"ם. הרמב"ם כותב: "ואם אי אפשר לו... יניחם וילך לו ויצוה לאחרים להנהיגם כראוי **להם**"! המילה "**להם**" נשמטה בדברי הפוסקים שציטטו את לשון הרמב"ם, כפי שהוזכר, והיא-היא המפתח, לפי הרב וולדנברג, להבנה נכונה את המצב המסוים שלגביו פוסק הרמב"ם ואת הנימוק לפסיקתו.

> ...ולפי דברינו מרומז ומאומת זה בלשונו המזוקק של הרמב"ם בעצמו במ"ש: ויצוה לאחרים להנהיגם כראוי להם. והיינו דאין רצונו לומר בזה לצות לאחרים לנהג כראוי ולספק להם כל הנצרך להם, **אלא רצה לומר שיצוה לאחרים לעשות מה שהוא לא יכול לעשות אע"פ שטובת העניין דורש זאת**, והיינו, שיצוה לאחרים להנהיגם כראוי להם **להם בדווקא, לפי מעמדם ושטותם**, לרבות האלימות בקשירה בחבלים וכדומה כפי הצווי הרפואי, כדי שישקטו על ידי כך וינוחו מרוגזם.

חשוב להדגיש שהרב וולדנברג דוחה את השגת הראב"ד לא ע"י הטיעון ה"פורמאלי" שהרמב"ם היה חייב לפסוק כפי שפסק משום התקדים התלמודי הוא מעדיף הסבר למהות ההלכה שכתב הרמב"ם: במצב המסוים הזה שההורים נמצאים בו **זו היא מצוות כיבוד הורים של הבן** שימנה אדם אחר שישגיח על הוריו כך פסק הרמב"ם וכך צריך היה לפסוק כדי שלא להכשיל את הבן במצווה חשובה זו. דווקא מתוך ההסבר של הרב וולדנברג מתעוררת שאלה בלתי נמנעת עליו ועל הפוסקים שלפי שיטתם הוא פסק: האומנם פסק הרמב"ם את ההלכה בעניין: "מי שנטרפה דעתו של אביו," על סמך "עובדא דרב אסי"? האם פרטי הסיפור כפי שהם

אסור לו להכותם ולקללם" כפי שכותב הרמב"ם בהלכות ממרים ה:יב. ויג וכפי שנפסק בשו"ע יורה
דיעה סימן רמ"א סעיפים ד, ה, כל שכן במצב זה שאין בהם דעת, יהיה אסור לו לעשות דברים אלו,
אלא עליו למנות מישהו אחר שיעשה להם דברים אלו לצורך רפואתם. ראה עוד על כך במאמר
המצויין בהערה 25.

[לט] ר' יחיאל מיכל הלוי אפשטיין, ערוך השולחן, יורה דיעה רמ, פיעטרקוב, תרס"ג.

[מ] שו"ת ציץ אליעזר, חלק יב, סימן נט, ירושלים, תשל"ו.

הדבר היא שהרמב"ם יכול לחדש עצה טובה מדעתו מתוך הנחה חזקה שכך נהג רב
אסי ולהורות שראוי לדאוג שמישהו אחר יטפל בהורה שלקה בנפשו אף שזה לא כתוב
מפורשות בתלמוד.

הסברו של ר' יוסף קארו תמוה ביותר: האם יתכן שהרמב"ם מתיר לבן לעזוב את
הוריו שלקו בנפשם ללא **הוראה מחייבת**—שעליו מוטלת החובה להמשיך ולדאוג להם
ע"י מינוי של מישהו אחר שיטפל בהם? הרי שחזרנו ל"זעקתו" של הראב"ד, אם בנם
לא ידאג להם למי יצווה לשומרם?

לסיכום התייחסויותיו של ר"י קארו לנושא דידן, ניתן לקבוע שהוא "מגן" על פסק
הלכה של הרמב"ם בטענה "פורמאלית-צורנית" שהרמב"ם פסק בהתאם לכתוב
בתלמוד, ואת הנקודה שבה קיימת אי התאמה בין פסק הרמב"ם לתיאור התלמודי
ניתן ליישב בקלות. חשוב להדגיש שר"י קארו לא מתייחס בדבריו לטענה **המהותית**
של הראב"ד "אין זו הוראה נכונה" במובן של: ראויה ומכוונת. האם נכון
וראוי לפסוק כפי שפסק הרמב"ם לבן שנמצא במצב עדין שכזה כאשר משתבשת דעת
ההורה שלו האומנם יש להתיר לו או אף לחייבו,[לו] לעזוב את ההורה ולמסור את
הטיפול בו לאדם זר? אפשר שר' יוסף קארו לא ראה צורך להתמודד עם טענתו
המהותית של הראב"ד, משום שלדעתו שיקול הדעת של פוסק ההלכה בשאלה הנדונה
מצומצם, שכן יש "תקדים" בתלמוד המחייב אותו לפסוק הלכה באופן מסויים.

הרדב"ז ר' דוד בן זמרה, שהיה ממגורשי ספרד, רבה של קהיר וראש רבני מצרים,
בראשית המאה ה-16, כתב פירוש על הלכות הרמב"ם. דרכו לנמק את פסק הרמב"ם
בעניין: "מי שנטרפה דעת אביו" היא כשל ר"י קארו בן דורו, אלא שהוא מסביר מהו
ההגיון העומד בבסיס **הדרישה** שהבן יעזוב את הוריו שנשתטו.

לדעתו, הרמב"ם פסק על-פי העובדא בתלמוד ולאחר שהוא מזכיר את השגת
הראב"ד וטוען שאין לה למקום, הוא כותב:

> ...אלא ודאי ציווה על אחרים לפרנסה **וזו תקנתה:** שיש לה על הבן געגועים, ולא מיכספא
> מיניה מה שאין כן באחרים, ולא מצי לגעור בה ואחרים גוערים בה ואפשר ע"י הכאה
> תחזור משטותה ומעשים בכל יום כיוצא בזה **והבן אי אפשר לו לעשות דבר מזה!**[לז]

נימוקו של הרדב"ז לפסק הרמב"ם דומה לנימוקו של בעל מגדל עוז שהורים לא
מתביישים מבנם ולכן הם מתנהגים בצורה פרועה, מה שאין כן אם מטפל בהם אדם
זר. אך הוא מוסיף דבר חשוב ביותר: להבנתו, הרמב"ם פסק שהבן **חייב** לעזוב את
הוריו משום שמצב זה של הורים שנטרפה דעתם דורש סוג כזה של טיפול שאסור
לבנם לעשותו, כמו גערה בהם או נתינת מכה. זוהי דרך הטיפול היעילה והיחידה
לעיתים, לאנשים שאיבדו את יכולת האבחנה בין טוב לרע. לכן ברור שכדי לא לעבור
על מצוות כיבוד ומורא הורים **חייב הבן לעוזבם.**[לח] דברים דומים מאוד ביחס להשגת

[לו] ראה הערה 25.

[לז] הרדב"ז, הלכות ממרים ו:י, ד"ה: "מי שנטרפה..."

[לח] הרדב"ז מבסס דבריו על קל וחומר פשוט—שהרי אפילו אם "היו אביו או אמו רשעים גמורים—

16. מביע דעתו בסוגיא הנדונה בשלושת חיבוריו: בית יוסף על ספר הטור, בחיבורו
ההלכתי השולחן ערוך, ובחיבורו כסף משנה על משנה תורה לרמב"ם. בבית יוסף,
מאשר ר"י קארו את נכונות פסק הרמב"ם והוא מבסס את קביעתו גם על דברי הר"ן
שהוזכרו:

דברי הרמב"ם נכונים וברורים הם מדגרסינן בפ"ק דקידושין, שם, רב אסי... וכן דעת הר"ן
דההיא עובדא מוכח כדעת הרמב"ם ז"ל ותמה על הראב"ד למה השיגו.[לב]

בשולחן ערוך החיבור ההלכתי הגדול והמקיף של ר"י קארו הוא מסכם את ההלכה
בעניין: "מי שנטרפה דעת אביו" ע"י ציטוט דברי הרמב"ם כפי שציטטם בעל הטורים
עם אותם שינויים שהצבעתי עליהם ללא התייחסות להשגת הראב"ד. בכותבו את
חיבורו כסף משנה שם לו ר"י קארו למטרה לא רק למצוא את המקורות להלכות
הרמב"ם ולפרש אותן אלא עיקר משימתו היא: להגן עליהן בפני השגות הראב"ד.
זאת ניתן ללמוד מהצהרת כוונותיו בהקדמתו לחיבורו.[לג] לעניינו, כותב ר"י קארו על
פסיקת הרמב"ם:

ומה שכתב: "ויצווה לאחרים להנהיגם כראוי" **עיצה טובה קא משמע לן, ואין ספק שכך**
עשה רב אסי. וכתב הראב"ד: אין זו הוראה נכונה... ואילו היה רבינו מוציא דין זה מדעתו
היה השגתו השגה אבל אחר שהוא מוציא אותו מעובדא דרב אסי שכתבתי אין מקום
להשגתו![לד]

בדומה לקודמיו גם ר"י קארו דוחה את השגת הראב"ד בטענה שהרמב"ם היה מחייב
לפסוק כפי שפסק בהתבססו על מאורע מחייב להלכה שמצוי בתלמוד, אך חשוב
להדגיש שהוא הראשון שמעיר שההתאמה בין "עובדא דרב אסי" ובין ההלכה של
הרמב"ם אינה מושלמת. ר"י קארו עומד רק על נקודה אחת באי ההתאמה ומסביר
אותה: הרמב"ם פוסק שגם כשהבן לא יכול יותר לטפל בהוריו, הוא אמור לדאוג
שמישהו אחר יעשה זאת, והרי בתיאור התלמודי אין זכר וסימן לכך שרב אסי בעוזבו
את אמו בבבל ובעלותו לא"י, דאג שמישהו אחר יטפל באמו. הסברו לתמיהה זו
מתפצל לשתי דרכים המתאחדות לאחת:

א. למרות שאין הדבר כתוב או מרומז בתלמוד אין ספק לדעתו, שרב אסי לא עזב
את אמו לפני שהוא דאג שמישהו אחר יטפל בה, לא יתכן שהוא לא עשה זאת!
ב. בדבריו של הרמב"ם: "יצוה לאחרים להנהיגם כראוי להם" **אין הוראה**
מחייבת שכך צריך הבן לעשות אלא **עצה טובה** של הרמב"ם שכך כדאי שהבן יעשה.
זוהי משמעות הביטוי שמשתמש בו ר"י קארו: "עצה טובה קא משמע לן."[לה] משמעות

[לב] בית יוסף, טור, יורה דעה, הלכות כיבוד אב ואם סימן רמ. וכן בשולחן ערוך, שם.

[לג] ר"י יוסף קארו, בהקדמה לחיבורו כסף משנה, על משנה תורה לרמב"ם, ד"ה: "ראה ראיתי את
אשר הואיל..."

[לד] כסף משנה, הלכות ממרים ו:י, ד"ה: "מי שנטרפה דעתו של אביו..."

[לה] ראה הגדרתו של נ. רקובר לביטוי זה, "ניבי התלמוד," ירושלים, תשנ"א, 298.

ללא נשוא ואם הוא יישאר איתם זה יגרום לו למכשלה גדולה ולכן במצב המיוחד שנוצר הוא לא יקיים את המצווה בגופו אלא בדאגתו לאדם אחר שיטפל בהוריו.

יכול להיות, שדברים אלו של בעל המגדל עוז היו בסיס לדבריו של פוסק מאוחר יותר ר' דוד פרדו בעל שו"ת "מכתם לדוד" שחי בארצות הבלקן במאה ה -18. ר' דוד רואה בהלכה של הרמב"ם יישום העיקרון ההלכתי "שלוחו של אדם כמותו".[כח] השליחות יכולה להיות לדבר-מצווה ולכן כפי שכל מצווה יכולה להיעשות ע"י שליח שהוא בא כוחו של השולח ונחשבת כאילו נעשתה בידי האדם השולח בעצמו,[כט] כך גם לגבי מצוות "כיבוד הורים" שהבן מכל מיני סיבות לא יכול לקיימה בעצמו, עליו לקיימה ע"י שליח:

> ועיין בהרמב"ם פ"ו מהלכות ממרים... ויצווה לאחרים להנהיגם כראוי במשמע דגם במה שמצווה לאחרים להנהיגם **קיים המצווה**! אלא בכל היכא דאפשר **מצווה בו יותר מבשלוחו** כמו כל המצוות שבתורה, וכל היכא דלא אפשר- יקיים ע"י אחר![ל]

הרב פרדו מדגיש שהאופן האידיאלי לקיום מצווה היא ע"י האדם עצמו אך במצבים שזה בלתי אפשרי ייחשב לאדם כאילו קיים את המצווה אם זו נעשתה ע"י שליח.

הר"ן, רבינו ניסים (בן ראובן) גירונדי שחי בספרד במאה ה -14, מקבל גם כן את הכרעת הרמב"ם, אלא שהוא מנסה להסביר באופן אחר את השגת הראב"ד. בחיבורו על הלכות הרי"ף, לאחר שהוא מצטט את דברי הרמב"ם ואת השגת הראב"ד הוא מגיב להשגה זו:

> ולא ידעתי למה דהא עובדא דרב אסי הרי מוכח אולי הוא ז"ל סובר דדווקא למיסק לא"י ואינו מחוור.[לא]

לדעתו, צריך היה הרמב"ם לפסוק ע"פ "עובדא דרב אסי." אך כדי להסביר את השגת הראב"ד הוא מציע שאולי הראב"ד סבר **שאין** לפסוק ממה שאירע לרב אסי הוראה **כללית** בעניין מי שנטרפה דעת הוריו משום שזהו מקרה פרטי ומיוחד בכך שרב אסי רצה לעלות מבבל (מקום מגוריו עם אמו) לא"י, ואולי רק מסיבה זו היה מותר לו לעוזבה, אך אם אין מדובר בעליה לא"י אסור יהיה לבן לעזוב את אמו שנשתבשה דעתה. יש להדגיש שהר"ן מסיים דבריו במילים : "ואינו מחוור" דבריו הם בגדר השערה שאינה מבוררת כל צורכה.

ר' יוסף קארו אחד מגדולי פוסקי ההלכה בכל הדורות, חי בא"י, בצפת במאה ה-

---

[כח] כלל הלכתי זה: "שלוחו של אדם כמותו" נלמד במדרשי הלכה שונים כדוגמת מכילתא דר' ישמעאל, מהדורת הורוביץ-רבין, ירושלים, תש"ל, פרשת בא, מסכתא דפסחא פרשה ה.

[כט] כך מגדיר זאת הפרופסור מ. אלון בספרו המשפט העברי, מהדורה ג, (ירושלים, תשמ"ח) חלק א, עמ' 288, 100.

[ל] ר' דוד פרדו , שו"ת מכתם לדוד, יורה דעה לב, ירושלים , תש"ל.

[לא] הר"ן, בחיבורו על הלכות הרי"ף. מסכת קידושין לא ע"ב, בסוף המסכת בדפוס וילנא של התלמוד הבבלי.

ההלכה הבאים אחריהם. כדי ליצור "תמונה הלכתית" יש לעיין בדבריו של כל אחד
מהפוסקים לבחון באיזו דרך הוא פוסק האם כדעת הרמב"ם או שהוא מקבל את
השגת הראב"ד, ובמיוחד יש לעמוד על דרכו של כל אחד מהם לעגן את שיטתו
ההלכתית בתיאור הגמרא את התנהגותו של רב אסי. ר' יעקב בן הרא"ש שחי באשכנז
ובספרד במאה ה-14 כותב לענייננו:[כ]

> כתב הרמב"ם: מי שנטרפה דעתו של אביו... ואם א"א לו לעמוד מפני שנשתנו ביותר,
> יניחם וילך לו ויצוה לאחרים לנהגם כראוי. וכתב הראב"ד אין זו הוראה נכונה אם הוא
> יניחם וילך לו למי יצוה לשומרם.

בעל הטורים בהכריעו את ההלכה מסתפק בציטוט דברי הרמב"ם והשגת
הראב"ד, אך את דברי הרמב"ם הוא מצטט בשינויים מסויימים:

א. הרמב"ם כותב "מפני שנשתטו" ובטור כתוב "מפני שנשתנו."
ב. הרמב"ם כותב: "ויצווה לאחרים להנהיגם כראוי **להם** "ובספר הטור נשמטה
המילה: "להם."

ר' שם טוב אבן גאון בעל חיבור "מגדל עוז" על הלכות הרמב"ם, שחי גם הוא
בספרד במאה ה-14, היה הראשון שניסה "להגן" על פסק ההלכה של הרמב"ם מפני
השגת הראב"ד:

> מי שנטרפה דעת אביו... כתב הראב"ד: "אין זו הוראה נכונה... ואני אומר תמה אני אם
> יצא דבר זה מפיו שהרי מעשה רב בכ"מ וגרסינן פ"ק דקידושין... דרב אסי הוי ליה ההיא
> אמא זקינה... ומה שהקשה הראב"ד ז"ל לאמר כי הבן כי עושה בחינם והממונה יעשה
> בשכר ועוד באב ואם לגבי הבן גייס דעתייהו טפי מלגבי הממונה שהוא נוכרי ומיכספי
> מניה.[כז]

ראש לכל, מקבל ר' שם טוב את הכרעתו ההלכתית של הרמב"ם שאכן הבן
יכול לעזוב את הוריו שנשתטו בהסתמך על "עובדא דרב אסי." לדעתו, אין כל דרך
להכריע אחרת לאור תיאור הגמרא את התנהגותו של רב אסי ויש להסיק מכך הלכה
בדיוק כפי שהסיק הרמב"ם. מעבר לכך מסביר ר' שם טוב את ההגיון הפנימי העומד
בבסיס הלכה זו. לדעתו, אכן על הבן מוטלת החובה הראשונית לטפל בהוריו, אך
כשהם הגיעו למצב בו נשתטו ביותר, **עדיף** שאדם זר יטפל בהם וזאת משום שכלפי
בנם דעתם גסה ולכן הם מתנהגים בצורה פרועה וחסרת שליטה אך אם יטפל בהם זר
הם יתביישו ממנו וישלטו בעצמם יותר.

לשאלתו של הראב"ד "אם הוא הוא יניחם... למי יצווה לשומרם" עונה ר' שם טוב
שאין כל קושי למצוא אדם זר שיטפל בהורים וזאת משום שאדם זר יתייחס לטיפול באותו
הורה שנטרפה דעתו כעבודה שהוא צריך לבצע ובתמורתה הוא יקבל שכר מהבן. כך
יוצא שהבן לא ייכשל בקיום מצוות "כיבוד הורים," שהרי התנהגותם מקשה עליו

[כ] טור, יורה דעה, הלכות כיבוד אב ואם רמ.

[כז] מגדל עוז, רמב"ם, שם, ד"ה: "מי שנטרפה דעת אביו."

משאיננו מסוגל יותר "מפני שנשתטו ביותר" "יניחם וילך לו" ובתנאי שידאג "לאחרים" שיטפלו בהוריו כראוי להם, זו נשארת חובתו של הבן כלפיהם!

שתי נקודות אינן ברורות בפסק זה של הרמב"ם:

א. מה משמעות הביטוי: "ואם אי אפשר לו" מהי הנקודה המסויימת שבה לדעת הרמב"ם, מסירה ההלכה מהבן את החובה לטפל בהוריו, במו ידיו? האם מדובר בקושי נפשי של הבן לראות את הוריו שנשתטו ביותר או שפיזית אין ביכולתו לטפל בהם במצב המסוים שבו הם נמצאים?

ב. לא ברור מלשונו של הרמב"ם האם הוא **מתיר** לבן במצב העדין שבו הוא נמצא לעזוב את הוריו ולדאוג ש"אחרים" יטפלו בהם או שהוא קובע שזוהי **חובתו** ההלכתית.

ר' יוסף קארו בכסף משנה והרדב"ז בפירושו למשנה תורה, מקדימים לפירושיהם את הלכות הרמב"ם חשיפה של מקורה התלמודי של כל הלכה. לגבי ההלכה הנדונה שניהם קובעים שהרמב"ם פוסק כיצד צריך בן לנהוג משנטרפה דעת אביו בהתבססו על תאור התנהגותו של רב אסי כלפי אמו כפי שהיא מתוארת בתלמוד הבבלי.[כג] משמעות הדבר היא שהרמב"ם לא המציא הלכה זו מדעתו, אלא הבנתו את פרטי "עובדא דרב אסי," הובילה אותו לפסוק שכך ראוי וצריך בן לנהוג בהוריו שאבדה שפיותם.

הראב"ד ר' אברהם בן דוד, שהיה בן דורו של הרמב"ם וחי בצרפת פרובאנס במאה ה-12, כותב בהשגתו על הלכה זו של הרמב"ם: "...א"א אין זו הוראה נכונה אם הוא ילך וינית לו למי יצווה לשמרו? עכ"ל."[כד] מדייק בלשונו של הראב"ד ניתן לומר שהוא סובר שהרמב"ם לא רק **מתיר** לבן לעזוב את הוריו אלא **מורה** לו לעשות כך שהרי הוא מכנה את דברי הרמב"ם: "הוראה,"[כה] אך בין אם זו הבנה הכרחית, ובין אם הרמב"ם רק התיר זאת לבן, ברור שלדעת הראב"ד **"אין זו הוראה נכונה"** **ואסור** להורות לבן שנטרפה דעת הוריו לעוזבם. ההגיון שעומד בבסיס דבריו של הראב"ד הוא, שעל הבן מוטלת החובה יותר מכל אחד אחר לטפל בהוריו ואם "אי אפשר **לו** יותר" ודאי שאין לצפות מאף אחד אחר שיסכים לעשות זאת. יש לשים לב שאין בדברי הראב"ד התייחסות למקור ההלכה של הרמב"ם אלא היא קביעתו היא עקרונית וחד משמעית רק ביחס למהות ותוכן ההלכה ולא ביחס לדרך בה היא נלמדה.

דברי הרמב"ם ומולם השגת הראב"ד מהווים בסיס להתייחסותם של פוסקי

[כג] יש להזכיר שוב את דברי תוספות ר"י הזקן על אמו של רב אסי "שנטרפה דעתה," קידושין, שם. וכן את דברי הגר"א בהגהותיו, שקובע בהתבסס על הרמב"ם, "מטורפת היתה," הגהות הגר"א, שם, הגהה א.

[כד] השגת הראב"ד, רמב"ם, הלכות ממרים ו:י.

[כה] ראה מאמרו של הרב שפרן, "טיפול רפואי בהורים בניגוד לרצונם," תחומין כרך יד (תשנ"ד) 351-333. בעמ' 349, כותב הרב שפרן "דיעה זו של הרמב"ם אינה רק היתר מללכת, אם הוא רוצה, אלא **הוראה מחייבת**."

שבו ולהבינו היטב . בשלב זה - יש לעמוד על שלוש נקודות שאינן ברורות בסיפור :

א. מה משמעות התאור : "אמא זקנה" האם מדובר באישה מבוגרת בשנים בלבד. או שמדובר באשה שגילה משפיע על יכולתה השכלית.

ב. מדוע דוקא לאחר בקשתה השלישית של האם : רצונה באיש יפה כמו בנה, מחליט הבן רב אסי, לעזוב אותה בבבל ולעלות לארץ ישראל? מה בבקשה זו יוצר אצלו את הרצון ו/ או הצורך להינתק מאמו?

ג. למה התכוון רב אסי באומרו, לאחר ששמע שאמו נפטרה : אילו הייתי יודע לא הייתי יוצא? אילו הוא היה יודע מה? מאיפה הוא לא היה יוצא? לאן ומדוע?

ר' יצחק הזקן, מבעלי התוספות שחי בצרפת במאה ה -12, כותב:[כא] "דשפיר–יפה, והכיר שנטרפה דעתה וברח שלא יוכל לצאת ידי שמים."

לפי דבריו ניתן להסביר באופן חלקי, את שתי הנקודות הראשונות שאינן ברורות : אמו של רב אסי לא היתה אישה זקנה בגיל בלבד אלא שמדובר באישה שאיבדה את שפיותה ורב אסי מבין זאת לאחר בקשתה השלישית, שימצא לה גבר יפה כמותו, הקשה שנראתה לו מאוד לא סבירה ונורמלית שאין ברצונו ו/או יכולתו להיענות לה ולכן הוא עזב אותה, מחשש שלא יוכל לקיים מצוות "כיבוד אם" כראוי ובכך למעשה ייכשל בקיום מצווה "לא יוכל לצאת ידי שמים."

על פניו ניתן להסיק מדברי ר"י הזקן שברגע שהבן תובע מבנו דברים שאינם סבירים ובגלל אי הסבירות שלהם הבן לא יוכל לקיים את מבוקשו של ההורה עליו לקום ולעזוב את אותו הורה וזאת כדי שהוא לא ייכשל בקיום מצוה כל כך חשובה: "כיבוד הורים." אין בדברי ר"י הזקן התייחסות לשאלה : מה יעלה בגורלו של אותו הורה שבנו עזב אותו האם בכך שאם מאבדת את חוש ההגיון הפשוט פוקעת אחריותו של בנה כלפיה? האם חובתו של בן במסגרת מצוות "כיבוד הורים" תלויה במצבו הנפשי של ההורה, ומשלקה ההורה בנפשו לא חלה עליו יותר מצוות "כבוד הורים"? כדי לענות על שאלה מורכבת זו יש לעיין בדברי פרשני התלמוד על "עובדא דרב אסי," ובמקורות ההלכתיים בעניין : "מי שנטרפה דעתו של אביו."

הרמב"ם ר' משה בן מיימון גדול פוסקי ההלכה, שחי בספרד, צפון אפריקה ומצרים במאה ה-12, כותב ב"הלכות ממרים" :

> מי שנטרפה דעתו של אביו או של אמו, משתדל לנהוג עמהם כפי דעתם עד שירחם עליהם.
> ואם אי אפשר לו לעמוד מפני שנשתטו ביותר יניחם וילך לו ויצוה לאחרים להנהיגו כראוי להם.[כב]

מאחר שדבריו של הרמב"ם מהווים בסיס להתייחסות של כל הפוסקים הבאים אחריו, בין מי שמקבלים את פסיקתו ובין מי שמתנגדים לה, יש להבין היטב את דבריו : בשלב ראשון מצווה הבן לטפל בהוריו שנשתבשה דעתם ככל יכולתו, אך

כא תוספות ר"י הזקן , קידושין לא ע"ב, ד"ה : "דשפיר."
כב רמב"ם, הלכות ממרים ו :י.

במצוות "מורא הורים."[יח]

חשוב להדגיש–אפילו כאשר התנהגות ההורה היא כל-כך בעייתית וחריגה אין הרמב"ם פותח פתח **בהלכה זו**, להתרחקות ממנו כתגובה מותרת של הבן אלא להפך, מהבן מצופה להישאר בקרבתו ולהבליג, בדיוק כפי שקבע ר' אליעזר כשנשאל על כך.

"מי שנטרפה דעתו של אביו" השתלשלות ההלכה עד המאה ה-16

במהלך רצף התיאורים בתלמוד הבבלי של "אנשים גדולים" ששימשו מופת בדרך קיומם את מצוות "כיבוד הורים," מסופר:[יט]

> רב אסי הוה ליה ההיא אמא זקנה, אמרה ליה: בעינא תכשיטין עבד לה, בעינא גברא נייעין לך, בעינא גברא דשפיר כוותך שבקה ואזל לארעא דישראל. שמע דקא אזלה אבתריה, אתא לקמיה ר' יוחנן אמר ליה: מהו לצאת מארץ לחוצה לארץ? אמר ליה: אסור! לקראת אמא מהו? אמר ליה: איני יודע. איתרח פורתא הדר אתא, אמר ליה: אסי, נתרצית לצאת-המקום יחזירך לשלום. אתא לקמיה דר' אלעזר, אמר ליה: דילמא מרתח רתח? אמר ליה: מאי אמר לך? אמר ליה: המקום יחזירך לשלום, אמר ליה: ואם איתא דרתח לא הוה מברך לך! אדהכי והכי שמע לארונא דקאתי אמר: אי ידעי לא נפקי![כ]

פרשנים ופוסקים שונים הבינו עובדא זו על הפרטים המרכיבים אותה באופנים שונים, כפי שיפורט בהמשך, לכן בשלב זה יובא תרגום בלבד.

רב אסי היתה לו אמא זקינה אמרה לו: רוצה (אני) תכשיטין עשה לה, רוצה (אני) איש אחפש לך, רוצה (אני) איש (שיהיה) יפה כמותך עזבה והלך לארץ ישראל. שמע שהיא הולכת אחריו. בא לפני ר' יוחנן (שאל) אותו: (האם מותר) לצאת מהארץ לחו"ל? אמר לו: אסור! (שאל) (האם מותר) לצאת לקבל פני אמא? אמר לו: איני יודע. המתין מעט, חזר ובא (לפני ר' יוחנן).

אמר לו: אסי החלטת שברצונך לצאת המקום יחזירך לשלום.

בא (רב אסי) לפני ר' אלעזר ואמר לו: חס ושלום שמא הוא כועס עלי! אמר לו: מה אמר לך?

אמר לו: המקום יחזירך לשלום. אמר לו: ואם יש (לומר) שכעס עליך לא היה מברך אותך.

עד שכך וכך שמע שארונה (של אמו) בא, אמר: אילו הייתי יודע לא הייתי יוצא!

עובדא זו אודות רב אסי מהווה את הבסיס התלמודי להלכה בעניין כיבוד הורים שנטרפה דעתם, כפי שיוכח בהמשך המאמר ולכן יש חשיבות עליונה לבחון כל פרט

[יח] פוסקי הלכה נוספים, פוסקים בספריהם את ההלכה בדיוק כפי שפסק הרמב"ם ואזכיר רק שניים מהם: ר' יעקב בן הרא"ש בטור, יורה דעה, סימן ר"מ ור' יוסף קארו בשולחן ערוך, שם, סעיף ג.

[יט] קידושין לא ע"ב.

[כ] לסיפור זה מקבילות בתלמוד הירושלמי, בשינויים קטנים ולא משמעותיים לענייננו של מאמר זה.

טפחה לו על ראשו וירקה לו בפניו ולא הכלימה!^{יב}

אמנם בחלק מכתבי היד של התלמוד הבבלי לא מתואר המעשה האצילי של דמה
בהגישו לאמו את הכפפה שנפלה לה,^{יג} אך די במילים : "ולא הכלימה" כדי להבין את
גודל האיפוק שנדרש לבן כשאמו נוהגת בו כך, ואת גדלות נפשו שעמד בכך. חשוב
להדגיש שוב, שר' אליעזר רואה בהבלגתו של דמא בן נתינה, דבר שקשה אולי לעמוד
בו, אך למרות זאת, מצופה מכל בן שכך ינהג כלפי הורה שלו אם חלילה יחווה חוויה
דומה לזו שחווה דמה.

בתוספות על אתר, מובאת מסורת : "יש במדרש שהיתה מטורפת מדעתה."^{יד}
ואכן במדרש דברים רבה מתוארת התנהגותה של אמו של דמה ושם כתוב : "והיתה
אמו חסרת דעת."^{טו} נראה שגם ללא מקורות אלו שבהם מאושר שמדובר באשה
שנטרפה דעתה די בבחינת מעשיה כדי להבין שאין אלו מעשים של אדם רגיל ומאוזן :
אמא המשפילה את בנה, שהיה אדם מכובד ביותר בצורה כל-כך קיצונית, וכל זאת
בפני אנשים המקורבים אליו התנהגות זו איננה התנהגות סבירה ונורמלית כלל
ועיקר. למרות זאת אימצו פוסקי ההלכה את גישתו של ר' אליעזר וקבעו שאפילו
במצב של התנהגות חריגה ולא מאוזנת של אחד ההורים ההבלגה על כך היא התגובה
הראויה והמצופה מהבן, וזאת בהסתמך על התיאור בתלמודים את הבלגתו הראויה
של דמה בן נתינה.

מי שהניח את הבסיס לתפישה הלכתית זו הוא הרמב"ם, שפוסק :

...ועד היכן הוא מוראן? אפילו היה לובש בגדים חמודות ויושב בראש בפני הקהל ובא אביו
ואמו וקרעו בגדיו והכוהו בראשו וירקו פניו, לא יכלים אלא ישתוק וייִרא ממלך מלכי
המלכים **שציווהו בכך**...!"^{טז}

ר' יוסף קארו בכסף משנה על משנה תורה וכן הרדב"ז ר' דוד בן זמרה בפרושו
לרמב"ם קובעים, שהרמב"ם פסק הלכה זו על בסיס התנהגותו של דמא.^{יז} נראה,
שאין הרמב"ם רואה באמו של דמה מקרה יוצא דופן של אם שנטרפה דעתה, שהרי
לכך הוא מייחד את ההלכה י שהיא עיקר עניינו של מאמר זה, משום שהוא קובע
כהוראה כללית: **בן חייב להבליג ולשתוק** אפילו כשהוריו עושים לו מעשים שייראו
לכל בר-דעת כמעשים לא נורמליים, ולדעתו, וזהו **חלק מהציווי של הקב"ה** הכלול

---

^{יב} בבלי, שם.

^{יג} יש גרסאות של התלמוד הבבלי שבהם מתואר המעשה הזה של דמא. כמו בגרסת העין יעקב:
"ונפל קורדקסין שלה והושיטו לה שלא תצטער." עין-יעקב, קידושין לא, הוצאת עם עולם,
ירושלים, תשכ"א.

^{יד} תוספות, קידושין, שם, ד"ה : "ובאת אמו וקרעתו."

^{טו} מדרש דברים רבה, פרשה א, ד"ה : "א"ר אבהו שאלו תלמידיו."

^{טז} רמב"ם, הלכות ממרים ו:ז.

^{יז} כסף משנה, שם, והרדב"ז, שם.

בנפשם, אלא לחשוף את מערכת השיקולים שעמדו לנגד עיניהם של כל אחד מפוסקי
ההלכה לתפוצותיהם וזמניהם השונים: הן השיקולים ה"פורמאליים-צורניים" והן
השיקולים התוכניים-מהותיים, בבואם להכריע הכרעה הלכתית בסוגיא כל-כך
מורכבת ורגישה: חובותיו ההלכתיות-מוסריות של בן שהוריו לא חלו בגופם אלא
שמחלתם היא בנפשם.

דמה בן נתינה העובדא והמשמעויות ההלכתיות שלה

בתלמוד הירושלמי, במסגרת לימודם של האמוראים את מצוות "כיבוד הורים"
מסופר:

> עד היכן הוא כיבוד אב ואם, אמר להן: ולי אתם שואלים, לכו שאלו לדמה בן נתינה. דמה
> בן נתינה ראש פטר בולי הוה, פעם אחת היתה אמו מסטרתו לפני בולי שלו ונפל קורדקסין
> שלה מידה והושיט לה כדי שלא תצטער!![ח]

"גיבורי" הסיפור הוא דמה בן נתינה גוי, מחשובי העיר אשקלון, עשיר מופלג ובעל
מעמד רם בעירו. וכפי שמפרש ה"פני משה"[ט]: "ראש פטר בולי הוה שר העיר וראש
החיילות והחשוב בהן היה." אירע המקרה ופעם אחת הגיעה אמו של אותו גוי חשוב
וסטרה לו על פניו בפני אנשים רבים שהיו סביבו, תוך כדי כך נפלה נעלה מידה
ובנה-דמה הרים את הנעל כדי שאם היא תמשיך לסטור לו על פניו ידה לא תכאב.
בעל פירוש "קרבן העדה" לירושלמי מעיר בפרושו: "הכי גרסינן שאלו לרבי אליעזר
עד היכן כיבוד אב ואם..."[י]

לפי גירסת הירושלמי שהייתה לפניו, סיפור קשה זה מופיע כתשובה של ר' אליעזר
לשאלה שנשאל ע"י חכמים עד היכן גבולותיה של מצוות "כיבוד הורים." ר' אליעזר
מתאר את הבלגתו המדהימה של דמה בן נתינה על ההשפלה שעבר מידי אמו כגבול
קיצוני לקיום מצווה זו. לדעתו, כך ראוי וצריך לנהוג כחלק מחובת כבוד הורים.
אותה עובדא מופיעה גם בתלמוד הבבלי בשינויים אחדים.[יא] גם לפי הכתוב בתלמוד
הבבלי נשאל ר' אליעזר עד היכן כיבוד אב ואם, אלא שבבבלי ר' אליעזר עונה תחילה
בסיפור אחר על דמא שכיבד מאוד את אביו (ולא העירו משנתו אף שדבר זה היה יכול
להסב לו הפסד ממון רב), ורק לאחר מכן מופיע התיאור של השפלתו בידי אמו. בנוסף
לכך התיאור בתלמוד הבבלי של מעשה ההשפלה, כולל מעשים נוספים ואף קיצוניים
יותר של האם, מהמתואר בירושלמי:

> פעם אחת היה לבוש סירקון של זהב והיה יושב בין גדולי רומי ובאתה אמו וקרעתו ממנו,

---

[ח] ירושלמי, קידושין, א:ז; פאה א:א.

[ט] פירוש פני משה ר' משה מרגלית, ירושלמי, שם.

[י] פירוש קורבן העדה ר' דוד פרנקל, ירושלמי, שם.

[יא] קידושין לא ע"א.

התקשה מאוד למצוא את המקור התלמודי להלכה שכתב, שקיימת בעייתיות בשיטת כתיבתו:

> וכן תמיד אני בצער מזה שיבוא השואל וישאל היכן נאמרו דברים אלו. פעמים אומר לו מיד במקום פלוני ופעמים לא. וחייך לא אזכור מקומן עד שנחפש אחריהן. ועל זה אני מצטער הרבה שאני אומר הרי אני המחבר ויתעלם ממני מקום דבר זה, מה יעשו שאר בני אדם?[ה]

מי שביטא בצורה חריפה את התנגדותו לשיטת הכתיבה של הרמב"ם במשנה תורה היה הראב"ד, ר' אברהם בן דוד שחי בצרפת במאה ה-12 וכתב השגות להלכות שונות שפוסק הרמב"ם בחיבורו. כתגובה להסברו של הרמב"ם שהחליט לקרוא לחבורו: משנה תורה, משום שיהודי יכול לקרוא את התורה ולאחר מכן לקרוא את המשנה וכך הוא יידע את התושב"ע כולה ואינו צריך ללמוד שום דבר נוסף, כותב הראב"ד בלשונו החדה:

> א"א סבר לתקן ולא תקן כי הוא עזב דרך כל המחברים אשר היו לפניו, כי הם הביאו ראיה לדבריהם וכתבו הדברים בשם אומרים והיה לנו בזה תועלת גדולה...ועתה לא אדע למה אחזור מקבלתי וראיתי בשביל חיבורו של זה המחבר, אם החולק עליו גדול ממנו הרי טוב ואם אני גדול ממנו- למה אבטל דעתי מפני דעתו...?[ו]

המתח בין שיטת הרמב"ם בכתיבתו וביקורתו החריפה של הראב"ד על שיטה זו, בא לידי ביטוי בשאלה ההלכתית שהיא נושא מאמר זה: חובותיו של בן במסגרת מצוות "כיבוד הורים," במקרה שדעתו של אחד מהוריו נטרפת עליו.

לרמב"ם דעה הלכתית מסויימת מאוד בעניין זה וכדרכו, אין הוא כותב על מה הוא מבסס אותה, והראב"ד מולו, חולק על מהות ההלכה שפוסק הרמב"ם וקובע: "אין זו הוראה נכונה."[ז]

מתוך הנחה שאין הרמב"ם בודה הלכות מלבו, סמכו נושאי הכלים שלו, את קביעתו ההלכתית בעניין: "מי שנטרפה דעתו של אביו," על תיאור מקרה שמובא בתלמוד הבבלי אודות רב אסי, ושלדעתם עליו התבסס הרמב"ם בקובעו את ההלכה. פוסקים שונים המאוחרים לזמנם של הרמב"ם והראב"ד מביעים דעתם בשאלה דנן, תוך שהם מתייחסים לפסיקתו של הרמב"ם ולהשגת הראב"ד על פסיקה זו.

במאמר זה תיערך סקירה כרונולוגית של הדעות ההלכתיות שקיימות בסוגיא זו מהמאה, ה-12 ועד ימינו, במרכזי ההלכה השונים בעולם. בניתוח דבריו של כל פוסק, ייבדק הקשר בין דעתו ההלכתית בשאלת: חובותיו של בן שנטרפה דעתו של אביו, לפרטים המרכיבים את "עובדא דרב אסי."

מטרת המאמר אינה לקבוע מסמרות להלכה בעניין חובות הבן כלפי הוריו שלקו

[ה] קובץ תשובות הרמב"ם ואגרותיו, א:קמ, ליפסיא, תר"כ.

[ו] השגת הראב"ד בהקדמת הרמב"ם למשנה תורה, ד"ה: "ויודע ממנו."

[ז] השגת הראב"ד על הרמב"ם, הלכות ממרים ו:י, ד"ה: מי שנטרפה דעתו... א"א אין זו..."

"מי שנטרפה דעתו של אביו או של אמו":
חובותיו ההלכתיות של בן כלפי הורה שלקה בנפשו

מלכה פיוטרקובסקי

הקדמה:

במסכת קידושין קיימת משנה המפרטת את ההבדלים בין חובת האיש וחובתה של
האישה בקיום מצוות מסוגים שונים, ביניהם סוג המצוות המכונה: "מצוות האב על
הבן," "וכל מצוות האב על הבן אחד אנשים ואחד נשים חייבין!"[א]
הגמרא בהסבירה את הכתוב במשנה,[ב] מסיקה שמצוות האב על הבן הן אותן המצוות
שחובתו של בן לעשות להוריו, המתחלקות לשני סוגים, על-פי שני הצווים שבתורה:
א. "כבד את אביך ואת אמך" (שמות כ:יב) **כיבוד הורים** משמע:
דאגה פיזית לכל צרכיהם של ההורים, כגון: אוכל, שתיה, לבוש, וכדומה.
ב. "איש אמו ואביו תיראו" (ויקרא יט:ג) **מורא הורים** משמע:
נתינת יחס של כבוד, והאיסור לזלזל בכבודו של ההורה. כגון: האיסור לשבת במקומו
של האב, או ההוראה שלא לסתור את דבריו. בחובות אלו-קובעת המשנה, חייבים
גברים ונשים כאחד.

במסגרת עיון מעמיק ומרחיב של האמוראים בעניין חובות הבן להוריו, מובאים
בגמרא סיפורי מופת המתארים את דרכם של חכמים ידועים בקיום מצווה מורכבת
זו. מטרת הסיפורים בגמרא היא, ככל הנראה, להמחיש ללומד כיצד ראוי ורצוי
לקיים את מצוות "כיבוד ומורא הורים" על כל גודלה, חשיבותה והיקפה הרחב, גם
כשלעיתים קשה לקיים מצווה זו.

הרמב"ם בחיבורו ההלכתי משנה תורה מתמצת בהלכות ממרים[ג] את כל אותן
ההלכות שקשורות במצוות כיבוד הורים, כפי שנלמדו בגמרא.[ד] כדרכו מתבסס
הרמב"ם בקביעותיו ההלכתיות על הכתוב בתלמוד, אך בהתאם למטרתו לכתוב
חיבור הלכתי מקיף, ממצה ולא מסובך להבנה כך שכל יהודי פשוט, יוכל לעיין בו
ולמצוא בקלות כיצד עליו לנהוג במצב זה או אחר אין הוא מפרט את המקור
התלמודי המסוים לכל הלכה והלכה שהוא פוסק.

מבקרים רבים קמו למשנה תורה, בגלל חוסר הקשר הנראה לעין בין ההלכה
למקורה, ואפילו הרמב"ם עצמו, מעיד, בעקבות מקרה שקרה לו, שהוא עצמו

[א] משנה, קידושין א:ז.

[ב] קידושין כט ע"א.

[ג] רמב"ם, הלכות ממרים ה:ו.

[ד] קידושין ל ע"ב—לג ע"ב.

האם לא ידע צוריאל על תיקוני הנוסח שנעשו על ידי המדפיסים מפני חשש הצנזורה? נדמה לי שקשה להניח הנחה כזו. הלוא הוא עצמו מזכיר את דברי ר' יו"ט ליפמאן, בעל דברי חמודות העומד על כך בפרושו?! דומה שצוריאל בחר במכוון שלא להזכיר את עניין תיקון הנוסח כדי שיוכל להסתמך "בתמימות" על הרא"ש והגר"א ולהוביל את המהלך ההלכתי בו היה מעוניין.

ישראל/ית" פוטר אותנו בדרך לגיטימית מהקשיים החינוכיים, הדתיים והמצפוניים
המלווים את הנוסח הקיים. נמצאנו מסתמכים על נוסח קדום, ובכך אף פטרנו את
אי-הנוחות המלווה את ברכת "שעשני כרצונו" שיש לאומרה לפי חלק מן הפוסקים
בלא שם ומלכות.[יז]

המהלך שהצענו מהווה דוגמא לאימוץ גירסא שנדחתה במהלך הדורות (כנראה
בגלל שראו בה גרסה ששובשה מטעמי צנזורה), אשר משתלבת יפה עם מגמות
שוויוניות של סוף המאה העשרים. האם פסיקת הגר"א מקורה בתקוני הצנזור שחלו
בגרסאות הרא"ש והטור שהיו בידו או שפסיקתו משקפת תפיסה עקרונית שונה זאת
לא נוכל לקבוע. אולם המצאותה של גרסת "שעשני ישראל" בתלמוד במנחות,
ברא"ש, בהגהות הרמ"א ולבסוף בדברי הברורים של הגאון מוילנא, גם אם בחלק מן
המקורות הללו היא עבודת הצנזור, מועילה לנו עד מאוד בחפשנו אחר יֵאִילֹן להתלות
בו' כדי שנוכל להמשיך ולומר בלב שלם מה שפינו אומר.

דוגמא מרתקת למהלך מסוג זה מצוי בהצעתו של צוריאל אדמנית[יח] המציע לומר
"שעשני ישראל" וכך הוא כותב:

> אין זה אמנם בדיוק לפי מה שנאמר בגמרא (מנחות מג ע"ב) שחייב אדם לומר שלוש
> ברכות. אך אם נקבל את הניסוח החיובי המצוי ברא"ש (סוף מסכת ברכות), נתקל בקושי
> שהברכה הראשונה בניסוח חיובי (שעשני ישראל) כבר כוללת את תוכן האחרות, כפי מעיר
> כבר בעל לחם חמודות [כוונתו כנראה לדברי חמודות] במקום. אך סטיה זאת היא קטנה
> לערך, מאחר שיש לנו אילן גדול כהגהות הרא"ש להתלות בו. וכן בהגהות הגר"א, או"ח,
> מו:ד.

הסידורים של היהדות הקונסרבטיבית. ברכות אלו למרות ערכן החינוכי (כמו הדגשת היסוד
האוניברסלי כבסיס ליסוד הלאומי) בעייתיות, וזאת בשל העובדה כי ברכת "שעשני ישראל/ית"
כוללת במשמעה, כפי שכבר צויין, גם את הברכות הנ"ל ומן הראוי שלא להוסיף בקלות יתרה
ברכות העלולות להיחשב כברכות לבטלה. ראו הרב שמחה רוט (עורך), סדור ואני תפילתי
(ירושלים: כנסת הרבנים בישראל והתנועה המסורתית, תשנ"ח) 17–בו מופיע נוסח "שעשני
ישראל" בלבד, ועמ' 587, בו מופיעה ההצעה לשלושת הברכות שהזכרתי, לעיל.

יז ראו הרב עובדיה יוסף, לעיל.

יח ראו הערה לב, לעיל.

מעידה על כך שבמשך כל הדורות היו שנטו לומר ברכה זו בנוסחתה החיובית שאם לא כן, קשה להבין את ההזהרות החוזרות ונשנות של הפוסקים הנזכרים מפני אמירת הנוסח "שעשני ישראל."

הצעה אחרונה זו ניצבת בניגוד לנוסח המסורתי הבנוי על שלילת האחר.[נב] הגדרת זהותו של האדם לא נעשית רק על ידי עמידתי כנגד הזר והשונה. ייחודו של אדם נבנה מתוך הגדרתו את עצמו, גם כשאינו עומד אל מול השונה. ואמנם נוסח דומה בא לידי ביטוי בברכת "אשר בחר בנו מכל העמים" המופיעה מיד לאחר ברכות השחר בהן אנו דנים. נדמה לי, כי דווקא הנוסח החיובי מתאים יותר לאופיין של ברכות השחר הנאמרות בכל יום על ידי היהודי המתעורר לעבודת יומו, ואין הן תלויות בראיית הגוי, העבד או האשה.[נג] בניגוד לברכות השחר האחרות אין ברכותינו תלויות במעשה ("מלביש ערומים," "זוקף כפופים") או בראיה ושמיעה ("כי שמע קול תרנגולא...").[נד]

יתרון נוסף של נוסח ברכה זה, חבוי בסיומת השונה לגברים ונשים: גבר מברך "שעשני ישראל," ואשה מברכת "שעשני ישראלית," כך אנו יכולים לשמר, בתוך העולם ההלכתי אורתודוקסי, משהו מרוחה של הצעה ג' ("שעשני אשה"), אשר לא מצאנו לה סימוכין במקורות פסיקה רבניים.

לסיכום, אני חושבת כי הגיעה השעה לאמץ את הנוסח המוצע בהצעה ד',[נה] ולפועל להחזירתו לקהילות התפילה השונות, או למצער לקהילות בהם נוצר זה מכבר נתק בין ה"אני מאמין" של אנשי הקהילה לבין נוסח ברכת השחר: "שלא עשני אשה" "שעשני כרצונו," אותו הם מחוייבים לומר מידי בוקר בבוקרו. יתרונותיה של גירסה זו עולים להערכתי לעין ערוך על חולשתה (הפחתת מספר הברכות).[נו] נוסח "שעשני

[נב] ראו ההסבר המוצע בב"ח, לעיל, ובמגן אברהם לנוסח הברכות השליליות וראו עוד בעניין העדפת הנוסח השלילי, אנצ. תלמודית ד:שעא-שעב.

[נג] דעה יוצאת דופן מציג ר' אברהם בן הרמב"ם. דבריו נמסרו על ידי ר' מסעוד חי רקח, מעשה רקח על הרמב"ם, ויניציאה 1742, א, עמודה ד. דיון בשיטתו היחידאית של אברהם בן הרמב"ם הטוען שגם תלויות אלו ברכות בראיה - מופיע בהרחבה תוך השוואה לכתבי-יד נדירים אצל וידר תשל"ט, עמ' 199-202, והערה 11 שם. ראו גם ברלינר המצטט את דברי אברהם בן הרמב"ם, ורואה בהם חיזוק לשיטתו, יעקובסון תשל"ז, עמ' 165.

[נד] ראו ברכות ס ע"ב. עלינו לציין כמובן כי כיום ברכות השחר נאמרות כחלק מתפילת הציבור בבית הכנסת, וממילא אין הברכות צמודות למעשה ההשכמה הטבעי. ראו את דברי הרמב"ם, הלכות תפילה ז:ו-ט.

[נה] הצעה דומה לשלי, מציע גם חגי בן-ארצי, הקורא לאימוץ הנוסח החיובי "שעשני ישראל/ית." אלא שבן-ארצי מתעלם לחלוטין מהחשש כי הנוסח המצוי במנחות הוא תוצאה של עבודת הצנזור, ואף אינו מתייחס לספק בגרסת **ר' מאיר** במנחות, אשר אולי היה צריך להיות **ר' יהודה**. הוא מתאר שתי תפיסות עקרוניות העומדות זו מול זו, שיטת ר' יהודה, ושיטת ר' מאיר. ראו חגי בן-ארצי, "ברכת 'שלא עשני אשה' האם יש אלטרנטיבה?" אקדמות, כתב-עת של לומדי בית מורשה, שבט תשנ"ח, עמ' 129-130.

[נו] קיימות היום הצעות נוספות לטיפול בברכות אלו, המבקשות לשמר את שלוש ברכות בלשון חיובית. למשל, "שעשני בצלמו," "שעשני בן-חורין," "שעשני ישראל," המופיעות בחלק מן

ברכות השחר ד).

אמנם פרשני הרא"ש, עליו מסתמך בין השאר הגר"א, מעירים כי נוסחו: "שעשני ישראל" מקורו "ממדפיסים שהגיהו,"[מט] אבל הגר"א שהכיר את שני הנוסחים, כפי שהוא כותב במפורש, בודאי הכיר את עבודת הצנזורה, ובכל זאת העדיף את הנוסח החיובי "שעשני ישראל," למרות שכנראה רוב הסידורים שהיו בידיו ורוב הפסיקות שהכיר בעניין העדיפו את הנוסח השלילי. בסידור הגר"א אנו מוצאים את ברכת "שלא עשני..." אך נפתלי הירץ הלוי שליקט את המסורות השונות המתייחסות לנוסח תפילתו של הגר"א מעיר: "משמע דגירסתו שעשני ישראל" (ב ע"א, הערה 3).[נ] מסתבר כי הגאון מוילנא העדיף אפוא, את הנוסח החיובי, למרות שהכיר היטב את הנוסח השלילי המקובל. סיבת הכרעתו אינה מפורשת, ואנו נוכל להסתמך על הכרעתו אם ברצוננו לשנות את נוסח הברכה הבעייתית "שלא עשני אשה."

ד. חיזוק מכיוון אחר לתוקפה של הגירסה החיובית, נמצא דווקא בדברי המתנגדים לנוסח זה ומזהירים כי מי שנכשל ואמר בטעות "שעשני ישראל" הרי אינו יכול לומר את הברכות: "שלא עשני גוי," "שלא עשני עבד," ו"שלא עשני אשה." ברכות אלו נעשות למיותרות. פוסקים רבים מזהירים מפני נוסח "שעשני ישראל" שיש בו כדי להפחית את מספר ברכות השחר,[נא] וכך כותב למשל הב"ח, ר' יואל סירקיס, במאה ה-17:

> יש המקשין אמאי לא תקנו לברך שעשאני ישראל ככל שאר הברכות שניתקנו על החסד שעשה בפועל, שנתן לב לב בינה, מלביש ערומים פוקח עורים וכן כולם. ומפרשים ע"ד מאמר רז"ל ינוח לו לאדם שלא נברא משנברא' וכו'... כלומר מי יתן שלא עשאני ועכשיו שעשאני אברך את ה'... **ונאה הוא לדרשא אבל אין כאן קושיה. דאם היה מברך שעשאני ישראל שוב לא היה יכול לברך שעשאני בן-חורין ושעשאני ישראל, ...ולא אשה דאשה נקראת ישראלית... ואם כן לא היה מברך ג'ברכות אלא ברכה אחת,** ואין זה כוונתינו לקצר אלא להאריך בהודאות ולברך על כל חסד וחסד ברכה בפני עצמה (ב"ח, טור או"ח, הלכות ברכות השחר מו).

התנגדות נחרצת זו מוכיחה על רציונותה ותקפותה של האלטרנטיבה, ואולי אף

[מט] ראו הערת יו"ט ליפמאן על הרא"ש והערת סידור הגאונים והמקובלים על הגר"א, הערה ג, לעיל.

[נ] סידור הגר"א, בתוספת פרשנות והערות על ידי נפתלי הירץ הלוי, ירושלים, תשל"ב. ראו גם חלק ג, "זה השולחן," עא, הערה שם.

[נא] לדעה זו מצטרפים המגן אברהם, ר' יו"ט ליפמאן על הרא"ש, המשנה ברורה שם, ס"ק טו, ועוד רבים מתנגדים לנוסח "שעשני ישראל" מתוך חשש שכך יתבטלו שתי ברכות ונמצאנו עוברים על דברי הברייתא, ואף מחסירים מאה ברכות ביום. וראו הטור המדגיש את החובה לשמר את מאה הברכות שחייב אדם לומרבכל יום: "תיקנו חכמים ז"ל אלו הברכות על סדר העולם והנהגתו להשלים ק ברכות בכל יום ודרך כל אדם ליזהר בהם והפוחת אל יפחות והמוסיף אל יוסיף על כל ברכה וברכה שנתקנה..." (טור או"ח, הלכות ברכות השחר מו :טז).

כאמור להצעה זו מספר סימוכין במקורותינו:

א. כפי שכבר ראינו, נוסח התלמוד במנחות משמר גרסא חיובית זו, וכן הרא"ש למסכת ברכות פרק ט (אשכנז-ספרד, 1250 – 1327 בקירוב). אכן, כנראה מקורה של גירסה זו בתיקון המדפיסים מחשש הצנזורה,[מה] אך עצם המצאותו של נוסח זה במקורותינו (גם אם "שלא לשמו") יכול להיות "קרש קפיצה" נוח למעניינים באסמכתה טקסטואלית "כשרה."

ב. יתכן והרמ"א, ר' משה איסרליש (מאה-16, קראקוב) קיבל אף הוא את גירסת "שעשני ישראל": בדפוסי השו"ע הרגילים (מו:ד) מופיעה הברכה בנוסח "שלא עשני גוי." אולם לאחר הברכה השלישית ("שלא עשני אשה") מופיעה הגהת הרמ"א האומרת: "ואפילו גר יכול לברך כך, אבל לא יאמר שלא עשני עכו"ם שהרי היה עכו"ם בתחילה."

הגהת הרמ"א אינה ברורה: כיצד יש להבין את דבריו שגר "יכול לברך **כך**"? הרי אינו יכול לומר "שלא עשני גוי"? וגם המשכה של ההגהה "**אבל** יאמר שלא עשני עכו"ם" אינו ברור, מדוע מנסח הרמ"א את הגהתו בלשון "אבל," הרי זה הנוסח ששיגרתי לפי השו"ע? אלא שכנראה לפני הרמ"א עמד נוסח **אחר** של השו"ע.[מו] מהדיר שו"ע השלם (הערה לג) עומד על כך שבדפוס מנטובה רפי"ז שינו את נוסח השו"ע מ"שלא עשני גוי" ל"שעשני ישראל." כנראה זוהי הגירסה שהיתה לפני הרמ"א ואם כך הערתו ברורה. גר יכול לומר "שעשני ישראל" אך לא יכול לומר "שלא עשני גוי." בדפוסים מאוחרים יותר הדפיסו כנראה את הנוסח הראשוני של השו"ע ומכאן נובע הבלבול.[מז] במידה והניתוח מדוייק,[מח] מסתבר שהרמ"א קיבל את נוסח "שעשני ישראל" שהרי לא השיג עליו ואף ראה בו נוסח המתאים גם לגר.

ג. עדות מעניינת אחרת התומכת בנוסח "שעשני ישראל" אנו מוצאים בדברי הגאון מוילנא. בהערותיו לשולחן ערוך הוא כותב:

שלא עשני גוי כן הוא ברי"ף ורמב"ם וכן הוא בתוספתא סוף ברכות וירושלמי שם. אבל גירסת ספרים שלנו **שעשני ישראל** וכן הוא ברא"ש וטור (ביאור הגר"א, א"ח, מו, הלכות

[מה] לעיל, הערה ג.

[מו] הסבר מאיר עיניים זה להגהת הרמ"א התמוהה על השולחן ערוך, מצוי במאמרו של ישי רוזן-צבי, מכון הרטמן, אשר יראה אור בקרוב. רוזן-צבי מביא את דברי המהדיר בשו"ע השלם, וחושף את הגרסא שעמדה, כנראה, לפני הרמ"א, ואני מודה לו על שהאיר עיני בעניין.

[מז] אולי זו גם הסיבה להזזת הערה זו לסוף הקטע, מכיוון שהערת הרמ"א לא הובנה עתה לאחר שחיברו בין שתי הנוסחאות הראשוניות של השו"ע ושל הרמ"א.

[מח] עוד בעניין זה ראו דברי ר' יוסף קשמן, בספרו נהג כצאן יוסף, תע"ח הענא (1718) התוקף גרסא זו בחריפות ואומר: "וההגהה שכתב הרמ"א לומר 'שעשני יהודי' הוא בדותא היא ועיין בדרכי משה..." ואמנם בדברי הרמ"א על הטור בחיבורו דרכי משה נאמר שגר יכול לברך "שעשני גר" ולפי זה כנראה פירש ר' יוסף קשמן את דברי הרמ"א בשו"ע: "ואפילו גר יכול לברך כך" אפילו גר יכול לברך "שעשני גר." עם זאת, לפי הסבר זה עדיין קשה הביטוי "ואפילו" המופיע אצל הרמ"א. (תודה לי. אחיטוב והרב ד. אסולין על הפניות חשובות אלו).

בהתאם לנוסח ברכות השחר המופיעות אצל יהודי איטליה,[מ] הגורסים "שעשיתני
איש ולא אשה," "מל ולא ערל" וכד' כותב ר' אברהם פריצול בסידור המיועד לאשה
"שעשיתני אשה ולא איש."

נוסח זה המנוסח על דרך החיוב ומדגיש את ההודיה האקטיבית ולא את הכניעה
הפסיבית הנרמזת בנוסח "שעשני כרצונו" הנזכר על ידי הטור ואבודרהם (כמאה שנה
מוקדם יותר), נראה בעיני הולם את תודעתן של נשים רבות בימינו. דא-עקא שהנוסח
הנ"ל ("שעשני אשה") מופיע בסידורי נשים בודדים בלבד ועד כמה שידיעתי מגעת אין
פסקי הלכה התומכים או מזכירים ברכה זו כגירסה נשית מוכרת. יתכן ויבוא יום
ונגלה סידורים נוספים התומכים בנוסח חיובי זה, אך כיום אין בידינו אלא דוגמאות
בודדות וחסרים אנו פסקי הלכה להתלות בהם בכדי לאמץ נוסח זה.

הצעה רביעית: החלפת נוסח הברכה השלילית בנוסח ברכה חיובית. נשים
תברכנה "שעשני ישראלית" וגברים יברכו "שעשני ישראל." יתרונה ההלכתי של
הצעה זו טמון בעובדה שיש בידינו מקורות הלכתיים מוקדמים ביותר התומכים
בנוסח זה (גם אם מקורו בפעולת הצנזורה): נוסח התלמוד, הרא"ש, ומאוחר יותר
גרסת הרמ"א והגר"א. חסרונה של ההצעה מצוי ב"הפסדן" של שתי ברכות, ובביטול
דברי התלמוד והתוספתא המצביעים על שלוש ברכות חייב אותן אדם לומר כל יום.[מד]
מבחינה חינוכית, יש בהצעה זו יתרון נוסף; אנו מודים על מה שהננו מבלי לפסול
את הזולת השונה, האחר, כדברי ברלינר:

> יש להמליץ בכל לשון של המלצה להנהיג בכל הסידורים את הנוסח "שעשני ישראל", כפי
> שהוא כבר נדפס בסידורים דפוס מנטובה שי"ח (1558), טינהינגן ש"כ (1560), פראג שכ"ו
> (1566), ...הגאון מווילנא ...והרב יעקב צבי מקלנבורג כולם דורשים בכל לשון של דרישה
> לקבל נוסח זה. הנוסח המוצע, המודה להשגחה האלוהית, על ששם חלקי בין בני ישראל,
> שנבחרו למלא תפקיד נעלה בעולם נוסח זה מביע הרבה יותר מאשר נוסח המקור בצורתו
> השלילית... אם הנוסח המוצע בזה יתקבל בכל תפוצות ישראל הרי בטלות מאליהן שתי
> הברכות האחרות: 'שלא עשני אשה' ו'שלא עשני עבד'; וכך פטורים אנו מלהשתדל
> להצדיק באיזה אופן שהוא שתי ברכות אלה. כן אין מקום למטבעות ברכה מאוחרים:
> 'שלא עשני גויה', ו'שעשני כרצונו'...

שבאוניברסיטה העברית. תודה לשלמה צוקר עובד המכון שהפגיש אותי עם כתב היד והרחיב
ידיעותי בנושא. (Heb. Ms. 8°5492 עשוי קלף, גודל מקורי 7X10 סמ', 362 דף, כתיבה איטלקית
מרובעת ורבנית, מעוטר בזהב ושלל צבעים.) הוכחה נוספת לכך שהסידור נכתב לצרכיה של אשה
שכנראה התפללה, כנשים רבות אחרות, בעיקר בביתה מצויה בעובדה המעניינת כי בסידור המקורי
נעדר נוסח הקדיש ורק הבעלים המאוחרים של הסידור הוסיף בכתב-יד את נוסח הקדיש.

[מג] ראו וידר תשל"ט עמ' 12–208.

[מד] ראו לנושא זה וידר, שם, עמ' 199, הערה 1. על המגמה לשמור על שלוש ברכות ולא לוותר על
על מספרן, ראו גם רש"י שצטטנו לעיל, מנחות מג ע"ב, ד"ה : "אלא מאי." וראו טור, או"ח הלכות
ברכות השחר מו:טז, ולהלן הערה נא.

בית-הכנסת הוא הפיך, ולכן נראה לי שצודק וידר המעיר כי מכיוון שברכות אלו הפכו במשך הזמן לחלק מתפילת הציבור, הרי שפרשוה המעשי של פסיקת ר' אהרן ווירמש, הוא ביטולה של הברכה. גם אם כוונת ר' אהרן ווירמש היתה להורות כי ברכה זו תאמר בלחש על ידי כל יחיד ולא על ידי החזן, סביר להניח כי תקנה מסוג זה היתה מביאה אט אט לשכחת הברכה.

דרך זו לדחיית הברכה על ידי אמירתה בלחש, לא התקבלה בקהילות ישראל ולא מצאתי עדויות נוספות למגמה זו. ההצעה להוציא את הברכה הנידונה מתפילת החזן, ואולי בעקיפין מן הסידור כליל, יש בה קשיים הלכתיים גדולים: בשל מקורותיה התלמודיים של ברכת "שלא עשני אשה" ובשל ניסוחו של רבי יהודה בלשון "**חייב** אדם לברך..." סילוק ברכה זו מסידורו של בעל-התפילה, ללא הצעת אלטרנטיבה הלכתית, תהווה פגיעה בברכות השחר המסגרת ההלכתית לפתיחת יומם של יהודים שומרי מצוות מזה דורות. העברת הברכה מסטטוס של ברכה הנאמרת ברבים, בקול רם, לברכת יחיד הנלחשת באופן אישי אינה אופציה הלכתית מכובדת.

הצעה שלישית: גברים יאמרו "שעשני גבר (ולא עשני אשה)" ואילו נשים תברכנה "שעשני אשה (ולא עשני גבר)." יתרונותיה החינוכיים של ההצעה ברורים: הצעה זו יוצאת מנקודת הנחה כי גברים ונשים מזדהים לרוב עם מאפייני מינם הביולוגים והמנטליים. הילד או הילדה הלומדים לברך ולהודות לאל על על בריאתם כגבר או אשה מפתחים את זהותם וייחודם המיני.

לפיכך, לברכה זו יתרון חינוכי חשוב במיוחד בדורנו, בו הבלבול בין המינים גובר בתרבויות מערביות שונות. בעיית הזהות המינית של צעירים הופכת לאחד הנושאים המרכזיים בחברה המודרנית המבלבלת לא פעם בין שוויון המינים לבין זהות המינים. זאת ועוד, הצעה זו אינה משקפת יחס היררכי בין גברים לנשים, אלא היא מגלמת תפיסה שוויונית המכירה בשונות שבין המינים.

ברכה זו מצויה, בשני נוסחים (לפחות) של סידורים עתיקים. האחד, בן המאה ה-14 או ה-15 מפרובנס והשני, בן המאה ה-15 מאיטליה:

הסידור מפרובנס הינו סידור אשה כתוב בניב יהודי-צרפתי באותיות עבריות. על כריכת הסידור נכתבה הכתבה ההקדשה: "אחותי את היי לאלפי רבבה" (הפסוק מבראשית כד:ס שונה ללשון יחיד). שלושת ברכות השחר המופיעות בסידור הן בלשון נקבה: "שלא עשני גויה," "שלא עשני שפחה," והברכה האחרונה מגלה אקטיביות מפתיעה "שעשני אשה" ("קי פיס מי פנה").[מא]

הסידור השני נכתב גם הוא לכבודה של אשה על ידי ר' אברהם פריצול באיטליה. "סידור שלם מכל השנה" כפי מנהג איטליאני, בפתיחת הסידור כתוב: "אני ר' אברהם פריצול מאבניו כתבתי סידור השלם אל הכבודה בנשים רבת התהלה מרת [שם האשה נמחק]..." (מנטובה, ר"מ—1480).[מב]

[מא] ראו תבורי 1998, המפנה למחקרו של:

G. Jochonwitz "...Who Made Me a Woman," *Commentary* 71.4 (1981) 63–64.

[מב] אני מודה לחנה לחנ ספראי שחשפה בפני לראשונה את מציאותו של הסידור זה במכון לכתבי יד

תפיסותינו החברתיות מתבקשת שוב בחינתה של הברכה הנידונה.

‏2.3. הצעות חליפיות:

בחלקו האחרון של המאמר ברצוני להציע מספר הצעות חליפיות לנוסח המוכר. אסדר את ההצעות "מן הכבד אל הקל," מן ההצעה הנועזת מבחינה הלכתית, (זו אשר חסרה תקדימים ממקורות הלכתיים) ועד להצעה ה"שמרנית" ביותר.

הצעה ראשונה: גם גברים וגם נשים יברכו "שעשני כרצונו." להצעה זו לא מצאתי סימוכין בכתובים, ובודאי שהיא רחוקה ביותר מהוראת ר' יהודה בתלמוד ובתוספתא. יתרונה של הצעה זו במשקלה החינוכי והפסיכולוגי. ברכה זו מבטאת את הרעיון כי גברים ונשים שמחים לרוב במינם. אין ספק כי ברכה זו, "שעשני כרצונו" יפה לשני המינים. אלא, שהנימה הכנועה שנלוותה לברכה זו מאות בשנים (אבודרהם, לעיל), העובדה כי היתה זו ברכה נשית מובהקת, העדרם של מקורות קדומים; תלמודיים או מימי הגאונים התומכים בנוסח זה (הרב עובדיה יוסף, לעיל) ולבסוף, חסרונם של פסקי הלכה המקבלים הצעה זו כל אלו מובילים לדחייתה של ההצעה.

הצעה שניה: יש המציעים שלא לומר ברכות אלו ("שלא עשני אשה" או "שעשני כרצונו") בציבור כלל. עדות מעניינת מביא וידר המונה שלושה כתבי יד בהם נשמטה ברכת "שלא עשני אשה" או תיבת "אשה,"[לח] והוא מוסיף ומעיר: "מכיוון שאין להניח שטעות נפלה בשלושה מקומות גם יחד, על כרחך אתה אומר שהשמטה מכוונת לפנינו. ונשאלת השאלה: השמטה זו טעמה מהו?" אמנם מעיד וידר כי לא מצא מי שנקט עמדה שלילית מפורשת נגד ברכת זו, במילים מפורשות, עד למאות האחרונות, אך יתכן כי "ביקשו המשמיטים למנוע עלבונה של האשה, שנחיתותה באה לידי ביטוי בברכה זו" (שם).

ערעור מפורש על אמירת הברכה "שלא עשני אשה" אנו מוצאים מהמאה ה-18 ואילך. בפסק הלכה מעניין של ר' אהרן וורמש (וורמס), ראש ישיבת מיץ משנת 1785‏-1836:[לט] "אכן נר' ש[אין] אומרים **ברבים** הברכות של"ע גוי שיש לחוש משום איבה וגם של"ע אשה היאך מלבין פניהן ברבים?"[מ]

הצעה זו שיש בה כביכול רק ביטול הברכות בציבור ואמירתן באופן אישי, בלחש, היא כמובן בעייתית מאד. קשה להניח שהמסלול שעברו ברכות השחר מן הבית אל

היוונים מהיהודים), ולבסוף הערותיו המעניינות על זיקתו הייחודית של ר' יהודה לתרבות היוונית.

[לח] וידר תשל"ט, עמ' 213‏-214, הערה 70.

[לט] על ר' אהרן וורמש, פעילותו בסנהדרין של נפוליאון ועוד פרטים מעניינים על חייו ראו משה קטן, "הרב אהרן וורמש ותלמידו אליקים כרמולי," נפתלי בן-מנחם ויצחק רפאל, עורכים, ארשת, כרך ב (ירושלים: מוסד הרב קוק, תשי"ד) 98‏—190.

[מ] באר שב"ע, שבת ברכות ערובין, 1818, כ ע"א. מצוטט אצל וידר, שם.

כתוב בתפילה ”ברוך שעשני כרצונו” לעומת ”ברוך שלא עשני אשה”? תכוון האישה
למחשבה: ”בסדר, הקב”ה. הגברים חיברו נוסח זה משום שהם באמת חשבו את עצמם
זכאים יותר מהאישה, וזהו ודאי הטעם ההיסטורי לנוסח ברכה זו. אבל אני ואתה הרי
שותפים לסוד הטעם האמיתי: שאת הגבר נאלצת לברוא כמות שהוא, על חולשותיו
הגבריות, כולל הצורך בטיפוח אשליית העליונות, אבל אותי בראת כרצונך ברייה מאושרת
עם עצמה כמות שהיא.”[לג]

קשה לי לקבל דרך מתחכמת זו. ייתכן ויש מי שייציקת תוכן חדש לתבנית הברכה
הישנה מספקת אותו/ה, אך, לדעתי, כל עוד נשארת על תילה ברכת ”שלא עשני
אשה,” קשה להעניק לברכת ”שעשני כרצונו” פרשנות מן הסוג שתמר רוס מציעה לנו
לאמץ.[לד] כפי שאראה בהמשך, נדמה לי כי ישנה דרך הלכתית־לגיטימית לאימוץ נוסח
ברכה אחר, הפוטר אותנו מפרשנות כזו. דווקא קריאתה של רוס, במאמר הנזכר,
לפעולת שינוי זהירה בתוככי המערכת ההלכתית מהווה תמיכה בהצעה שאפרט
להלן.[לה]

ב. הנימוק החינוכי־חברתי: גם אם נניח כי רשימת ”שלא עשני” הכוללת גוי, בור
או עבד ואשה אינה משקפת משהו ממעמדה הנחות של האשה בתקופת חז”ל, וכי כל
מטרת הברכה היא לחנך את הגבר להודות על זכייתו הגדולה בתרי”ג מצוות ללא כל
פטור ממצוות שהזמן גרמן ואחרות הרי שנותרת השאלה הסוציולוגית־חינוכית:
האם ניתן לחנך ילדים ונערים לייחס של כבוד לאשה, לתפיסה המכירה בשונותם של
המינים אך גם בערכם השווה, כאשר נוסח זה הוא מנת חלקו של כל גבר? בעוד הילד
הצעיר מתפלל בכל יום, מגיל הגן או בי”ס היסודי, ”שלא עשני אשה” מתחנכת הילדה
הקטנה ”לקבל את גזר דינה” בכנעניות והשלמה ”שעשני כרצונו.” (ברכה זו, כמובן,
לא היתה מעוררת תחושה של כניעה והשלמה אילולא היה מולה הנוסח הגברי ”שלא
עשני אשה”) האם ניתן לחנך באמת לשוויון בין המינים בעוד אנו משננים נוסח ברכות
עתיק זה, אשר נכתב בתקופה אחרת, ובעולם בו ”אדם” פרושו גבר?

עוד יש לטעון, כי דווקא הקירבה הקיימת בין ברכותינו לברכות היוונים
הקדמונים, כדברי גינצבורג: ”היוונים מזכירים ג’ ברכות שהיה אפלטון (או לפי גרסא
אחרת: סוקרטיס) נוהג לברכן והן: ש נ ו צ ר א ד ם ו ל א ב ה מ ה, א י ש ו ל א א ש ה, י ו ן
ו ל א ב ר ב ר י.”[לו] יש בה כדי להדגיש את השפעותיה של תרבות הסטורית תלויית
הזמן והמקום על מטבע ברכות שטבעו חז”ל.[לז] על כן עם שינוי הזמנים ושינוי

[לג] תמר רוס, ”מעמדה של האשה ביהדות כמה השגות על תפיסתו של ליבוביץ לגבי מנגנון התיאום
בין הלכה ומציאות,” בתוך אבי שגיא, עורך, **ישעיהו ליבוביץ עולמו והגותו**, ירושלים: כתר, 1995,
עמ’ 156.

[לד] וראו ביקורתי על פרשנויות אפולוגטיות דומות, לעיל, סוף פרק ב.

[לה] ראו להלן הצעה רביעית. ודברי ת. רוס, שם, עמ’ 157.

[לו] ראו גינצבורג, חלק ג, עמ’ 229, וראו הערה טז לעיל.

[לז] ראו תבורי 1998, המשווה בין הנוסחים השונים של נוסח תפלתינו ונוסח תפילת אפלטון כפי
שהוא מופיע אצל פלוטרד, וכן ראו דיונו הנרחב בשאלה מי הושפע ממי (היהודים מהיוונים או

שלא עשאﬧ גוי או עבד (או בור לפי חלק מהנוסחים), כך הוא גם משבח אותו על שלא
עשאו אשה, וקשה מאד בעיני הוצאת ברכה מהקשרה והפיכתה לתאור שבחי
האשה.

ג. הצעת נוסח חליפי: "שעשני ישראלי/ישראלית"? שעשני אשה?
ג.1. מדוע יש צורך להחליף את נוסח הברכה "שלא עשני אשה" לגברים ו"שעשני כרצונו" לנשים?

א. כנות וﬧושר אישי: נדמה לי כי רוב המתפללים יסכימו להנחה כי אסור להן
לתפילות או לברכות שתתפוכנה להיות מס שפתיים שאﬧש לא מאמין בו. יש בברכה זו
סכנה חינוכית גדולה הפוגעת בכנות ובתפילת אמת. אם אחת ממטרותינו בחינוך
הדתי היא לחזק את הﬧחס הרציני למילים היוצאות מפינו, ובודאי בשעת תפילה -
כיצד זה נלמד את בנינו ובנותינו לומר ברכה שאﬧנה משקפת את תפיסתינו? האם אנו
הנשים מרגישות "כמודות על הרעה"?! או "כמצדיקות את הדין עלינו"?! האם אנו
חיﬧם בעולם בו שמחים הורים על הולדת בן יותר מאשר להולדת בת? האם רוב
הגברים הנמנים על מה שנהוג לכנות "ציונים-דתיﬧת" או "דתיﬧם-מודרניים" מודים
באמת כל בוקר על ששפר גורלם ונמנע מהם האסון הנורא של "להﬧות אשה"?! האﬧן
אנו עושים שקר בנפשינו בהפטﬧרנו כאשתקד, מבלי להתﬧﬧחס למהפכה העצומה
שהתחוללה בעשרות השנים האחרונות[לא] בתפיסת האשה ותפיסת הﬧחסים בין
המינים? מן הראוי לצטט כאן את דבריו הנוקבים של צוריאל אדמנית: "ברכת 'שלא
עשני אשה' בחברה שלנו נעמוד לפני הברירה: או שנאמר אותה **בסילוף תוכנה** או
שלא נאמר אותה כלל. אני מעדﬧף את הדרך השניה."[לב]

אמנם, יש המציעים לפטור את הקשﬧם שמעלה נוסח הברכה "שעשני כרצונו" על
ידי העני קת פרשנות חדשה למילים העתﬧקות. כך תשתנה משמעות הברכה וזאת,
מבלי להכנס לשטח המסוכן' של שﬧנוי מטבע ברכות שנקבעו על ידי חז"ל והשתרשו
בנוסחי הסﬧדורים בתפוצות ישראל. כך למשל כותבת תמר רוס בﬧﬧחס לברכת "שעשני
כרצונו":

[לא] על הפולמוס הסוער הסובב ברכות "שלא עשני אשה," אשר התעורר בעת החדשה עם התעוררות
ההשכלה והביקורת על אורח החﬧים היהודי-מסורתי, ראו למשל, ריב"ל (יצחק בער לוﬧנזאהן),
זרובבל, ורשה, תר"ן (1890) עמ' 70-68. תגובה לדברﬧם אלו ראו הלל צייטלﬧן, אל"ף בﬧﬨ"ﬨ של
יהדות, תרגם וערך רועי ברש, ירושלים: מוסד הרב קוק, תשמ"ג (1983) עמ' 130-123. צייטלﬧן
פותח את מאמרו במﬧלותיו של פושקﬧן "ﬧﬧשנו עם אחד, נבער מדעת, שהגברﬧם שבו מברכﬧם ומודים
לאלוהﬧהם שלא עשה אותם נשﬧם" שם, עמי 123. תודﬨﬧ לﬧהודה נﬧמן חברﬧ לעבודה ב"מרכז
הרצוﬧג" שחשף בפני קצה קצהו של פולמוס מרתק זה.

[לב] צוריאל אדמנית, "מעמד האﬧשה בהלכה ובחברתנו," בתוך הזרם הזרם ונגדו (תל-אביב: הוצאת
מזכﬧרות הקﬧבוץ הדתﬧ, תשל"ז) עמ' 105. (התפרסם לראשונה בעמודﬧם, תשט"ז/ﬧ"ז ובדעות,
תשל"ג.) צוריאל קורא גם הוא לאמץ את הנוסח החﬧובﬧ ולומר "שעשני ישראל," על פﬧ נוסח
הרא"ש, ראה דﬧון להלן, הצעה רביעﬧת.

מאחר ולגברים יש יותר דעת, הם נוטים להיות מותאמים יותר לפרטי העולם החילוני,
החיצוני. על כן הם צריכים תזכורות חיצוניות לחשיבות הזמן המקודש. לנשים יש ריתמוס
ביולוגי פנימי המשיג אותה מטרה. מחזור הוסת הנשי אינו נחשב על ידי היהדות לתאונה
של הטבע. הוא נוצר בכוונת מכוון על ידי האל כדי ללמד אותנו מספר לקחים. ...על כל
פנים, נשים וגברים יהודיים מגיעים לאותה מטרה תוך שימוש בדרכים שונות, המותאמות
באופן השלם ביותר לכל מין (שם, 35.).

איקין מניחה הנחות בדבר כוונת האל, בדבר הטבע הביולוגי-פסיכולוגי של האשה,
ועוד הנחות מסוג זה, אשר כמובן אי אפשר לאשר ואי אפשר לשלול. כמו כן, אין היא
נותנת כלל משקל לסביבה התרבותית-חברתית המשתנה ולהשפעותיה על הנחות כמו,
"לגברים יש יותר דעת," או "האשה פחות נוטה לפיתויים חיצוניים" וכו'. הסברים
אלו, גם אם הם משקפים רגישות למעמדה של האשה, סובלים משני ליקויים:
הראשון, מתגלה, בהנחות המטאפיזיות על מהות האשה או הגבר, המשוקעות
בתפיסות כגון אלו. הרב מונק, ליסה איקין, הרב אהרן סולובייצ'יק[כט] ורבים אחרים
הנוקטים בשיטה דומה מניחים הנחות אשר אינן ניתנות לאימות משום שהן אינן
ניתנות לבדיקה בכלים המדעיים שברשותינו, מתחום מדעי החברה או מדעי הטבע.

החסרון השני של הסברים מסוג זה טמון ביסוד האפולוגטי המצוי בהם.[ל] מתוך
מגמות הרמוניזציה והרצון לתאם לתאם בין הברכה ה"בעייתית" והתודעה המודרנית
הרואה באשה אדם שלם בפני עצמו, צומחת ספרות אפולוגטית המטשטשת את
הקשיים, אף במחיר סילוף המקורות. במקום להודות בבעיות שמעורר נוסח הברכה
"שלא עשני אשה," מעדיפים להעלים את הפער בין הברכה העתיקה לבין תודעתינו
ואורח חיינו המודרניים. המעיין בתלמוד או בתוספתא רואה כי הקונטקסט בה
מצויה ברכה זו אינו מתאים לפרשנות שמציעים הללו הרואים בברכה זו עדות
לגדולתה של האשה: מן המקורות התלמודיים עולה כי כפי שמברך הגבר את אלוהיו

[כט] ראו מאמרו של הרב אהרן סולובייצ'יק הטוען כרב מונק לעליונותה של האשה, הזקוקה
לפחות מצוות משל הגבר.

Rabbi Ahron Soloveitchik, *Logic and Reflection on Topics of Our Times* (Jerusalem:
Genesis Press, 1991) 92–97.

ולענייננו, ראו הסברו לברכת "שעשני כרצונו," עמ' 96

ראו גם דברי המהר"ל מפראג וש. ר. הירש, המובאים על ידי יעקובסון, תשל"ו, עמ' 166. עיינו
גם בדברי הרב קוק בסידורו "עולת הראיה," עא-עב, ברכת "שעשני כרצונו," הגרר לנימה
אפולוגטית בנסיונו למצוא את מעלתה של האשה "הנפעלת."

[ל] ראו הרב נתן אורטנר, עורך, סידור בני יששכר, על פי ספרי הרב צבי אלימלך, ירושלים, תשנ"ג.
לאחר שהוא מצטט את דברי הטור האומר "נהגו הנשים לברך שעשני כרצונו וכו' שהוא כמצדיק
עליו את הדין" הוא מתחבט בניסוח בעייתי זה ואומר: "הרי זה לא אפשרי דמשמע שהיה בידה
איזה חטא קודם בריתה ועל כן נבראת נקבה?!" והוא נכנס לדרשה מפולפלת על רצונו של האל,
תוכניתו הראשונה והשניה... וראו שם, עמ' קע-קעא. ראו גם דברי הרב שמעון יצחק הלוי
פינקלשטיין, בסידורו סדר תפילה עם באור שיח יצחק, ירושלים, 1968, עמ' יג-יד.

לי כי מן הראוי יהיה להמנע מתפיסות המצביעות על היררכיה 'מהותנית,' גם כשמדובר בגברים ונשים.

כמובן, אם ברצוננו לשמור על עקביות, יהיה עלינו לשלול גם פרשנויות 'מהותניות' המניחות הנחות הפוכות על מהות האשה. כלומר, תאוריות המדגישות דווקא את **גדולתה** של האשה ועליונותה על הגבר, כפי שנראה להלן.

ב.2. האשה משוחררת ממצוות שהזמן גרמן בשל 'עליונותה' על הגברים

בספרות העת החדשה ובעיקר בספרות הפופולרית מצויות גרסאות שונות של פרושים המסבירים את טעמה של הברכה "שלא עשני אשה," ואת שחרורן של הנשים ממצוות שהזמן גרמן כעדות לעדיפותן של הנשים על הגברים. לפי תאוריות אלו, עליונות הנשים היא הסיבה לשחרורן מן הצורך במצוות רבות, שתפקידן לשמור על הגבר ולעצבו לדמות היהודי השלם. הרב אליהו מונק, למשל, כותב בספרו "עולם התפילות" את הדברים הבאים:

> האשה היהודיה במיוחד, שאותה פטר החוק האלוהי מקיומן של "מצוות עשה" מרובות, היא ביחוד חייבת לראות בשחרור זה מחלק ניכר של אמצעי החינוך שכולם יפים כלפי הגברים, הבעת אמון אלוהי במשמעותה המוסרית העצמית. החוק היהודי מבוסס איפוא על ההנחה, שלנשים יש בדרך כלל יותר נכונות פנימית להתמסר לעצם מטרתן, יותר אמונה נלהבת לגבי תפקידן היהודי, וסכנת הפיתויים המזדמנת להן בעת מילוי תפקידן קטנה יותר. לכן אין צורך להשתמש כלפיהן בכל התקנות המרובות המיועדות להזהיר אנשים. ...האשה מסמלת גם את המלאך השומר על ניצוץ הקדושה, על גחלת הטהרה והמוסר במשמע העליון שלהם. ברוח זו אומרת האשה היהודיה כל בוקר ובוקר את הברכה: "שעשני כרצונו," לא רק מתוך הכנעה סבילה כקבלת החלטות ה', שאין אנו רשאים למרוד בה, כי אם מתוך ברגשות חיוביים בהחלט, בתודה עמוקה ובשמחה כנה, שבוראה עשה אותה "כרצונו," כלומר, לפי הרצון והחפץ שלו יתברך, בצורה שמצאה חן בעיניו... (שם, עמ' לו).[כו]

כאמור תשובות מסוג זה נמצא לרוב בספרות התורנית החדשה, בעיקר בספרים המיועדים לנוער, או המיועדים לתת בידי הנוער הדתי מענה נוסח "דע מה שתשיב."[כז] כמו כן, בשנים האחרונות מעין "כתבי הגנה" ביחס למקומה של האשה ביהדות, המגייסים הסברים פסיכולוגיים להצדקת מקום האשה במסורת היהודית. דוגמא מאלפת לכיוון זה ניתן למצוא בדברי ליסה איקין, הכותבת בין השאר:[כח]

[כו] הרב אליהו מונק, עולם התפילות, כרך ראשון, תירגם פ. גלבסקי, ירושלים: מוסד הרב קוק, תשמ"ט.

[כז] ראו למשל, ישראל הס, אמונות (ירושלים: הוצאת "תחיית ישראל," תש"י) 60 וכן מאמרו בכרך שני של אמונות, "ברוך שלא עשני אשה האמנם?" עמ' 38-39.

[כח] Lisa Aiken, "Men and Women in Traditional Judaism," *To Be a Jewish Woman* (NY, 1993) 27–43.

אריסטוטלי.[כד] יחס הגבר לנקבה כיחס הצורה לחומר. בשפה ימי-בנ״יימית זו ההבדל
בין החומר והצורה אינו הבדל כמותי, אלו מושגים המבטאים את פניה השונים
(והמנוגדים) לחלוטין של ההוויה; הצורה היא הייחודיות והאיכות המיוחדת של כל
עצם, ואילו החומר—אינו מאּפיֵיך, והוא חסר כל ביטוי עד שמתלבשת בו הצורה.
כלומר האשה ממהותה חסרה את הצורה, את הייחוד המתבטא על ידי "נפש
הכובש." האשה יכולה לבוא לידי ביטוי רק על ידי הגבר המטביע בה חותמו כי היא
מטבעה בריה "הנכבשת והמתדברת בהנהגתו של איש."

רבים, כיום, יתקשו עד מאד לקבל תפיסות מטאפיסיות אלו. הוגים ופרשנים
המצויים בהגות המודרנית הבתר-קאנטיאנית, המושפעים מזרמים, כמו ה'פוזיטיביזם
הלוגי', ובוודאי הוגי סוף המאה החשופים לביקורת הפוסט-מודרנית ימנעו מלקבל את
ההנחות המטאפיסיות המצויות בבסיסן של הפרשנויות הללו. החשיבה המודרנית
ובוודאי הפוסט-מודרנית, אינה עוסקת יותר בתכלית העולם ומרכיביו, או בתכלית
האדם, היא מסתפקת בתאורים של תהליכים הניתנים לניתוח מדעי בלבד.[כה]
בטקסטים שראינו לעיל, מסתתרות יותר מידי הנחות שאינן ניתנות לאימות; לשלילה
או לאישור. לפיכך הייתי מעדיפה תאוריות הלכתיות מן הסוג הראשון אשר אינן
בהכרח מניחות ידיעה על "נשמתי" האשה ומהותה "העצמית."

אם יורשה לי להוסיף הערה נוספת מן התחום הערכי, אומר, כי בסופה של המאה
העשרים, מאה בה סבלנו, יותר מכל, מתפיסות גזעניות, עלינו להתרחק מכל מיון
המתבסס על צבע עורו של האדם, מוצאו האתני, מינו, דתו או לאומיותו. כיום, מאה
וחמישים שנה לאחר ביטול העבדות באמריקה, לאחר המאבקים הקשים
בדרום-אפריקה סביב נושא האפלייה הגזעית, לאחר מאבקיה של התנועה
הפמיניסטית כשתפיסת השוויון הבסיסי בין בני אדם שונים הולכת ומתפשטת נדמה

[כד] ראו רמב״ם, מורה-נבוכים, חלק ראשון, פרק יז: "ואפלטון וכל מי שקדמו היה קורא את
החומר—נקבה, והיה קורא את הצורה—זכר" ועיינו עוד שם, וכן חלק ראשון, פרק סט.

[כה] לא כאן המקום להכנס לביקורת פילוסופית מפורטת על תפיסות מטאפיסיות, התרות אחר
מהות נצחית של האדם בכלל או האשה בפרט. אפנה את הקוראים המעוניינים למאמרו המפורסם
של רודולף קרנאפ על "דחייתה של המטאפיסיקה," בתוך ליאו ראוך, עורך, מקראה לפילוסופיה
בת-זמנינו, תל-אביב: יחדיו, תשנ״ג 1983, עמ׳ 40-52. ניתוח תמציתי של המהפך החשיבתי הנ״ל
מצוי גם במאמריו השונים של אליעזר גולדמן על הצורך ב"גיוס" חשיבה מסוג שונה
לחלוטין לדיונים "תאולוגיים" כיום ראו קובץ מאמריו, ד. סטטמן וא. שגיא, עורכים, מחקרים
ועיונים, ירושלים: מאגנס, תשנ״ז, "על האמונה הבלתי אשלייתית" עמ׳ 361-371, "מושג האמונה
של ישעיהו ליבוביץ׳" עמ׳ 256-257, "על ההשגחה" עמ׳ 351-357. וכן ראו רורטי:

R. Rorty, Contingency, Irony and Solidarity (N.Y.: Cambridge Univ. Press, 1989)

בעיקר עמ׳ 4-24, 73, 81. סיכום תמציתי על הביקורת הפוסט-מודרניסטית, ראו במאמרו של עדי
אופיר, "פוסטמודרניזם עמדה פילוסופית" בתוך אילן גור זאב, עורך, חינוך בעידן השיח
הפוסטמודרני (ירושלים: מאגנס, תשנ״ו) 148-160. ראו גם מאמרי "הגות יהודית-אורתודוכסית
נוכח עולם פוסט-מודרני" אשר יראה אור בקרוב בקובץ מאמרים בעריכת אבי שגיא, דוד שווארץ
וידידה שטרן, יהדות—הדיאלוג בין הפנים לחוץ, בהוצאת מאגנס.

ו[גם] אם הן שייכי במצוות והן מזרע ישראל **אין נשמתן כנשמת הזכר**.[כא]

דוגמא שניה, מראשית המאה הנוכחית, אפשר למצוא בפרושו של הרב קוק לסידור, וכך הוא כותב בהסברו לברכת "שלא עשני אשה":

> הנשמות בגורל חייהן, מחולקות הן לפעולות ונפעלות, לרשומות את החיים ואת הויתם בכל מכמניהם, ולנרשמות מהם. וזהו ההבדל העצמי, שיש בין נפש האיש, הפועל, החוקק, הכובש והמדביר, ובין נפש האשה, הנרשמת, הנפעלת, הנחקקת והנכבשת והמתדברת, בהנהגתו של איש. וכמה מדות עליונות וטובות, **וכמה אושר ומרחב יש בחלק הטוב הזה, של היות הנשמה נשמת איש פועל, יוצר, מחדש... על פי עצמיותו הפנימית במערכי קדושתו, הנעלה מנפש האשה, הנחשבת כחומר לגבי צורה, לעומת נשמת האיש הצורתית**, ורבה היא ההודאה המחויבת ליוצר הנשמה מכל איש ואיש, שלא עשני אשה (עולת ראיה, עא).[כב]

דוגמא שלישית ואחרונה אביא מפוסק בן זמנינו, הרב אליעזר ולדנבג, הדן בספרו שו"ת "ציץ אליעזר" בשאלה: האם מותר לשנות יעודו של מקום ולהפכו מעזרת גברים לעזרת נשים. לדעתו, בפעולה זו, בה הופך מקום שבו פעלו אנשים למקום תפילתן של נשים יש משום 'הורדה' בקודש' והדבר אסור, כלשונו: "ודאי **הזכרים עדיפיא מנשים**, דהרי מברכין בכל יום שלא עשני אשה, לכך פשוט דהוי **הורדה**" (ציץ אליעזר ט:יא).

כלומר, ברכת "שלא עשני אשה" נתפסת על ידי ה"ציץ אליעזר" כעדות לעדיפותם העקרונית של גברים על נשים, ועל כן הפיכת עזרת אנשים למקום תפילה עבור הנשים מהווה הורדה בקדושת המקום.

פרשנויות אלו חושפות תפיסה מטאפיסית מובהקת, הטוענת להכרת המהות הנשית; הכרת "עצמיותה" כלשון הרב קוק, או "נשמתה" כלשון הרב יהושע אבן שועייב. מהות נשית זו אינה משתווה לזו של הגבר והאשה נועדה, על כן, לעולמי עולמים, להיות בדרגה נמוכה מן הגבר. הרב יהושע אבן שועייב מתאר תמונה היררכית של היש', כפי שעשו רבים בימי-הביניים. דרוג זה מבטא הערכה אונטולוגית שונה ליש' שהוא דומם, צומח, חי, מדבר,[כג] או ל'מדברים' השונים גוי, עבד כנעני, אשה, גבר יהודי. מדרג זה, מבטא לשיטתו, עדות לבריאת סוגים שונים של בני-אדם, אשר מהותית שונים זה מזה. לפי תפיסה זו אין בכוחם של מאמצים חברתיים וחינוכיים, גדולים ככל שיהיו, לשנות היררכיה אונטולוגית זו.

גם הרב קוק, מאות שנים מאוחר יותר, מאמץ תפיסות מטאפיסיות, בעלות גוון

כא ר' יהושע שועיב, דרשות על התורה, קרקא, של"ג, מח, עמודה ב. מצוטט על ידי וידר תשל"ט, עמ' 214, הערה 70.

כב הרב אברהם יצחק הכהן קוק, עולת ראיה (ירשלים: מוסד הרב קוק, תרצ"ט) עא.

כג ראו למשל ר' יהודה הלוי, **הכוזרי**, מאמר ראשון סעיף כו-מג ומאמר חמישי, סעיף כ, "ההקדמה הרביעית." (במהדורת הרב מרדכי גניזי, הכוזרי המפורש, תל-אביב, תשכ"ט, עמ' 26-29, ועמ' 366-369).

בברור הנחות מטאפיסיות בייחס למהות האשה, לאופיה, יכולתה ותפקידה בעולם. בחרתי להביא מספר דוגמאות שונות להסברים שניתנו לברכת "שלא עשני אשה"; כל הפרושים שיובאו להלן מכירים ב**נחיתותה** של האשה לעומת הגבר, וכולם מנסים להסביר מדוע פטרה ההלכה את האשה ממצוות שהזמן גרמן, אלא שהראשונים מדגישים את הנחיתות ה**חברתית** של האשה ואילו האחרונים מצביעים על תפיסה **מהותנית** הרואה בנחיתות הנשית עניין הקשור ל"נשמתה" ו"מהותה" של האשה.[ט]

ב.1.1. דוגמא מפורסמת להסבר הסוציולוגי על מעמדה הפרובלמטי של האשה ניתן למצוא בדברי אבודרהם בפירושו לסידור. כפי שכבר ראינו, אבודרהם מסביר את ברכת "שעשני כרצונו" כברכת "מי שמצדיק עליו את הדין על הרעה הבאה עליו," רעה זו נובעת לדעתו משעבודה של האשה לבעלה, וכך הוא כותב, בהקדמתו לסידורו:

> והטעם שנפטרו הנשים מהמצוות עשה שהזמן גרמא, לפי שהאשה משועבדת לבעלה לעשות
> צרכיו, ואם היתה מחוייבת במצות עשה שהזמן גרמא, אפשר שבשעת עשיית המצוה ציוה
> אותה הבעל לעשות מצותו, ואם תעשה מצות הבורא ותניח מצותו אוי לה מבעלה. ואם
> תעשה מצותו ותניח מצות הבורא אוי לה מיוצרה. לפיכך פטרה הבורא ממצוותיו, כדי
> להיות לה שלום עם בעלה (שם, כה).

הסבר זה שרבים העתיקוהו והסתמכו עליו בפרושם לסידור[2] נשען על הכרת המציאות המשפחתית והחברתית שבה היתה נתונה האשה ברוב קהילות ישראל עד לפני כמאה שנה. אם אין בהסבר זה יותר מאשר תאור מצב חברתי, ואם אין כאן רמז לתפקידה הנצחי של האשה כמשרתת הבעל הרי שדבריו של אבודרהם כמו דברי רש"י שראינו לעיל, עשויים להוות נקודת מוצא למי שדורש/ת שינוי בנוסח הברכה כיום, וארחיב כיוון זה בהמשך.

ב.1.2. המגמה השניה העולה מן ההסברים לברכת "שלא עשני אשה" היא הפרשנות ה'מהותנית'. אדגים גישה זו על ידי מספר דוגמאות: הראשונה, דברי ר' יהושע אבן שועיב, לפני כ-400 שנה:

> לכן מברכין בכל יום שלא עשאני כותי ושלא עשאני עבד ושלא עשאני אשה... כי נשמתן של
> ישראל הן קדושות יותר מן האומות, ומן העבדים הכנעניים הפחותים, ואפילו מן הנשים.

[ט] יש להזכיר כי פה ושם נתקלתי גם בפרשנויות (מאוחרות) התולות את ברכת "שלא עשני אשה" בסבלה הפיזי של האשה היולדת. כך ז. יעבץ בסידורו עבודת הלבבות, ירושלים: הוצאת "קריה נאמנה," תשכ"ד, עמ' 8 "שלא עשני אשה שהיא עלולה לפגעים יותר מן האיש ככתוב 'הרבה ארבה עצבונך' וגו' (בראשית ג:טז) וכך מפרש ריב"ל בזרובבל (למראה מקום מדוייק עיין בהערה 32, להלן), ואולם נדמה לי שאין לעמדות אלו על מה לסמוך. התוספתא מבארת את טעם הברכה באי-מחויבותן של נשים במצוות ולא בעניין ביולוגי. וכבר כתבתי במקום אחר (עמודים, תשרי תשנ"ו "מאחורי הפרגוד" עמ' 15) כי אחת הזכויות שלנו הנשים היא דוקא היכולת להיות שותפות פעילות למעשה הבריאה. אולי דוקא חווית הלידה היא אחת מזכויותיה של האשה, (שעשני אשה!) במיוחד בעידן המודרני כאשר הלידה אינה כרוכה על פי רוב בייסורים ובסכנות כבעבר.

[2] ראו טור או"ח, ברכות השחר מו:לה, ברכות השחר מו:לה, יום-טוב ליפמאן, דברי חמודות על הראש, ברכות לט ע"ב, ומן החדשים, למשל, הרב י. יעקובסון תשל"ו עמ' 166. הרב יוסף דוב (בער), תשט"ז, עמ' 41.

להזהיר מאד את המורות והמדריכות בבתי הספר הדתיים... להורות לתלמידותיהן
לבל יברכו ברכת שעשני כרצונו אלא בהשמטת הזכרת שם ומלכות... כדי שלא יכשלו
באיסור ברכה לבטלה, שהוא איסור חמור מאד (שו״ת יחווה דעת חלק ד׳, סימן ד).

לא כאן המקום להכנס לדיון הארוך בנושא הטעון של הוספת ברכות לאחר
תקופת הגאונים. נושא זה רחב ועמוס בתוכו מחלוקות עקרוניות ועמוקות. עמדתו
החריפה של הרב עובדיה יוסף נגד אמירת ברכת ״שעשני כרצונו״ בשם ובמלכות
קשורה, ללא ספק, להתנגדותו הנחרצת להוספת ברכות (לאחר תק׳ הגאונים), וכדרך
פוסקי ספרד הוא רואה בכך ברכה לבטלה. לענייננו, דברי הרב עובדיה יוסף
מבהירים שני דברים: ראשית, את איחורה של ברכת ״שעשני כרצונו.״ ושנית, את
הפיחות הקיים ביחס למעמדה של ברכה זו, בין השאר, בשל מקורותיה המאוחרים.

עם זאת מעניין לציין כי נשים רבות מברכות בשם ובמלכות ברכת ״שעשני
כרצונו,״ וכך נוהגים ברוב בתי הספר הדתיים בארץ. נדמה לי כי מאבקו של הרב
עובדיה בעניין לא נחל הצלחה רבה ברוב מקומותינו (למרות שבסידורים הספרדיים
לרוב מופיעה הברכה ללא שם ומלכות).[יח] יתכן כי עובדה זו מעידה על השתרשותה
המהירה והעמוקה של הברכה ״החדשה״ בקרב בנות ישראל.

ב. האשה בעיני פוסקים בדורות השונים לאור עמדתם ביחס לברכת ״שלא עשני אשה״ ו״שעשני כרצונו״

ב.1. ברכת ״שלא עשני אשה״ מעידה על מעמדה הנחות של האשה

ראינו כי התוספתא מסבירה את ברכת הגבר ״שלא עשאני אשה״ בגלל שחרורה
של האשה ממצוות (שהזמן גרמן). הפוסקים ופרשני הסידור מציעים הסברים שונים
לשאלה מדוע שוחררו הנשים ממצוות אלו. עיון בפרשנויות שהתפתחו לאחר התלמוד,
לאורך הדורות, אינו מגלה, על-פי-רב, האם לפנינו גישה **מטאפיסית**, שתכונה מעתה
הגישה ה׳מהותנית׳ (אסנציאלית) זו החותרת לגילוי מהות האשה, הגבר, או שלפנינו
גישה **הסטורית**, המתארת את מצבן של הנשים מבחינה סוציולוגית בתקופות נתונות.
כמו כן, נדמה לי, כי לרוב, הפרשן אינו מודע להבחנה זו, ועל כן הוא חושף את
עמדתו בעניין.

נסיון למיון השיטות השונות לפי מגמות פרשנות; הסטוריות-סוציולוגיות או
מטאפיסיות-׳מהותניות׳ היה תורם רבות לשאלה שתעסיק אותנו בחלקו השלישי של
המאמר, בדבר שינוי נוסח הברכה. להבחנה זו, בין סוגי הפרשנות השלכות מרחיקות
לכת לגבי נכונותו של הפוסק לפעול לשינוי הלכות הקשורות למעמדה של האשה,
ככלל, ולגבי נכונותו לשנות מטבע ברכה זה שבו אנו דנים, בפרט. אולם, כאמור, קשה
להכריע, על פי רוב, בשאלה זו בבואנו לחשוף את ה׳אני מאמין׳ של הפרשן.

עם זאת, למרות העמימות הרבה, נוכל להצביע על חלק מן הפרשנויות כחושפות

יח ראו, למשל, סידור תפילה למשה, לפי מנהג הספרדים ועדות המזרח, ערוך בידי משה רבי,
רמת-גן, תשל״ב, ברכות ״שלא עשני גויה...שפחה״ נאמרות בשם ומלכות, וברכת ״שעשני כרצונו״
ללא שם ומלכות.

שלי, ג.ז.).[ט]

בסדור אבודרהם השלם, מן המחצית הראשונה של המאה ה-14, אנו קוראים:

> מברך אדם בכל יום שלש ברכות אלו: ...והשלישית, שלא עשני אשה מפני שאינה מצווה במצות עשה שהזמן גרמא..., ועד שאימת בעלה עליה ואינה יכולה לקיים אפילו מה שנצטוית. והנשים נהוגות לברך במקום שלא עשני אשה, **שעשני כרצונו כמי שמצדיק את הדין על הרעה הבאה עליו.** (שם, ירושלים, תשי"ט, עמ' מא–מב)

הטו"ר ואבודרהם נוקטים לשון מנהג ביחס לברכת הנשים. היכן התעורר מנהג זה? האם נשים חיברוהו מדעתן? אין אנו יודעים. אך ממקורות אלו נראה כי ברכת "שעשני כרצונו" התחילה כנוהג בין נשים, ולא נכנסה מתוקף פסיקת רבנים. ניתוח זה של התפתחות הברכה מקבל אישור מעדותו של ר' יוסף בן משה בספרו "לקט יושר" (מאה ה-15):

> ...ואמר זה הסדר עם הקהל, לשכוי בינה, גוי, עבד, אשה. ואמר אשה אומרת במקום שלא עשני אשה שלא עשני בהמה. **אבל שמעתי מאשה שאומרת במקום שלא עשני אשה שעשני כרצונו,** [וכמדומה לי שלא הודה לה הגאון זצ"ל כי אמו של הגאון זצ"ל הקדושה בגזרת אושטריך הי"ד, היתה אומרת שלא עשני בהמה...] (לקט יושר, חלק א או"ח, ז, ב).

הווה אומר, בעל ה"לקט יושר" מעיד כי בזמנו, בבווריה, נהוגות שתי ברכות על ידי נשים: "שלא עשני בהמה" ו"שעשני כרצונו," ודווקא הראשונה זוכה לאישור של רבו, "הגאון זצ"ל" ר' ישראל איסרלין, בעל "תרומת הדשן" (שנפטר ב-1460, כ-30 שנה לפני תלמידו). מן העדויות שבידינו נראה כי ברכת "שלא עשני בהמה" נאמרה רק על ידי נשים מעטות בקהילות ישראל לדורותיהן ונעלמה כיום כליל מסדר הברכות,[ט] ואילו ברכת "שעשני כרצונו" כבשה את מקומה עם הזמן והפכה לנחלת כל הנשים.

הרב עובדיה יוסף, פוסק כי נשים אומנם חייבות בברכות השחר (ואין הן בכלל מצות עשה שהזמן גרמא), אך לגבי ברכת "שעשני כרצונו" כותב הרב עובדיה יוסף כי מכיוון שברכה זו **מאוחרת** ונתקנה הרבה שנים אחרי תקופת התלמוד ואף לאחר תקופת הגאונים הרי שאין לברכה בשם ומלכות. ואלו דבריו:

> אולם ברכת שעשני כרצונו, אף על פי שבכמה סידורים נדפסה בהזכרת שם ומלכות, נראה שמכיון שברכה זו [אשר מקורה בטור ואבודרהם, וראה ספר מעבר יבוק, שפתי צדיק סוף פרק טי"ו][יז] לא הוזכרה בתלמוד ולא בספרי הגאונים, יש לחוש באמירתה לאיסור ברכה לבטלה. ...לכן נראה שהנשים יאמרו ברוך שעשני כרצונו בלי שם ומלכות. ...לפיכך יש

[ט] מעתה, כל ההדגשות שלי בקטע מצוטט בכתב מעובה.

[ט] על ברכת "שלא עשני בהמה," ועל השוואתה לברכה היוונית אשר על פי מסורות שונות נאמרה על ידי אפלטון, ראו ליברמן בפרושו הארוך, עמ' 120, גינצברג תשי"א, עמ' 229 וראו גם נ. וידר תשל"ט, עמ' 206-214 להשתלשלותה של ברכת "שלא עשני בהמה" וכן תבורי 1998.

[יז] "מעבר יבוק" נכתב על ידי ר' אהרון בר משה, איטליה, נפטר ב-1639.

או שרש"י משקף תפיסה מטאפיסית בייחס לאשה, שנבראה מן צלע, כדי לשמש את
הגבר ועל כן היא כ"שפחה לבעלה"? מן המקורות שהבאנו לעיל אי אפשר להסיק
מסקנות ברורות.

על כל פנים מן המקורות שראינו עד עתה בגמרא ובתוספתא, מדברי רבי מאיר[יא]
ורבי יהודה ברור כי הביטוי הפותח: "חייב **אדם" אינו כולל נשים**. המינוח הכוללני:
"חייב אדם" פרושו: חייבים **הגברים**. הם הנמענים של נושא התפילה ובהם אנו
עוסקים. משמעותו של ביטוי שגרתי זה מעידה, בראש וראשונה, על העולם הגברי
המובהק שבו מתנהל השיח התלמודי. אך יתכן ויש כאן אף עדות לתפיסה
מטאפיסית, הרואה בגבר, דווקא, את התגלמותו המלאה של האדם,[יב] ואילו האשה
נתפסת כ"עזר כנגדו" או אדם מסוג ב', שאין בו את כל היכולות של אדם הגבר.

אי לכך, מעניין לציין כי יש מי שאסר על נשים לברך את שלושת הברכות ("שלא
עשני גויה," "שלא עשני שפחה," ו"שעשני כרצונו") בשם ובמלכות. כך כותב ר'
יעקב עמדין בסידורו "בית יעקב": "נראה לי שהאשה תברך שלא עשני גויה, שלא
עשני שפחה. אכן מאחר שלא נזכר בגמרא, נכון שלא תזכיר בהו שם ומלכות. וכן
בשעשני כרצונו נכון בעיני שלא תברך בשם ומלכות."[יג] דומה שעמדה הלכתית זו
מעידה כי ר' יעקב עמדין וההולכים בדרכו מבינים את המונח "אדם" במקורות
שלפנינו כמכוון לגברים בלבד.

א.2. מקורותיה של ברכת "שעשני כרצונו"

עיון במקורות התלמודיים ואף במקורות מאוחרים יותר (כולל תקופת הגאונים)
מגלה כי ברכת "שעשני כרצונו" **נעדרת** ממקורות אלו. ברכה זו הנהוגה כיום על ידי
רוב הנשים בציבור האורתודוקסי נתחברה כנראה בתקופה מאוחרת. העדות הקדומה
ביותר,[יד] היא, כנראה, זו המצויה בפסקי הטו"ר, ר' יעקב בן אשר (ספרד, 1270-1340)
ואלו דבריו: "...**ונהגו** הנשים לברך שעשאני כרצונו, ואפשר שנוהגים כן שהוא כמי
שמצדיק עליו הדין על הרעה." (טור, או"ח, הלכות ברכות השחר, מו:לה) (הדגשה

[יא] ראו הערה ד לעיל.

[יב] דוגמא מובהקת לתפיסה מסוג זה אפשר לראות בדבריו המפורשים של פרשן התורה דון יצחק
אברבנאל לבראשית א:כז: "כי עיקר הבריאה היא בזכר, והוא אשר נברא בצלם א-להים, וכמו
שאמר בלשון יחיד "בצלם א-להים ברא אותו" לפי שהוא היה זה מי שיראה תעלומות חכמה, לא
הנקבה, שאין חכמתה אלא בפלך... שהאדם נברא לבדו ראשונה בשלמות והיא נעשית אחר כך
ככלי תשמישו."

[יג] הרב יעקב עמדין, סידור בית יעקב, לעמברערג, תרס"ד (1904), עמ' 32, וראו להלן דברי הרב
עובדיה יוסף ופוסקים אחרים הקובעים כי רק ברכת "שעשני כרצונו" תאמר על ידי הנשים ללא
שם ומלכות.

[יד] מעניין לציין כי בסידור רש"י (עם פרוש ר' שלמה באבער ובעריכת יעקב פריימאן, ירושלים:
הוצאת קריה נאמנה, תשכ"ג, עמ' 1 - 4), לא נזכרת כלל ברכת "שעשני כרצונו" לנשים.

הנוסח במנחות סבל מיד הצנזור[ו] הרי יתכן כי דווקא נוסח התוספתא והירושלמי משמר את הגירסא הקדומה. כלומר על פי התוספתא והירושלמי, הגבר מברך על כך שזכה להיות מחויב במצוות, ואינו כאשה הפטורה ממצוות. רבי יהודה אינו מפרט מאילו מצוות פטורה האשה אך סביר להניח, וכך פרשו כל פרשני התוספתא והתלמוד, כי כוונתו לפטירתן של הנשים ממצוות עשה שהזמן גרמן.[ח]

מן ההקשר (גוי, בור, אשה) ומהסברים הנילווים לנוסח הברכה עולה כי פטור זה של נשים ממצוות עשה שהזמן גרמן מעיד על **נחיתותן** של הנשים. הגברים מודים כל יום לאל על שזכו לדרגה הגבוהה של 'המחוייבים במצוות', ואינם (חס ושלום) נשים. אומנם, הסיבה לפטירתן של נשים ממצוות אלו לא נאמרה במקורות שציינו לעיל, אך מן ההקשר כולו נובע, כי שחרור זה אינו מעלה וזכות לאשה, אלא להפך; אי-שיחרורם של הגברים ממצוות מוכיח על עליונותם ביחס לנשים. חיזוק להבנה זו מצוי בגמרא, ב'מנחות', בהמשך הקטע שציטטנו נאמר: "רב אחא בר יעקב שמעיה לבריה דהוה קא מברך; 'שלא עשאני בור'. אמר ליה; כולי האי נמי? אמר ליה; ואלא מאי מברך שלא עשאני עבד, היינו אשה?! עבד זיל טפי" (שם, מג ע"ב–מד ע"א). כלומר בנו של רב אחא בר יעקב עונה על תמיהת אביו מדוע העדיף את ברכת "שלא עשאני בור"[ט] על ברכת "שלא עשאני עבד": **"עבד היינו אשה"** ברכת "שלא עשאני עבד" היתה בעיניו זהה לברכת "שלא עשאני אשה." לכן כדי להשלים לשלוש ברכות כפי שדרש רבי מאיר, הוסיף "שלא עשאני בור." מדוע האשה והעבד היו שווים בעיניו? מסביר רש"י: "דאשה נמי שפחה לבעלה כעבד לרבו. לשון אחר: היינו אשה דלעניין מצוות אשה ועבד שוין." כלומר, על פי הסברו הראשון של רש"י, המשתלב טוב יותר עם תשובת הגמרא בסוף הדיון,[י] האשה גם היא משועבדת לאדונה לבעלה, ומעמדה דומה לזה של עבד.

אנו שואלים: האם לפנינו עמדה מטאפיסית התופסת את האשה כנחותה מטבע בריאתה, או שמא דברי הגמרא מצביעים על תמונת מצב חברתי-חברתי מוכרת? כך גם לגבי רש"י, האם פרושו הוא עדות למצבן ההסטורי-סוציולוגי של הנשים בתקופה נתונה,

───────────────────────────

שם: "שלשה דברים צריך אדם לומר בכל יום. ברוך שלא עשאני גוי, ברוך שלא עשאני בור, ברוך שלא עשאני אשה. ברוך שלא עשאני גוי שאין הגויים כלום, כל הגויים כאין נגדו. ברוך שלא עשאני בור שאין בור ירא חטא. ברוך שלא עשאני אשה שאין האשה מצווה על המצוות." ברכות ט:א.

[ו] ראו הערה ג, לעיל.

[ח] ראו ליברמן בפרושו הארוך, ניוארק תשט"ו, עמ' 121, המביא נוסח המאירי הגורס: "שאין אשה חייבת ב כ ל המצות," ועוד גרסאות דומות.

[ט] רש"י נותן שני הסברים לתמיהת רב אחא בר יעקב. הראשון, כיצד מעיז אתה להתגאות ולשבח עצמך שאינך עם-הארץ? והשני, ניתן להבין מדוע שמח אתה שאינך גוי ואשה, שהרי הללו "לא בני מצוה נינהו," אבל מדוע אתה מברך "שלא עשני בור" והרי "בור בר מצוות הוא?!"

[י] תשובת הגמרא, אומנם, מבחינה ואומרת "עבד זיל טפי," יש בכל זאת הבחנה בין עבדות העבד ועבדות האשה. כדברי רש"י: "אפילו הכי מזולזל העבד יותר מן האשה," אולם גם כך נשארת האשה בדרגת עבדות כלשהי.

מקורותיה המאוחרים של ברכת "שעשני כרצונו." בחלק השני, אסקור את ההסברים
העקריים שהוצעו לברכות אלו, תוך נסיון לחשוף את תפיסת האשה המסתתרת
מאחורי ההסברים השונים ללשון הברכה. בחלק השלישי והאחרון של המאמר,
אתייחס לקשיים החינוכיים והדתיים שברכה זו מעלה עבור המתפלל/ת בימינו ואציע
נוסחים חליפיים לנוסח הברכות המקובל, תוך הסתמכות על מקורות הלכתיים
שנדחו, עד עתה, ברוב קהילות ישראל.

א. מקורותיהם של הברכות: "שלא עשני אשה" ו"שעשני כרצונו"
א.1. מקורותיה התלמודיים של ברכת "שלא עשני אשה"

במקורות התלמודיים מופיעה לראשונה ברכת "שלא עשני אשה" בברייתא
הנזכרת בתלמוד הבבלי: "רבי מאיר אומר: חייב אדם לברך שלש ברכות בכל יום.
אלו הן? שעשאני ישראל[ג] שלא עשאני אשה, שלא עשאני בור" (מנחות מ"ג ע"ב).
בתוספתא המקבילה (ברכות פ"ו) מופיעה הלכה זהה משמו של רבי יהודה[ד] ושם אף
מתלווה נימוק לברכות אלו, וזה לשון התוספתא: "רבי יהודה אומר: שלוש ברכות
חייב אדם לברך בכל יום; ברוך שלא עשני גוי, ברוך שלא עשאני בור, ברוך שלא
עשאני אשה. גוי שנאמר 'כל הגויים כאין נגדו כאין מאפס ותהו נחשבו לו', (ישעיהו מ:יז)
בור שאין בור ירא חטא, אישה שאין הנשים חייבות במצוות."[ה]

נוסח דומה אנו מוצאים גם בירושלמי, ברכות (ט:א)[ו] אם נקבל את ההנחה כי

[ג] מסורת הש"ס, שם, "בתוספתא איתא שלא עשני גוי וכן העתיקו הרי"ף והרא"ש." ואמנם רוב
חוקרי נוסח התלמוד מצביעים על עבודת הצנזור שגרמה לשינוי הנוסח המקורי "שלא עשני גוי."
נוסח התוספתא המוסיף את הפסוק מישעיהו מ:יז, "כל הגויים כאין נגדו..." מוכיח גם הוא על כך
שהמלה "גוי" בברכת "שלא עשני גוי" היא המקורית. יש להעיר כי נוסח הרא"ש שבידינו, משמר
דווקא את גירסת "שעשאני ישראל" ויתכן שנוסח הרא"ש המקורי צונזר גם הוא. לעניין זה
מעניינת ההערה המופיעה בסידור הגאונים ומקובלים (ר' משה ווינשטוק, ירושלים תשי"ל) המעירים
על נוסח הגר"א, "שעשני ישראל" (עוד אתייחס אליו בהרחבה בחלק ג' של המאמר) - "נראה
שהגר"א ז"ל לא ראה את הרא"ש והטור מדפסים הראשונים שלא בהם חלו בהם ידי הצענזוריא, וכתב
על פי הנוסחא שבאה בספרים שחלו בהם ידיים." וכן ראו הערה דומה על הרא"ש ר' יום-טוב
ליפמאן "דברי חמדות" על הרא"ש, ברכות לט ע"א: "עיקר הנוסח שלא עשני גוי כמו ב' ברכות
האחרות שהן בלשון שלילה... ומה שכתוב שעשני ישראל אין זה אלא ממדפיסים שהגיהו כן
הספרים. כך נראה לי ברור ובדפוס ישן שלא עשני גוי." וכן תלמוד ירושלמי, ברכות ט:א. וכן ראו נ.
וידר תשל"ט, עמ' 212 הערה 58, אנצ. תלמודית, ערך "ברכות השחר" עמ' שעא, הערה 112.

[ד] ואמנם במסורת הש"ס במנחות מג ע"ב, כתוב: "צ"ל רבי יהודה" וכן איתא בתוספתא דברכות
פ"ו, וכ"א ברי"ף ורא"ש סוף פ"ט דברכות." ראו בעניין זה גם תבורי 1998, במיוחד הערה 7. הדיון
השולי, לכאורה, בשאלת שמו של התנא מקבל משמעות חשובה בבואנו לדון בשאלה האם
לפנינו שתי מסורות שונות או שלפנינו מסורת אחת שעברה שינויים והתפצלה לשתי גרסאות.
למסקנותינו בעניין זה עשויות להיות השלכות גם לגבי שאלת הנוסח המקורי. כלומר, האם
"שעשאני ישראל" הנו תיקון הצנזורה או גרסה מקורית. ראו להלן הערה 56.

[ה] תוספתא, הוצאת שאול ליברמן, ברכות ו:יח, עמ' 38 (ללא שנת הוצאה).

[ו] בנוסח הירושלמי קיימים מספר הבדלים דקים בהשוואה לנוסח התוספתא, וזה הנוסח המופיע

"שלא עשני אשה" ו"שעשני כרצונו": הצעה לברכה אחרת

גילי זיוון

מדי בוקר, זה מאות בשנים, אומרים יהודים שומרי מצוות בברכות השחר "ברוך
אתה... שלא עשני גוי... שלא עשני עבד... שלא עשני אשה," ואילו נשים מברכות
"שעשני כרצונו."[א] רבות כבר נכתב על שלוש ברכות אלו, על מקורותיהם, על זמן
אמירתן, על הסדר שבו יש לאומרן, על משמעותן ועל חילופי נוסחים שנשתמרו
בקהילות ישראל השונות.[ב] במאמר זה אתמקד בברכה האחרונה בסידרה זו: "שלא
עשני אשה" הנאמרת על ידי הגברים, ו"שעשני כרצונו" הנאמרת על ידי הנשים.

ללא ספק, העיסוק הרב בברכה זו בעשרות השנים האחרונות, כמו גם דברי כאן,
נעוץ במהפך הפמיניסטי של המאה הנוכחית. נוסח ברכות השחר קשור, להערכתי,
לתפיסת מקומן של הנשים במשפחה ובקהילה, להבנת מקומן בהיררכיה ההלכתית
ולהבנת היעוד הנשי בדורות קודמים. השינוי שחל בתחומים אלו אמור להוביל אותנו,
נשים וגברים, לבדיקה מחודשת של נוסח הברכות הללו; חברה המניחה כאחת מאבני
היסוד שלה את עקרון השוויון בין בני האדם למרות שונותם (בתחומי גזע, דת, מין)
לא תוכל לקבל בשלוות נפש ברכה בה משתבח הגבר שאינו אשה ואילו האשה, מנגד,
משלימה, כביכול, עם גורלה.

המאמר שלפנינו חותר, על כן, לבחינתן המחודשת של ברכות אלו. בחלקו הראשון
של המאמר אצביע על מקורותיה התלמודיים של ברכת "שלא עשני אשה" ועל

---

* תודות ליוסק'יה אחיטוב, למשה לביא, וליהודה נוימן, שטרחו ועזרו לי במציאת מקורות
חשובים למאמר זה, רוחב ידיעתם והערותיהם היו לי לעזר רב. תודה מיוחדת לרב דוד אסולין
ולמיכל וולף שקראו את המאמר כולו בנוסחו הראשוני.

[א] בייחס לשאלה הדקדוקית האם יש לכתוב "שעשני" או "שעשאני" נקטתי בדרך הבאה. בכל
מקום שציטטתי שימרתי את הכתיב המצוי במקור, ובשאר המקומות נקטתי בכתיב המקובל
בסידורים מודרניים וכתבתי "שעשני."

[ב] ראו למשל, אנצ' תלמודית, כרך ד, ערך "ברכות השחר," עמ' שסג-שעח, הרב י. יעקובסון, נתיב
בינה, א, תל-אביב, סיני, תשל"ו, עמ' 89-91, 164-166, גינצבורג, פירושים וחידושים בירושלמי,
חלק ג (ברכות ד:ב, [ז:ד] ניוארק תשי"א, עמ' 229-230, נפתלי וידר, "על ברכות 'גוי-עבד-אשה',
'בהמה' ו'בור', ברכות שנשתקעו ונשתכחו, סיני, פה, תשל"ט, עמ' 199-218.

עם סגירתו של המאמר הגיע אלי מאמרו המקיף של יוסף תבורי:

"The Benedictions of Self-Identity and The Changing Status of Women and of
Orthodoxy"

מאמר זה הינו עיבוד מהרצאה אשר נשא י. תבורי בקונגרס העולמי למדעי היהדות בירושלים
בשנת 1997, (מעתה, תבורי 1998).

IV. עסקי הפרט

אחד המאפיינים המובהקים של ההלכה היהודית הוא העיסוק בהלכות פרט. קדושה יהודית לעולם לא צימצמה עצמה לבית הכנסת בית המדרש ובית הדין אלא חבקה זרועות עולם. כל חייו של אדם, מראשיתם ועד סופה מוקפים הם במצוות, מצוות הפרט ומצוותיו של הציבור. בנקודה זו נפגשת ההלכה בתודעה המודרנית המתיחדת בחיפוש אחר מקומו של היחיד הגדרתו והערכתו. 'רצונו של אדם כבודו' שוב איננה מימרה יהודית מובהקת, היא הפכה לחלק מהוויית היחיד בן המאה העשרים. אך במסגרת היהודית אין היא מתפרשת כפריקת עול, אלא כחלק מהותי של תפיסת ההלכה והקדושה.

כל שלושת המאמרים ביחידה זו בוחנים כל אחד בדרכו, את המפגש שבין מסורת הלכתית ורצונו של הפרט. האשה המודעת למקומה בעולמה של קדושה, תפקידם של ילדים, בנים כבנות בטפול בהורים שאבדו את שפיותם, והחיפוש אחרי חשיבה הלכתית נוכח האפשרויות הביו-טכניות בנות זמננו, והשינויים החברתיים החלים בחיי הפרט בעולם המודרני. בכולם יש נסיון לבחון את העמדות הקיימות מזה כבר בעולמה של הלכה, מחד ולהציג נוכח אפשרויות הלכתיות שעדיין לא נבחנו עד תומן.

תוכן חלק העברית

נשים בדיון הלכתי

בעריכת
מיכה ד. הלפרן וחנה ספראי

אורים הוצאה לאור
ירושלים תשנ״ח